LOCATION AND WELL-BEING

LOCATION AND WELL-BEING
AN INTRODUCTION TO ECONOMIC GEOGRAPHY

THOMAS J. WILBANKS
Oak Ridge National Laboratory

Harper & Row Series in Geography
D. W. Meinig, Advisor

HARPER & ROW, PUBLISHERS
SAN FRANCISCO

Cambridge London
Hagerstown Mexico City
New York São Paulo
Philadelphia 1817 Sydney

Sponsoring Editor: Bhagan Narine
Project Editor: Carol Pritchard-Martinez
Production Coordinator: Marian Hartsough
Designer and Cover Artist: Karen R. Emerson
Cartographer: Robert E. Winter
Compositor: Interactive Composition Corporation
Printer and Binder: R. R. Donnelley & Sons Company
Display and Body Typeface: Melior

Additional credits are located on page 454.

LOCATION AND WELL-BEING: AN INTRODUCTION TO ECONOMIC GEOGRAPHY

Library of Congress Cataloging in Publication Data

Wilbanks, Thomas J
    Location and well-being.

    Bibliography: p.
    Includes index.
    1. Geography, Economic.   I. Title.
HF1025.W58   330.9   79-26646
ISBN 0-06-167404-4

CONTENTS

Preface   vii

PART I. INTRODUCTION   1
1. Prologue   3
2. Perspective   16

PART II. SITUATION AND SCARCITY   41
3. The Location of Opportunity and Benefit   43
4. Place and Economic Activity   60

PART III. THE "WHERE" OF ECONOMIC DECISIONS   73
5. Why a Location Has Some Activities and Not Others   74
6. Why an Activity Chooses Some Locations and Not Others   94
7. Systems of Activities at Systems of Locations   116

PART IV. LOCATIONAL ADVANTAGE   147
8. The Basis of Locational Well-being   148

v

9. Environments and Locational Distinctiveness 163

10. The Geography of Locational Advantage 188

PART V. **INTERACTION AND DEPENDENCE** **211**

11. The Locational Environment 212

12. Linkages and Well-being 231

13. Linkage and Vulnerability 256

PART VI. **PUBLIC POLICY AND ECONOMIC PATTERNS** **275**

14. Government as an Actor in an Economic-Geographic System 276

15. Government as a Shaper of an Economic-Geographic System 311

PART VII. **PLACE PLANNING AND WELL-BEING** **345**

16. Objectives in Spatial Planning 347

17. Evaluating the Prospects of a Place 371

18. How a Place Changes Its Prospects 395

19. The Implications of Place Planning 412

PART VIII. **IN CONCLUSION** **421**

20. Questions That Remain 422

Glossary 430

Bibliography 438

Credits 454

Index 458

PREFACE

*T*his book began as an attempt to resolve a paradox. Because of my interest in such subjects as economic development and the kindred field of economics, I found that I was labeled an "economic geographer" and, as a young faculty member at Syracuse University, was expected to teach a course or two carrying that label. Yet in becoming a geographer I had found the standard text materials for economic geography—and the standard kinds of course presentations—uninteresting. Given a chance, I read and did other things.

What was it about economic geography that was so compelling that I ended up in it, in spite of my lack of immediate interest in so much of it? Could I communicate that to my students? Could I even explain it to myself?

In the summer of 1969, needing to pay the family grocery bills, I agreed to teach a couple of introductory courses, one of which was economic geography. Organizing that course was the beginning of this book. As it turned out, the course was scheduled five days a week at 7:30 A.M., and no one enrolled. I was considerably more relieved than disappointed (I got paid anyway).

But I found two keys to resolving my paradox: (1) the appeal of ideas and (2) the motivations associated with issues. For me, ideas spark curiosity, and curiosity stimulates learning. Unless an academic subject has a core of fruitful *ideas, it is hard for me to sustain an interest in it. But, to me, it is hedonistic to be preoccupied with ideas for their own sake. Our world faces immense challenges in reaching such objectives as peace, justice, and "quality of life." We as individuals must grapple every day with the realities of making a living, getting along with each other, and relating to large institutions with goals of their own. Unless a subject's ideas are useful in dealing with such real-world issues, it is hard (for me) to justify making them one's life work.*

My problem had been that what I read in economic geography was so set on communicating facts (about what was where, etc.) or considering techniques for analyzing facts that it didn't tell me enough about ideas or their relevance. I had gone into the cognate fields of geography to explore the issues that I thought were important and, in investigating the role of location with respect to the issues, had discovered the ideas of my own discipline. The ideas had been there all along, of course—effectively hidden by written materials in geography which assumed that a student needed to learn the facts and the techniques before addressing the ideas and issues.

The unused course preparation in 1969 was a first attempt to focus an introductory course on the ideas of economic geography as they help us to cope with the problems of life and society. The approach was refined a little in intermediate courses at Syracuse and then finally tried in elementary courses at the University of Oklahoma. There, it was so successful in exciting students about the subject matter—and about geography in general—that I thought it was worth turning into a book.

The main change in the material in this book, compared with its beginnings, reflects a marked change through time in how students define relevance. In 1969, the classroom responded to my own concerns about social welfare; in fact, the students pushed me in developing my social conscience. But by the mid-1970s in Oklahoma, and I believe elsewhere in the United States, most students were far more interested in questions of individual economic well-being. The concepts of economic geography are useful in either connection, of course, and I tried to respond to the different kinds of questions I was asked. This book, then, is a blend of my attempts to communicate with both kinds of people.

But my aim is not to convince students of a particular point of view. I am not that certain myself which single view, if any, is right in all respects. My hope is to open up for readers a vista of powerful, interesting ideas and some of their applications, so that some of the readers will choose to go on to learn the facts and techniques necessary to develop and validate their own points of view. I believe that the ideas of economic geography can be useful to most people in addressing many of the major issues in their lives, if we as teachers can get their attention.

In seeking to communicate about ideas with the beginning college student, some compromises were necessary. A philosopher once said: "The art of teaching is careful lying" (because there is too little time "to tell the whole truth"). Over the years, the text material has been simplified several times; instructors will note the lack of technical material and rigorous precision. The richness of the factual knowledge of geography is only suggested, a limitation that can perhaps be remedied by instructors in the classroom. And the fascinating array of techniques available to people doing research in economic geography has been left for later books and courses.

But in choosing to emphasize ideas, concepts, and perspectives (realizing the costs), I believe that this book is in tune with an exciting trend in North American higher education. Recent curriculum reforms at Harvard and elsewhere can be considered experiments in helping students to cope with an information explosion. In their own lives, in school or out, the students are surrounded by facts and figures, by books and magazines and microfilms and television and newspapers. They cannot absorb it all; in fact, they cannot make sense out of very much of it without a set of perspectives. And college courses cannot teach all the facts; for one thing, the world changes too rapidly. Instead, the main role of general higher education will be to introduce students to ideas and ways of thinking, while at the same time the learners find out how to locate and use important facts that are readily available in libraries, computers, and other resource centers. I hope that the book will help to point the way for geographers who want to try to explore this educational frontier with their colleagues in other disciplines.

Many people have influenced this book, some unknowingly. At Syracuse, Don Meinig, Ed Hammond, Preston E. James, and Dick Dahlberg showed by example that introductory courses are important—that they deserve at least as much care and commitment as advanced courses. John

Thompson, Bob Jensen, Jerry Karaska, Bob Colenutt, and Lalita Sen encouraged and helped me to find economic geography on my own. And David Sopher made learning exciting. Visitors to the department, such as Fred Lukerman, John Borchert, Ed Ullman, William Garrison, and Walter Isard, contributed to my perspectives on economic geography. At Bristol, Peter Haggett, Barry Garner, and Michael Chisholm introduced me to a new world of geography, with the help of my student colleagues Keith Bassett, Andy Cliff, Bob Colenutt, Glen Norcliffe, Pat O'Sullivan, Roly Tinline, Iain Wallace, and Rodney White. And at Oklahoma, I continued to learn from faculty colleagues, including Robert Hanham, Mike Libbee, Ed Malecki, Chris Smith, Gary Thompson, and Bill Turner (and from my students).

More specifically, I need to acknowledge the influence on this book of Peter Haggett and Peter Gould, who gave me my first glimpses of the real satisfaction to be gained from explaining something so that students understand it; of Eugene P. Odum and Edgar M. Hoover, whose introductory texts gave me ideas on format and style (and O. H. K. Spate, who showed that a text need not be devoid of personality); and of Ron Mallis, who first encouraged me to write it.

In addition, the book was improved substantially by the comments and suggestions of a number of reviewers of various drafts of some or all of the chapters. I would particularly like to mention the assistance of:

Robert G. Jensen
Syracuse University

Kingsley Haynes
The University of Texas at Austin

Allan Pred
University of California, Berkeley

Ralph A. Sanders
Syracuse University

Iain Wallace
Carleton University

D. W. Meinig
Syracuse University

Donald A. Gandre
University of Wisconsin, Green Bay

Jon A. Glasgow
State University of New York at New Paltz

Mario P. Deliso
  Boise State University

Dennis R. Mock
  Ryerson Polytechnical Institute

Marshall A. Worden
  The University of Arizona

Of course, the staff at Harper & Row were invaluable, including Carol Pritchard-Martinez, their spirited and vigilant project editor. But none of these individuals, of course, should be held responsible for what I did or did not do.

Finally, my family. Kathy provided the motivation for the book, and Lisa and John were patient, positive, genuinely interested. And my wife, Kay, was my associate in every way. She typed manuscripts, told me when something didn't make sense, mailed permission letters, put up with piles of books and papers around the house, helped, pushed, believed. The book would not have been done without her.

T. J. W.

LOCATION AND WELL-BEING

PART I

INTRODUCTION

*T*he purpose of this book is not to look at questions or facts unique to economic geography. Problems and events (and even things) are seldom the exclusive territory of any single academic field. Such objectives as peace, quality of life, stability, and survival lie behind all that we do. Neither is the purpose of the book to offer an authoritative statement of truth. Different people see different truths in the subject matter we will deal with, and you will have to seek your own there.

The purpose is to introduce you to a perspective on the world, a view that sees shifting "geometries" in the things and events that shape our lives and which looks for answers to larger questions with these geometries in mind. This is the perspective of geography. The special emphasis of the book will be on the major concepts that have developed from attempts to apply this perspective to issues of scarcity and well-being. This is where geography overlaps with economics, becoming "economic geography."

But why bother? What difference will it make? Part I of this book will describe our concerns (Chapter 1) and our perspective (Chapter 2). Part II will illustrate why the perspective has turned out to be useful, and it will review some economic concepts that are helpful in applying this viewpoint to economic questions. Part III will investigate how the perspective is put to work by individual economic decision makers as they try to improve their well-being. Part IV will show why the resulting decisions give some areas certain advantages whenever particular kinds of economic activities are considered. Part V will explain how, because of this "locational specialization," a wide variety of things and people move between areas. Part VI will describe some of the ways that governments shape all of these kinds of decisions. Part VII will reconsider the concepts of economic geography from the standpoint of the well-being of areas rather than of individual decision makers. And we will conclude with a brief chapter that notes some important questions that remain.

You see, like any other subdivision of knowledge, economic geography is first and foremost a group of ideas, and this book is an introduction to those ideas: about the economic importance of location, the reasons why some locations have advantages over others, the economic role of movement, and the well-being of places and the people who live there. In your own life, you will be making location decisions, moving from place to place, and joining with other people in a complicated web of linkages between locations. You will be living in many of the kinds of situations that these ideas were developed for. Although a nontechnical book such as this can give you only a glimpse of the richness and rigor of many of these notions, you can use it to pick out the ones that interest you most, that seem likely to help you most. Then you can go on to other books and papers, including the ones listed in the Bibliography, to learn more about the ideas that you want to master.

CHAPTER 1

PROLOGUE

*T*here are mansions in this world and there are shacks. A mansion and a shack are seldom found next to each other, except occasionally when people who live in the shack work for people in the mansion. Areas in a city where shacks are clustered are clearly identified by those who live there and by those who do not. Depending on the local vocabulary, the name may be "ghetto," "shantytown," "slum," "bustee," or something else. But regardless of the name, the area is never confused with other areas where mansions are clustered.

Just as living environments differ from place to place within cities, the area around one city may differ from the area around another. A city is a kind of mosaic of opportunities and satisfactions, and the world at large can also be viewed as a mosaic, where most pieces are larger than a city. These larger areas—which may be called New England, the Riviera, Appalachia, or Chota Nagpur—can differ in their opportunities and satisfactions as much as a mansion differs from a shack. Certainly, no observer would confuse eastern Kentucky with eastern Connecticut, much less India's central Gangetic plain with the New York City metropolitan area.

This fact has profound significance. It means that most people in some areas have a strikingly better material standard of living than most people in other areas. A person's material welfare is not just a matter of how hard he or she works and where individual aptitudes lie. It is partly a matter of where he or she lives. If people in both rich and poor areas are fully aware of the contrast, the poor areas are likely to resent their poorness and the rich areas may fear the loss of their richness. "Peace in our time" is undermined by many things, but none is more fundamental or persistent than inequities from place to place in the material benefits of life and work.

These differences also affect choices we make as individuals. Where should we seek jobs? As would-be entrepreneurs, where are the things to be done, the demands to be met? As people concerned about comfort and convenience, what are our options for getting things that we want but do not have where we live? Is it possible that if we know more about how the differences arise we can cope better with this complicated, often impersonal and unresponsive world? Can this knowledge get us better jobs, make us more money, give us better financial security, help us to anticipate trends? It may help.

Let's get a little closer to what these differences from place to place in material well-being really mean. The usual practice, and one that we will follow in Chapter 3, is to use numbers to compare areas: gross national product, per capita income, per capita energy consumption, and similar indicators. But the impact on people's lives of differences in the numbers can be better appreciated by reading some descriptions of different places.

Case 1: Badajoz, Southwestern Spain   *Most of the land was barren, with no trees at all. The soil was rocky and red from decomposing ferrous elements. At times a stream-bed, empty of water for the past five months, crawled like a wounded snake across the plain, but often there was not even this to watch. I longed for at least a buzzard to mark that merciless sky, but none appeared. "Sleeping," the driver said. "Everything is sleeping!"*

We came to a village, a truly miserable collection of adobe huts clustered about an unpaved square. One bar was open, apparently, for its doors were not closed, but no men were visible behind the strands of beads that served as a curtain for keeping out the flies. Farther on there was a town, and since it was now nearly five in the afternoon people were beginning to move about, but the heat was so intense that no work was being done. It was a town that had little to commend it except its longevity; Roman legions had known this town, and when their expedition had ended in the years before the birth of Christ, Caesar Augustus had allowed the oldest veterans to take up land here. Over the ravine at the edge of town ran a stone bridge that had been used in its present form for more than two thousand years.

"You want to stop for a drink?" the driver asked.

"Not in this town," and we pushed on.

We came now to fields that looked as if they might have been cultivated and to a series of oak and olive forests that were well tended. "We're getting close to Badajoz," he said, pronouncing the word with respect. As evening approached, the heat grew more bearable and in one river valley we actually felt a breeze. We climbed a hill, turned west and saw below us the Rio Gaudiana, which farther on would form the border between Portugal and Spain, and in its valley stood a city without a single distinction: no tower, no ancient walls, no exciting prospects. The eastern half looked old and unrepaired; the western half, new and unrelated to the rest; and there was no apparent reason why a man in good sense would descend the hill to enter that particular city, for this was Badajoz, the nothing-city of the west.

JAMES A. MICHENER, IBERIA

Case 2: Texas As invited, we arrived at the ranch on the afternoon before the Thanksgiving orgy. It is a beautiful ranch, rich in water and trees and grazing land. Everywhere bulldozers have pushed up earth dams to hold back the water, making a series of life-giving lakes down the center of the ranch. On well-grassed flats the blooded herefords grazed, only looking up as we drove by in a cloud of dust. I don't know how big the ranch is. I didn't ask my host.

The house, a one-story brick structure, stood in a grove of cottonwoods on a little eminence over a pool made by a dammed-up spring. The dark surface of the water was disturbed by trout that had been planted there. The house was comfortable, had three bedrooms, each room with a bath—both tub and shower. The living room, paneled in stained pine, served also as a dining room, with a fireplace at one end and a glass fronted gun case against the side. Through the open kitchen door the staff could be seen—a large dark lady and a giggleful girl. Our host met us and helped carry our bags in.

The orgy began at once. We had a bath and on emerging were given a scotch and soda, which we drank thirstily. After that we inspected the barn across the way, the kennels in which there were three pointers, one of them not feeling so well. Then to the corral, where the daughter of the house was working on the training of a quarter horse, an animal of parts named Specklebottom. After that we inspected two new dams with water building slowly behind them, and at several drinking stations communed with a small herd of recently purchased cattle. This violence exhausted us and we went back to the house for a short nap.

We awakened from this to find neighboring friends arriving, they brought a large pot of chili con carne, made from a family recipe, the best I have ever tested. Now other rich people began to arrive, concealing their status in blue jeans and riding boots. Drinks were passed and a gay conversation ensued having to do with hunting, riding, and cattle-breeding, with many bursts of laughter. I reclined on a window seat and in the gathering dusk watched the wild turkeys come to roost in the cottonwood trees.

As the darkness came the window became a mirror in which I could watch my host and his guests without their knowledge. They sat about a little paneled room, some in rocking chairs and three of the ladies on a couch. And the subtlety of their ostentation drew my attention. One of the ladies was making a sweater while another worked a puzzle, tapping her teeth with the eraser of a yellow pencil. The men talked casually of grass and water, of So-and-So who had bought a new champion bull in England and flew it home. . . .

I awakened early. I had seen two trout rods leaning against the screen outside our room. I went down the grassed hill, slipping in the frost to the edge of the dark pool. A fly was ready fastened on the line, a black gnat, a little frayed but still hairy enough. And as it touched the surface of the pool the water boiled and churned. I brought in a ten-inch rainbow trout and skidded him up on the grass and knocked him on the head. I cast four times and had four trout. . . .

JOHN STEINBECK, TRAVELS WITH CHARLEY

Case 3: Huddersfield, Yorkshire, England . . . the long huddle of the textile mills, creeping away to the moor's edge; the marching file of tall brick chimneys, their vapors drifting into the dusk; the conveys of cramped terrace houses, jammed hugger-mugger against the hillsides; the dingy red brick everywhere, the patina of dirt, labor, and middle age . . . the wind blows chill and bluff off Wessenden. The buses lumber sadly by to Leeds and Slaithwaite, Oldham and Crosland Moor, the housewives in kerchiefs peering wanly out of their misted windows. The evening sky is gray and melancholy. Somewhere a steam locomotive blows its lonely whistle, and there is a distant clanging of couplings in a freight yard.

JAMES MORRIS, THE ROAD TO HUDDERSFIELD

Case 4: Between Kasganj and Fatehgarh, Uttar Pradesh, India Now, once again, I was on the train to Fatehgarh. It was the same time of day more or less; only the season was different. Now it was December; then it had been the end of March. Then I had looked out on a monotonous and desiccated landscape that sizzled under a sky that was as drab and dusty as an army blanket. Now, all the crops were low and green and the absence of sunlight intensified their greenness. Only the rice harvest was finished and those fields that until recently had been the greenest of all were now rectangles of brown stubble, separated from one another by low banks of earth. In the whole landscape there was not a hedge to be seen. The horizon seemed illimitable; only when there were trees on the rim was it possible to guess whether it was a mile or twenty miles distant.

In the irrigation channels which cut straight through the plain, pairs of men were using the swinging basket, as they had always done, to lift the water into the fields, a bamboo basket suspended by four cords. Sometimes the difference in level was too much for them to manage by themselves—about six feet was the limit to which they could raise it with a single throw; more than that and there would have to be two or three pairs of men, each with a basket, standing one above the other, lifting the water from one scooped-out basin to the next until it reaches the top and could flow down into the fields by its own gravity where two or more men turned it into the different beds. In this way a team of eight men with two baskets can irrigate an acre a day, but it is very hard work.

There were wells at which the bullock-drivers urged their beasts up and down the ramps, backing them up and then sitting on the rope as they went down to keep it taut until the leather bucket appeared dripping over the well-head; then a second man took it and poured it into a hollow in the platform from which it ran glistening into the channels from which yet a third man distributed it over the fields. And in the sandy places there were Persian wheels with earthenware pots attached to them, alternately ascending, overturning and descending, worked by blindfolded bullocks doomed to circle the well as long as water was needed.

The train chugged on, past brilliant fields of mustard and deep green garden crops; past shrines and small white temples and, more rarely, a mosque. On the dusty roads wretched-looking ponies drew ekkas loaded with six or even eight persons, together with their belongings. It went on and on past groves of mangoes, clipped-looking toddy palms, plantations of yellow flowering pulse, nim, acacia and shisham trees; villages of houses that were dun-colored rectangles of dried mud, windowless and roofed with sagging thatch; villages surrounded by piles of dung and stacks of twisted grass; villages shaded by ancient trees festooned with the funnel-shaped nests of the tailor birds now empty and with red flags hanging limply, high among the greenery. . . .

The day was nearly over now. The crows were going home, mournfully. The people in the fields were beginning to straighten their backs. At Kaimganj people boarded the train carrying young trees, sugar cane, bundles on the ends of sticks, brass pots, baskets containing hens and long bamboo poles with murderous iron axeheads attached to them; men from the country who had invested in shoes of European design limped past—the more sensible carried them in their hands; spotted dogs lay comatose in the dust; Muslim girls in tight trousers squatted drinking from a tap with their head coverings thrown back.

Dusk fell. The sky changed from khaki to muddy grey; the bullock-carts were squeaking their way home now; but the drawers of water were still working their beasts at the wells; all but lingering lovers had gone from the fields; little yellow fires were burning in the rice stubble; in the clearings among the trees by the villages long, horizontal ribbons of smoke from the cooking fires on which the evening meal was being prepared hung motionless in the air; high-pitched, mournful whistles came from the engine of the train. How sad India was at this moment; like a person afflicted with melancholia. In a few more minutes it was quite dark.

ERIC NEWBY, SLOWLY DOWN THE GANGES

Case 5: Westchester County, New York Wealth continues to be apparent in Westchester, where building lots—considerably smaller than the seven-hundred-acre tracts of the old estate builders—can, depending upon location, cost as much as half a million dollars each. Money nowadays, however, is not so much spent upon gigantic houses as it is on landscaping and interior decorating. A collection of good paintings carries more weight, socially, than a private squash court, and an electronic kitchen and air-conditioned garage ("so much better for the car," one resident insists) can mean more than a ninety-foot banquet hall. To be sure, the more city a man builds into his "country place," the less "country" it becomes, and, in Westchester, nature has been systematically subdued, rearranged, clipped, manicured and, in many cases, forced to do an about-face. Brooks have been made to reverse their courses, mountain laurel and dogwood have been japanned with plastic sprays to give their leaves a hard green gloss.

A number of Westchester residents have radiantly heated driveways to melt the winter snow. A woman in Ardsley has installed a specially built vacuum cleaner to dust her shrubbery. A house at the edge of the Sound has an ingenious watering system designed to launder the grass; salt spray from the Sound was being unkind to the lawn. A special filtering device removes the salty taste from the swimming pool water. James Russell Ashley of Scarsdale built, in his backyard, not only an outsize swimming pool with a sandy beach at one end, but a brook and waterfall, and what Mr. Ashley christened "an underground cave above ground" in which to have parties. At night, concealed floodlights simulate moonlight. Nor does the era of great estate building appear to be completely over. Only a few years ago, the Edgar Bronfmans—he is the son of the liquor potentate—built a sprawling handsome Georgian house that might have been lifted right out of the last century, and surrounded it with all the traditional estate trimming, including pool, pool house, tennis court, and—to be up-to-date—had the whole house air-conditioned.

STEPHEN BIRMINGHAM, THE RIGHT PEOPLE

For purposes of comparison, various kinds of numbers are used to describe such living conditions. The most widely used indicator of the standard of living has to do with a "typical" level of

TABLE 1.1
A Measure of Standard
of Living

NOTE: All estimates are in current dollars as of the cited year. Because of differences in the estimation procedures in the two references, the figures for the U.S. states must be multiplied by 1.09 for a truly accurate comparison.

Place	Date	Estimated Per Capita Annual Income
Spain (Badajoz)	1970	$884[a]
Texas (Panhandle ranch)	1970	$3,576[b]
United Kingdom (Huddersfield)	1970	$1,991[a]
India (Uttar Pradesh)	1969	$88[a]
New York (Westchester County)	1970	$4,714[b]

SOURCE: [a] United Nations. *Statistical Yearbook, 1973*. New York: U.N., 1974, pp. 590–594; [b] U.S. Bureau of Economic Analysis. *Survey of Current Business*. Washington: U.S. Government Printing Office, July 1973.

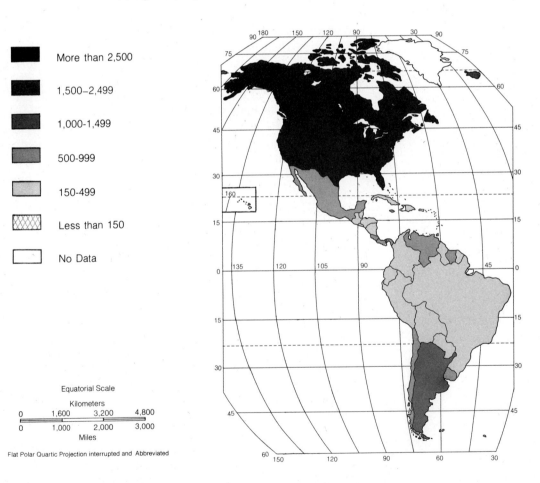

Legend:
- More than 2,500
- 1,500–2,499
- 1,000-1,499
- 500-999
- 150-499
- Less than 150
- No Data

Equatorial Scale

Kilometers
0   1,600   3,200   4,800
0   1,000   2,000   3,000
Miles

Flat Polar Quartic Projection interrupted and Abbreviated

FIGURE 1.1
Estimated Level of Per Capita Income in 1970 (based on U.N. data).

money income. Table 1.1 shows typical incomes for people in the places described above. A more comprehensive picture of the worldwide pattern of material well-being, based on one of these measures, is shown in Figure 1.1. To this indication of *levels* of benefit, we can add Figure 1.2, which displays estimates of the *rate* at which benefits are improving. It can be instructive to study these maps, to see what questions they raise. Are there regularities? Does the rate of change in the level of the material quality of life seem to relate to location, physical environmental setting, political or economic system, historical experience, population density?

A problem in trying to answer these questions is that a country, taken as a unit, may include considerable diversity in any of

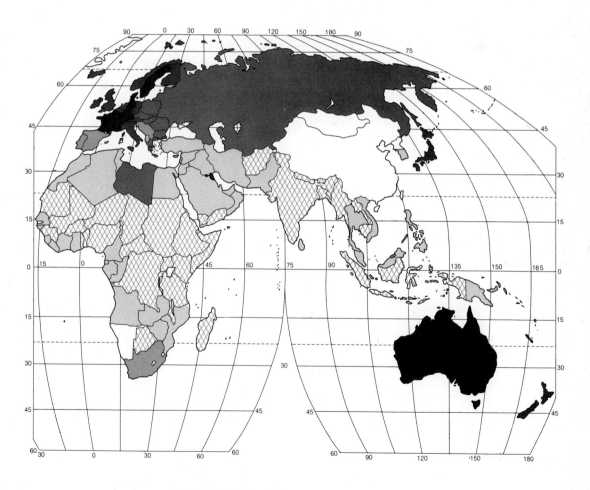

FIGURE 1.1 (cont'd.)

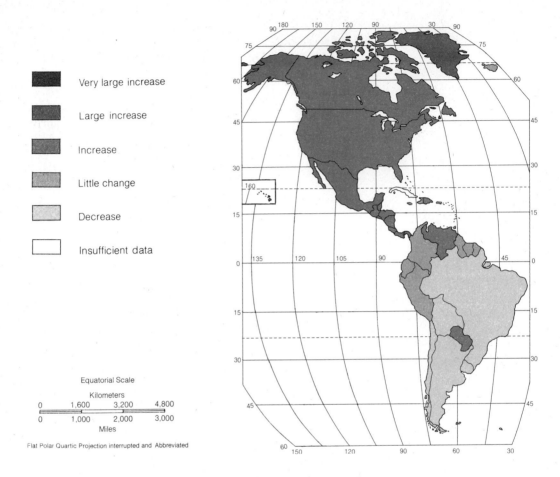

■	Very large increase
■	Large increase
■	Increase
■	Little change
■	Decrease
□	Insufficient data

Equatorial Scale

Kilometers

0	1,600	3,200	4,800
0	1,000	2,000	3,000

Miles

Flat Polar Quartic Projection interrupted and Abbreviated

FIGURE 1.2

Estimated Change in Per Capita Income, 1960–1973, with buying power held constant (based on U.N. data). Note (a) the rise in European and Japanese incomes from a 1960 level well below Canada and the United States to a 1973 level that is comparable; (b) the effect of population increases in South Asia; (c) the effect of inflation in certain South American countries; and (d) the effect of the demand for oil from the Middle East.

these factors. The Soviet Union is both accessible and inaccessible. India is both desert and jungle. China is both ancient culture and recent political possession. The United States is both crowded and sparsely settled. It all depends on where a person looks, and from what perspective. Within an individual country, there is also a pat-

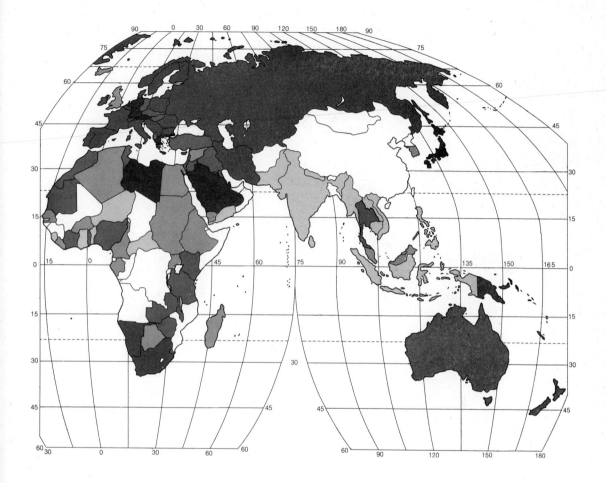

FIGURE 1.2 (cont'd.)

tern of well-being. Figure 1.3 illustrates the sorts of contrasts that exist in the United States. Again, depending on one's knowledge of the country, a person can make some guesses about what might lie behind these patterns. *The observation that there is some order to the patterns, something more than just a nonsensical shotgun blast of light and dark shades, is of fundamental importance.*

But each one of these mapping units, no matter how small, includes diversity within it. A city is itself a very intricate mosaic of standards of living, as we have said, and there is order to the pattern at this scale as well. Because of a shortage of income data at a

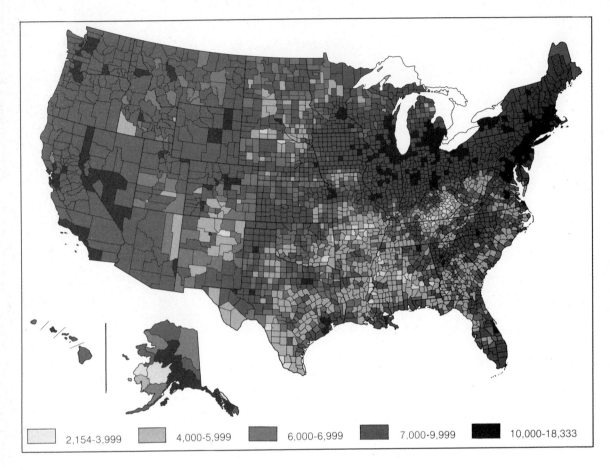

| | 2,154-3,999 | | 4,000-5,999 | | 6,000-6,999 | | 7,000-9,999 | | 10,000-18,333 |

FIGURE 1.3

Median Family Income for 1969 by Counties of the United States.

very localized scale, maps of these patterns are scarce, but an example is provided by Figure 1.4.

The contrasts indicated by these maps are important at any scale; just as in focusing a camera, however, an attempt to cover all scales with one picture is likely to result in something being blurred. As a consequence, it has been common to consider what happens to areas larger than a city separately from what happens within a city. Whether or not the basic processes are truly different is not very well known, partly because of this separation, but this book will keep its length manageable by emphasizing the larger areas. A selection of references covering similar topics at the urban scale is included in the Bibliography.

FIGURE 1.4

Median Family Income for 1969 by Census Tract in St. Louis, Missouri (based on U.S. Census data). Can you imagine differences in the "typical day" of people who live in different parts of St. Louis?

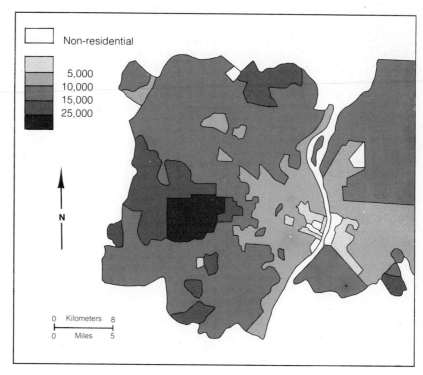

CHAPTER 2
PERSPECTIVE

*A*s a book about economic geography, this text presents a view of the world that is based on a particular perspective. Geography is centrally concerned with *location* and its significance. Economics is centrally concerned with *scarcity* and its significance. Our perspective will stem from the ways these two concerns overlap. This chapter is mainly about geography—not as a compendium of information about places but as a viewpoint for understanding what is happening in and between places. This discussion is placed at the beginning of the book for two fundamental reasons: (1) it is as important to learn to ask good questions as to answer them; and the perspective is a valuable one for stimulating inquiry, both as the book is read and as the world is observed; and (2) the perspective underlies many of the concepts we will be encountering later on, and it is only fair to make clear where the ideas come from. We are introducing a frame of mind. Try it on for size, and see if it doesn't help you to put the concepts of this book to work in your own life.

2.1 THE USES OF CONCEPTS

It is important to understand that neither of our basic concerns, location and scarcity, is limited to particular kinds of things: mineral resources or agricultural crops or heavy industries. The perspective can be applied whenever two conditions exist: (1) something is scarce—this means that it is not so abundant that people can get all they want without any particular effort; and (2) something is less scarce in some places than in others—it is more abundant, easier to get. The subject can be legal services or Sicilian pizza or clean air, and the reason for using the perspective may be one of many: Why? What difference does it make? What can I do about it? How can I use it? Is it right that it be this way?

To be able to study something from this perspective, it is necessary (at least in theory) to be able to accomplish two tasks: (1) to define the locational attributes of the subject—where it is, its extent, shape, distance, direction, overall pattern of distribution and movement; and (2) to measure how much the subject is worth. Since some scarce things are easier to value than others, and since more information is available about the locational attributes of some things than others, our current knowledge about economic geography is dangerously incomplete, often extrapolated a long way from observations of what happens with a very few things in a very few places.

In simplest terms, though, the line of thinking goes like this. Something is both scarce and useful, a condition that motivates acquisition. Who worries about collecting things (or providing them to those who want them) if they are available everywhere in unlimited supply? The urge to acquire things not immediately available, whether they are necessities or luxuries, promotes certain kinds of activities to meet the demand. For example, someone collects, constructs, or otherwise produces the barrel of oil or rice, ripe peach or aspirin tablet that is in demand. Someone else consumes it. And an intermediary may help to get the two together.

The producer (or potential producer) locates at a place where production is possible, preferably where it is easier than anywhere else. The consumer (or potential consumer) locates at a place where life is possible, preferably where it is as rewarding as possible, overall. Linking the producer and the consumer so that an exchange takes place requires connecting the two locations.

A major aim of economic geography is to develop general understandings about these kinds of situations, for example about efficient arrangements in space or the cost of distance, that can be applied to a very wide range of things. These understandings can serve many different purposes:

1. to predict—to say: if you observe that, you can expect this to follow

2. to optimize—to say: if you want to do this, here is the best way to go about it

3. to express an influence—to say: if you observe that, you are going to know that there is some pressure on the situation in this direction

4. to provide a basis for comparison—to say: if you observe that, you can talk about it clearly to other people by saying it differs from this ideal case in these ways

5. to provide a guide for study—to say: if you observe that and want to know more about it, these are the things you need to find out more about

6. to provide a basis for discussion—to say: until something better comes along, here's something we can start talking about

7. to summarize—to say: this is the way things usually seem to be

In common usage, a *theory* is just a clearly stated idea that has been shown to have some utility for one of these purposes. A *hypothesis* is a possible theory on the lookout for a little support. A *model* is a simplified version of reality, a definition that includes theories, hypotheses, and generalized descriptions.

The danger in learning about theories is that they are invariably both true and not true: correct and useful in some ways, under certain conditions; incorrect and misleading in other ways. When the theories are based on a narrow range of evidence, the usual case in economic geography, the possibility of misuse is great. Therefore, as you read this book, *beware. Think. Question.* Use the ideas only after you have checked them out to your complete satisfaction. Clearly, the world is too complex to summarize in the chapters to follow; so remember to ask yourself what has been left out.

2.2 *LOCATION: THE CONCEPTS WE START WITH*

The special concern here will be with the part of the perspective that has to do with location: recognizing patterns in distributions and asking good questions about them. This is not something that comes automatically for everyone. Accordingly, let's get in the right mood for what is to come.

2.2.1 *Space as Dimension versus Space as Context versus Space as Contingency*

Figure 2.1 displays the way homes are distributed in the United States: their location relative to other residences, their spatial ar-

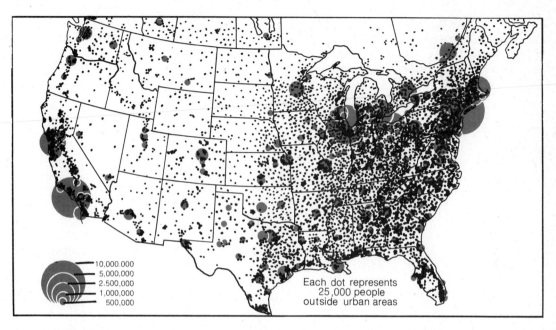

FIGURE 2.1
1970 Population Distribution in the United States (based on U.S. Census data).

rangement as a whole. The information on this map can be used in two very different ways: (1) to estimate how many people reside in a particular state or county (counting dots in an area and multiplying by the number of people a single dot represents); or (2) to get a picture of where the people are: a simplified mental image of how concentrations are arranged with respect to emptier areas. These goals illustrate two basic ideas about space as a useful concept in studying the world: space as *context* and space as *dimension*.

Using space as a dimension, we focus on characteristics of things. The people are concentrated or dispersed. Two concentrations are near or distant from each other. One is large but the other is small in extent. A long, narrow concentration has a sharp border in one direction but gradually fades away in another. If you look at the map, you can see that the population distribution can be discussed in terms like these.

Using space as context, we focus on characteristics of places. For example, Alabama has this many people; Connecticut has a greater population density than Wyoming. Since other things also are known about these places, we can use this focus to explore what factors may account for the densities that we see.

Both of these ideas have been a part of geography for as long as the term has been used. Space as a dimension can be traced back to the concern of early mapmakers with the precise measurement of locational relationships, and space as a context is a descendant of

TABLE 2.1
Space as Dimension and as Context: Examples of Titles of Professional Journal Articles in Geography

Space as Dimension

"Distance and Direction Bias in Inter-Urban Migratory Streams," *Annals AAG,* 1967, pp. 605–616.

"Market, Location, and Site Selection in Apartment Construction," *The Canadian Geographer,* 1968, pp. 211–226.

"Interprovincial Interaction Patterns," *The Canadian Geographer,* 1970, pp. 372–376.

"Economic Impulses in a Regional System of Cities," *Regional Studies,* 1969, pp. 213–218.

Space as Context

"The Rank Size Structure of the Agricultural Holdings in Finland, 1959," *Acta Geographica,* 1968, pp. 175–184.

"The Energy Balance Climatology of a City-Man System," *Annals, AAG,* 1970, pp. 766–792.

"Cross-Sectional Analysis of Canadian Urban Dimensions," *The Canadian Geographer,* 1966, pp. 204–224.

"A Regional Analysis of the Effects of Age, Education and Occupation on Median Income," *Journal of Regional Science,* 1966, pp. 35–48.

Space as Dimension and Context

"The Prediction of Trade Center Viability in the Great Plains," *Papers of the Regional Science Association,* 1965, pp. 87–115.

"The Economic Implications of the Pattern of Urbanisation in Nigeria," *Nigerian Journal of Economic and Social Studies,* 1965, pp. 9–30.

"Toward a Geography of Economic Health: The Case of New York State," *Annals, AAG,* 1962, pp. 1–20.

"Cultural Differences in Consumer Travel," *Economic Geography,* 1965, pp. 211–233.

the descriptions of unfamiliar areas by early travelers. Both are clearly a part of understanding our world; they complement each other (see Table 2.1). Using one does not foreclose the possibility of using the other.

Since academic disciplines are administrative conveniences rather than logical intellectual subdivisions, these ideas have been used and elaborated in many fields other than geography. It is difficult, for example, to use any kind of census data without paying attention to space as context, and anyone interested in movement must consider space as dimension. Historically, economic geography has carved a niche for itself by (1) contributing to a search for theory about space as a dimension, often by concentrat-

FIGURE 2.2
A Map of a Portion of the Northeastern United States.

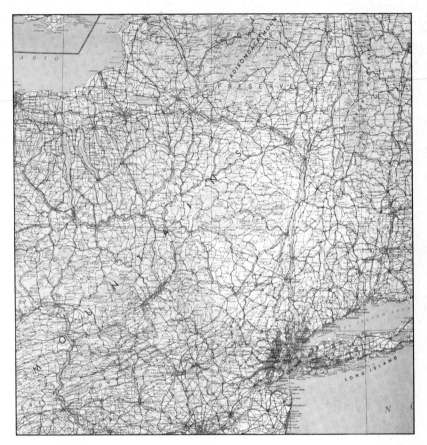

ing on a description of spatial arrangements; and (2) crossing boundaries between other academic subdivisions, especially between the social and natural sciences, in investigating space as context. But the important thing is not the niche but the perspective, and what it enables us to do.

Returning to the title of this section, note that it includes a third element in addition to dimension and context. Locations and activities are related to each other, but they are also related to time. They cannot be separated from it. Think about your own life; it has a kind of "trajectory" through both time and space. It is marked by key events that take place in a particular sequence at particular locations: birth, graduation, marriage, employment, promotion, fam-

FIGURE 2.3
Geographic Information
Contained in Figure 2.2:
(a) the pattern of larger
urban areas shown
on the map;
[continued on next page]

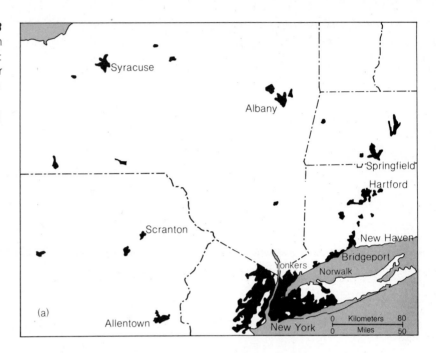

(a)

ily achievements, death. The significance of these events depends on who is involved in them, a factor that in turn is affected by when and where the events take place. And, at any specific time, what you do—what you *can* do—is limited by time and space constraints. There is only so much time to work with. There are only so many places you can get to quickly. There are only so many opportunities open to you within a limited time and limited range of distance—your "daily-life environment."[1] There is only one place where you can be at a time.

Furthermore, each event—involving a particular activity at a particular place at a particular time—affects our range of choice the next time around. Lives, economic activities, and landscapes develop as a "series of contingent events."[2] Because we experience A instead of B, we end up experiencing C. If we had experienced B, we eventually would have experienced D. Understanding this space-time aspect of economic geography as well as the other two aspects is a major part of the research frontier of the field.

2.2.2 *Recognizing Spatial Structure*

What do we—or can we—see when we look at a map? Sometimes the elements of an understandable pattern get lost in the busyness of it all. Consider Figure 2.2. We can see small urban concen-

FIGURE 2.3 (cont'd.)
(b) the pattern of limited access highways; and (c) the pattern of major rivers and lakes. Note how the various patterns agree (or disagree) with each other, and note how much easier it is to make such comparisons if each pattern is extracted from the much more comprehensive map.

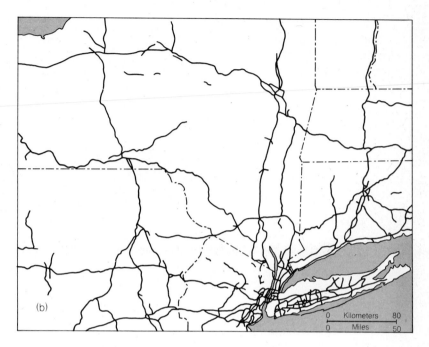

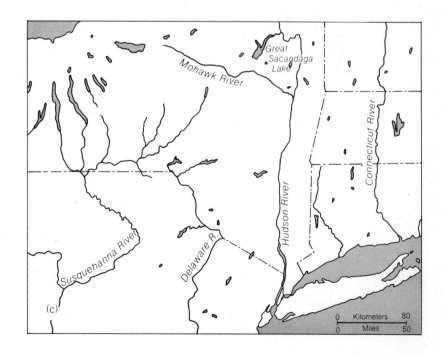

FIGURE 2.4
A Choropleth Map: Total
Gasoline Consumption per
Gas-Powered Vehicle,
1976. This map shows the
percentage above or
below the national mean
(764.91 gallons).

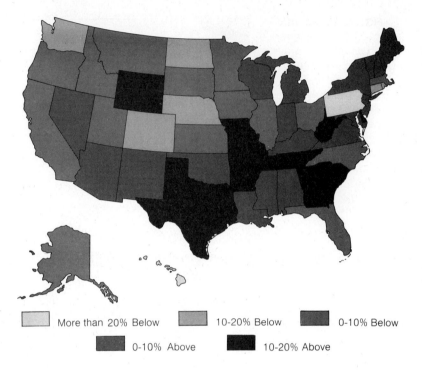

More than 20% Below   10-20% Below   0-10% Below

0-10% Above   10-20% Above

trations as dots, and bigger ones as areas with size and shape.
When this information is extracted from the rest of the map, it is
easier to examine it for its own coherence, rather than simply using
the map as an aid for navigation, as you might use Figure 2.3(a).
Similarly, there is pattern to the road network as in Figure 2.3(b),
and this pattern differs in many ways from the configuration of the
drainage network shown in Figure 2.3(c). Working directly from
the map, we could also identify the pattern of political boundaries,
the rail network, inland water bodies other than rivers, and other
categories of information. With a book or two about the area to tell
us what is where, we could locate radio stations, pipelines, public
lands, universities, migrant labor camps, metal fabricating industries, and Holiday Inns. In each case, we could lift the pattern off
the map to study it for its own sake, identifying concentrations and
gaps, getting ideas about factors that might explain what we see.

    We can go another step. Information about areas can be con-
verted to numbers, and differences between the numbers can be
displayed on a map as a mosaic of colors or shades; Figure 2.4 is an
example. And there is still one more step. This information can be
interpreted, with the interpretations then shown on a map (for in-

FIGURE 2.5
General Economic Health in New York State in the 1950s.

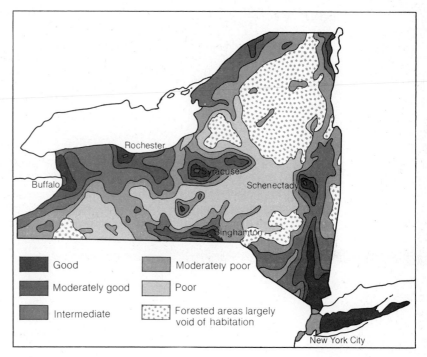

Good

Moderately good

Intermediate

Moderately poor

Poor

Forested areas largely void of habitation

stance, Figure 2.5). In any case, the aim is to go beyond a list of characteristics of particular places to see how that information is arranged in space. In part, the reason is to allow special kinds of measurements to be made and techniques of analysis to be applied; but in a more profound sense, for many of us a graphic display of information stimulates more ideas and suggests more insights than a table or an equation.

What we are doing is recognizing that location is a *relative* characteristic. Try telling someone where you are without referring to somewhere else. It is impossible. We say we are in Room 425 of Smith Hall of Jones University, or at 1010 Montgomery Street, or 2 miles south of downtown, or at 60° E., 40° N. More formally it is said that location is relative to a larger *spatial structure*, which includes the positioning of a lot of elements with respect to each other. A spatial structure is the product of a *spatial process*: it reflects the fact that something is going on. As we will see, it also influences what will go on thereafter. We start to make sense out of the structure (and to understand the process) by looking for a *pattern*: a characteristic shape or geometric form in the information displayed on a map.

	Type	Nature	Examples
TABLE 2.2 Map Types	*Qualitative Maps*	Indicate characteristics of places but not quantities, using distinctive symbols	Highway maps
	Quantitative Maps	Indicate quantities	Weather maps showing temperature or pressure patterns
	Point and/or Line Symbols	Use dots, lines, or sized figures or lines to indicate quantities	Figures 2.6 and 2.7
	Choropleth Maps	Use a shading or a color to indicate the approximate quantity for a statistical unit (such as a county or a state)	Figure 2.4
	Dasymetric Maps	Use a shading or a color to indicate an approximate quantity, crossing boundaries between statistical units	Figure 2.8(b)
	Isarithmic Maps	Use lines that pass through all points with the same quantitative value ("isarithms") to indicate quantity; in theory only possible when variation is uninterrupted	Figure 2.9(b)

Table 2.2 summarizes the different kinds of maps that can be made, and the Bibliography lists some references that discuss how to make and interpret maps. An important alternative to a map is an aerial photograph, which shows what an observer could see rather than displaying the selective judgments of a mapmaker about what to put on the map.

If we review the maps we have considered so far, it is possible to distinguish four kinds of possible components of a map, seen as a combination of patterns.

1. **Points.** Some of the information appears on the map as dots: urban places, sites of industrial plants, locations of warehouses or particular retail stores, locations of trees in a forest that are ready to be turned into lumber (for example, see Figure 2.6). Regardless of what the dots represent in a given case, certain questions arise in interpreting the pattern. How were the dots located? Do they all represent the same value? Is there any discernible order in their arrangement—clustering,

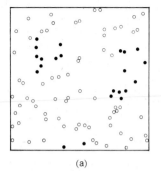

(a)

FIGURE 2.6

Examples of Point Patterns. (a) Two species of plants growing in an uncultivated area. Together, the plants are distributed unpredictably, neither evenly spaced nor clustered; but the darker dots, seen separately, are somewhat clustered; and the two species do not overlap each other in location. (b) Groups of physicians' offices in the Chicago metropolitan area, 1965. Note how the dots are concentrated toward the center of town (compare with Figure 12.3). This can be considered an indication that physicians prefer to locate their offices close to hospitals, even if they are not so close to where many people live.

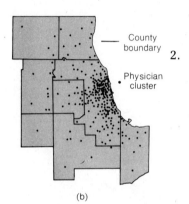

County boundary

• Physician cluster

(b)

regular spacing, linearity? What is the significance of dots being located close to each other? Of empty spaces? Is the pattern the same as it was a year ago? Ten years ago?

2. **Networks.**   Some information is depicted by lines, which may join places (networks) or separate them (cells). Although any connected system of lines can be considered a network, for convenience we will use the term for lines along which something moves: highways, rail lines, pipelines, power lines, communication lines, rivers (see Figure 2.7). Again, general questions are raised. How were the lines located? What is the meaning of the width of a line? Do lines of the same width mean the same thing? What is the meaning of the degree of straightness of the lines? Of their lengths? What is important about where they meet? Or end? Is there any discernible order in the overall arrangement? How densely does the pattern cover the space? Is the pattern changing?

3. **Cells.**   Lines that separate places form "networks" of boundaries, converting a larger area into a mosaic of smaller areas: counties, sales territories, market areas, development regions (see Figure 2.8). But how were those boundaries decided? Do they represent sharp breaks or the midpoint of a gradual change? Do they sometimes mean one and sometimes the other? Are all of the bounded areas, or cells, comparable? Is there any discernible order in the way they are shaped and arranged? How densely are they packed? Is a bounded area the same everywhere within its boundaries? How much variation and structure exists within a cell shown as a uniform patch? What does it mean if two cells are next to each other rather than distant? Is the cell patterns changing?

4. **Surfaces.**   When working with information about points and using lines as symbols, it is often useful to visualize continuous variation as a surface: land values, prices, transportation costs, typical individual or family income. A high value be-

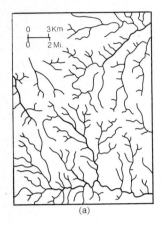

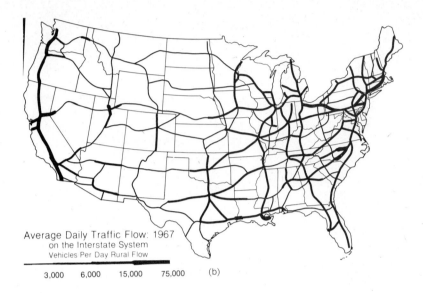

Average Daily Traffic Flow: 1967
on the Interstate System
Vehicles Per Day Rural Flow

3,000   6,000   15,000   75,000   (b)

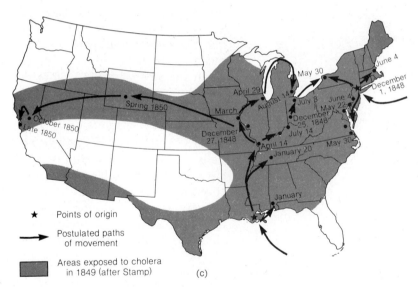

★ Points of origin

→ Postulated paths
of movement

▨ Areas exposed to cholera
in 1849 (after Stamp)   (c)

FIGURE 2.7

Examples of the Network Patterns: (a) a drainage pattern in West Virginia; (b) the interstate highway system of the United States; and (c) the spread of cholera in 1849. Similar to Figure 2.6, the links in (a) mean something different than those in (b) or (c), but each pattern contains useful information. Note that in the case of (b), the width of a link indicates the average daily flow along it, and that in (c), arrows are used to show the direction of movement. There are many such ways to add further information when a pattern is displayed.

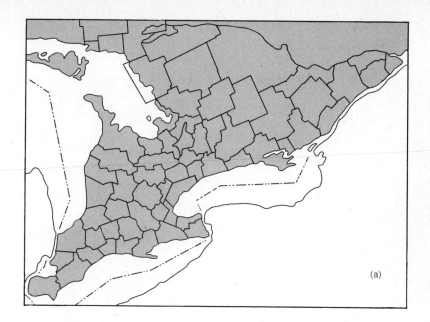

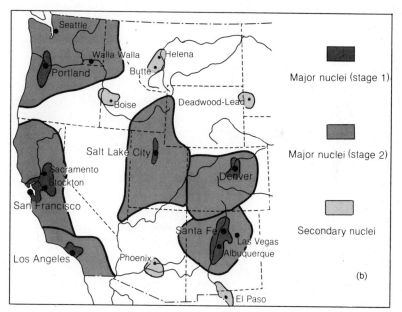

FIGURE 2.8

Examples of Cell Patterns: (a) administrative areas in Ontario; and (b) major nuclei and regions of the West in the Nineteenth Century. Other examples could include urbanized areas and drainage basins. Note that cells may be bounded precisely, as in (a) or a bee-hive. Or their boundaries may have to be approximated by single lines, as in (b), even though such precision is known to be a little misleading (consider the single line on a map showing the boundary between land and sea, when the true boundary varies with the tides).

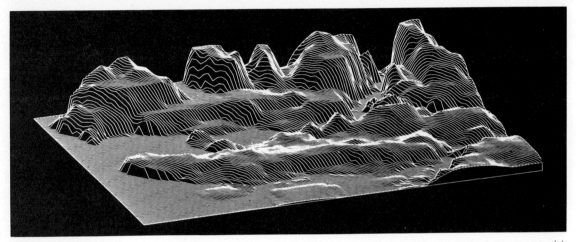

(a)

FIGURE 2.9

Examples of Surface Patterns. (a) A cartographic representation of Vancouver, drawn by a computer. Does it show land surface form? Land values? Population density? Are you sure? (b) The spread of settlements in a part of New England in the seventeenth century, shown in the form of a simplified surface. Areas on the eastern coast and to the south were settled by 1630, and settlement expanded (in a sense, flowed downhill) into the area in between. Notice how the same kind of pattern that tells us about land surface form in an atlas or atmospheric pressure on a weather map can give us information about a wide variety of subjects.

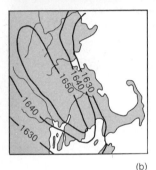

(b)

comes a high point, a low value a low point (see Figure 2.9). What is the general level and slope of the surface? How rough is it? How peaked? How complex? What is the significance of a slope—steep versus gradual? Is there any discernible order in the way peaks, ridges, valleys, and sinkholes are arranged? Is the surface changing?

Table 2.3 lists some examples of how these categories of patterns show up in studies of topics in economic geography. But some of the most interesting questions involve relationships between several pattern components (see Figure 2.10). For instance:

1. **points with networks:** McDonald's restaurants with street and highway networks, warehouses with rail lines or interstate highways, cities with power lines

2. **surfaces with networks:** land values with transportation lines

3. **networks with cells:** national boundaries as barriers to roads and rail lines

4. **cells with points:** cities and their market areas

TABLE 2.3
Components of Patterns:
Examples of Titles of Professional Journal Articles
in Geography

Point Patterns

"Temporal Land-Use Pattern Analysis. . . ," *Annals, AAG,* 1964, pp. 391–399.

". . . The Pattern of Urban Settlements in Selected Areas in the U.S.," *Tijdschrift voor Economische en Sociale Geografie,* 1962, pp. 1–7.

"The Spacing of River Towns," *Annals, AAG,* 1960, pp. 59–61.

Network Patterns

Structure of Transportation Networks: Relationships Between Network Geometry and Regional Characteristics, University of Chicago Department of Geography, 1963.

Highway Development and Geographic Change, Seattle, 1959.

"Ribbon Developments in the Urban Business Pattern," *Annals, AAG,* 1959, pp. 145–155.

Cell Patterns

"Zone Preference in Intra-Regional Population Movement," *Geografiska Annaler,* 1968, pp. 133–141.

"Scale and Economic Factors Affecting the Location of Residential Neighborhoods," *Papers of the Regional Science Association,* 1962, pp. 161–172.

". . . The Regionalization of Economic Development," in *Essays on Geography and Economic Development,* University of Chicago Department of Geography, 1960.

Surface Patterns

"The Spectrum of U.S. 40," *Papers of the Regional Science Association,* 1969, pp. 45–52.

Toward a Geography of Price, Philadelphia, 1959.

"A Topographical Model of Consumer Space Preferences," *Papers of the Regional Science Association,* 1960, pp. 159–173.

Other interesting questions may arise from relationships between different cases of the same pattern component, such as points with points, and networks with networks. For example, consider a comparison of a land value surface with an income surface. The important thing is to see not just maps but patterns, to learn to ask good questions about the patterns you see, to be able to ask your own questions about new topics and make your own maps to help answer them.

2.2.3   *Location and Behavior*

There is no reason to worry about pattern unless it makes a difference. Geography operates with the expectation that it does, en-

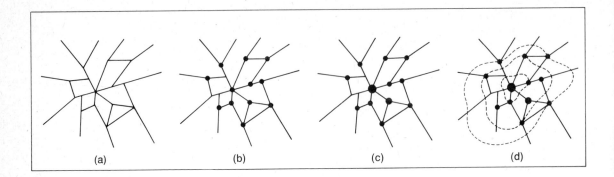

(a)   (b)   (c)   (d)

FIGURE 2.10

Stages in the Analysis of Spatial Structure: (a) networks, which indicate and facilitate movement; (b) nodes, which are the origins and destinations of most of the movement; (c) hierarchies, which indicate how the nodes and networks are organized with respect to each other (the concept of hierarchies will be discussed in Chapter 7); and (d) surfaces, which show how characteristics of the spatial system vary across the entire area, including locations between nodes and links.

deavoring to develop a body of concepts about what the difference usually is. Since this effort has not progressed very far, it is impossible to relate location and pattern to human behavior in a truly logical and general way. A number of specific concepts will be introduced in each chapter, as particular topics in economic geography are addressed. The entire discussion, however, will be based on decades of research by scholars who have made certain assumptions about the way people behave. These assumptions have become so intermingled with the concepts that we need to keep them in mind.

The first assumption is that in a world of scarcity a person tries to live as well as possible. The head of a household tries to earn as high an income as he or she can. The business owner tries to make as much profit as possible. Each of us acts in the way that maximizes our own material interest, usually defined in monetary terms. Clearly, this is a rather crude assumption (for example, it may be more appropriate for some cultures than others), but it is central to the economic ideas that economic geography incorporates. Therefore it is common to assume that a person will choose to locate wherever his or her income will be the highest.

A second presumption is that if a job can be done in more than one way, a person will do it the way that requires the least effort, that is, money, energy, and time. Since greater distance normally means more effort, this assumption offers a way to make predictions about patterns. For instance, a fast-food restaurant will do better if it is located near a lot of people than if most of the customers have to make a long trip. This seems so self-evident that it is not very interesting, but it is more complicated than it appears. What about multipurpose trips? What if the choice is between two locations, and the more distant one is slightly more desirable for other reasons? At any rate, it is usually assumed that, other things equal, a shopper will choose the nearer market. Minimizing effort usually

FIGURE 2.11

Examples of "Mental Maps." (a) To a map-maker, Sweden looks like the map on the left. To an individual at Asby in the center of Sweden (where the X is located), who is thinking about how much effort would be required to migrate to different destinations, Sweden is more like the transformed map on the right. A move of 102 kilometers instead of two kilometers—a difference of 100—is a greater mental distance than a move of 300 compared with 200. Consequently, nearby distances are "stretched" in the migrant's mind, while far-away distances are condensed. (b) Residential preferences from the perspective of college students in central Pennsylvania. Note that the students' home area is rated high, along with the West coast, Colorado, Florida, and New England. The Deep South is rated low. College students from Alabama, on the other hand, rate Alabama and Florida very high but Pennsylvania and New York very low.

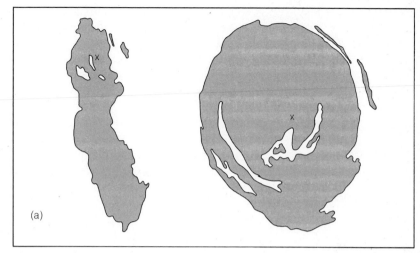

(a)

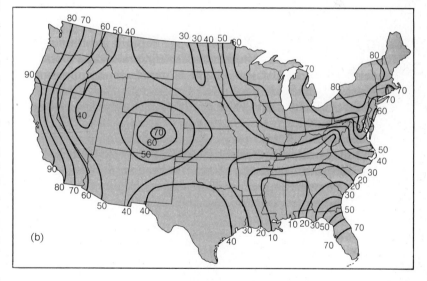

(b)

means minimizing distance, which encourages related activities to locate close to each other.

Third, when factors such as distance and concentration or spacing are important, it usually is assumed that the measurements that you and I can make from a map or on the ground are similar to the impressions held by the people making locational choices. If the map tells us that a farmer is closer to City A than to City B, we assume that the farmer sees it that way too. Actually, though, it has been found that it is not so easy to predict people's "mental maps" (see, for example, Figure 2.11). An important direction of research is concerned with the possibility that although mental maps may be different from physical maps there may be some predictable relations between the two. If so, it is possible to apply unambiguous rules to reshape, or "transform," a physical map to resemble a mental map more closely—and thereby to anticipate better the connection between pattern and behavior.

2.2.4 *Interpreting Spatial Structure*

Without trying to be formal or thorough at this point, let's see where these behavioral assumptions and our common sense lead us in thinking about what a difference a pattern makes. As you read, refer back to Figures 2.6–2.9 for examples, and see if the interpretations make sense.

1. **Points.** On a map that covers a large area, where we live is a point. Places where we get the things that we want—jobs, food—are points. The "least-effort" arrangement is one where our residence point is close to our job and market points, which suggests that a number of kinds of points are likely to cluster together. There is an urge to be close to things that we need. Thus, any point that offers goods and services has a relationship with an area around it that contains consumers: the consumers need the point and the point needs the consumers. When points representing many providers of the same thing are clustered densely together, this suggests a dense clustering of consumers—and, because the points represent opportunities, it encourages consumers to group nearby. On the other hand, too many points in a cluster may mean too much competition for consumers; therefore clustering may suggest that some points will be unable to survive in the long run. Widely scattered points suggest lack of a market, a shortage of opportunities, and perhaps a likelihood that new points will arise in the future.

2. **Networks.** Likewise, linkages mean opportunities, and they often reflect needs that exist, or once did. In our own least-effort behavior, we find that distance can be overcome by technology, but the technology costs money. The fewer links we have, the less it costs to provide and maintain the network. The more links we have, the more movement can be handled and the easier it is to get to a large number of different places. Since we can observe how completely linked a network is, we can make judgments about how these trade-offs have been resolved, and we can make decisions about using the network in a least-effort manner.

3. **Cells.** According to the case, we may be able to interpret boundaries as movement divides or barriers. Since certain efficiencies result from regularity in the form of a system of cells (beehives are a familiar example), we may be able to suggest that eventually the form of a cell will become more regular and more similar to other cells.

4. **Surfaces.** This is perhaps the most evocative category of form. Reflect on the patterns displayed in Figure 2.9. High or low points on a surface suggest that points are spreading an effect around them: they are having an impact on their surrounding areas. Ridges or valleys suggest effects from links. Cliffs in the surface indicate effects from boundaries/barriers: things are different on one side of a line than on the other. A slope indicates a direction of variation, and it may suggest a likelihood of future changes to reduce the slope.

These are some examples of the way the perspective works. It does not provide answers. It suggests questions that still need to be answered. But the secret to success in most fields, whether in scholarship or entrepreneurship, is the ability to ask good new questions, and this perspective is often a fruitful one, especially when a subject involves locational decisions.

2.3 A FOCUS ON PLACE OR A FOCUS ON PEOPLE

A sticky problem with the perspective, however, is that it seems all wrapped up in sterile geometries rather than in people. Who cares if a cell is a regular hexagon or not? Will the people there have better lives? Will it help me get the right job? Let's consider this from three points of view: the individual, the producer, and the development planner.

2.3.1 The Individual's Perspective

An important individual decision is where to live, especially when choosing a location for the first job in what is to be a long career. It is not just a question of whether to be an engineer or a musician. Do I settle in Maryland or British Columbia or Sussex or New Zealand? Where can I maximize my quality of life?

We all start with an impression about which areas are more attractive than others (see Figure 2.11(b)). Usually this impression is based on a combination of fragmentary information about climate, job opportunities, recreational opportunities, and social and political opinions, along with the present locations of friends. And we seek a list of job opportunities from newspaper classified advertisements, placement services, and other sources. In a sense, we map job openings as points against locational attractiveness as a surface. How often is one's choice between a less attractive job in a more attractive location and a more attractive job elsewhere? Why is it that employers, such as research laboratories, who depend on highly skilled employees, often prefer to locate in attractive places like Colorado and California?

We may go on to consider specific factors that have a spatial pattern. Wage rates are an obvious example, but the cost of living may also be important. Or the degree of concentration of similar kinds of employers nearby, so that job mobility is less likely to require a move. Or transportation and communication networks, to enlarge the range of leisure-time opportunities. Or, especially for an entrepreneur, *trends* in the patterns: where will markets be larger in ten years than they are now? What is the direction of money flows? Where am I most likely to meet people who can open doors for me? Where are the places where my cultural and educational background are likely to be advantages, or at least not disadvantages?

It turns out that the locational choice is imbedded in a variety of information about *places*—space as context—but also about *patterns*—space as dimension. Not only *there*—but *close to there*.

2.3.2 *The Producer's Perspective*

The producer wants to maximize total profits, if we accept the assumptions discussed earlier. He or she views the world as a pattern of inputs to production (points, cells, and networks) and their costs (often as surfaces); a pattern of consumers for the outputs of production (and the offered prices); and a pattern of linkages for acquiring inputs and delivering outputs. Distance means cost, but more for some kinds of shipments than others. Inputs cost more at some supply points, and more are available at some points than others. Consumers are willing to pay more at some market points, and there are more consumers in the vicinity of some places than others. Deciding where to locate production requires a balancing of many of these bits of information, especially when some of them are inclined to change from time to time. For some producers, a locational decision is just the difference between a 15 percent annual profit and a 12 percent profit. For others, it is the difference between survival and failure.

2.3.3   *The Development Planner's Perspective*

As an example of this perspective, let's assume that an aim of regional development is to assure that each person with the same skills and experience has an opportunity to get about the same level of material benefit from work regardless of where he or she lives, even though economic advantage is unevenly distributed from place to place. If material benefit is in fact unevenly distributed (for instance, Connecticut having a higher level than Mississippi), there are at least two types of remedies. Households (points) from Mississippi (a cell) can move to Connecticut (via a network), reducing the number dividing up the limited benefits in Mississippi by shifting some of the people to a place where there is a lot more to go around. The result is a benefit surface that is less uneven. Or the pattern of total benefits might be changed in some way, so that Mississippi's level of benefit relative to Connecticut's is increased. The first solution requires changing a lot of individual perspectives, for example by supplying new information (so that Mississippi residents know about the opportunities in Connecticut) and making transportation cheaper (so that they can afford to get there). The second calls for changing the perspectives of producers and marketers. This could be accomplished by subsidizing production in Mississippi or injecting money into the local economy so that consumers can buy more, thus improving the business of retail stores and spreading jobs and money throughout most communities. Both are difficult and delicate, and both need to be based on a real understanding of how location decisions are made by individuals, producers, and marketers, if the government is to be able to meet development goals without imposing many of the decisions itself.

There are other development goals, of course. One might be to assure that economic production is located so that the national economic system is as productive or efficient as possible. Another could be to distribute activities and benefits so that existing political-economic institutions are supported. Others might be to redistribute the population in some way; or to integrate a bunch of diverse areas into a larger whole; or to preserve traditional landscapes, artifacts, and ways of life. All of these call for a knowledge of a sizeable number of patterns and what they mean and how they are changing—and how they respond to different kinds of stimuli.

2.3.4   *Conclusion*

It is clear that a focus on pattern is a means to an end, not an end in itself. Since many important aspects of our lives are influenced by locational decisions—ours and others—we may be able to better our lives by being able to apply a spatial perspective. And since for many people the perspective is an essential part of doing a successful job, individuals who can apply it professionally—with a complete grasp of concepts and a full bag of tools of analysis—can make a good living providing services to those who need them.

Footnotes for Chapter 2

1.   Hägerstrand, Torsten. "What About People in Regional Science?" *Papers of the Regional Science Association*, vol. 24: (1970), pp. 7–21.

2.   Curry, Leslie. "Chance and Landscape." In English, P., and Mayfield, R., (eds.), *Man, Space and Environment*. New York: Oxford University Press, 1972, pp. 611–621.

PART II

SITUATION AND SCARCITY

In order to use the perspective of economic geography, we need to focus on valued goods and services that are more scarce in some places than in others. This section starts with some examples of the place-to-place variation of opportunities and benefits, to illustrate why the perspective is so widely applicable, and it introduces ways a person can identify this variation on his or her own (Chapter 3). Then in Chapter 4, it introduces some of the vocabulary and concepts that are helpful in talking about scarcity. These building blocks are still close to the foundation of our subject, but they anticipate the structure of the beams in the attic.

Chapter 3 also introduces a format that will be used in most of the remaining chapters. After a brief introductory paragraph, a few situations are described. Each one is a plausible real-life circumstance—one in which you might someday find yourself. In most cases, it shows how a knowledge of the concepts of the chapter might help you to deal with an important decision; in a few others, it illustrates an important concept. The situations are followed by a discussion of basic concepts or procedures. (If you think carefully about the situations, you will find that you can discover many of the ideas by yourself, and you can use the following sections mainly to confirm your hunches, pick up some professional terminology, and provide some more illustrations.)

After the concepts are outlined, examples are given, and a further section offers some final thoughts on the subject matter of the chapter.

In some chapters, an additional section will present a little more technical detail about an item discussed less precisely in the main body of the text. After most chapters, the major concepts and terms that have been introduced will be listed, for easy reference. In summary, although we will not be prisoners of an arbitrary format, the usual presentation will be situations, then concepts, then examples, then a brief reconsideration and a listing of major concepts and terms introduced.

CHAPTER 3

THE LOCATION OF OPPORTUNITY AND BENEFIT

*I*n Chapter 1 it was suggested that most people in some places live better than most people in other places: incomes are higher, opportunities are easier to find, and life is more exciting and fulfilling. If we ignore for the moment those who are rich enough to make their own opportunities and choose their own locations without constraint, the lives of most of us are lived out on a kind of carpet of opportunity and benefit. Like an ant on an Oriental rug, we can appreciate that there are differences in the texture of the carpet as we move from one place to another, but it is difficult for us to get an image of the overall pattern, to decide the most interesting and promising location of them all.

3.1 SITUATIONS

3.1.1 The Transferred Employee

You are a middle-level executive with a large electronics firm. After a good career in management and sales, you are now happily located in Southern California, managing a plant that makes component systems for the aerospace industry.

Out of the blue, you are told that the plant is being shut down because of cutbacks in aerospace production, and you are to be transferred to West Virginia to manage a plant for pollution measurement instruments. You have children in junior high school, family in the Southwest, and a vacation home in Oregon; and your wife has a good job teaching in a local high school. You are not sure that you want to take the new assignment. If you turn it down, though, you will have to look for a new job, and there are already a lot of unemployed executives in Southern California.

What would it be like to live in West Virginia? How are the schools for your kids? Where do graduates of West Virginia high schools go to college? Is health care adequate? What would you do for summer vacations? What about job opportunities for your wife? How much permanence would there be in the new location? The answers will determine a decision that will shape your family's life.

3.1.2   *The Entrepreneur*

You and a friend will finish your time in the Air Force in about three months. Your training has been in electronics and your friend's in security. In your spare time, the two of you have developed an electronic security system for private homes that you believe is something people will buy, and you have decided to set up business. By pooling your savings, you can probably scrape by for as long as two years without breaking even, but that's all. You have no particular ties with any one part of the country.

The question is where to locate the business. You could choose any city, rent some office and workshop space, and start advertising. But where is the best prospect for success? You have dreams of a merchandising miracle—national advertising, franchises across the country, retirement to Puerto Vallarta—but first you have to have a solid start.

There are several factors to be considered. You want to be able to reach a large number of householders from a single location; so you are looking for a place where a single television station or newspaper can contact millions and those millions can call or visit your office without difficulty. You need a place where as many people as possible live in single-family homes rather than apartments, and the home owners need to be fairly affluent because your system will be expensive. And, frankly, you think your sales will be better in a place where property crimes are a serious problem.

Is there a place that fits this description better than any other? Are other firms already providing home security services there?

3.1.3   *The Trucker*

You are one of the last of the truly self-employed: the new owner of a large, modern truck rig, making a living by hauling cargoes in semitrailers on a freelance basis. If you can keep your truck full and rolling, you will make a good living. If it is idle, you will be making payments on a very expensive piece of equipment without income. If you get stuck somewhere far from home without a cargo, you will have to choose between waiting for something to turn up and paying your own expenses to drive empty to another location.

At least several times a month, you find that you are faced with difficult decisions. From your location in central Indiana, do you take a lucrative long-haul job to Texas even though you are unsure that there will be a return cargo, or do you take a short-haul assignment to Chicago, with a return load guaranteed? Do you wait for a load where you are or do you move to find one elsewhere? After a month on the road, how can your route yourself back home for a while?

Actually, you need to know more than most people about the movement of goods across the country: what moves, when it moves, where it moves from and to, how it moves, who moves it, who makes decisions about these things. But how do you find out?

3.2   BASIC PROCEDURES FOR LOCATING OPPORTUNITIES

Obviously, there are many times when each of us needs to know about the distribution of opportunities and benefits from place to place. Section 3.3 will illustrate how pervasive this variation is, but first let us consider how we can find out about it when we are starting from scratch.

Remember that most of the maps that have already been made were intended to answer the mapmaker's questions, not necessarily our own questions. If we are to be able to use the concepts of economic geography to meet our own needs, we need to be able to acquire, display, and analyze information that has not been used that way before. And we need to understand how other people have arrived at their conclusions.

This section is a very brief introduction to the kinds of "detective work" that lie behind the maps in the next section and the examples in the chapters that follow. It should give you some notions about how to get (and process) information for your own purposes. First, it will indicate how a person finds information; then, it will suggest some of the things that are often done with it. Actually, given the perspective of economic geography, a lot of information, some common sense, and a good deal of hard work, many of you could invent the rest of the book if it did not already exist. And a few of you will discover concepts that are not in the book— because they will be brand new, never before known. One of the most challenging frontiers of all is the research frontier.

3.2.1 *Finding Data*

Because so many people need information so often, a great deal of information is readily available at any time. Governments spend money for censuses and other kinds of recordkeeping because they need the data themselves and because citizens can make good use of them. Businesses collect information for their own purposes, and some firms—ranging from private investigators to publishing companies—even specialize in providing it for a price. Any good reference library contains a vast store of information available to any patron.

Some of the most useful sources of information are the following:

1. **National censuses.** Most countries organize a comprehensive program of data gathering at regular intervals, focusing especially on a count of the population by village or city, region, and the country as a whole. For example, every ten years, the U.S. Bureau of the Census conducts a census of population, socioeconomic characteristics of the population, and housing. Data are made available for units of many different sizes and kinds: the country, states, counties, metropolitan areas, urbanized areas, cities, towns and villages, census tracts, and census blocks. Other periodic censuses of the United States include manufacturing (every four to six years), agriculture, government, and business. The U.S. Census Bureau also publishes reports on special subjects and prepares estimates of data for some intercensal periods. An example is the *Annual Survey of Manufactures and Current Industrial Reports* (monthly, quarterly, and annually). For easier reference, the most commonly used categories of information from all the censuses are collected periodically in a *County and City Data Book.* An annually updated book entitled *Statistical Abstract of the United States* provides a guide to past censuses.

   Similar kinds of information are available for many other countries, although there are variations in their comprehensiveness and in the intervals between censuses. Sweden, for example, has been a gold mine for social scientists because its social and economic data are unusually detailed and reliable.

2. **Other national government publications.** Other agencies of national governments gather and publish information; in fact this is one of the traditional ways for a public agency to justify its existence. In the United States, for example, the Departments of Labor, Agriculture, and Interior are prolific data producers, along with other agencies of the executive branch and committees of Congress. A guide to government publications

is the *Monthly Catalog of United States Government Publications,* and a number of other reference books summarize sources of statistical data. Examples are *County Business Patterns,* published every three years by the Department of Commerce, and the *Quarterly Financial Report for Manufacturing Corporations,* issued by the Federal Trade Commission. Along with numbers, government publications often provide interpretations of the information, descriptions of technologies and policies, and other useful material. And they are usually bargains, since taxes have already paid most of the bill.

3. **United Nations publications.**   Information about many countries is collected and published by the United Nations. For example, a *United Nations Statistical Abstract* is released annually, and U.N. agencies such as the Food and Agricultural Organization (FAO) and the U.N. Educational and Scientific Organization (UNESCO) have separate information services. Specific documents are listed in the *United Nations Documents Index.*

4. **State and local publications.**   In the United States, each state generates information as well: data on state services, especially in education, health, and welfare; and data on tax revenues and budget expenditures. Much of the information is provided annually in the form of a state statistical handbook, which includes numbers from federal sources.

   Local governments, particularly of larger cities, also gather and provide numerical data of certain kinds. Planning agencies are often a fruitful source of this information.

   A further source, and a very important one, is state and municipal universities. State universities, for instance, usually include a Bureau of Business and Economic Research (or the equivalent), and the so-called land grant universities—usually identifiable by their strong academic programs related to agriculture—perform impressively in providing information about agronomy, farm economics, and other very practical subjects.

5. **Privately published references.**   The reference section of a library also contains reference books published by private firms or nonprofit agencies, including indexes of more specialized books and articles in periodicals. These may range from annually updated compendia of information, such as the *World Almanac* or the *Stateman's Yearbook,* to the telephone directories of large cities, travel books, Dun & Bradstreet evaluations of the financial condition of firms, a *Polks Directory* of the occupations of householders in a city (by street address),

estimates by the J. Walter Thompson advertising agency of the market potential of communities in the United States, and population data from the Population Reference Bureau. The subject index of a library card catalog can be augmented by the *Subject Guide to Books in Print,* and the intimidating mass and complexity of the periodical literature can be dealt with by using a wide variety of subject indexes. Examples are the *Business Periodicals Index* and *The New York Times Index.* It can be useful—and even profitable—to become well acquainted with the information services that are locally available.

In addition, with a little more effort (and sometimes money) a person can get access to more specialized information. National, state, and local nonprofit foundations often publish valuable materials related to their special interests. And private firms often specialize in certains kinds of information. An example is the comprehensive coverage of information about oil shale and coal resources provided to subscribers, for several hundred dollars a year, by an engineering firm in Denver.

6.   **Other documentary sources.**   Many other kinds of information are never published. They reside in filing cabinets or basement storage rooms or computer memory banks and are used as needed, then stored or destroyed. Property tax records are an example of facts that are publicly available but seldom printed and distributed.

Most government agencies maintain files of data for their own use. In some cases, an agency is legally obligated to make the information available on request; in a few others, it may be legally forbidden to allow access to it. But most often it is up to the agency, which means that a person may or may not be allowed to use the data, depending partly on how the request is made.

Private firms are repositories of information as well, from the results of mineral exploration by energy companies to the market research efforts of manufacturers and the property value files of savings and loan associations. Most of this is proprietary—owned by the firm—and is used to give the owner an advantage over competitors. In fact, if a firm shares the information with its competitors, in some cases it can be subject to antitrust action. Consequently, firms are very cautious about allowing access to their own funds of facts, but an individual can occasionally arrange to use some of the data if a firm sees the possibility of some kind of economic or public relations benefit from the proposed study.

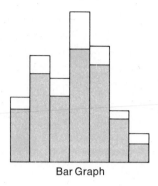

Bar Graph

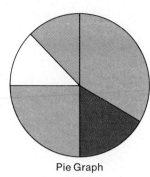

Pie Graph

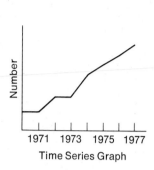

Time Series Graph

FIGURE 3.1

Four Types of Graphs: (a) bar graph; (b) pie graph; (c) time-series graph; and (d) graph of the relationship between two variables.

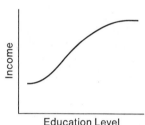

Graph of the Relationship
Between Two Variables

7.   **Original data.** If it proves to be impossible to find all the information a person needs, all is not lost. When the focus is local and well defined, some new data can be generated, for example (1) by observation: traffic counts, indicators of housing quality, prices, land uses; and (2) by survey (asking questions): occupations, educational levels, product or service preferences.

　　　If original data gathering is to result in dependable information, it must be done according to some well-tested rules of procedure (some references are listed in the Bibliography). But it may be the only way to acquire data that nobody else has.

3.2.2   *Analyzing Data*

Now that you have it, what do you do with it? In many cases, others have already interpreted the information and published studies of it: government agencies, university bureaus, private firms. But in some cases it is necessary to fill gaps or to go farther.

　　　Going beyond a visual inspection of tables of numbers, a person usually has three kinds of options: graphs, statistical analysis, and maps. A good study in economic geography often combines all three.

1.   **Graphs.** Most of us are familiar with a variety of types of graphs (for example, see Figure 3.1). A form that is widely used in economics and economic geography is represented by Figure 3.1(d): expressing a relationship between two quantitative values.

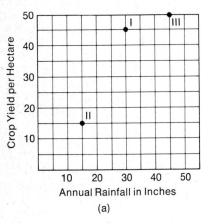

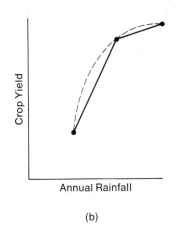

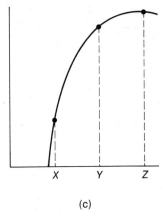

(a)

(b)

(c)

FIGURE 3.2

Constructing Graphs of Relationships. Although a relationship cannot be established reliably from three observations, this illustrates the general approach.

Figure 3.2 shows how such a graph is constructed. For three years, a farmer keeps careful records of the yield per hectare of the crop and the annual rainfall on the farm. The records show this:

Year	Yield	Rainfall
I	45	30
II	15	15
III	50	45

In Figure 3.2(a), each year is plotted on the graph as a dot. Let's say that the farmer is trying to decide whether to invest in an irrigation system that will assure a water supply each year equivalent to 40 inches of rainfall. What kind of yields can he or she expect? Unless there has been something unusual about one of the three years, the general relationship between water supply and crop yields should be approximately as shown in Figure 3.2(b), predicting a yield of 45–50 bushels per hectare with irrigation.

It is generally desirable to base such a general prediction on as many observations as possible, and statistical analysis is commonly used to define the "best-fitting line" for a *scatter diagram*, a graph with a large number of observations indicated by dots.

A line or curve on a two-axis (or two-dimensional) graph can be defined by a series of observations, but its basic form can often be identified ahead of time by logic. In Figure 3.2, for example, it is reasonable to expect that the crop yield will be zero even if rainfall is at some level above zero and that the

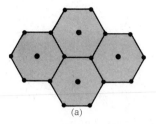

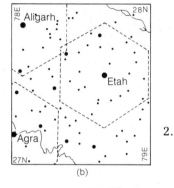

FIGURE 3.3
Theory and Reality: (a) theoretical pattern of settlements; (b) actual pattern of villages in the Gangetic Plain, India.

crop yield will stop increasing if rainfall gets too heavy. In fact, the yield may even decrease beyond a certain point because of flooding or erosion. Figure 3.2(c) indicates the kind of relationship that corresponds with these expectations. Knowing this basic form, even without having specific numbers on the axes, allows us to make general statements: the farmer will not apply more irrigation water than Z; for the crop we are considering, an investment in an irrigation system will probably be repaid more quickly if the average annual rainfall is Y than if it is Z, because the added production will be greater.

Much of the theory of economic geography is built on the use of graphs like Figure 3.2(c), particularly with distance as the label on the horizontal axis. Calculus has proved to be a highly useful tool of analysis because of its eminent suitability for reasoning about this special class of graphs.

2. **Statistical analysis.**   Statistics is a branch of mathematics that studies how a person can use a limited number of observations to make general statements about things not observed. It includes the calculation of averages and typical variations from the average, but it also deals with such matters as fitting the best line or curve through a scatter diagram, measuring the closeness of the relationship between two quantitative factors, and deciding whether two qualitative classes (such as countries or soil regions) show a significant difference in some quantitative characteristic.

3. **Maps.**   With its special focus on location, economic geography characteristically uses maps as tools of description and analysis (see Chapter 2). These maps can be used to communicate information to others, or they can be studied for insights and questions. They can be combined with other maps to suggest further ideas. And the patterns on them can be described and analyzed, using techniques first applied in such diverse fields as plant ecology, psychology, geology, econometrics, and mathematical cartography.

Just as scatter diagrams relate to generalized graphs, maps can be associated with schematic spatial diagrams. For example, using the logic that will be developed in Chapter 7, a person could expect towns on a flat plain to be arranged in the evenly spaced pattern indicated by Figure 3.3(a). Villages in a part of the flat Gangetic Plain of India are in fact distributed in a very similar way, as shown in Figure 3.3(b).

These idealized diagrams are a convenient way to investigate general concepts about location, and we will use them frequently in the chapters that follow.

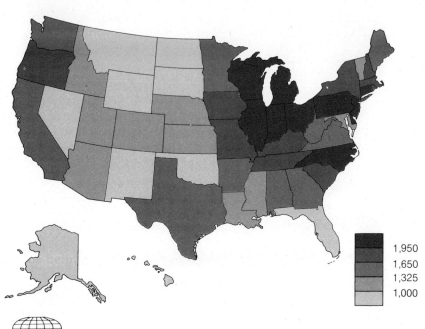

FIGURE 3.4
Economic Characteristics of the United States: I. (a) Value added by manufacturing, 1972, in dollars per state per capita—a measure of where manufacturing activity is concerned; [continued on next page]

Legend:
1,950
1,650
1,325
1,000

3.3 EXAMPLES

When various kinds of information about opportunity and benefit are displayed on maps, it is easy to identify similarities or differences between the patterns, and with these observations we can do several useful things; for example, suggest relationships between similar patterns and form general impressions about the characteristics of areas.

Figure 3.4 shows the distributions of two different characteristics of the United States: manufacturing activity and predominantly urban areas. And the caption refers you to two additional maps: of population and highway traffic. There are some similarities among these maps. As a group, they begin to characterize some parts of the country; for instance, the urban, industrial, economically intensive Northeast. And small differences among them are worth studying; note the east-west highway traffic through North and South Dakota, where urban areas are sparse.

The same kind of comparison can be made of economic characteristics throughout the world. Figure 3.5 provides an example: urban population as a proportion of the total population in a country.

For any collection of similar maps, there is another collection of maps that display contrasting patterns. Figure 3.6 shows two dis-

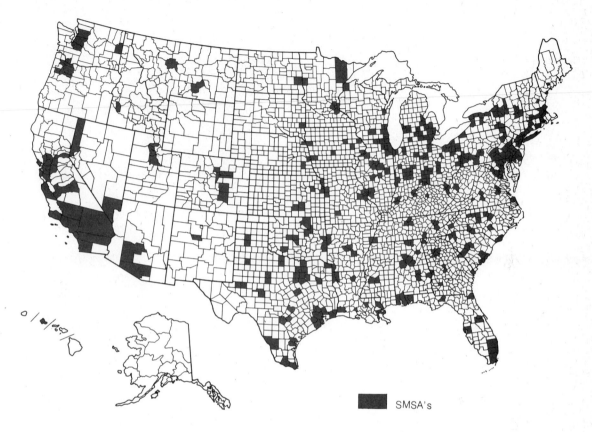

SMSA's

FIGURE 3.4 (cont'd.)
(b) Standard Metropolitan Statistical Areas in the United States—areas associated economically and socially with a large population nucleus. Also see Figures 2.1 (population distribution) and 11.7 (highway traffic flows). Many indicators of economic activity show a concentration in the northeastern part of the country, although 3.4b shows that the concentration is less pronounced now than it once was.

tributions that are quite different from those in Figure 3.4. In general, these two characteristics have high values outside the Northeast, focusing on either the Southeast or the Southwest. Note, for example, that where manufacturing is concentrated now is not the same as where the new manufacturing is going. Also note that some of the less urban, less industrial areas are less poor and hungry than others.

Because the world is a combination of so many varied patterns, it is very difficult to develop a single map of opportunity and benefit. Figure 3.7, for example, shows three maps of aspects of "quality of life," each based on a combination of several factors. "Technological change" reflects patents issued, research activities, and levels of vocational education. Which of the three maps is the best indicator of the location of opportunities? Can a map be made that combines them all?

Generally, a single map is less useful than several maps that illustrate distinctively different distributions—one the type of Fig-

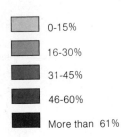

- 0-15%
- 16-30%
- 31-45%
- 46-60%
- More than 61%

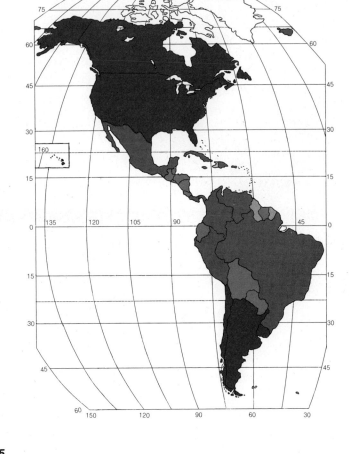

Equatorial Scale

Kilometers

| 0 | 1,600 | 3,200 | 4,800 |

| 0 | 1,000 | 2,000 | 3,000 |

Miles

Flat Polar Quartic Projection interrupted and Abbreviated

FIGURE 3.5

An Example of a Map of an Economic Characteristic of Countries of the World: Urbanization (urban population as a percentage of total population).

ure 2.1, but also one of each of the other kinds of patterns that occur repeatedly. The price of the convenience of one map is a loss of information.

But there are times when a single map is a necessity. Many countries designate certain areas with economic problems as development regions, which receive special assistance from the national government. This designation makes it necessary to reduce all the patterns of economic disadvantage—ranging from low fam-

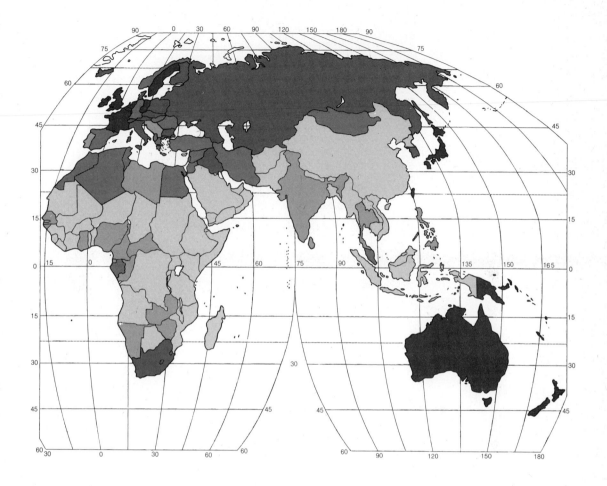

FIGURE 3.5 (cont'd.)

ily incomes to high unemployment—to a single pattern of "cells."
States and counties inside a cell are eligible for aid. Areas outside
the cells are not. Figure 3.8 indicates how the "development regions" of the United States were defined in 1968 by the U.S. government. Related to specific objectives and shaped by political accommodation, this is not an all-purpose "best" map, because no
such thing exists. It is a single map to serve a general purpose,
developed because decision makers required one.

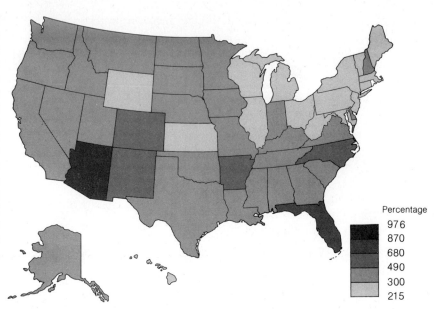

FIGURE 3.6
Economic Characteristics of the United States: II. (a) Value added by manufacturing in 1972 as a percentage of the value added in 1954, in current dollars—a measure of the trend in the location of manufacturing activity (where activities are going); and (b) hunger in the United States. These maps show different dimensions of economic opportunity and benefit from Figure 3.4.

Percentage

976
870
680
490
300
215

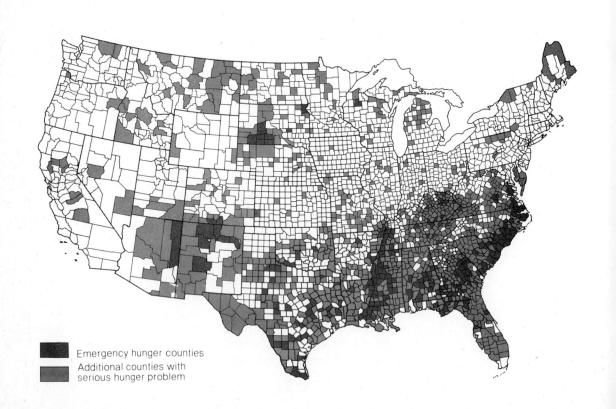

Emergency hunger counties

Additional counties with serious hunger problem

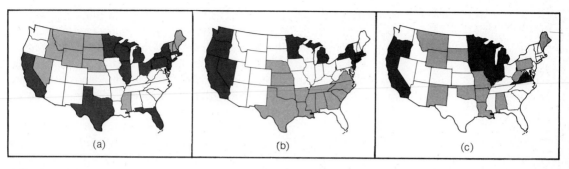

FIGURE   3.7

Three Indicators of "Quality of Life" in the United States. The dark area shows the top twelve states and the lighter area shows the bottom twelve states based on measures of each indicator: (a) technological change; (b) living conditions; and (c) economic growth quality.

FIGURE   3.8
Economic Development Regions in the United States, 1968.

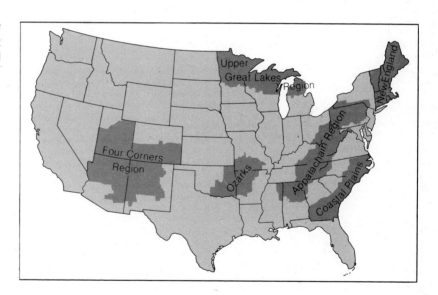

3.4   A RECONSIDERATION

When we look around us to get an organized conception of where to seek opportunities and benefits, and we study available data with the help of maps and graphs, we find that some places interest us more than others. Before long, these places come to dominate our mental maps, which stretch to accommodate our special concerns. For example, the views that a manufacturer and a retailer might have of the United States could resemble Figure 3.9. And it is with this kind of view of the world that we proceed to make a living. If the mental map is well informed, we may have an advantage in seeking out the interesting and rewarding things to be done. If it fails to correspond with the facts, there are likely to be unpleasant surprises ahead.

As the pace of life—and the pace of change (see Alvin Toffler's *Future Shock*)—increases, it becomes especially important to resolve as many uncertainties as possible by having as much good information as we can. In fact, "the dominant commodity in society . . . is not corn or grain or agricultural products or petroleum. It is not automobiles, housing, or transportation. The dominant commodity of American society is information."[1]

Footnote for Chapter 3

1. Coates, Joseph F., "Why Think About the Future: Some Administrative-Political Perspectives." *Public Administration Review,* vol. 36 (1976), pp. 580–85.

FIGURE 3.9
Different Views of the United States: (a) manufacturing; and (b) marketing in which areas of cities and states are shown in proportion to their (a) employment in manufacturing, and (b) retail sales.

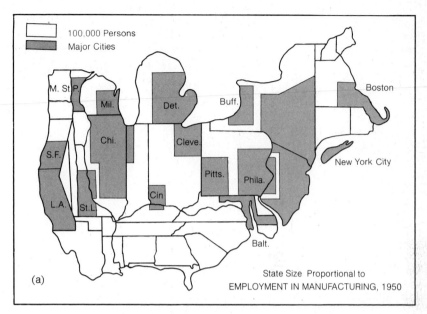

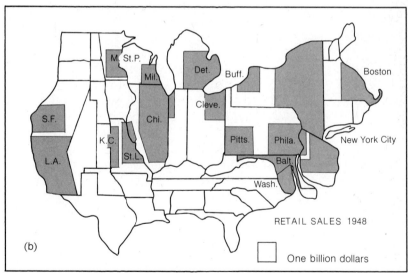

CHAPTER 4

PLACE AND ECONOMIC ACTIVITY

*R*eflect on your personal experience. Each of us is a focus of the economic-geographic system that operates around us. If every article of clothing and food that we use in a day could tell us where it has been, we would be able to trace a web of connections that spreads to many parts of the world. That shirt or shoes or breakfast food or banana has passed through a lot of hands in moving from the farm or mine or forest . . . to the factory or warehouse . . . to the shopping center or grocery store . . . to you.

There is a geographic pattern to this series of transfers, reflecting the hard-nosed logic of economic decision makers. And we can begin to understand the reasons for the pattern—why it gives some locations advantages and others disadvantages—by beginning to understand the logic. After all, if we want to really *understand* the distributions of opportunity and benefit that are important to use, to make them work for us, we have to do more than memorize them, because the maps may change. If we understand what causes the distributions, we can predict changes in the map before they happen. We can anticipate the maps that people will make of future distributions—guessing at the nature of maps to be made.

This section will help us take some first steps toward understanding economic-geographic patterns by (1) introducing some terms that are commonly used by people who talk about such things (so that you can understand their language when you hear or read it) and (2) relating some standard economic concepts to the geographer's concern with places.

4.1 *ELEMENTS OF ECONOMIC-GEOGRAPHIC SYSTEMS*

We can start this effort by identifying some important types of economic activities and, in very general terms, how they relate to each other. A conventional distinction, for example, is among *producers* of goods (such as electric can openers or paint) and services (such as schools and massage parlors), *marketers* of these goods and services, and *consumers* of them. Alternatively, we might speak of providers, intermediaries, and users.

This kind of classification tends to hide the fact that most of the goods and services that reach us in our home locations are the end of long sequences of exchanges. Most providers are also consumers, and most consumers are also providers. Not only this, most of the transactions are aided by intermediaries—transporters, brokers, advertisers—who are themselves providers of services and consumers of both goods and services. Clearly we could make a map of the process for a particular instance if it would be helpful.

Since the term *goods and services* covers such a range of possibilities, it is often helpful to divide provision types of activities into categories, or *sectors of an economy*, as well. The usual method is this:

1. **primary activities:** those that acquire "building blocks" from our physical environment: hunting, fishing, mining, farming
2. **secondary activities:** those that convert building blocks into other products: manufacturing
3. **tertiary activities:** those that get products to users and supplement the products with other services that people want

There is considerable variation in the use of the term *tertiary*, which is often subdivided. Some experts limit tertiary activities to business services and identify government services as quaternary. Others separate retailing and wholesaling from the rest of the business activities. And it is sometimes useful to divide transportation activities from others. It is common to worry a great deal about such matters, but for the sake of simplicity we will simply use the term *tertiary* to refer to all the activities that are not primary or secondary.

Although it is dangerous to make too much of the difference, in general the location of primary activities is linked closer to characteristics of the physical environment than the other sectors are. Petroleum is where the geological history of the earth has caused it to form (and where people have found it). Bananas are usually grown in places with a certain kind of climate. Shrimp are found in certain parts of the sea.

Secondary activities are less closely linked in their locations to such characteristics of the environment—hard to move and expensive to find substitutes for. Part of the reason is that they often use a variety of inputs from different locations, giving them more factors to consider in choosing a location.

Tertiary activities—in the broad sense of retailing, wholesaling, consumer services, and government services—are even less closely linked to the physical characteristics of places, because they are more oriented to consumers than to producers. They can be wherever the people are, not just where the oil or shrimp are.

Remember that large firms often include activities in more than one sector. An international energy company, for example, may produce oil from oil wells (primary), refine it into gasoline (secondary), and sell the gasoline in service stations (tertiary). In such a firm, activities in one sector are often located with respect to related activities in other sectors—suppliers, markets, complementary activities of many types.

4.2 *LOCATION AND CIRCULATION*

The key to most economic systems is *exchange.* If you have something that I want, I need to find something that you want so that we can make a trade. The special interest of economic geography is in the way this process involves exchanges between places as well as exchanges between components that can be identified in other ways. Figure 4.1 is a very simplified version of the way economic-geographic exchanges work. Consider three places, each with one product to trade, but each wanting some of what the others have to offer. The needs of a place are satisfied by exchange; for example, if New York City wants more cars, it has to publish more books to trade for them. (If you think carefully about this, you may be able to anticipate one or two of the most important theories of regional development.)

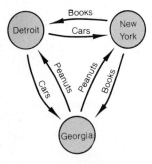

FIGURE 4.1

A Schematic Diagram of Economic-Geographic Exchanges.

Note what this example means. When individual location decisions lead to *specialization,* so that some places do some things and others do other things (and they nearly always do), then a consequence is not only exchange but *circulation.* Goods, services, and people must move from place to place, so that people at locations that provide one kind of thing can make use of other things as well. Just as exchange is central to the concepts of economics, circulation is central to the concepts of economic geography.

4.3   *DECISIONS IN ECONOMIC-GEOGRAPHIC SYSTEMS*

Section 2.2.3 mentioned that economic geography usually assumes every economic decision maker is trying to maximize his or her well-being, which is defined by material things rather than by qualities such as emotional peace. These assumptions allow an elaborate framework of theory to be built. Although we will not try to follow this process of construction, it is important to touch on the most important concepts because they give us insights into the way business decisions are made and because they are associated with a vocabulary that we will need to be able to use.

4.3.1   *Preference and Exchange*

In choosing a place to live, we compare the alternatives and decide which one we prefer and why. The same mental activity is a part of every exchange. For example, perhaps your choice of a location for your residence is influenced by a desire to be as far as possible from (1) a noisy, smelly industrial concentration in your city; and (2) your spouse's parents, who are the source of social friction in your family. You are comparing ten different houses to decide which is preferable, and the house with the most *utility* for you will be the one that, on balance, is farthest away from both these places.

Table 4.1 shows your measurements for the alternatives. J is clearly the best because it is farther from either location than any of

TABLE 4.1
Bases of Location Preference

House	Miles from Relatives	Miles from Heavy Industry	Classification of Preference
A	1	4	IV
B	2	2	IV
C	3	1	IV
D	4	4	III
E	3	5	III
F	5	3	III
G	6	6	II
H	7	5	II
I	5	9	II
J	9	10	I

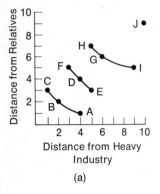

Distance from Relatives

Distance from Heavy
Industry

(a)

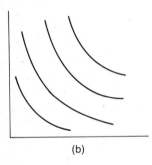

(b)

FIGURE 4.2
Representation of Prefer-
ences on a Graph. (See
text for explanation.)

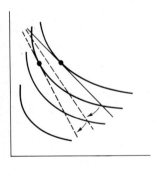

FIGURE 4.3
Relating Cost to
Preference. (See text for
explanation.)

the other houses. But what if it is too expensive? G, H, and I are preferable to the rest of the houses because each is at least as far away from one target location as A through F, and farther away from the other. It is not clear whether G is preferable to H or I; therefore we can say that you would be more or less indifferent about a choice between them. Similarly, D, E, and F are preferable to A, B, and C.

When we put this information about the utility of the ten housing options on a graph, a pattern starts to emerge, as shown in Figure 4.2. When the alternatives to which you are indifferent are connected by a solid line, showing that different combinations of distance can give you approximately the same utility, the graph becomes a representation of how different characteristics of places are weighed in determining our preference for places. We prefer greater distance to lesser, but at a given level of utility we are willing to give up some distance from the relatives to get farther from the industrial center, and vice versa. One can be substituted for the other, as long as the overall utility is not changed.

The dotted lines in Figure 4.2(a) can be called indifference curves, and for convenience they usually are assumed to take the convex shape shown in Figure 4.2(b). The more convex (bent toward the point where the axes join) the curves are, the more difficult it is to substitute one advantage for another: as one characteristic gets scarcer and scarcer, it takes more of the other to take its place. For instance, being a mile closer to the industrial concentration may not mean a big loss in utility if it is 8 miles rather than 9, but it would take a sizeable collection of other advantages to equal the difference between 1 mile and zero.

What if for a variety of reasons you find that the locations with higher utility have houses that are more expensive? Others also want to be distant from the industries, and other young families are interested in moving away from their parents' neighborhood. In Figure 4.3, the cost of housing—related to the two dimensions of preference—is represented by a straight line. Any indifference curve that falls to the right of the cost line is a level of utility (or a standard of living) we cannot afford. Any indifference curve that falls—even in part—to the left of the cost line is a lower standard of living than we can afford. Therefore the best option is the one where the highest possible indifference curve just touches the cost line. But what if, because of the general desire to be distant from the heavy industry, the cost of being distant goes up? The cost line moves to the left as shown by the dotted lines in Figure 4.3, reducing the level of utility available on a fixed budget and also leading

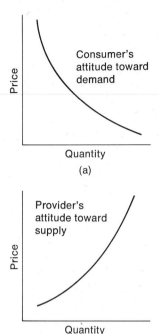

Consumer's attitude toward demand

Quantity

(a)

Provider's attitude toward supply

Quantity

(b)

Supply

Price paid

Quantity supplied

Demand

Quantity

(c)

FIGURE 4.4
How Supply and Demand Usually Relate to Price, Quantity, and Each Other.

to a best solution that places less emphasis on distance from the industrial area.

This gives us a very important behavioral concept. As the *price* of distance from heavy industry goes up, the *demand* to be distant will go down. Figure 4.4(a) shows this concept graphically: as price rises, quantity decreases; as price drops, quantity increases. And this, from a consumer's point of view, is the usual relationship between price and preference (except where a higher price carries with it the appeal of conspicuous consumption or the promise of other intangible benefits).

A provider sees things differently. As the price of housing rises in an area, a home owner may find it more attractive to build a new home elsewhere, especially if property taxes rise as well. If the price of housing drops, there will be less economic incentive for selling. This suggests a supplier's view of the relationship between price and preference, as seen in Figure 4.4(b). If the price is higher and other things are equal, more will be supplied, affecting the supplier's preference for providing this rather than something else.

Combining Figures 4.4(a) and 4.4(b) gives a graph with an intersection: a price and quantity that both a supplier and a consumer can agree upon, as shown in Figure 4.4(c). At a higher price, more houses will be on the market than there are buyers available, and the sellers of houses will compete with each other by lowering their prices (with some owners choosing not to sell so cheaply). At a lower price, there will be more buyers than houses available, and some of the buyers will offer a higher price to try to persuade people to sell their houses to them. In either case, the price and quantity will move toward the intersection, or *equilibrium*, amounts (the level of exchange where there is no excess supply or excess demand).*

The equilibrium can change if either the supply or the demand curve changes. For example, a sudden interest in a fashionable new housing development may make home owners in an older area more eager to sell, sliding the supply curve for the older area to the right. Or an increase in the average incomes of potential buyers may make them better able to buy, shifting the demand curve to the right.

---

* Technically, because this equilibrium refers to only one kind of good or service, it is only a partial equilibrium solution for the market. A general equilibrium solution would simultaneously remove excess supply and demand for all goods and services. Because, for example, the equilibrium for housing may depend partly on the equilibrium for transportation, it is unrealistic to think of an equilibrium in one sector of an economy as independent of the rest of the economy.

4.3.2 *Types of Markets*

The concepts we have been considering, and especially the supply-demand equilibrium illustrated by Figure 4.4(c), grow out of a sequence of logic that assumes that markets are *competitive*. No single provider or consumer can set the price, because there are many providers and consumers interacting in an ongoing process of bargaining—each provider competing with other providers to serve consumers, and each consumer competing with other consumers to get what is in demand. It is assumed that every provider and user has perfect knowledge of the alternatives and that providers and consumers can move in and out of the bargaining process without any difficulties. For example, if demand will support a higher level of production, the current providers cannot force prices up by refusing to produce more because new providers will jump in immediately to meet the need.

Obviously, this is not the way very many economies work; for example, as Section 2.2.1 pointed out, competition is limited by some basic constraints on how and where a person can act within a short period of time. As a result, theories have also been developed to describe the behavior of providers and consumers when the market is *monopolistic* (one provider or consumer sets the price) or *oligopolistic* (a few large providers or consumers join together to set the price). There are some near-monopolies in the United States (such as Amtrak, ATT, the Postal Service) and in the past there have been many others (for example, duPont for some years in cellophane and the 3M Company in adhesive tape). Monopolies usually indicate one of three kinds of situations: (1) the company moved into a field early, getting so much of a head start that it has been hard for others to compete; (2) the company was granted an exclusive right to something for a while (by getting or buying a patent); or (3) the only way a company could come close to breaking even was to be so large that there was room for only one in the country. Many countries in the world organize their economies so that most activities are government-owned monopolies. Examples of what often appear to be oligopolies in the United States are the automobile industry and the retail gasoline industry. If the large U.S. automobile manufacturers were to decide to set price levels for new cars that are higher than the theoretical equilibrium prices in a competitive market, it would be hard for someone who has not previously been making cars to decide to jump into the market by selling cars at a cheaper price. The start-up process is too big an investment.

A great deal of study has been devoted to the influence of the type of market on individual economic behavior and well-being.

For example, is the price for an item more or less under a monopoly than in a competitive market system? Two general principles have come out of all this study, and, carried to extremes, they disagree about the merits of unrestricted competition:

1. It can be argued that the more competitive a market is the better people will fare economically. A monopoly or oligopoly, by avoiding the bargaining process, ends up setting price levels that benefit the few who have the power to set them rather than being a fair reflection of the preferences of all individuals. In the long run, this results in a loss of productivity for the entire economy by discouraging new ideas, shutting people out of the system, and often reducing demand because of unduly high prices. In addition, some experts argue that monopolies, since they lack competitors to keep them on their toes, tend to get inefficient, administratively top-heavy, and slow to make progress.

2. On the other hand, it can be argued that in a purely competitive individual market, the highest level of productivity may not be the result. If everyone is doing "what's best for me," what one person does may reduce the productivity of someone else. Smoke from a smokestack may hurt the business of the owner of a tree nursery, for example. This kind of effect is called an *external diseconomy*. In the same way, something that restricts individual productivity or profits in the short run may turn out to have economic benefits in the long run: an *external economy*.[†]

Suppose, for instance, that there are eight multifamily rental houses on a block in a run-down neighborhood, all owned by absentee landlords. Each owner is trying to decide whether to spend money rehabilitating the houses. Each one, acting independently, decides not to improve the house. Since the area is unattractive to prospective renters who could pay higher rents, the owner would not be able to recover the invested money in this way.

But perhaps if all eight owners got together and agreed to rehabilitate all eight houses, the area might become attractive enough to support higher rents, benefiting all the owners. The problem is that the only way to bring this about is for each owner to do exactly what his or her judgment as an independent competitor would say

[†] Some references call these "technological" economies and diseconomies to distinguish them from another kind of external effect. If one tree nursery doubles the size of its operation, and the additional supply of trees pushes the price per tree to a lower level, then a second tree nursery, which has changed nothing at all, is the recipient of a "pecuniary" external diseconomy.

is wrong. Long-range benefit might be better served by cooperation than competition. (But would this benefit the renters?)

In other cases, what is best for a group might in fact not be best for a few of the individuals, even in the long run. Land use restrictions adopted by a city council may limit the amount of money a real estate developer can make from a parcel of land, for example. And this poses questions of fairness that are difficult for most political systems to resolve.

Much of the ideological debate in the world today concerns the apparent conflict between one principle, which says that pure competition is the most efficient kind of market, and another principle, which says that pure competition may mean diseconomies for the community as a whole. Many people outside the United States define capitalism as a belief in the first and socialism as a belief in the second; this is especially true in the developing countries.‡ The answer of most American or European economists (and many in Africa, Asia, and Latin America) has been to look for some form of regulated capitalism or modified socialism that keeps the efficiency of a high degree of individual supply-demand decision making but provides some mechanism to put limits on individual decisions when they adversely affect others.

Chapters 5–13 of this book summarize a group of concepts stemming from a sequence of logic that includes an assumption of unrestrained competition. Chapters 14–16 then consider some of the ways that governments participate in economic decision making, which is often by shaping the way private decision makers put the concepts to work.

4.3.3   *The Geography of Prices*

As an illustration of how the economic concepts introduced so far can result in a geographic pattern, let us consider a map of prices. We will assume a classic competitive economy, where a demand exists for a scarce primary product—an agricultural good. What follows is a simplified version of a very complex process. A base price is set in one or more big-city central markets, where a lot of buyers and sellers meet, compete, and bargain—"market" in the traditional sense. This base price is an attempt to find a level where price is high enough to encourage supply but low enough to encourage demand, indicated in Figure 4.4(c). It reflects such factors

---

‡ Professional social scientists distinguish between capitalism and socialism in terms of a difference in the ownership of the means of production and distribution of goods and services in society: privately owned and collectively (i.e., government-) owned, respectively.

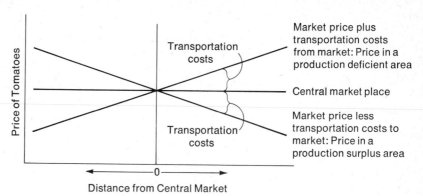

FIGURE   4.5

A Fundamental Principle in the Geography of Prices: local prices are related to a "base price" at a central market and to transportation costs to or from that market.

Price of Tomatoes

Transportation costs

Market price plus transportation costs from market: Price in a production deficient area

Central market place

Transportation costs

Market price less transportation costs to market: Price in a production surplus area

—0—

Distance from Central Market

as quality and scarcity (shortages of the commodity in the area served by the central market, which are in part seasonal). Consequently, the base price for tomatoes might be higher in the winter than in the summer and higher for vine-ripened garden tomatoes than for prepackaged, unbruisable, tasteless space-age tomatoes.

Figure 4.5 shows how local prices are determined with respect to the base price. If the local area has more tomatoes than it will buy at the base price less transport costs to the market, the farmers will ship the excess to the market. The local price will be that lower price (approximately). If the local area has fewer tomatoes than it will buy at the base price plus transportation costs from the market, the market will ship tomatoes to it. The local price will be that higher price (approximately).

The means that the map of tomato prices will reflect three kinds of geographic variation: (1) the amount of local tomato production, which is affected by local decisions about the best deployment of land, labor, equipment, and money; (2) differences between the base prices at different central markets, which depend mainly on regional differences in the scarcity of the product (but also on such variables as regional diet preferences); and (3) transport costs to and from the central markets.

The result is usually a "price surface" showing a low basin in the region where production of the agricultural commodity is concentrated, other basins or valleys where supplies exist, and peaks or high ridges in areas where large deficits are combined with long distances from centers of production.

4.4   A RECONSIDERATION

Although this has been a very superficial introduction to the way economic decision makers think, it may give you a first glimpse of how it is decided that one place is a better place to be (for economic reasons) than another.

Places are complex entities, offering combinations of advantages and disadvantages ranging from proximity to factors of production to a desirable type of market to many other characteristics. But an activity must be *somewhere*. There is a *where* to an economic decision as well as a *what*, and the concepts in the previous section are applied to locational choices as well as to choices between activities.

Part IV of this book will consider locational advantages related to the distinctiveness of a place, and Part V will discuss advantages related to the way a place fits into the system of circulation that arises from such differences. But first, Part III will outline the most widely accepted ideas about how locations and economic activities get together.

MAJOR CONCEPTS AND TERMS

For *definitions*, see the Glossary.

Circulation	External economy	Secondary activities
Competition	Monopolistic	Specialization
Competitive	economy	Supply
economy	Oligopolistic	Tertiary activities
Consumers	economy	Utility
Demand	Price	
Equilibrium	Primary activities	
Exchange	Producers	
External dis-	Productivity	
economy	Scarcity	

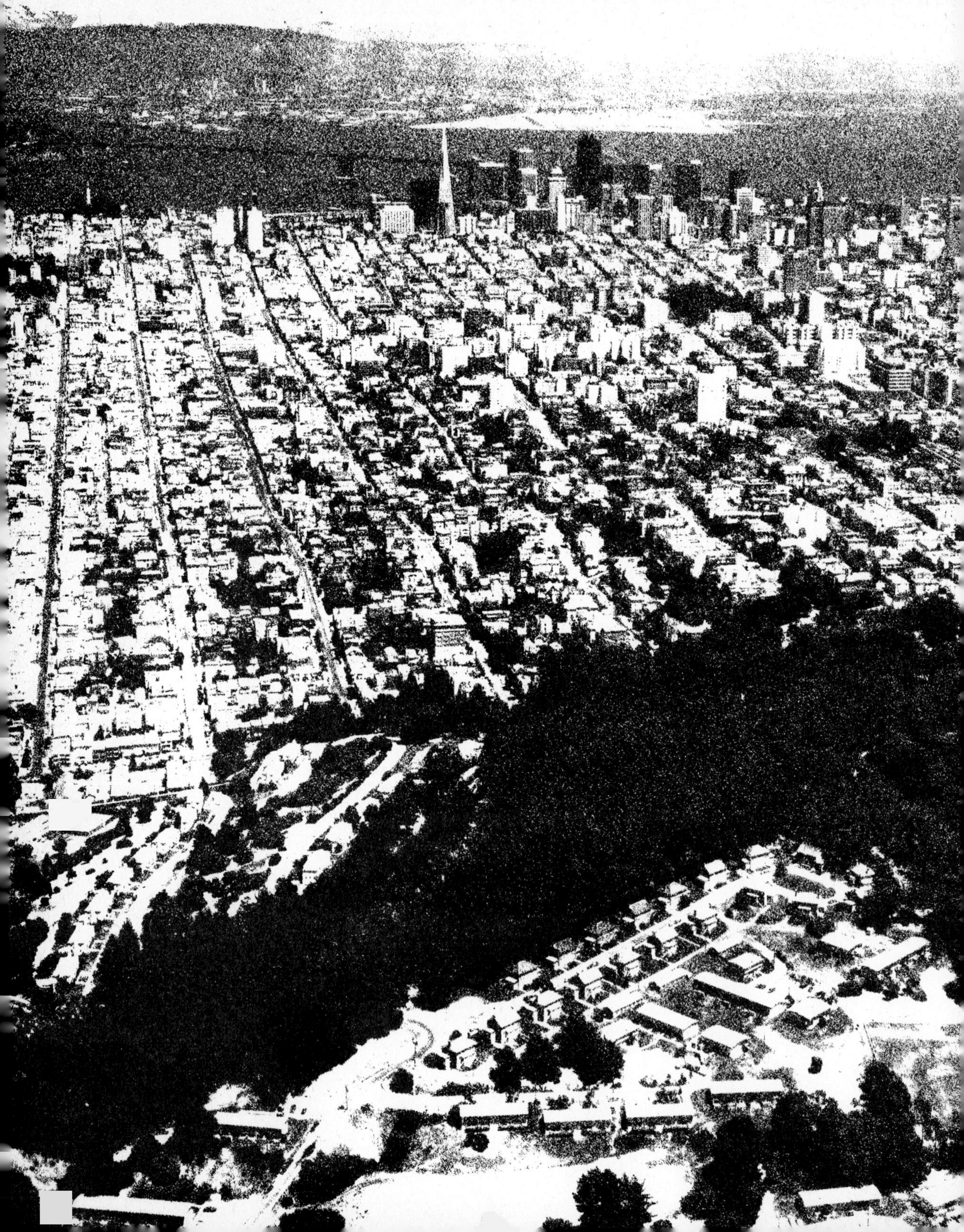

PART III

THE "WHERE" OF ECONOMIC DECISIONS

*O*ur well-being is the result of a host of decisions (mostly by other people) about where to locate economic activities. Whether we are preparing to make locational decisions ourselves or simply trying to understand why things are the way they are, it is useful to understand the underlying logic of these decisions that affect us all. This section will be concerned with the choices made by private individuals and firms, motivated by profit in an economy that consists at least partly of competitive markets.

Chapter 5 will consider the question: given a location, what will probably be the activity? Chapter 6 will deal with the other side of the coin: given an activity, what will probably be the location? And Chapter 7 will discuss how the answers to these questions combine in an economic system that includes a great many different activities and locations.

Whether you read these chapters as an introduction to profitable decision making, a window to how some people think, or a part of the explanation of differences in the distribution of economic benefits, it is important to remember two things: (1) the material is selective and much simplified; and (2) there are other very different ways of viewing the same processes, equally logical given their assumptions but leading in radically different directions.

CHAPTER 5

WHY A LOCATION HAS SOME ACTIVITIES AND NOT OTHERS

*F*rom the previous sections, we already know that there is a relationship between place decisions and economic activity. An activity must locate somewhere. One location may be preferred over others if it means closeness to something desirable: shoppers, resources, transportation. *Proximity* has *utility* because it reduces the effort involved in doing desirable things, such as reaching customers, which means that places with this quality of proximity are going to be in greater demand than those without it. And higher demand means higher value. From this simple idea, we can develop some notions about why a location has some activities and not others.

5.1 SITUATIONS

5.1.1 The Sicilian Farmer

You are a young Sicilian man, one of two sons of a farmer. Part of the way through your higher education, you receive word that your father has died unexpectedly. Each of the sons was left a piece of farmland, and in order to help support the family you return to your town of 20,000 to farm the land. Being a progressive sort, you

FIGURE 5.1
Land Use Around a
Sicilian Town.

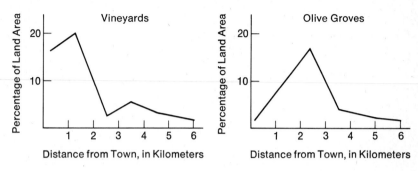

intend to do the best a person could do with the farm, and being a skeptical sort, you doubt if your father was doing that well.

The first question is how to use the land—what to grow on it. The farm is about 3 kilometers from the town, where you will be living in the big old family house (in this area, farmers nearly always live in town and commute out to their land). There is no money for a car or truck, and the path to the field is too rough for a bicycle. You know that two crops that can usually be sold for a good price are grapes and olives. The profit per hectare is higher for grapes, but your father had the land mainly in olive groves. The vineyards near the town, in fact, are concentrated on farmland 2 kilometers from the village or less, except for some very large vineyards farther out than your field, owned and operated by cooperatives (see Figure 5.1). Although you know that a vineyard takes about twice as much work as an olive grove because it requires a lot more trips to and from the field, you decide to try the higher value crop, and you spend time and money switching to vineyards.

It is now three years later. You are tired, less affluent than you had hoped, and a little unpopular with some of the other farmers. It seems as if you are spending your entire life going back and forth to that large field, carrying fertilizer and insecticides and tools out, bringing grapes in. Time that other farmers with land closer to the village spend pruning their vines or enjoying their families, you spend in transit. Farmers who own the olive groves around your land seem to be doing fine without working nearly as hard as you. What's more, your switch to vineyards increased the amount of grapes offered in the town to buyers for a wine-making company. Since the buyers were not especially interested in buying more grapes, this meant you had to compete with other farmers by offering to sell at a lower price, reducing your income and making the other farmers unhappy because they had to drop their prices as well. The price is continuing to drop, and it is approaching a point where the income from your vineyards is just not worth the effort. Maybe the situation calls for a shift back to olive groves.

5.1.2   *The Upstate New York Entrepreneur*

You are a young woman with business sense and a wealthy uncle. Your uncle, believing in your ability, has offered to loan you enough money to set up your own business. Since you come from a small town about 80 miles southeast of Syracuse, New York, and you have worked most of your life for dairy farmers in the area, you decide that what you know best is the production and processing of milk—but that you certainly do not want the work schedule of a dairy farmer. In order to take advantage of your contacts with dairy farmers near your home, you decide to go into milk processing. But what should be the product? Milk itself? Butter? Cheese? Whatever it is to be, you want it to be big.

First, you consider milk. The New York City area is not too far away, and such a large population concentration must consume a lot of milk. But you find that your costs would be too high to match the going price: milk producers closer to the city have lower transportation costs, and some other producers in the Midwest are able to operate on such a massive scale that they can ship low-cost milk to the city in tank trucks on interstate highways.

Next, you study butter, cheese, and similar milk products, also for large regional or national markets. This is a possibility, but you foresee problems: a shortage of labor in the local area experienced in making cheese, competition with other producers who already have established reputations, the added cost factor of refrigerated trucks and storage facilities.

In the end, you settle on a factory to produce dried milk, on long-term contract to a national brand. The product is easy to store and transport. The processing technology is well tested and requires only a small labor force. And, although the product is not quite as valuable as liquid milk, fresh butter, or cheese, you seem to have a niche where you can compete with an excellent chance of success.

5.1.3   *The Land Speculator*

A cousin of yours named Ralph owns 160 acres of land 40 miles from a large city. Since the land adjoins an interstate highway leading to the city and is only about 2 miles from a highway interchange, he thinks that the property might be worth more money to him if it were used in a different way (it is now leased on a short-term basis to a neighboring farmer, who grows corn on it). Ralph knows very little about such things; so he asks you for advice, offering to pay you 10 percent of any increase in value over the next five years. With this incentive, you decide to give the matter your full attention.

You conclude that the chances are not very good of using the land for an activity that serves the city specifically, like houses for commuters, except possibly for the production of crops (such as tomatoes) that bring less per acre than houses but more than corn. Your advice to Ralph is that he try to find someone to grow perishable vegetables on the land, and in the meantime that he persuade the little town nearby to join him in seeking a small industry to locate on the property. It is possible that a firm might be attracted by easy access to the highway and city, lower land prices than found nearer the city, and the willingness of some members of farmers' families to work for moderate wages.

5.2   BASIC IDEAS

Let's consider what general points we can extract from these examples. In all three cases; (1) the decision about what to do with a parcel of land was related to the distance of the parcel from a place that might serve as a market location for some of the possible goods and services; (2) closeness to the market meant easier and cheaper transportation of products and people to and from the market; and, therefore, we can conclude that (3) if there are several alternative land uses and locations, and one use has heavier or more difficult movement requirements than the others, then that most demanding use will be located closest to the market.

The logic of this is simple and persuasive. Everybody would rather be close to the market than farther away because it is easier and cheaper to make a living that way. This means that everybody will be willing to buy land near the market if it is available at a very low price. As the seller of a parcel raises the price, however, because it is in such great demand, some of the buyers will begin to drop out of the competition (see Box 5.1). Why?

Say that there are ten prospective buyers of a piece of land: five corn farmers and five wheat farmers. Each farmer has studied his or her transportation costs for moving fertilizer and other inputs to the farm and harvested crops to a market in the town. Each finds

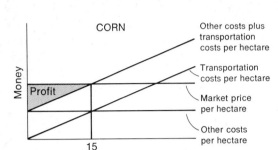

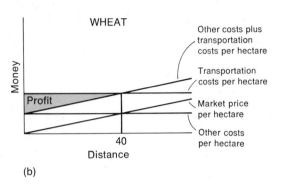

(a)

(b)

FIGURE 5.2

An Illustration of Differences Between More and Less Intensive Crops. A more intensive crop brings a higher price per hectare farmed, but it requires more inputs (such as fertilizer) per hectare. If the inputs are bought in the town, this means that the transportation effort is greater per kilometer for the more intensive crop (the line rises more steeply).

that the situation is this: if the farmer owned all the land, he/she would first plant the land right next to the market. Then he/she would move farther out—fertilizing, cultivating, harvesting—until at some distance the transportation costs mean that it is costing more to raise the crop than it can be sold for.

We know that corn is usually farmed more intensively than wheat (that is, it requires more inputs per unit area cultivated). For its maximum yield, it requires more fertilizer and water. It then yields more bushels per hectare. Suppose that the corn farmers find that if they locate more than 15 kilometers away from the town, and prices and costs remain the same as at present, they will earn too small a profit to make the effort worthwhile. Farming less intensively, the wheat farmers find that they can locate as far as 40 kilometers away and still get by. Figure 5.2 illustrates the difference.

Taking a closer look at the relationship between profit and distance gives us Figure 5.3. At a distance from the market less than X, a corn farmer can pay more for a parcel of land than a wheat farmer can because he has a larger profit margin to work with; thus the

BOX 5.1   "RENT" AND LAND USE

A piece of land can be used for almost anything, if people are willing to spend enough to make it possible; but we know that priorities do become established. In general, the *highest and best use* of the land should prevail, however this is defined. When the mechanism for making the decision on priorities is a price system, the use with the highest priority is the one that is able to pay more for the use of the land than any other. Since a land owner, acting to maximize his or her economic well-being, will make sure that this happens, the highest bid will establish the value of the land.

It is common to refer to this value as *rent*. A map of "land rent" is a map of the land values set by a price system.

FIGURE 5.3
Land Use Domains, as Defined by Figure 5.2. *X* is the distance from town where wheat and corn are equally profitable (vertical slices through the darker wedges in Figure 5.2 are equally long).

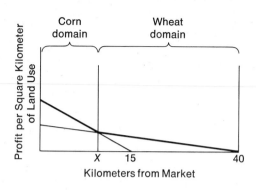

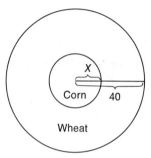

FIGURE 5.4
Land Use Domains, converted from Figure 5.3 to the way they would appear on a map or aerial photograph.

price of land will move up to a point where only corn farmers are bidding for the land. Wheat farmers will be left to compete for the land more distant than 15 kilometers, where corn farmers cannot make a profit, or for the land between *X* and 15, where the profit per square kilometer from wheat is greater than from corn. The land use around the market will look like Figure 5.4, and the value of land will decline with distance as shown by the heavy line in Figure 5.3. (Also see Box 5.2).

As we have seen, the same kind of idea applies to land uses other than agricultural ones. Land values in and around urban areas usually show the same kind of relationship to distance from centers of activity, because the general model works well for industrial and commercial land uses (although not so well for residential areas). For instance, face-to-face contacts among business executives are considered important enough that offices tend to cluster in commercial centers. For a more formal statement of the general concept, see Section 5.6.

BOX 5.2   RENT GRADIENTS

If we expand Figure 5.3 to include more than two competing land uses, the heavy line indicating "land rent" at any distance from the market becomes more and more like a smooth concave curve, as shown in Figure 5.5(a). This curve, or *rent gradient,* can be discussed in terms of its steepness or flatness, its concavity, or its smoothness. Think about how a rent gradient might be affected by each of the factors mentioned in Section 5.3.

Combining all the rent gradients that spread out from the location that has the highest rent, we can define a *rent surface—* usually very peaked, cone-like, with ridges showing the flatter gradients along better transportation routes and bumps or dents indicating the effect of local advantages or problems (see Figures 5.13 and 5.14).

FIGURE 5.5

Von Thünen's Model, in Graphic Form: (a) is an expanded version of Figure 5.3; (b) is an expanded version of Figure 5.4. If "distance" in (a) is replaced by transport costs, and transport costs are influenced by nearness to a river or highway as well as to a market town, (b) becomes (c).

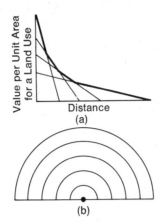

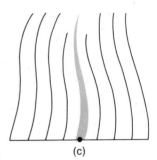

BOX 5.3 THE VON THÜNEN MODEL

Early in the nineteenth century, a young north German estate owner named Johann Heinrich von Thünen decided to study how to make the most efficient use of the land in his estate. His meticulous records led him to conclude that the best arrangement of the land uses on his estate was in a series of zones, with the more intensive activities closer to the market. In 1826 he published a book, *Der Isolierte Staat in Beziehung auf Landwirtschaft* (The Isolated State . . .), which turned his observations into a theory of agricultural location. He assumed that:

1. there is an isolated area without any outside contact

2. there is a single large city that serves as the only market

3. the area around the city is a feature-less plain, uniformly fertile, in which movement is equally easy everywhere

4. the city receives agricultural goods from farmers and supplies them with indus-trial and other goods

5. the farmers transport all goods between city and farm and the transportation costs are directly proportional to dis-tance

6. farmers respond to the needs of the cen-tral market in whatever way maximizes their economic well-being.

Under these conditions, he showed that agricultural land uses would arrange them-selves in a series of concentric ring-shaped zones around the city, as shown in Figure 5.5(a) and (b).

He also considered some more compli-cated situations. For example, introducing a navigable river through the area to the city, which offered reduced transport costs, he proposed that the zones would stretch out along the river, as shown in Figure 5.5(c). And he related this zonation to rural land values as discussed in Sections 5.2 and 5.6.

After a century and a half, von Thünen's models remain the basis of a great deal of our current urban and agricultural location theory.

5.3   *ELABORATING THE BASIC IDEAS*

Hidden within this line of reasoning are a lot of unrealistic assumptions, some of which can be removed by a slightly more complicated model. As originally suggested by a German farmer named von Thünen in 1826, the basic ideas described his surroundings: a flat plain with no high-speed roads, an orientation of farmers to a single market town (see Box 5.3 and Figure 5.5). But, as von Thünen himself recognized, there are other factors that can disrupt the simple concentric ring model of land use.

5.3.1   *Accessibility**

Because it is easier and quicker to travel on roads and rivers than across fields and fences, the relationship between effort and distance is simpler than Figure 5.4 indicates. Figures 5.2, 5.3, and 5.4 all assume that straight-line distance from the market and transportation cost are so directly related that a single straight line on a graph will suffice.

But consider Figure 5.6. A single road, making it possible to travel farther at the same costs, can extend the distance from the market to a land use boundary for an activity near it, as shown in Figure 5.6(a). Taking this into account, Figure 5.4 becomes something like Figure 5.6(b).

FIGURE   5.6
Land Use Domains, as
Modified by Accessibility.

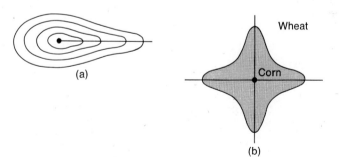

(a)

Wheat

Corn

(b)

---

* These ideas will be discussed in more detail in Chapters 11 and 12.

5.3.2 *A "Non-flat Plain"*

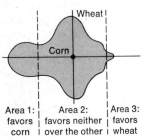

Area 1: | Area 2: | Area 3:
favors | favors neither | favors
corn | over the other | wheat

FIGURE 5.7

How Different Environmental Conditions Can Affect Land Use Patterns.

All that has been said so far assumes that locational decisions are taking place in a perfectly uniform area: a flat land surface with no differences in soil types and with water equally available everywhere. Except for distance and the presence of transportation facilities, every place in the area is just like every other. This is a rare situation, to say the least (see Chapter 9).

The fact is that the estimates of market price per hectare and fixed costs per hectare indicated in Figure 5.2 may be different for different physical, social, political, and technological surroundings. With some exaggeration for the sake of emphasis, Figure 5.7 shows how clear-cut variations in physical conditions can change the expected pattern of land use.

5.3.3 *A Bounded Plain*

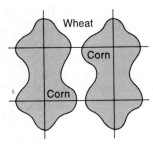

FIGURE 5.8

How Nearness of Market Towns Can Affect Land Use Patterns.

An extreme case of a nonuniform plain is a land/sea boundary, where conventional land use comes to a halt. So far, we have assumed that activities can spread out from a market center without interruption, but physical boundaries are a clear exception. Another exception has to do with the following kind of situation. Earlier, we found that in a simplified case wheat could be grown profitably as far as 40 kilometers from the market. But what if there are other markets less than 40 kilometers in every direction, each with its own pattern of land use around it? It is clear that some of the land use domains will intersect—and that the least intensive activities will be the ones most likely to get squeezed out. Figure 5.6(b) can become something like Figure 5.8.

5.3.4 *The Capacity of the Market*

Two more of the seemingly endless string of assumptions have been that (1) market prices for corn and wheat are fixed, as are prices for purchased items such as fertilizer; and (2) whatever corn and wheat are grown can be sold at the constant price, regardless how much or how little. But we know from Chapter 4 that scarcity tends to raise prices and abundance to lower them.

Let's consider a situation in which there are just not enough people buying at the market center to consume all the corn produced in the area indicated in Figures 5.3 and 5.4. There are two implications here. One possibility is that the surplus will cause the market price to drop, as corn farmers compete to sell their produce.

In Figure 5.2, as the market price comes down, the break-even distance (where corn and wheat are equally profitable) comes in toward the market, and over a period of time the corn domain will become smaller, reducing production. The other possibility is that a surplus can be transported to another market center; if this added transport cost is the same for everyone, it raises the "other cost" and total cost lines, which also reduces the break-even distance.

In the same way, if the corn producing area is not large enough at the given market price to satisfy the desires of consumers in the market center, some consumers will be willing to pay more, and the market price will rise, which will tend in the long run to move the break-even point outward.

Anticipating future price levels is a very difficult business, but it is an important part of choosing the best activity for a location. Since prices may fluctuate, a boundary between land use domains often shifts within a zone of year-to-year change—a zone where risk and uncertainty are greater than elsewhere. This can itself have an effect on locational decisions, since some activities are more conveniently transient than others. Corn can be shifted to soybeans from year to year, but it may be harder to change a boundary between irrigated and nonirrigated land. In an urban case, a parking lot can be changed to another activity pretty quickly, but an apartment building is hard to change into a factory. Consequently, it is logical for activities with large fixed costs (very expensive to locate at a particular spot in the first place) to avoid land use boundary zones, with all their uncertainties, unless they are versatile in shifting quickly from one product or service to another.

Just as a change in the market price for a farm product has an effect on the rent gradient, an increase or decrease in a production cost (for, say, fertilizer or transportation) makes a difference as well. Generally, technological progress reduces production costs through time, while market capacities increase as the size of the population grows. Both of these tendencies move the boundaries of land use zones outward, pushing extensive activities such as forestry and grazing farther away from market centers.

5.3.5   A Problem of Classification

It is simple enough to talk about rent gradients for an area around a market if (1) all the land uses are oriented to one and only one center and (2) the land use alternatives are easy to rank—each one clearly more or less intensive than every other. But the place where a farmer sells wheat may not be where pesticides or tractors are usually bought. The urban dweller may shop at a place that is not very near his or her job. Or a person may use several markets from time to time, since none of us lives in an "isolated state." Consequently, a location that gives access to several desirable centers may end up with high rent, even though it is not right next to any of them. And, for this and a variety of other reasons, a location that seems central on a map may have a lower rent level than other places nearby, and the "market" for a multipurpose land use may be hard to identify.

As for the distinguishability of land uses, how do we rank a "mixed" farm: corn, alfalfa, pigs, chickens, eggs, and vegetables—all in a single property? How do we handle the difference between a maize field that gets careful irrigation and fertilizing and one that has to get by on its own between planting and harvesting? These kinds of real-world complications can make it difficult to apply the simple model in specific cases, although the basic insights continue to be helpful.

But this is only the beginning. When von Thünen developed his theory, most economic activities (farms, firms, and so on) were small and specialized, relatively easy to classify. Now, most activities are large and diversified; specialization is more often found within activities than between them. For instance, instead of being oriented toward a nearby market town, a farm growing potatoes may be operating on contract to a potato chip manufacturer in a city much farther away, using seed supplied by the company—which also pays to have the fields sprayed with insecticides. In such a case, proximity to the local market town is less important.

5.3.6   *The Highest and Best Use*

There is one final complication, and a very important one. This entire discussion has assumed that priorities are defined strictly in economic terms. The highest bidder, the biggest moneymaker, gets the land. The owner of the land cares only about monetary profits. And the economic trade-offs are always clearly defined and fully known.

Clearly, these conditions do not always describe the way our world works. For one thing, people are not this predictable—and not always this knowledgeable. For another, if every land-use decision is made in the way that maximizes individual profits, the overall effect may be less than the optimum for the region or country as a whole. The activity offering the highest bid for a particular piece of seaside property might be a chemical processing plant that would pollute the sea so much that it would reduce the value and productivity of resort hotels nearby. Or the residents of an urban area might want city parks enough to put some controls on the use

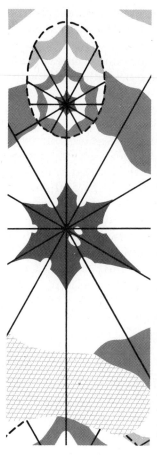

FIGURE 5.9
A Composite Land Use Pattern, showing zones around market towns of different sizes, transportation routes, and environmental conditions (such as swamps, lakes, or mountains) that disrupt more regular patterns.

of certain parts of the city, even though the parks will earn less per square meter than skyscrapers.

As a result, land use patterns reflect the value systems of cultures and the policies of governments as well as the economically motivated decisions of individuals (see Part VI). In fact, the von Thünen-type model can be used as a basis for evaluating the importance of these other factors—and, in some cases, the economic cost of basing decisions on them.

Summary

The ideas that develop from a von Thünen-type framework of thought are applicable to any economic pattern that is oriented toward nodes and connections between nodes. For these patterns, they lead us to expect a relation between land value and distance from markets (or other locations that offer something important), and they suggest a kind of layering of activities around central locations, with high-intensity, high-value activities nearby and successively less intense activities arrayed farther away. Taking into account a transportation pattern, anomalous physical situations, and the presence of a variety of centers of different sizes, we can begin to approach an understanding of the kinds of complex land use patterns that we observe in the world (see Figure 5.9).

5.4   EXAMPLES

These concepts are the result of attempts to generalize about what we observe in the world around us, and they have been widely accepted because the careful study of many actual situations has led to the same basic conclusions. To illustrate this and to add some detail to a very spare framework, let's consider some examples.

5.4.1   Hops in Kent

In the nineteenth century, as before and since, a great deal of beer was produced and consumed in England. An important ingredient was hops, and a central part of the county of Kent in southeastern England came to be a focus for the cultivation of this crop. Why?

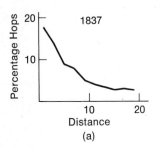

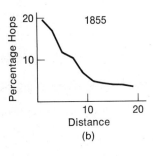

FIGURE 5.10
Decline in Density of Hop Cultivation with Distance in miles from Wateringbury, a center of hop cultivation (from Harvey).

To find out, David Harvey mapped the density of hop cultivation in Kent at several times during the nineteenth century, showing the increasing concentration of production in a core area.[1] He found that the distance of a parish (a small administrative unit) from the center of the core had an effect on whether or not the parish increased or decreased its production faster than other parishes. It was clear that the density of cultivation was related to this distance factor (see Figure 5.10), but how about trends through time? Looking at a period when hop production was growing overall (1820–1861), Harvey found that there was more growth close to the center, as shown in Figure 5.11(a); and in a period when hop production was declining (1885–1899) he found less decline near the center, as shown in Figure 5.11(b). Both periods showed that the degree of concentration was increasing.

On the basis of soil and climate, there was no particular reason why there should be an association between specialized agricultural production and distance from the center of the specialized area. Studying the history of the area, Harvey found that three factors seemed to be especially important in focusing hop cultivation in an area:

1. There were advantages to concentrating the production somewhere: for example, the chance to share storage and processing facilities, the benefits of having an experienced labor force available to cultivate a difficult crop, and the opportunity to develop a reputation for high-quality hops sold in a particular market center. And the closer a piece of land was to the center of the concentration, the easier was access to the whole range of nodal advantages.

2. Hops were a high-value crop, requiring a heavy investment in fertilizer but bringing high prices. Once hop production was established in central Kent, it began to force out less valuable crops, partly by causing the value of land to rise. Landlords began to require tenants to make payments on the basis of what the land could earn by growing hops, an especially valuable crop, which meant that a farmer growing something less valuable might lose money. In addition, hop growers could pay more for agricultural labor, which raised wages, also encouraging conformity. The general effect was to reinforce a tendency toward concentration, with hops an equivalent of the "inner-ring" crop in Figure 5.4.

3. But there was a limit to how concentrated the production could get. For instance, it took so much fertilizer to grow hops that a farmer had to use most of the land to feed the cattle that provided manure. Consequently, it was very difficult to grow

FIGURE 5.11
Relationship between Hop Acreage Change and Distance from Yalding (from Harvey). Yalding is less than three miles from Wateringbury; the center of the hop cultivation region varied between the two towns during the nineteenth century. (a) Absolute change 1829/1835 to 1856/1861; (b) Percentage change 1885 to 1899.

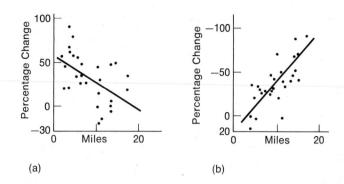

(a)   (b)

hops on more than one-third of a farmer's land (15 percent was the usual proportion). Generally, the center of the area went up to a maximum density of hop cultivation, then the adjoining sections grew to that level, and outlying areas declined gradually from that density. Even with this limit on the center, however, the growth or decline of hop production took place with reference to distance from the center.

As a result, although there were some unpredictable factors involved in the selection of the center of the hop-growing area, once the production got started it evolved very much as the von Thünen model would have predicted for a high-value, central market-oriented crop.

5.4.2   Other Studies

Many other cases have been documented, especially by Chisholm.[2] For example, he reports research by three Finnish investigators, all of whom found that production per hectare (a measure of land use intensity) declined with distance from a town to farm plots (Table 5.1). Couper found that crop production zones in the Fiji Islands

TABLE 5.1
Output per Hectare for Farms in Finland, as It Related to Distance of the Parcel of Land from the Farmstead. Output is measured in monetary terms and adjusted so that land next to the farmstead has a value of 100. Net output equals gross output less gross input.

| Distance in Kms. | Wiiala | | Virri | | Suomela |
	Gross Output	Net Output	Gross Output	Net Output	Net Output
0–0.1	100	100	100	100	100
0.5	92	78	89	67	83
1.0	84	56	80	50	68
1.5	77	34	73	40	56
2.0	69	13	67	33	46
3.0	. . .	. . .	57	25	32
4.0	. . .	. . .	50	20	. . .
5.0	. . .	. . .	44	17	. . .

resembled the concentric-ring model, in this case focused on the market center of Suva.[3] The same tendency can be seen in Figure 5.12, which shows the actual pattern of land uses in a part of West Africa.

A dramatic illustration of rent gradients is a three-dimensional map of land values in Topeka, Kansas (see Figure 5.13), which

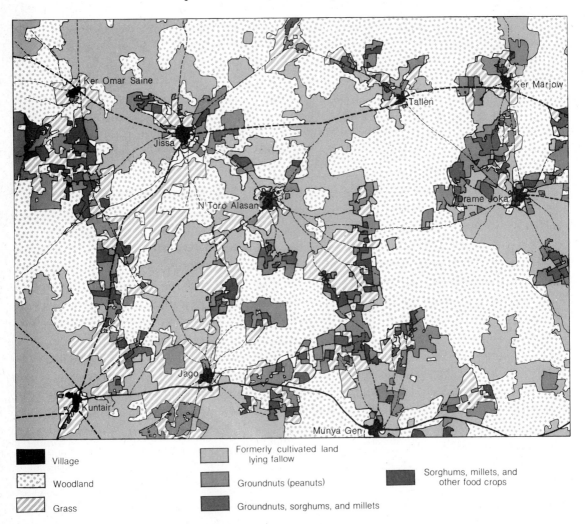

| | Village | | Formerly cultivated land lying fallow | | Sorghums, millets, and other food crops |

Village

Woodland

Grass

Formerly cultivated land lying fallow

Groundnuts (peanuts)

Groundnuts, sorghums, and millets

Sorghums, millets, and other food crops

FIGURE 5.12
Rural Land Use in Gambia, West Africa. The total distance across the map is about 3 miles (5 km). Groundnuts (peanuts) are a cash crop for the farmers, and sorghum and millets (grains) are consumed locally for food. Departing from the concentric-zone pattern is the use of newly cleared, relatively fertile land on the margins of the woodland for higher value crops.

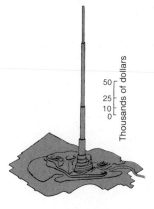

FIGURE   5.13
Urban Land Values in
Topeka, Kansas.

shows how peaked the rent surface usually is when the center is an urban place of any size. For larger cities, the rent surface looks more like a large circus tent, with ridges extending along the main roads and smaller peaks showing the location of neighborhood shopping centers, usually where the roads intersect (see Figure 5.14).

There have also been studies of the shifts of land use boundaries with time. For example, Table 5.2 shows the average distances that some British agricultural imports were transported during several periods between 1831 and 1913. It is easy to see that the distances increased steadily, but it is also possible to see when technological breakthroughs in transportation took place (look for sharp increases from one period to another in the average distance—and how they differ in time from one product to another). Another study found that with the growth of the Hong Kong population after World War II the expanding cultivation of perishable vegetables, which Chinese cooks insist be fresh, steadily displaced less perishable rice as the crop planted in fields near the city.[4]

5.4.3   *Further Examples*

Along with consulting the studies in the academic literature, we can form our own conclusions by looking at maps that show where different land uses are located. This is complicated a great deal by the classification problems mentioned in Section 5.3.5, but Figure

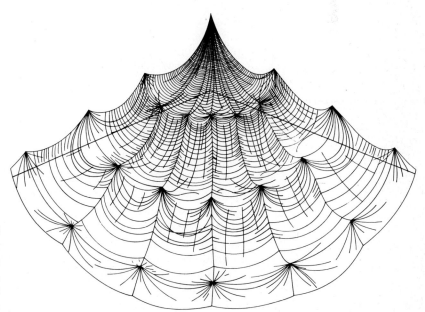

FIGURE   5.14
The Urban Rent Surface:
land values in a city shown
in the form of a surface,
where higher points mean
higher values.

TABLE 5.2   Transport Distances for British Agricultural Imports

Import	Average Mileage from London to Source Regions of Import				
	1831–1835	1856–1860	1871–1875	1891–1895	1909–1913
Fruit and vegetables	0	324	535	1,150	1,880
Live animals	0	630	870	3,530	4,500
Butter, cheese, and eggs	262	530	1,340	1,610	3,120
Feed grains	860	2,030	2,430	3,240	4,830
Flax and seeds	1,520	3,250	2,770	4,080	3,900
Meat and tallow	2,000	2,400	3,740	5,050	6,250
Wheat and flour	2,430	2,170	4,200	5,150	5,950
Wool and hides	2,330	8,830	10,000	11,010	10,900
Weighted Average of All Imports	1,820	3,650	4,300	5,050	5,880

SOURCE: Cox, Kevin R. *Man, Location, and Behavior*. New York: Wiley, 1972, p. 276.

5.15 shows some of the kinds of relationships that we could find in working with any good atlas. In each of the four cases, the more intensive, highest value activity is grouped closer to the densely populated northeastern quadrant of the United States.

The same thing can be observed from maps of urban land uses, where the highest value activities—commerce and services—often form a core that is surrounded by successive land use zones (for example: old industry/warehousing, older residential, newer industry, newer residential). But in most of these cases, the multiplicity of "markets," the cost of converting old land uses to new ones rather than developing new areas, and the different considerations that affect residential choice distort the rent gradient so that it resembles a smooth concave curve very little.

5.5   A RECONSIDERATION

In general, what we have been considering is the relationship between an area (in von Thünen's framework, an area of agricultural land use) and a point (a market). Because of the economic advantages of proximity, a consequence is a land value gradient that slopes downward away from the point. Lösch has pointed out that there is a reverse side to this. From the point of view of the market, the gradient is one of *price* to the consumer, and it slopes upward from the central point: regardless of whether the consumer comes to the market or the seller goes to the consumer, the price of an

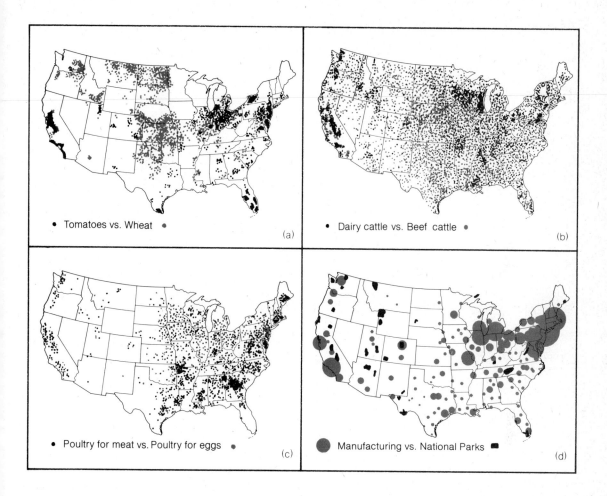

FIGURE 5.15
Contrasts in the Degree of
Consumer Market Orienta-
tion of Selected Activities.
See text for interpretation.

item is the base price at the market location plus the cost of movement. The land value "cone" is associated with a price "funnel"; as
we have seen, higher prices usually reduce demand, which arrives
from a different direction of thought at our prediction of a decreasing intensity of land use with distance from the market.

5.6   *TOWARD GREATER PRECISION*

Many of the concepts introduced in this and later chapters can be
expressed much more formally. Here is an example. According to
the model proposed in Section 5.2, accepting von Thünen's as-

sumptions, the value of land for a given activity at any distance from the market can be calculated by:

$$L = Y(P - C) - YDF$$

where

    L = the value, in dollars per km²
    Y = the amount produced, in tons per km²
    P = market price, in dollars per ton
    C = production cost, in dollars per ton
    D = distance from the location to the market, in km
    F = the cost of transportation, in dollars per km

Beyond some distance, for any land use, production will take place at a loss because the cost of transporting the product to market is higher than the net return at the market. Dunn has shown that if the ratio between $Y(P - C)$ for two uses i and j has a value in a certain range, the two uses will occupy distinct zones, with i closer to the market:[5]

$$1 < \frac{Y(P - C)_i}{Y(P - C)_j} < \frac{Y_i}{Y_j}$$

A rent gradient with respect to distance from the market is given by:[6]

$$R = a(b - 1)\left(\frac{P - DF}{ab}\right)^{\frac{b}{b-1}} - F$$

where

    R = rent per km²
    a and b = parameters of the equation

$$C = F + aY^b$$
$$\text{with } b > 1$$

    F = fixed cost per acre

From differential calculus, it is easy to see that this formula defines a rent gradient that slopes downward from the market location and is concave.

MAJOR CONCEPTS AND TERMS

For definitions, see the Glossary.

Accessibility	*Proximity*	*Uniform surface*
Highest and best use	*Rent*	*Von Thünen model*
Intensive land use	*Rent gradient*	*Zones of land use*
Nodes	*Rent surface*	

Footnotes for Chapter 5

1.   "Locational Change in the Kentish Hop Industry and the Analysis of Land Use Patterns." Institute of British Geographers, *Transactions,* vol. 33: 1963, pp. 123–44.

2.   Chisholm, Michael. *Rural Settlement and Land Use.* London: Hutchinson, 1962.

3.   Couper, A. D. "Rationalizing Sea Transport Services in an Archipelago." *Tijdschrift voor Economische en Sociale Geografie,* vol. 58: 1967, pp. 203–208.

4.   Yu, Christopher. Unpublished M.A. thesis, Department of Geography, Syracuse University, 1972.

5.   Dunn, E. S. *The Location of Agricultural Production.* Gainesville: University of Florida Press, 1954.

6.   For a derivation of this formula, see Hoover, Edgar M., *An Introduction to Regional Economics.* New York: Knopf, 1971, p. 115.

CHAPTER 6

WHY AN ACTIVITY CHOOSES SOME LOCATIONS AND NOT OTHERS

*T*here are times when a decision maker is not worried about choosing the best activity or land use for a particular location. He or she has already picked the activity: dude ranch, dog food factory, paper mill, legal services. The question is where to put it.

To deal with this question, we need again to see activities both as users of things—goods and services—and as providers of things. Consider a manufacturing firm as an example. It uses certain materials, such as steel, and produces certain goods, such as boilers, for a market. The problem in deciding where to locate the manufacturing plant arises from the fact that the location of the source of steel and the location of the market for boilers may not be exactly the same. If they were (for instance, both limited to Detroit), the decision would be an easy one: the plant would be in that same place.

But what about a plant that will produce copper wire using ore from Utah to meet the needs of electronics companies on Long Island? Should the plant be in Utah, on Long Island, or somewhere in between? Where?

6.1 SITUATIONS

6.1.1 The Development Planner
You work for an international development organization, such as the International Bank for Reconstruction and Development (World

Bank). Your organization has received a request from a country that just completed its first careful resource inventory, showing the presence of larger than expected quantities of iron ore and coal. Since most users of iron and steel in that part of the world are now importing them at great cost from far away, the economic planners in the country believe that a large iron and steel production center is feasible to serve nearby customers, and they need a loan to make it possible to construct the complex.

The planning staff of your organization has studied the situation, and they have advised that there is very little margin for error. Unless the new facility can keep costs to a minimum, it will have a hard time competing with the current suppliers of iron and steel to neighboring countries because the large international steel companies are prepared to cut their prices for a time in order to protect their dominance of the markets. Consequently, the country requesting the loan has invited the lending organization to advise it how to organize the activity so that costs are minimized. Your job, which is among the most important ones, is to determine what location for the production complex will involve the least operating costs per unit of output. If you are right, the activity will probably succeed, bringing new jobs and income to the country and changing the world's pattern of flow of iron and steel. If you are wrong, the activity may fail, crushing the hopes of the people, affecting their confidence in the leaders of the country, and probably causing the country to default on repaying the loan.

The country is a small one, with a simple layout, and there are three key locations: an inland source of iron ore, an inland source of coal, and the port from which products will be exported to neighboring countries. (The port city is also the location of most of the firms that will buy iron and steel for use inside the country.) These locations are connected to each other and to other places by a rail network that will be used to transport the large quantities of goods that will have to be moved. The requirements are to get the iron ore and coal together at a production point, to get the products to the port, and to do all this at least possible cost.

Someone hands you a thick folder containing transport costs per unit weight of coal, iron ore, and iron/steel; the amounts of coal and iron ore needed to produce a unit weight of iron and steel; wage rates in each of six cities and at several intervening points; and the costs at each location of supplying power, water, and other support items. What do you do now?

6.1.2   *The Printing Business*

All your life you have been interested in printing as a vocation. In your spare time you like to design new typefaces. You take pride in knowing about the pros and cons of different kinds of paper stock. You collect books with rare bindings. After years of saving, you are now ready to go into the printing business—not stationery and wedding announcements but hardbound books. You believe that with your knowledge you can offer a combination of quality work and reasonable prices that will be attractive to major publishers across the country. But first you have to decide where to build your plant.

What are the considerations? For inputs, you know that the major bulk item will be paper, and the sources are pulp and paper mills, usually located where lumbering is a big industry (in the United States: the Pacific Northwest, the Southeast, or perhaps at a point near the Canadian border or on a seacoast where transportation costs for imports are kept to a minimum). Another important input item will be contact with the publishing houses: the receipt of manuscripts, the shipment of proofs for reading and editing, frequent consultation about the design of the products. You decide to concentrate on the eastern U.S. publishing group, where the largest number of potential clients seems to be, and this puts the Northwest at a disadvantage as a source of paper. You are also concerned about such items as the availability of skilled labor, the cost of electricity, and the cost of land for the plant site. As for outputs, it seems to you that you can ship books from anywhere. The buyers are spread across the country. Your main concern is the presence of convenient truck and rail transportation, along with at least a small airport for emergency connections with New York, Boston, and other client locations.

After careful study, you decide to look for a piece of land in the Bristol/Kingsport/Johnson City section of eastern Tennessee. And, when you visit there to talk to a realtor, you find that others have had the same idea before you.

6.1.3 *Liquid Fuel from Coal*

Several years ago you accepted a job offer from a small independent oil company. For several years you have been trying to persuade your bosses that the future lies in liquid fuels, not necessarily just in crude oil. You believe that the major international energy companies are moving so slowly into the field of synthetic fuels that your company might be able to sneak ahead of them if it moves aggressively—and you believe that this represents a tremendous growth potential for the company over the next twenty or thirty years.

Largely because they are tired of hearing your arguments, you suspect, your bosses have given you the go-ahead to choose a process for coal liquefaction, develop a preliminary engineering design for a liquefaction plant, and take the necessary steps to make it possible to begin construction (although they haven't agreed yet to build it). An old college friend of yours, a chemical engineer working for the U.S. Bureau of Mines, has had experience with the Synthoil process, and you hire her to help.

What you find is that a major requirement will be an environmental impact statement for the proposed liquefaction facility. The statement will have to be thorough. It will be expensive and will take a long time, both to do and to get approved (or disapproved). No construction can start until it is approved. And it will not be possible to go very far in preparing the statement until a site is selected, because most of the environmental impacts have to be evaluated for the characteristics of a particular place. Clearly, an early requirement will be to choose a location.

The major material requirement, obviously, is coal. Major sources of coal in the United States are Appalachia, including western Pennsylvania; the central part of the country (Illinois, southern Indiana, western Kentucky); and the northern Great Plains (Wyoming, Montana, and North Dakota). According to your thinking, the market for the coal liquids will be the current users in the United States of imported crude oil, since you expect the U.S. government to reduce imports sharply by 1995. The largest of these markets is in the Northeast, now served by oil tankers from Venezuela and the Middle East and by pipelines from the Gulf Coast. Although you will face competition from offshore oil production, you decide to focus on this market rather than compete with Alaskan oil in the smaller Pacific Coast market. This makes Appalachian coal attractive because it is closest to the market, and you are assured by Consolidation Coal Company that it can meet your needs from coal fields in this area.

By this time, the choices have been reduced. Do you locate near the coal mines in Kentucky or West Virginia and ship crude oil by pipeline to refineries on the East Coast? Do you move the coal to the East Coast by train and liquefy it there? Do you locate somewhere in between—moving the coal, let's say, to an intermediate place offering a good linkup with an existing pipeline?

Besides all the environmental, social, and political issues involved, how do the options compare in strictly economic terms? You must find out because the decision makers in the company will ask you to defend your recommendation.

6.2   BASIC IDEAS

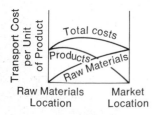

FIGURE   6.1

A Simplified Depiction of
the Relationship between
Location and Transport
Costs for an Activity Needing Both a Raw Material
and a Market.

As in Chapter 5, the fundamental issue here has to do with movement costs. If the activity is located at the market center, the inputs
for the activity have to be transported from their sources. If the activity is located where the inputs are produced, the goods or services from the activity have to be transported to the market. The
concerns are: where do the necessary inputs come from? Where can
the goods and services be sold? How do the movement costs of the
inputs compare with the movement costs of the outputs?

As a start, consider the simplest case: one place as the source
of materials for a manufacturing activity and one location for the
market. If the cost of shipping the *product* is high, for example
because it weighs nearly as much as the materials and is more
fragile, the best location is close to the market. If it costs a lot more
to transport the *raw material*, for instance because the product
weighs one-thousandth as much as the raw material, the best location is near the source of the material.

But the situation is seldom this simple. For one thing, the
costs of the inputs and outputs may be too similar for the decision
to be obvious. Figure 6.1 shows how the various transportation
costs can be summarized for the simple case. In actual cases the
curves are frequently not very smooth. For example, materials or
products may need to be transferred from one container to another
along the way (sea to land, train to truck), and the different modes
of movement may have different individual curves to and from the
point of transfer. But given a single material source and market center, along with good information about movement costs, it should
be possible to find the place that means minimum transport costs.

Most often there is more than one source of input or more
than one market—or both. Two possibilities have simple solutions.
If there is one market center and materials can be obtained anywhere, the best location is at the market. If there is only one source
of materials but the product can be sold anywhere, the best location
is where the materials are found.

These ideas indicate that the *locational attraction* or *pull* of a
place—material source or market—relates to two characteristics of
the activity being considered: (1) the effort (cost) involved in moving materials versus products; and (2) the range of alternative locations of materials or markets.

Let's investigate a case that is slightly more complex, though
still fairly simple. Instead of one material source and one market,
we will consider an industry's use of two materials, each of which

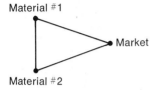

Material #1

Market

Material #2

FIGURE 6.2

A "Locational Triangle."
(For explanation, see text.)

is located at a single place—but the places are different. There is still just one market location. We will assume that the product costs less to move than either of the materials, so that the location of the materials makes a difference.

Figure 6.2 shows how the three locations can be mapped, reducing the range of plant locations that need to be considered. If there are no special circumstances, the best location will be somewhere within the *locational triangle*. The specific location depends on the relative cost of transporting the items (for example, the difference in weight or bulk of one material compared with the product and the other material). Logically, the most costly item to move exerts the most locational pull (see Box 6.1). Coming up with an

BOX 6.1   WEBER'S THEORY OF INDUSTRIAL LOCATION

In 1909 a German economist named Alfred Weber published a book entitled *Theory of the Location of Industries*, in which he proposed a theory (as the title says) about the location of industries. His assumptions, which lie behind many of the ideas in this chapter, were these:

1. The area is uniform physically, culturally, politically, and technologically.

2. Sources of raw materials and centers of consumption are known.

3. Labor is located in a certain number of places, and the addition of a new activity in any of them will not affect wage rates.

4. Only one product is considered at a time.

5. Transportation costs are a function of weight and distance, increasing in direct proportion to either.

Working with these assumptions, he arrived at a framework of thought that is an ancestor of this chapter and that includes several concepts that we will refer to (the *isodapane*, the locational triangle). He was especially interested in the weight of materials versus products (*weight loss*), the case of industries with several raw materials but only one market, and the roles of economies of scale and agglomeration (discussed in Chapter 7).

In dealing with one material/one market and two material/one market cases, assumption 5 led Weber to emphasize the role of weight loss in industrial location: a *material-source orientation* with a sizeable weight loss, a *market orientation* with a weight gain (for instance, the conversion of soft drink syrup into bottled drinks by adding water, usually considered to be available everywhere). His solutions for least-cost locations in these cases have persisted in the location theory literature because of their logic and simplicity, and the isodapane has been widely used as a descriptive device.

Motivated partly by an unease about Weber's assumptions and omissions, Palander, Hoover, Isard, and others have developed more comprehensive industrial location theories since the mid 1930s. Some references to their work are listed in the Bibliography.

Inputs	Number of Markets			
	1	2	3	4 or More
1	If raw material more expensive to transport, at input location; if product more expensive to transport, at market location	Within locational triangle	Probably at input location	Almost certainly at input location
2	Within locational triangle	Within locational polygon	Within locational polygon	Probably at the location of the input that is more expensive to transport
3	Probably at market location	Within locational polygon	Within locational polygon	Almost anywhere, but influenced by relative costs of transportation
4 or more	Almost certainly at market location	Probably at the location of the larger market	Almost anywhere, but influenced by relative costs of transportation	Anywhere, but influenced by relative costs of transportation

TABLE 6.1
Least-Cost Location for an Industrial Facility, if Weber's Assumptions Are Accepted

exact calculation of the best location is not too difficult for this simplified triangle case if movement costs are directly proportional to distance, but it can become cumbersome for a more realistic situation (see Section 6.6).

Similarly, we could figure out the solution for one input location and two markets, and, at least in general terms, for many other kinds of situations. It is simply a matter of applying the same Weberian assumptions (Table 6.1).

6.3   *ELABORATING THE BASIC IDEAS*

Again, these straightforward ideas can be misleading because they unrealistically assume an uncomplicated world. Basing a locational decision merely on movement costs makes sense only if all the other costs of an activity are the same wherever it might be located. Moreover, it can be difficult to take into account all the costs involved in the movement of each item. Furthermore, the number of possible material sources or possible market centers can be so large that the range of locational alternatives is intimidating.

6.3.1   *Locational Differences*

A private economic decision maker is concerned with making a profit, not with minimizing transport costs for their own sake. If a location is more expensive from a transportation point of view but less expensive from some other point of view, it may turn out to be a better one than the least-cost transportation point (regarding other kinds of locational advantages, see Part IV).

An example of a complicating factor is labor costs, which may vary from place to place. This is not simply a matter of wage rates. A worker making $4.00 an hour, producing 50 units an hour, costs 8 cents per unit. A second worker, making $3.60 an hour, producing 40 units in the hour, costs 9 cents per unit. The second worker, though paid less, is more expensive. Because of the importance of this fact to a producer, a location with low unit labor costs can compete successfully for activities even though it is far from both markets and raw materials. Japan, Hong Kong, South Korea, Taiwan, and Singapore are well-known instances.

How does a decision maker decide how much of a labor cost savings is needed by location in order to overcome transportation cost disadvantages? With a lot of good information, it is possible to draw *isodapanes* on a map—lines of equal total transport costs for an activity (see Figure 6.3 and Box 6.2). Figure 6.4 illustrates how this might look for a one-market, one-material case in which the material is more expensive to move than the product (giving the source of the materials a transport cost advantage). For instance, at

---

BOX 6.2   CALCULATING ISODAPANES

To map isodapanes, the procedure is this:

1. Locate the input sources and output markets as points.

2. For each point, map lines of equal transportation costs (*isotims*) for that commodity: material for the input source, finished product for the market.

3. Connect the points that represent the same total transportation costs.

The examples that are cited in textbooks nearly always show isotims as concentric circles around point locations, usually with the circles evenly spaced (for example, Figure 6.3). This pattern of isotims follows from Weber's assumptions 1 and 5. If an area is not uniform, the isotims will not be circular, and if transportation costs are not directly proportional to distance, the isotims will not be evenly spaced. Although these conditions add to the effort required to calculate isodapanes, they do not reduce their utility.

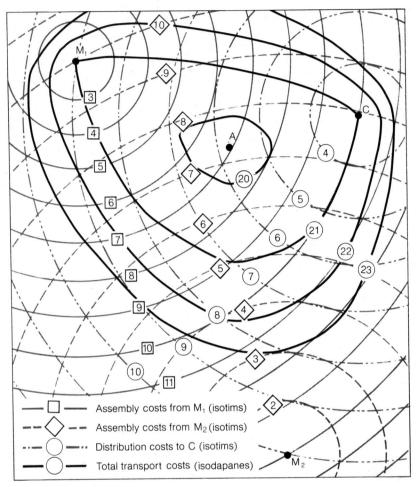

FIGURE 6.3

Isotims and Isodapanes for a Firm with Two Materials and One Market. M_1 and M_2 are the resource locations, and C is the market location. The squares are movement costs from M_1, diamonds from M_2, and circles containing numbers 10 and less from C. The circles containing numbers above 10 are total transportation costs, declining to A, the least-cost location.

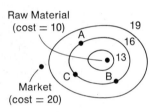

FIGURE 6.4

A Schematic Diagram of Isodapanes.

Legend:

☐ Assembly costs from M_1 (isotims)

◇ Assembly costs from M_2 (isotims)

○ Distribution costs to C (isotims)

○ Total transport costs (isodapanes)

location A, B, or C, the total cost of transporting the material to a manufacturing plant at that place and then transporting the product from there to the market is 16. These lines, although they are difficult to draw for a more complex case, make it clear how much of a cost savings a place has to offer to overcome transportation disadvantages. If location A or B has unit labor costs of 11 (11 + 16 = 27), while the raw material source location has costs of 20 (20 + 10 = 30), the material source is not actually the least-cost point.

In the same way, isodapanes can be used to evaluate the effect on production costs of terrain modification, taxes, acquiring necessary power, and other factors that may vary from place to place.

FIGURE 6.5
Total Movement Costs at
Locations Between a Raw
Material Source and a
Market.

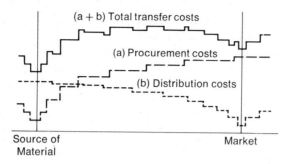

Source of
Material

Market

6.3.2 *Movement Costs*

In referring to Figure 6.1, we cruised blithely past the very complicated nature of movement costs. Weber's simple model ignored the cost of maintaining transportation terminals and of transshipment: shifting cargoes from one carrier to another. In general, it missed the fact that movement is network-oriented and that, as a result, terminals and junctions on networks have special cost saving advantages. And it took later critics to point out the importance of freight rates, as well as weight and distance, in calculating the movement cost of a commodity.

Part V will consider movement costs in more detail, but for the time being let us simply note that movement costs are not directly proportional to distance, because freight rates are usually not—and because terminal and transshipment costs are not usually related to total distance at all. A more realistic estimate of costs can change the relative attractiveness of alternative locations a great deal. For example, Figure 6.1 is biased in favor of terminal points by assuming that movement costs for both the material and the product increase less than proportionately with distance (convex curved lines), when a more typical situation is a kind of stepped line that is sensitive to the attractions of intermediate points (see Figure 6.5).

There are still more issues. The capacity of a transportation network may be in question because congestion can affect the time of movement. The return trip of the transportation carriers can have an impact on costs: if they must return empty, the total trip will be more expensive to the shipper than if they can return carrying a cargo for a paying customer. Some modes are faster than others. Some connections offer more flexibility than others. Because of congestion or other reasons (including government regulations), the cheapest route may not be the most direct one.

Given full data about movement costs, though, there are well-tested methods for identifying not only the least-cost location of an activity but the best combination of material sources, markets, and movement routes (see Section 6.6).

6.3.3 *A Location as an Area*

The development of our basic ideas so far has assumed that each input is obtained from one place, and the place is usually interpreted in theory and example as a point—a dot on a map. But whether the input is coal or wheat or lumber, in many cases its source is an extended area, not a point. When one material or service can be substituted for another (for instance, scrap iron for iron ore), the source area for an input can be even larger. In the same way, a market can be an area rather than a point.

This can add a new dimension to a location decision: (1) if the demand for the material or market is small, its pull as a location factor is reduced because it is available throughout an area of some size; or (2) if the demand for the material or market is large, the fact that it is scattered will increase the costs of collection or distribution, and this can limit the profitable size of the activity.

6.3.4 *Location as Teamwork*

Most industrial location decisions are made by large diverse firms rather than by specialized firms worried only about a single facility. A firm with scores of plants and products may have a variety of concerns, such as using buildings vacated by another of its divisions or sharing facilities with the head office. It may be concerned about the movement of people for face-to-face coordination as well as the movement of raw materials and finished products. For the company as a whole, emphasizing teamwork may be better business than what theory would say is the best location for an individual facility (see Chapter 7.)

6.3.5 *An Uncertain, Constrained, and Changing World*

A problem with a map of isodapanes, no matter how carefully prepared, is that it is already out of date. Another problem is that some of the numbers in it are more dependable than others.

For example, the costs that are used to define the best location are usually estimated from current (or recent) costs and prices. But the new activity will increase local demands for transportation, labor, and other items, and this can raise prices. Since these effects are subtle and often localized, they can be practically impossible to

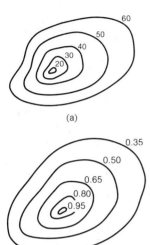

FIGURE 6.6
Interpreting Isodapanes
as Probabilities: (a)
isodapanes indicating es-
timated movement costs;
(b) probability surface indicating likelihood of success of new enterprise (a
probability of 0.50 predicts
success one time in two
tries; 0.80 means success
four times out of five tries).

estimate at more than a few locations, but they can mean that the best place for long-term operation is not the same as the best place on the basis of current prices. If, for instance, a study shows that a town with attractively low unit labor costs has such a tiny local labor supply that the proposed new activity will have to raise wages to hire the labor away from other local employers, then the labor cost advantage must be discounted.

Some directions of likely change in a pattern of isodapanes can be guessed at. As transportation technology improves with time, a general effect is to widen the spacing between isodapanes, and processing technologies usually increase in efficiency, reducing the locational pull of material supply points or areas.

But it is important to understand that a precise single optimum location is seldom what a person is looking for. The aim is to find an *area* that is relatively attractive: lower in total processing and movement costs than other areas. Within the prime area, the differences are not very great, and the decision depends on very practical matters such as where properties are for sale. Converted into three dimensions, the map of isodapanes looks more like a bowl than an inverted cone.

It is also important to appreciate that isodapanes are, in a sense, *probability estimates*—estimates of the chances of success in an uncertain world. If, (1) in Figure 6.6(a), the isodapane showing a total movement cost of 50 is considered a break-even boundary because any greater costs will mean that the industry cannot stay in business; but (2) the isodapanes are considered subject to error (and they certainly are); then (3) the same map can be seen as a pattern of the likelihood of getting a minimum net benefit, as illustrated in Figure 6.6(b). This is especially true if, instead of limiting the map to movement costs, it is expanded to represent overall expected net benefits, including processing costs and market prices.

Finally, a decision maker's options are limited by his or her daily-life environment (see Section 2.2.1). Any person is likely to have limited time, a limited range of contacts (for getting information, making decisions, and arranging for actions), and a limited range of possibilities (for example, not every parcel of land can be purchased). This focuses attention on where and how the decision is being made as well as where and how the facility will be located. Why an activity chooses some locations and not others depends in important ways on the location of whoever is choosing.

6.3.6 Summary
The Weber-type framework of thought is a way of dealing with a locational decision when any economic activity is being pulled in

Company	Finished Steel Production, M.T.	Iron Ore		Coke		Oil		Market Scrap	
		Total Consumption, M.T.	Consumption per Ton of Finished Steel, Kg.	Total Consumption, M.T.	Consumption per Ton of Finished Steel, Kg.	Total Consumption, M.T.	Consumption per Ton of Finished Steel, Kg.	Total Consumption, M.T.	Consumption per Ton of Finished Steel, Kg.
Fundidora	110,000	213,389	1,940	153,900	1,400	29,000	263	22,000	200
						107,000 [a]	974 [a]		
Altos Hornos	102,000	172,500	1,691	108,000	1,059	95,000	931	33,000	323
Total	212,600	385,889		261,980		202,000		55,000	
Weighted average			1,820		1,235		953		259

TABLE 6.2[1]
Consumption of Principal Materials per Ton of Finished Steel, 1950
[a] Assuming oil to be the only fuel used at Fundidora.

several directions: different places are important to its operation as sources of inputs or markets for outputs. Its main value is to remind us how much the costs and benefits of an activity can vary from one place to another. In general, it points out that when an input is costly to move there is an economic advantage to locating close to its source. When an output is costly to move it makes economic sense to locate close to the market. If there are only a few input sources and output markets, the best place is usually at a source or market location. If there are many sources and markets, the best place is often at a centrally located point where transportation systems intersect. Combining a pattern of movement costs with a map of other processing costs (labor, power, taxes, and others), it is possible to come up with a comparison of total activity costs at alternative locations. And this is an important basis for deciding the best location for the activity.

6.4 EXAMPLES

Some examples may help to show how these concepts do in fact reflect the way locational decisions are made in our world.

6.4.1 The Steel Industry in Mexico

A careful comparison of the *actual* location and the theoretically *optimal* location of the steel industry in Mexico was carried out in the early 1950s by R. A. Kennelly.[1] At the time, there were two primary steel plants in the country: Fundidora, at Monterrey, and Altos Hornos, at Monclova (about 200 kilometers northwest of Monterrey). Tables 6.2 and 6.3 show the major inputs of the plants, their sources, the principal markets of the finished steel, and the

Iron Ore

Source, Amount, Distance to Plant, and Freight Cost

Company	Consumption per M.T. in Kg.	Durango Kg.	Km.	P.	Dinamita Kg.	Km.	P.	Rinconada Kg.	Km.	P.	Golondrinas Kg.	Km.	P.	Castanos Kg.	Km.	P.	Sol y Luna Kg.	Km.	P.	Ciudad Guzman Kg.	Km.	P.	Freight Cost per M.T. in Pesos
Fundidora	1,940	1,352	637	19.33	91	414	1.11	144	58	.50	165	120	1.07	37	200	.32	151	222	1.82				24.15
		1,940[a]	637	27.74																			27.74
Altos Hornos	1,691	1,437	677	20.90	254	455	3.23													81	1,343	1.42	24.38
		1,691[a]	677	24.60																			24.60

Coke

Source, Amount, Distance to Plant, and Freight Cost

Consumption per M.T. in Kg.	Sabinas Kg.	Km.	P.	Freight Cost per M.T. in Pesos
1,400	1,400	340	31.57	31.57
1,059	1,059	122	8.63	8.63

Oil

Source, Amount, Distance to Plant, and Freight Cost

Consumption per M.T. in Kg.	Reynosa Kg.	Km.	P.	Tampico Kg.	Km.	P.	Freight Cost per M.T. in Pesos
263	0	247	0	263	521	9.42	9.42
973[b]	486	247	9.099	486	521	17.40	26.49
931	465	465	15.11	465	739	21.06	36.17

Market Scrap

Source, Amount, Distance to Plant, and Freight Cost

Consumption per M.T. in Kg.	United States Kg.	Km.	P.	Mexico City Kg.	Km.	P.	Monterrey Kg.	Km.	P.	Freight Cost per M.T. in Pesos
200	100	268	2.42	50	999	3.23	50	0	0	5.65
323	162	238	3.23	81	1,093	5.37	81	218	1.49	10.09

Finished Product

Consuming Center, Amount, Distance from Plant, and Freight Cost

Freight Cost on Materials in Pesos	Steel to Market in Kg.	Mexico City Kg.	Km.	P.	Monterrey Kg.	Km.	P.	Freight Cost per M.T. of Finished Steel, P.	Total Transported Weight in Kg.	Total Transport Cost per Metric Ton of Finished Steel T.Km.	P.
70.79	1,000	500	999	39.14	500	0	0	39.15	4,523	2,141	109.94
87.86[b]									5,517[b]	2,341x	127.01
79.27	1,000	800	1,093	64.92	200	218	4.64	69.56	5,008	2,740	148.83

TABLE 6.3[1] Sources of Materials, Amount from Each Source, and Transportation Cost on Materials and Finished Steel for Fundidora and Altos Hornos, 1950.

([a] Assuming Durango to be the source of all ore, and [b] assuming oil to be only fuel used at Fundidora.)

FIGURE   6.7
Isodapanes Based on
Weight and Distance.

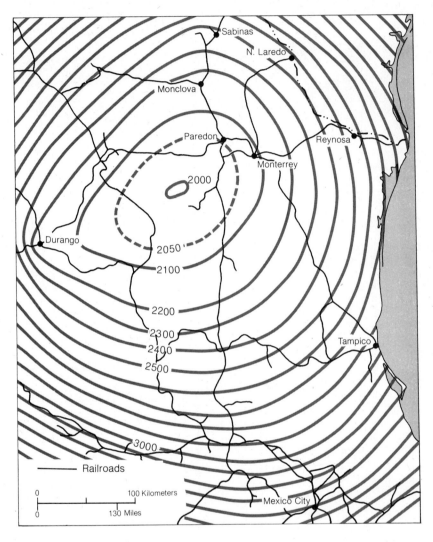

transportation costs of the different items; and Figure 6.7 locates
the major places mentioned in the table. The four materials were
obtained from at least seven locations, and the products were
oriented to two markets, one fairly distant (Mexico City). As the
table indicates, Fundidora had a lower cost location than Altos
Hornos (its total transport costs per metric ton of steel were less).

Using this information about the weights, distances, and
freight rates for moving the commodities that were essential parts
of the steel industry, Kennelly constructed isodapanes. Figure 6.7
displays the pattern of transport costs when only weight and dis-

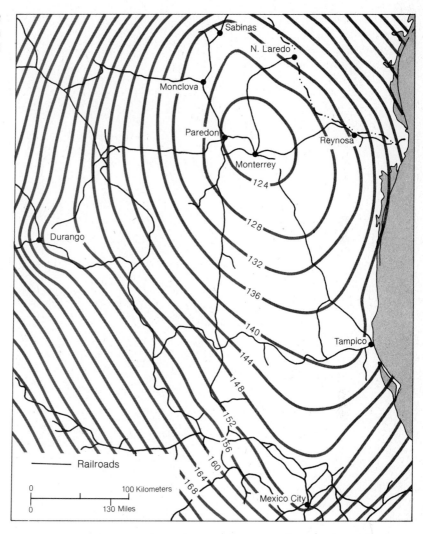

FIGURE 6.8
Isodapanes Based on
Weight, Distance, and
Freight Rates.

tance were considered, and Figure 6.8 shows the pattern when frieght rates were added. Durango, the source of the heaviest input, iron ore, shows a strong influence when only weight and distance were included. Since the freight rates for iron ore were relatively low, however, the pull of the source of ore was replaced in Figure 6.8 by Mexico City, a market for finished products that had a relatively high freight rate.

Considering the material supply points and markets for Mexican steel production in the early 1950s, Kennelly found that the industry was located very efficiently, with one plant right at the

FIGURE 6.9
Isodapanes: Location of
paper mills in Sweden
(For interpretation,
see text.)

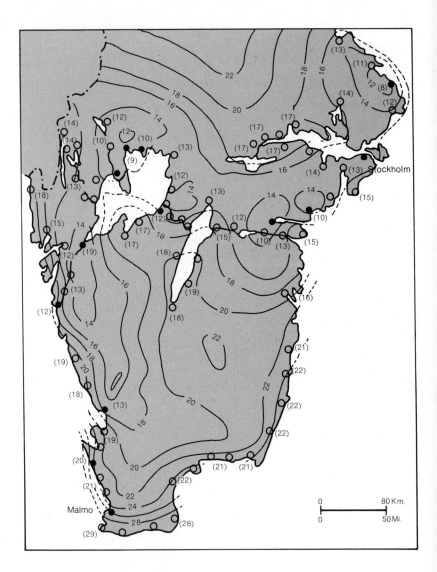

minimum transport cost point and the other at a rail junction near
the minimum point. Clearly, the best place for steel production was
in the northern part of Mexico. And since the same factors are
operating today, it is not surprising that the plants at Monterrey
and Monclova remain the dominant locations for steel production
in Mexico.

6.4.2 Other Studies

The professional literature includes studies that range from elaborations of the Weber model to the development of techniques for solv-

ing more complicated location choice questions, the historical study of how locations change as conditions change, an evaluation of the prospects of particular locations, and the identification of particular activities as input-oriented or market-oriented.

For example, in looking at the location of the paper industry in Sweden, Lindberg estimated that isodapanes had the pattern shown in Figure 6.9, giving the least-cost advantage to coastal areas in the east and west, along with a band of territory across a lowland area in the center of the country.[2] In this case, even though there is a great deal of weight loss in turning lumber into paper, the material source—forest land—covers an extensive area; and in fact the production of paper is more oriented toward locations with easy access to the sea (the most important market is exports from port cities).

A case in which the input source exerts a very strong locational pull is sugar beet refining, where the sugar weighs about one-ninth as much as the sugar beets required to produce it. A study of the French experience with industrial location has shown that, as Weber might have predicted, the material orientation is less clear for the production of pig iron than for sugar beet refining; iron ore weighs only three or four times as much as the product.[3]

6.4.3 Further Examples

We can add to the meaning of the concepts in this chapter by studying maps that show the distribution of economic activities, their input sources, and their markets. Consider Figure 6.10, which indicates some of the locational pulls on petroleum refining in the United States. The refineries are oriented toward areas where crude oil is produced and (less clearly toward) seacoast locations, where large markets can be served by processing imported crude oil (which should tell you something about the spatial distribution of the market).

Another type of energy production is the generation of electricity, which—except for large hydroelectric developments on the Columbia River (in and near Washington state) and the Tennessee River (in and near Tennessee)—has a pattern very much like a map of population density. Since electricity can be created from a variety of power sources, nearly every place is close to a source of some kind. In contrast to oil, the product is difficult to store and expensive to move long distances.

There are many examples of the locational advantage of intermediate places. Port cities in Europe often became industrial cities because of their access to raw materials from other parts of the world, moved at low cost by sea. In the United States, transshipment points historically have been important in steel production in the Great Lakes area, where the lake transportation of iron

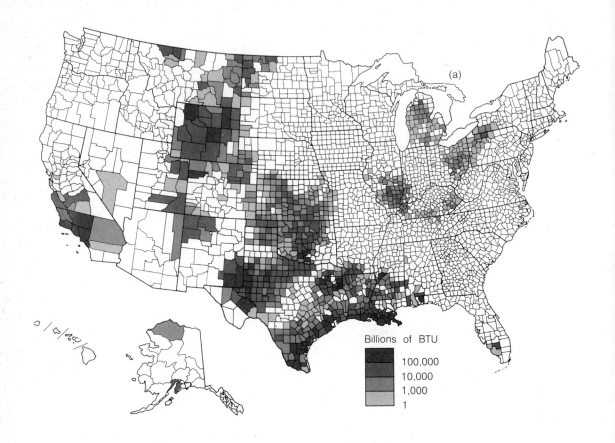

FIGURE 6.10 Locational influences on Petroleum Refining in the United States: (a) petroleum production (BTU means *British Thermal Unit,* which is a way of measuring quantities of energy; one barrel of oil contains about 5,800,000 BTUs of energy);

[continued on next page]

ore met rail lines carrying coal. And aluminum is a case involving two steps, each with weight losses. Bauxite from Caribbean islands and South America is refined at Gulf Coast ports to get alumina (aluminum oxide); and then the alumina is shipped cheaply by river barge to locations closer to market concentrations in the Northeast (generally those with a relatively abundant supply of electricity), where the aluminum is extracted.

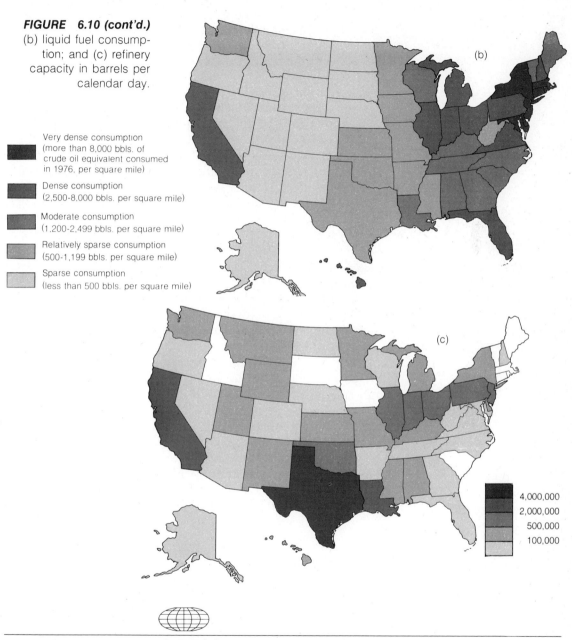

FIGURE   6.10 (cont'd.)
(b) liquid fuel consumption; and (c) refinery capacity in barrels per calendar day.

Very dense consumption (more than 8,000 bbls. of crude oil equivalent consumed in 1976, per square mile)

Dense consumption (2,500-8,000 bbls. per square mile)

Moderate consumption (1,200-2,499 bbls. per square mile)

Relatively sparse consumption (500-1,199 bbls. per square mile)

Sparse consumption (less than 500 bbls. per square mile)

4,000,000
2,000,000
500,000
100,000

6.5   A RECONSIDERATION

A realistic situation for a location decision might be something like this: seven materials or services used in production, each of which has three to fifty possible sources; markets of different sizes and prices in twenty major cities spread around the country; a variety of movement possibilities and an even larger number of possible combinations of the options; and maybe ten major cost items to be considered in addition to transportation. Given unlimited time and information, a person eventually can determine that one location for the activity is probably better (slightly) than any other.

For a problem like this one, though, the process is a cumbersome one, and a major interest (both practically and theoretically) has been to find ways to simplify the choice—that is, to eliminate locations that are probably not the best ones so that the decision is more manageable. But there is generally a gap between theory—spare, simple, and elegant—and application in the complex, uncertain, risk-laden, often data-poor world of the business decision maker. For instance, it took a surprisingly long time for theorists to realize that their models were overemphasizing transportation costs as part of the total costs of most economic activities.

Regardless, the concepts in this chapter are important because a map of isodapanes is in fact a map of spatial inefficiency:[4] locations distant from the optimum are more and more inefficient, from the point of view of transportation costs. Unless other efficiencies can compensate for this, the decision maker is throwing away benefits if he or she ignores the facts.

This concept needs to be used with caution, however. Although movement costs are dominant in some location decisions, they may be insignificant in others. For instance, a large firm might be more interested in acting quickly than in minimizing movement costs; as a result, it might locate a new activity on property it already owns, regardless of location. Or movement costs might amount to less than 2 percent of the total operating costs of the firm, in which case it simply might not be worth undertaking an expensive study of alternatives.

6.6 *TOWARD GREATER PRECISION*

The literature of industrial location theory has given a great deal of attention to ways to solve a Weber-type problem for the best location, and there are several approaches available for simple cases: geometric solutions and mechanical analog solutions (which can be converted to problems for an analog computer). But because their assumptions are so unrealistic, these methods are very rarely used by actual decision makers.

A more helpful tool is *spatial allocation analysis* (also called location allocation analysis or optimal location analysis), which uses a digital computer to deal with a complex system of suppliers, consumers, and flows to and from production points. Essentially, with this method the total transportation costs at each of a large number of possible locations for a facility are very quickly calculated, and the least-cost location is therefore identified. More complex objectives can be handled as well, such as minimizing total operating costs (including wage and tax rates as well as transportation costs).

Although it is also hard to use this approach without simplifying the world a little, the level of realism can often be quite high. For example, transportation costs between two real locations can be based on actual freight rates or on an actual rail line that connects them. And unrealistic solutions can be avoided by the use of "constraints"; for instance, the computer can be asked to identify the lowest cost location *not* in a large city, or the lowest cost location *not* in an area where that kind of industry is not welcome.

Spatial allocation analysis is useful not only in locating economic activities for private decision makers but in locating government services, where an objective might be to locate a service facility so that it minimizes distance to the people who need the services, subject to a number of constraints (see Chapter 14). Finding the best location for an activity is a kind of problem-solving activity that has very wide application.

MAJOR CONCEPTS AND TERMS

For definitions, see the Glossary.

Isodapane	*Locational triangle*	*Optimal location*
Isotims	*Market orientation*	*Spatial efficiency*
Location factor	*Material-source*	*Weight loss*
Locational pull	*orientation*	

Footnotes for Chapter 6

1. Kennelly, R. A. "The Location of the Mexican Steel Industry." *Revista Geografica*, vol. 15: 1954, pp. 109–129; vol. 16: 1955, pp. 199–213; vol. 17: 1955, pp. 60–77.

2. Lindberg, Olof. "An Economic-Geographical Study of the Localisation of the Swedish Paper Industry." *Geografiska Annaler*, vol. 35: 1955, pp. 28–40.

3. Clout, H. D. "Industrial Relocation in France." *Geography*, vol. 55: 1970, pp. 48–63.

4. Abler, R., Adams, J. S., and Gould, P. *Spatial Organization.* Englewood Cliffs, N.J.: Prentice-Hall, 1971, p. 333.

CHAPTER 7

SYSTEMS OF ACTIVITIES AT SYSTEMS OF LOCATIONS

*S*o far, we have been acting as if each location has only one activity and each activity has only one location. But we can define either a location (for example, a city) or an activity (for example, Woolworth's) in a way that makes this untrue. An important characteristic of a place—and a strong influence on the well-being of the people in it—is the number and kinds of activities that collect there. Likewise, an important dimension of an activity is the way it is spread among different locations.

This leads us to some new ideas, stemming from the fact that an economic activity has to have a market. It can survive only if it helps to remedy some sort of scarcity by finding a niche that no one else is filling. Consequently, if everyone wants dry cleaning services, and one city is full of them while a second city has only a few, then there are better opportunities for a new dry cleaning establishment in the latter place. What could be simpler? But from this simple idea come some powerful notions about how cities are arranged with respect to each other, why cities differ in size and services, and why particular activities are located in many places versus a few.

7.1 SITUATIONS

7.1.1 The Home Security Entrepreneur Revisited

In section 3.1.2 you were planning to start a business of providing electronic security systems for private homes. Having made a good choice for the location of your initial office and workshop, you have been very successful, and the enterprise has expanded to two nearby cities.

Now you and your partner think the time is right to become a national operation. While the partner minds the store, it is your job to draw up a plan that can be used to get a loan to finance the move to a national scale. If the plan makes sense, your chances of finding support are good. If it is unsound, the bankers will probably dismiss you as naive young dreamers who lack a good understanding of business principles.

As you see it, the plan will have to be a complex one. It will include the location of offices for local sales and service, warehouses for larger assemblies and all kinds of parts, service centers for more specialized repairs, and possibly some regional headquarters to tailor marketing efforts to the special interests of different parts of the country. For each of these activities, there are questions about how many to have and where to locate them. For example, is the idea to locate a local sales office in every city with a population of 100,000 or more? Larger? Smaller? How big does a metropolitan area need to be to provide a big enough market for an office? In the same way, you have to decide how many warehouse centers and how many centralized service centers to have. If there are too few of the service centers, you will spend too much money transporting assemblies back and forth for repair. If there are too many, one or more of the centers may sit idle for lack of enough to do. Either case means inefficient operation; so what is the right balance?

7.1.2 The Fast-food Chain

A new alternative to hamburgers, hot dogs, and pizza is becoming popular in the United States and Canada: chunks of meat grilled on a skewer over a charcoal fire, served with a variety of accompaniments. A fast, efficient, low-cost process for this has been patented; an advertising firm has come up with a catchy name, jingle, and design for the drive-in stands; and franchises are now being sold.

Along with a large group of old college friends, you have borrowed a lot of money and bought the right to all franchises in the states of Kentucky and Tennessee. Your intention is to build drive-in restaurants and lease them to operators who will agree to purchase meat, condiments, and other supplies from you. You will provide the advertising and will use a team of inspectors to assure that the local outlets are kept clean, cheerful, and responsive.

But at the moment you have spent a great deal of money without building anything, and you need to get things going: to buy property on which to build the restaurants, to arrange contracts with builders, to find operators for the local outlets, and to get ready to provide the promised products and services. The first thing is to decide how many local restaurants to build and where to build them. Should there be two in Louisville—or four or six or eight? How close together is too close (making it hard to find an operator because he or she will have to share the business with too many nearby competitors)? How far apart is too far (missing people who would buy if they did not have to go so far)? What about locations on the interstate highways? Is every third interchange too many or too few?

After the plan is developed for the local outlets, there are also decisions to be made about the support activities. How many meat processing and storage locations will be needed? What about warehouses for bottled sauces, charcoal, and brand name paper products? If you end up with one meat processing facility and central warehouse and four centers for meat storage and smaller warehouses, how should these be located?

7.1.3 *The New Town*

The state of Colorado has become concerned about the increasing concentration of activities and people just east of the Rocky Mountains between Colorado Springs and Fort Collins, centered on the city of Denver. In order to encourage people who insist on relocating in Colorado to consider places outside the Denver area, the state government has decided to sponsor the creation of three new towns in the state: model residential communities with their own industries and other employers. The towns, located in attractive parts of the state away from the Denver area, will be linked with the Denver airport by regularly scheduled small aircraft. Most of the cost of the new town developments will be covered by fees to be collected from new residents of the Denver area (for example, a substantial fee paid to the state by new public utilities customers at the time that service is first provided), so that the cost to long-time Colorado residents will be minimal.

You are the chief planner for the decentralized development authority that has been established by the state to administer this program, and the first job is to identify locations, sizes, and functions for the new towns. Should they be towns of 10,000 or 20,000 or 50,000 people? Should they concentrate on being market centers for the surrounding area—farming, ranching, mining, recreation—or should they emphasize new industries attracted from other parts of the country?

Since the state wants to limit its financial support to the initial phase, the challenge is to distribute these towns so that they can eventually thrive on their own at the intended places and sizes. If a town is poorly located, after the subsidies disappear the activities and people may drift away—many of them to Denver. If the intended size is unrealistically large, it may prove impossible to attract enough people to fill the houses and provide employees for the economic activities. The potential for failure is great. How can you get started on this project?

7.2   BASIC IDEAS

What do these three cases have in common? At least two things. First, a home security company office, a fast food outlet, a new town—each of these has a special kind of "territorial imperative." It needs some kind of surrounding area to serve; if it were bounded by high walls without doors, it could not survive. Second, some kinds of economic activities are suited for larger territories than others: a big warehouse versus a small retail outlet, a town of 50,000 people versus a town of 5,000 people. These ideas are where we start in understanding location decisions for multifacility, multilocation activities.

It is clear that the size of an economic activity—whether it is a factory, a specialized retail store, or a consulting firm—depends on the size of its market. When there are many buyers, a store can be large. When there are few, it must be small to avoid a waste of resources. Because there are costs involved in movement, our examples and our common sense tell us that consumers more distant from a producer or seller are less likely to be part of its market. Consequently, we can begin to talk about a *market area*, an area in which the market for certain goods and services will be located. And the size of this area has an effect on the size of an activity.

In addition to the basic impulse of making more money rather than less, there are some strong economic reasons, called *economies of scale,* for trying to make an activity as big as possible. When a firm is big, it can more easily afford expensive equipment (such as computers) or specialized employees (for example, Ph.D.s for research) that may give it an advantage over competitors. It can afford specialized subdivisions, such as market research sections, and more sophisticated advertising campaigns. It may be able to introduce more efficient operating procedures, such as an assembly line in production. Maybe there is some size at which an organization becomes administratively cumbersome, but we can assume that up to that point a decision maker wants his or her activity to be as large as possible and is in competition with others wanting the same thing.

FIGURE 7.1
A Theory about How Ice Cream Sellers Would Locate on a Beach. Stars represent sellers. (For explanation, see text.)

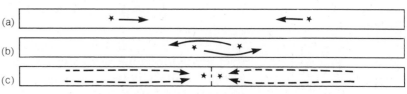

FIGURE 7.2
Other Concepts Regarding the Location of Ice Cream Sellers on a Beach. (For explanation, see text.)

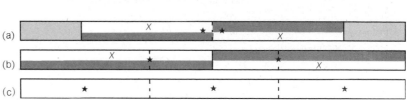

If the consumers of a good or a service are evenly spread from place to place, a larger market area (in square miles or kilometers) will include more consumers than a small one; therefore the activity can be larger. This means that each producer/seller of something is presumably trying to enlarge its market area at the expense of its competitors.

What does this suggest about the spatial arrangement of activities offering the same kinds of goods and services? The classic illustration is the case of ice cream sellers on a beach. Assume a long, narrow beach with swimmers and sunbathers distributed uniformly along it. If there are two sellers, each trying to assure that as large a portion of the beach as possible will belong to him or her, the sequence of location and relocation might be similar to that shown in Figure 7.1, leading to a back-to-back location at the center of the beach.* This is the seller's optimum, in theory, although an uncertainty factor might operate as well: if the two sellers are right next to each other, one cannot be sure that people from each one's territory, having come to the center, will not buy from the other. The greater the concern about this, the more likely it is that there will be some separation.

But what if the distance from the end of the beach to the center is so great that the people near the ends decide it is not worth the effort to buy ice cream? Perhaps the farthest that most people will go is the distance shown in Figure 7.2(a) as X. The lightly shaded areas are a potential market not being served; thus the seller's optimum becomes Figure 7.2(b). In this sense, the sellers could

---

* A less convincing argument can also be made for a sequence of decision making that results in each seller being one-quarter of the way (or a little more) from his or her end of the beach—at least if each seller wants to operate from a fixed structure. A key question has to do with the mobility of each seller.

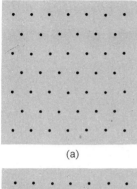

(a)

(b)

FIGURE   7.3

Two Arrangements of
Regularly Spaced Points.

be expected to cluster near the center if demand is not affected by the requirement that a consumer walk a long way; they could be expected to separate if demand is affected by distance.

And what if a third ice cream seller arrives at the beach to compete with the other two? Even if there is no "melt factor" limiting the distance consumers are willing to travel, the three sellers would end up evenly spread, as in Figure 7.2(c) after a long series of shifts, as each sought an advantage over the others. In general, an activity tries to enlarge its market area by finding a location that makes it the closest provider for as many consumers as possible. This usually means putting space between it and its competitors. And if every competitor tries to get as far as possible from every other, the activities will end up evenly spread. Figure 7.3 shows two familiar types of regular spacing.

Just as we have seen for ice cream vendors on a beach, it is possible to figure out a theoretical optimum for the arrangement of any kind of competing activities in any large area, when each activity is trying to maximize the size of its market area. The activity may be Kentucky Fried Chicken or Western Auto or Household Finance Company. But the need for a market area encourages the competing activities to disperse. If the population is evenly distributed and each fried chicken franchise is equally well run, the eventual arrangement should be a regular spacing of the activities.

The issue then becomes this: how far apart are the activities spaced? The separation may be relatively small for some activities, like grocery stores, but very large for others, like restaurants that charge $50 a person for a meal. Although there are a number of reasons for the spacing in any actual case, two are especially important: (1) how far a person is willing to go to get the good or service—which can be called the *range* of a good and sets an outer limit on the size of the market area; and (2) the minimum size of a market that it takes to make an activity worth operating—which can be called the *threshold* for a good. For example, it is difficult to operate a grocery store for three families. This sets an inner limit, or minimum size, for the market area, defined by a minimum number of consumers. The size of the *area* that meets the minimum requirement depends on the *density* of consumers in the market area: the number of consumers per square mile or kilometer. Nearly everyone in a county in Iowa is a consumer of groceries; therefore a relatively small area can provide a large enough market to support a grocery store. But only a small percentage of the population would be regular patrons of the expensive restaurant, which means that its market area must include a much larger number of people, either by covering more territory or by finding a place where people are more densely packed together.

Type of Speciality	Threshold Population
General practitioner	2,500
Pediatrician	6,000
Internal medical, surgery, eye and ear	10,000
Obstetrician	7,500
Ophthalmologist, radiologist	20,000
Urologist, orthopedist, neurologist	40,000

SOURCE: Garrison, W. L. and others, *Studies of Highway Development and Geographic Change.* Seattle: University of Washington Press, 1959.

An individual house in Iowa is thus a part of countless different market areas: large ones for fancy restaurants and specialized magazines, small ones for grocery stores and local newspapers; stable market areas and shifting ones (for example, see Table 7.1).

This does not mean that there is an infinite number of possibilities for locating an activity. Chapter 5 suggested that many location decisions are influenced by spatial *nodes* or foci of activity: markets, central business districts, cities. Chapter 6 mentioned the special advantages of junctions in transportation networks. Economic activities tend to be located with reference to these focal points, which offer so many marketing conveniences.

For simplicity, let's assume that all economic activities can be divided into three categories: those with small market areas, those with medium-sized ones, and some with large ones. This would suggest a need for nodes, which can be called *central places,* having three different levels of outreach (for example, large cities serving large areas; small cities; and villages). At each scale, it is reasonable to expect that the characteristic activities would evolve toward some kind of regular spacing; so the end result should show an evenly spaced arrangement of nodes at three scales. Since a node serving large market areas could also serve smaller ones, the most logical outcome would be a *hierarchy* of central places, reflecting and facilitating a hierarchy of market areas (see Box 7.1):

1. large cities containing activities that require large, medium, or small market areas

2. small cities containing activities that require medium or small market areas

3. villages containing activities that can manage with small market areas

The large cities would be separated by about the same distance from each other, as would the small cities from each other

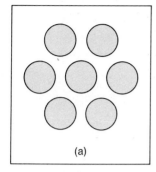

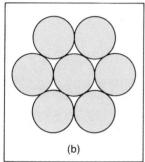

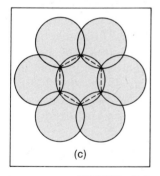

FIGURE   7.4
Space Packing. The circular market areas in (a) expand until they meet in (b), but small gaps still remain between them. In principle, they remove the gaps by expanding still further: (c). If the resulting overlaps are divided equally, the market area of the central point becomes a hexagon.

and the large cities. Likewise, the villages would be scattered evenly. On a perfectly flat, unbounded plain, the market areas of places of a particular size should be roughly circular, limited by the range of the goods and services the place offers. In order to avoid leaving some consumers without service, the circular market areas squeeze together as shown in Figure 7.4, and the circles become *hexagons* as the overlaps are evenly divided. These hexagons can be arranged into a system of locations containing a system of activities, looking like Figure 7.5(a). This is the arrangement that puts an average consumer as close as possible to a large, medium, and small central place; and it provides that the market area of any central place is three times as large as the market area of a place at the next lower level in the hierarchy. For instance, small cities serve three times as large an area as do towns.

The problem is that this arrangement is inefficient for *connecting* places. In Figure 7.5(a), a straight line joining the city in the middle with a small city at the center of a neighboring market area misses the town that lies between them. Figure 7.5(b) shows how the hexagons can be shifted so that intermediate places lie directly between larger places. Although transportation is more efficient, the consumers pay a price because the market area of a place is now four times as large as the next lower category of places. This means that consumers generally have to travel farther to reach a market center.

But what if the "small cities" in this case happen to be locations of the only high schools, and the "towns" just provide education through junior high school? Because the market areas of small cities divide those of the towns, a town must send some of its young people to one small city and others elsewhere, which is administratively complicated. It is possible to rearrange the hexagons again, so that the market area of a larger place includes all of the market areas of the smaller places around it, as shown in Figure 7.5(c). Larger market areas are now seven times as large as the next smaller ones, which means that the students may have to travel farther to high school in exchange for the administrative convenience. The transportation situation is now less efficient than in Figure 7.5(b), and the average distance to market (or high school) is greater for the consumer than in either Figure 7.5(a) or 7.5(b).

Each of these three ways of interlocking central places of one size with smaller and larger places nearby has advantages, and each has disadvantages. In most instances, the consumer located outside the central places themselves would prefer the 3:1 solution. Individuals and firms located in the central places who mainly interact with other central places, rather than the surroundings of their own

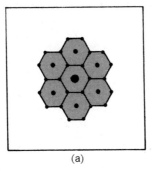
(a)

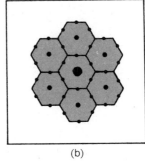
(b)

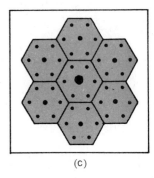
(c)

FIGURE 7.5
Three Alternatives for Arranging Central Places in a Regular Pattern: (a) marketing principle; (b) transportation principle; and (c) administrative principle.

BOX 7.1   HIERARCHIES

It is common for us to think of roads in several convenient categories—perhaps limited-access highways for interstate travel, other highways used for travel between towns, and local roads used to reach homes within a town. This kind of system of categories, ranging from larger to smaller items, can be called a *hierarchy*. Hierarchies are especially interesting when a group of smaller items can be associated with each larger item because structure is added to what would otherwise just be bushels of apples and bushels of canteloupes. For example, for every Mississippi River, there are Ohio, Missouri, Tennessee, and Arkansas Rivers. For every Ohio River, there are smaller rivers feeding into it. And each of the smaller rivers is the destination of still smaller streams.

Urban places are another example of this kind of situation. In studying hierarchies, a frequent interest is in identifying a "typical" number of items connected to each larger item; for example, 3:1, 4:1. Walter Christaller suggested that hierarchies of

urban places show a consistent relationship between the numbers in higher and lower categories—about 3.3:1. Michael J. Woldenberg has proposed a more complicated formula that fits the real-world evidence better, and he has found that the numerical relationships that describe systems of cities also describe an astonishing variety of other hierarchies: branched stream systems, veins and bile ducts in bovine livers, branches of some species of trees, and others.*

If there is some numerical relationship that is characteristic of a well-balanced system of urban places, as Woldenberg hypothesizes, then a country or region can identify gaps or redundancies by comparing its numbers with the "ideal." Some developing countries, for instance, have fewer urban places in middle-sized categories than do developing countries, a fact that may indicate a kind of "urban underdevelopment" (see chapter 16, especially Table 16.1).

*"Energy Flow and Spatial Order," *Geographical Review*, vol. 58: 1968, pp. 553–574.

places, would prefer the 4:1 arrangement. Political and administrative interests might prefer the 7:1 situation (see Box 7.2).

It is likely, in fact, that these different solutions compete for predominance and that each one makes a contribution to the pattern that eventually appears. A map shaped when urban-rural relationships were dominant (as in many parts of Europe) may resemble Figure 7.5(a) most closely, while a map outlined at a later period, when rapid transportation between cities was more important (as in many parts of the United States), may look more like Figure 7.5(b).

In any event, this idealized kind of economic landscape is characterized by a kind of spatial rhythm, a rising and falling of economic intensity at regular intervals. Figure 7.6 illustrates how a cross section of one of the patterns in Figure 7.5 would appear, defined perhaps by the density of traffic or the value of land.

BOX 7.2 WALTER CHRISTALLER AND AUGUST LÖSCH

The principal ideas of this chapter were developed independently by two German geographer-economists in the 1930s: Walter Christaller and August Lösch.

In 1933 Christaller published his Ph.D. dissertation at the University of Erlangen, entitled *Central Places in Southern Germany*. Thoroughly developed and documented, this pioneering work introduced the concept of hexagonally shaped trade areas and showed how these areas arrange themselves into a hierarchical system of central places. Although at the time there was little interest in the book in Germany, it gradually became known in the United States and Scandinavia after World War II, and during the 1960s Christaller's *central place theory* became a major topic of study by economic and settlement geographers.

Lösch, who worked independent of Christaller, presented a remarkable variety of ideas about the spatial pattern of economic activities in a book, *The Economics of Location*, published in 1940. As Valavanis has said:

> *The Economics of Location* belongs to that class of works, of which each generation produces very few, that both introduce a new subject and exhaust it. . . . The main ideas are few and appear utterly simple once popularized. They are *fortunate* ideas; that is, they have many consequences that matter and that are not obvious.*

Among these ideas were the same hexagonal trade areas and hierarchies suggested by Christaller, and Lösch also found a way to combine the 3:1, 4:1, and 7:1 (and higher) arrangements into the richer pattern illustrated in Figure 7.9(b). But this is only one part of a book that is so full of interesting notions that, even now, a reader can still find fresh insights.

*Valavanis, Stefan. "Lösch on Location." *American Economic Review*, vol. 45, 1955, p. 637.

FIGURE 7.6
A Cross Section of a Central Place Pattern. Higher points might represent greater population density or higher land values.

BOX 7.3 HOW A THEORY IS DISCOVERED

The following are the words of Walter Christaller.

> When I was at the age when one uses a school atlas, my mother suggested to our well-to-do aunt that she send me an atlas for Christmas. . . . My aunt was quite disappointed that she "just" sent a "useful" gift, and not something to play with, which really would make one happy. However, it turned out otherwise: when I saw the atlas on the gift table, and its many-colored maps, I was quite bewitched. I didn't play ball, or walk on stilts, but rather was only engrossed in the study of my atlas. The atlas then became a plaything, not only something to look at and study. I drew in new railroad lines, put a new city somewhere or other, or changed the borders of the nations, straightening them out or delineating them along mountain ranges. However, I . . . never thought to study geography. I didn't want to become a teacher—and what other profession could one then take up as a geographer besides that of a teacher?

> So I studied national economy. Geography was almost forgotten as I witnessed the efforts of my teacher Alfred Weber in Heidelberg to create an industrial location theory. My interest in the national economy tended to be theory-oriented: . . . How can we find a general explanation for the size, number and distribution of cities? How can we find laws? The relation of the site to geographical and natural conditions can neither explain the distribution nor the number, nor the size of cities.

> I studied not only these . . . theoretical questions. At the same time, I continued my games with maps: I connected cities of equal size by straight lines . . . in order to determine if certain rules were recognizable in the railroad and road network, whether regular traffic networks existed, and . . . in order to measure the distances between cities of equal size. Thereby, the maps became filled with triangles, often equilateral triangles . . . , which then crystallized as six-sided figures (hexagons). Furthermore, I determined that, in South Germany, the small rural towns very frequently and precisely were 21 kilometers apart from each other. . . . My goal was staked out for me: to find laws, according to which number, size, and distribution of cities were determined. . .

> I . . . followed exactly the opposite procedure that Thünen did: he accepted the central city as already having been furnished, and asked how the agricultural land was utilized in the surround-

7.3   *ELABORATING THE BASIC IDEAS*

Although the logic that leads to one of the honeycomb patterns of market areas shown in Figure 7.5 is certainly part of the truth (see Box 7.3), our places seldom look like this. As any atlas will tell us,

---

BOX 7.3 (cont'd.)

ing area, whereas I accepted the inhabited area as already having been furnished, and subsequently asked where the cities must be situated. . . . Thus, I first of all . . . developed an abstract model.

The truly geographic aim was to be to verify the abstract theory within the reality of a specific landscape, and to show that, in reality, number, size and distribution of the central places correspond to the theoretical model to a considerable extent. . . . I wanted to use all of Southern Germany for the field of investigation of my theory; an area where almost purely agricultural utilization of the land very much predominates (whereas in other portions of Germany industry is very widespread), where there are mountain ranges and plains, and also distinctly marked tourist traffic landscapes. . . . I picked out the number of telephone connections in the various places as the criterion of the central function of a settlement— related to the number of inhabitants of these places, in order to determine the significance of surpluses (of people) in respect to the surrounding land. . . . So, I was able to assign to all central places in South Germany value indication numbers and I was able to mark the central places in South Germany, ac-

cording to their significance as central places, on a map, to measure the distances among them, and to determine the rank in the hierarchy of their "complementary areas" which belonged to them. . . . I was able to find surprising concurrences between geographical reality and the abstract schema of the central places (the theoretical model) especially in the predominantly agrarian areas of North and South Bavaria.

On Saturday and Sunday, I used to hike around in the beautiful landscapes of the Frankish Alps. While hiking, I mentally developed the progress of my work. . . . Many an idea which helped me progress . . . gave me the happiness of a discoverer; it was connected in my memory to some forest path or other, just where I was, where the sun cast its light patches through the foliage onto the earth, or with some view or other from a rocky height, or with some field path of no importance. . . . In general, the opinion predominates that creative scholarly work is born at the desk. It must not be so. Mine was created while hiking, in nature. I am glad to consider myself a geographer.

SOURCE: Translated in English, Paul Ward, and Mayfield, Robert C. (eds.), *Man, Space, and Environment.* New York: Oxford University Press, 1972, pp. 601–610.

the spacing is not always uniform. For example, there are reasons for activities to cluster together as well as separate; the "plain" is not unbounded and undifferentiated; economic activities are not always easy to classify into discrete groups according to size of markets; and an activity is not always operating in a situation where competition is as perfect as the theory assumes.

7.3.1 *Agglomeration Economies*

As we have seen, economies of scale give bigger activities an advantage. Because bigger activities need larger market areas, the activities are encouraged to disperse as much as possible. There are other economies, however, that may favor their concentration:

1. There are reasons why a lot of *similar activities* may locate in the same vicinity. They have the same needs for labor supply and other inputs, for markets and transportation facilities, and for specialized services. Consequently, fast food outlets and publishing firms and other activities may concentrate in a few places rather than spreading out evenly.

2. There are certain advantages for *different activities* to locate in the same vicinity. It can reduce the cost of general services, such as transportation, power, and education, when they can be concentrated and operated at a grander scale. Some activities are buyers from or sellers to others; so a concentration of activities can mean savings in transportation and communication costs, leading activities to be more clustered in larger central places than logic would otherwise suggest. This is true, by the way, both for buyers in the concentration and buyers from outside, who benefit from the fact that a multipurpose trip has the same economic effect as a reduction in the price of goods and services offered at a center (because the cost of the trip is spread among many items).

Because of the benefits of concentration, proximity, as well as separation, is desirable, and activities compete for proximity, giving it value. If everyone wants to be in one place, at the center of a concentration, the land values are likely to rise until there are only as many buyers as there are openings. Further, concentration may mean crowding and congestion. And it can mean a need to get rid of a lot of garbage. Consequently, there can be diseconomies to proximity along with its benefits; and they can combine with the advantages to give a net advantage to areas near, but not quite at, the central point (see Figure 7.7). A familiar example of this is the "doughnut ring" tendency in the location of industry in urban areas: early industry in a ring near the city center, and new industry in a larger diameter ring out beyond the older residential areas

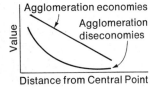

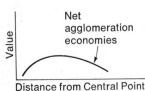

FIGURE 7.7
A General View of Economies and Diseconomies Associated with Nearness to the Center of an Agglomeration.

(reflecting an outward movement of the point of greatest net agglomeration economies as the city has grown).

Proximity may play an especially strong role if a number of different production activities are all part of the same large, integrated organization, one supplying another. Because a market is guaranteed, a subdivision that makes component parts for a second subdivision that assembles, say, automobiles or television sets does not worry very much about separating itself from other plants making the same components. In any event, when a large organization is involved, it is clear that agglomeration economies are evaluated in terms of the multifunction, multilocation company rather than in terms of individual categories of activity.

7.3.2 *Equilibrium Spacing of Activities and Places*

We have now identified two ideas that seem to be opposites: (1) there are good reasons for activities to locate close together; and (2) there are good reasons for activities to seek maximum separation. Transport costs and the distribution of consumers encourage activities to disperse to gain competitive advantage by being closer to potential consumers. New firms enter the competition for markets by serving areas disadvantaged by being far from suppliers, leading to smaller market areas for all, thus smaller activities. Economies of scale and agglomeration, on the other hand, encourage the activities to become larger and more concentrated, requiring larger market areas. Economies of scale exert a *push*; if there were not advantages from size and agglomeration, the economic landscape would be entirely one of small local activities. Transportation costs exert a *pull*; if there were no effort required in movement, there would be no reason to be close to potential customers. Somewhere between the two is a balance, indicated by a degree of dispersion of similar activities and reflecting the relative importance of transportation costs versus economies of scale and agglomeration for that class of activities. This balance, or *equilibrium*, should remain constant as long as conditions stay the same (for instance, transportation costs do not change).

Since the equilibrium identifies the most efficient pattern for the activity (any other pattern is wasteful, at least of profits), defining it is a matter of great theoretical and practical interest. The definition for a particular kind of activity looks something like Figure 7.8, and the result is a vast difference in the way, say, grocery stores are spaced compared with the way large movie studios are spaced.

As Section 2.2 indicated, however, "dispersed" or "clustered" can itself be difficult to define. For example, how do we indicate on the vertical axis on Figure 7.8 an industry such as moviemaking,

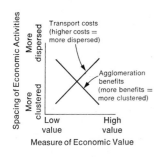

FIGURE 7.8

A General View of the Ideal Spacing of Individual Cases of a Particular Kind of Economic Activity.

fashion garments, or national network television, which usually operates in widely dispersed clusters? It is important to be careful and consistent in defining one's terms.

Also remember that for the same multifacility economic activity, there is a different equilibrium for each level of the hierarchy of operations; beer manufacturing plants are usually more widely spaced than beer warehouses, which are more widely spaced than retail sales locations.

7.3.3   *Uniform Spacing of Activities and Places*

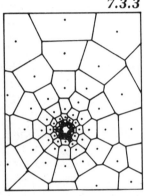

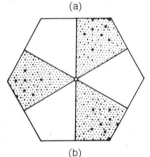

FIGURE 7.9
Spacing of Central Places In and Near a City: (a) the spacing of central places if population density increases toward the center and each center serves the same number of people; and (b) central-place-rich and central-place-poor sectors around a very large agglomeration.

If we look carefully at central places on a map, we see that they seem to be partly concentrated, partly dispersed, and partly unpredictable in location. How much of this is equilibrium and how much is accident or inefficiency? In the United States, the overall pattern is not very regular, although the smaller the class of central places, the closer one gets to regularity. The reasons for a departure from the regularity of Figure 7.5 include these:[†]

1. **Theory.** Activities are spaced according to their market areas, but since the population that makes up the market is more densely concentrated near an agglomeration, the areas there can be smaller. This means that nodes of a given size, serving market areas of a given population size, will be closer together in or near big cities, as in Figure 7.9(a). Further, Lösch has shown that if overlays of the 3:1, 4:1, and 7:1 arrangements of central places are superimposed so that as many nodes as possible overlap exactly, a pattern appears where the places around the big central node show a sort of radial banding, as in Figure 7.9(b); this tendency is in reality reinforced by transportation patterns. At any rate, it is hard to conceive of central places without recognizing an uneven distribution of population, which necessarily distorts the simple honeycomb pattern of Figure 7.5.

    Other things than population may be unevenly distributed as well; for example, natural resources and the physical and cultural characteristics of areas and the people who live in them. According to the theory, each distinctive area may have its own distinctive equilibrium, and any regularity may be discernible only after the different areas are separated so that they can be studied individually.

2. **History and inertia.** The historical beginnings of patterns of settlement and economic activity may have had little connec-

[†] Also see Section 6.3.5.

tion with current market forces. Given a group of small villages, some will grow and some will not. Only some will become market or administrative centers. The initial push for growth may be advantage or accident, but the result is a skeleton that shapes the morphology of the pattern to follow. Because of the selection that takes place, with some locations in a concentration thriving and other settlements fading while empty areas begin to fill, there is some impetus toward a greater regularity in the spacing of settlement nodes of a given size. But agglomeration economies work in the opposite direction, giving well-established places an advantage, regardless of their spatial pattern. Consequently, any pattern of settlements that we observe on a map is a continuing compromise between historical circumstance and theoretical ideals, because the economic and social costs of fundamentally reshaping the pattern are often harder to accept than its inefficiencies.

7.3.4   *The Classification of Activities and Places*

Figure 7.5 assumes a clearly distinguishable three-level hierarchy of economic activities and the central places that influence their locations. Actually, our expectation is more like what we see in Figure 7.10(a): that there is simply some relationship between the size of a place and the greatest degree of specialization of the activities located there.

Studies of actual data for American cities have shown that there are some discontinuities in the graph: the actual relationship is not an unbroken, smooth one—as seen in Figure 7.10(b). This evidence supports the idea that there are *orders* of central places (for example, large cities, small cities, towns, villages, hamlets) and the idea that the orders fit into a hierarchy of nodes. And these are key ideas in theory that we have been considering.

On the other hand it can be hard to find discontinuities in a range of central place population figures. For several decades scholars have considered the fact that the population of a city or town can be approximately predicted by a *rank-size rule:*

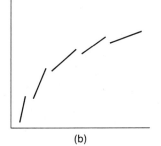

Size of Central Place

Degree of Specialization of Most Specialized Activity

(a)

(b)

FIGURE 7.10

The Relationship between the Size of a Place and Its Economic Specialization: (a) the general expectation (Toronto has more specialized restaurants than Crooked Creek, Alberta); (b) the actual evidence: the relationship is not one smooth curve; it consists of portions of a number of different curves, each one of which describes the relationship for central places within a limited range of sizes.

$$\frac{\text{Population of}}{\text{a city or town}} = \frac{\text{Population of the largest city}}{\text{Rank of the city or town in a}}$$
descending order of cities
and towns

If the largest city has a population of 5 million, then the one-hundredth largest city would be expected to have a population of 50,000. This indicates that central places, at least in their population sizes, follow a kind of gradient rather than being arranged into a hierarchy. Such an inconsistency has been perplexing, especially when there was logic behind the hierarchy idea but none behind the rank-size rule.

Martin Beckmann seems to have resolved the paradox by suggesting that, for any single level of the central place hierarchy, local factors will cause the population of the numerous places at that level to vary above and below an "expected" size—some places larger, some smaller; some a little, a few a lot. If this provision for population variation is added to central place theory (which is concerned with the nodal provision of goods and services rather than with the populations of central places as such), the apparent inconsistency with the rank-size rule disappears (see Figure 7.11).

7.3.5 *Equilibrium and Perfect Competition*

Resolving the various "push" and "pull" influences in the way that best balances the interests of all, as proposed by the theory, assumes that perfect competition is taking place. If two activities, focused on economies of scale, are giving poor service to consumers midway between them, a third activity can arise to meet the need. Further, all consumers and all providers are fully informed and absolutely rational (economically) in making their decision.

As we have noted before, the world is not this simple. A monopoly may arrange itself however it wishes, although a hierar-

FIGURE 7.11
Reconciling the Rank-Size Rule with the Concept of a Hierarchy of Orders of Central Places. Each horizontal step is an order with an *average* population size, but the population of the central places in that order varies around the average. Consequently, the population sizes of *all* central places take the form of a fairly smooth curve.

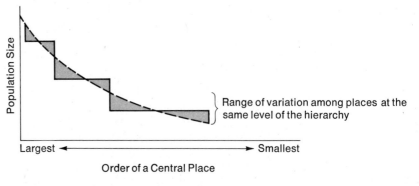

chical spatial organization usually means greater profits for it. Fears of monopolies may lead to limits on the scale of activities (such as antitrust laws), maintaining a degree of freedom of entry by new competitors by foregoing the possible benefits of greater economies of scale. Some potential entrepreneurs find it easier to get development money than others.

Moreover, our judgments are nearly always uncertain and less than perfectly informed. They involve guesses about the future as well as documentation of the past. They include valuations of friends and scenery as well as monetary profits. Consequently, central providers of goods and services may be closer together or farther apart than the ideal. Market areas may overlap substantially, partly because it is not entirely clear whether the goods or services are exactly the same. When such economic inefficiencies exist, however (understandable, and even perhaps admirable, as they are), they often present opportunities for better informed entrepreneurs to enter the competition successfully.

7.3.6 Equilibrium and Changing Conditions

Central place theory is a static theory. It predicts an equilibrium under a constant set of conditions. But what if conditions change: distance shrinks because of transportation improvements, or market areas shrink because of an overall increase in population density or purchasing power? The theory is very limited. It does not tell us how a regular arrangement of service centers, as shown in Figure 7.5, accommodates a need to add another center. Where should it go? Surely, all the centers do not have to shift locations so that we can retain the honeycomb pattern in a slightly more dense form.

For this reason, central place theory works better as a body of basic principles than as a specific plan of action. It suggests, for example, that a customer-oriented new activity is most likely to do well if it can locate a group of potential customers distant from all the competing providers. It also suggests that if conditions allow market areas to expand, some activities will be squeezed out—with the remaining pattern showing much of the spatial rhythm diagrammed in Figure 7.6. It is clear that a change that makes market areas larger can cause overlaps (or reduce gaps), and a change that shrinks their size will open up gaps. Anticipating either effect can be useful to an economic decision maker. But remember that there may be a considerable difference between the spatial *range* and the spatial *threshold* of an activity—the maximum and minimum size of the market area. In responding to changed conditions, it makes a difference whether a previously stable condition was based (1) on market areas nearly as large as the range (local shrinkage can be accepted without disrupting the overall pattern, but there is little

FIGURE 7.12
Market Areas for Different Functions of Central Places. Lines connect a place of residence with the places where the residents shop. Longer lines mean longer shopping distances, thus larger market areas. (a) shopping for food; (b) shopping for clothing; *[continued on next page.]*

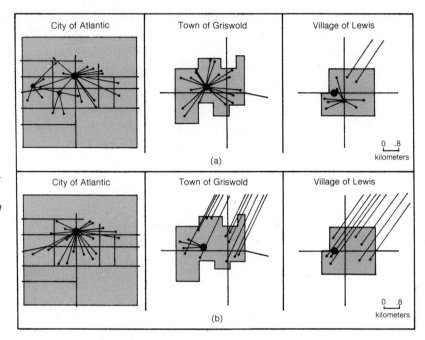

potential for expansion); or (2) on market areas nearly as small as the threshold (local expansion can be handled easily, but there is little potential for shrinkage without forcing some centers out of business).

7.3.7   Intermittent Functions

Sometimes, particularly in a less developed area, a special kind of situation arises: the range is smaller than the threshold. For instance, in parts of West Africa the local transportation system, the climate, and the lack of refrigeration combine to make it difficult to transport fresh beef very far. The range is short because the meat spoils quickly, and people move relatively slowly by bicycle and foot. But within this range, too few people have enough money to keep a large daily meat market in a centrally located village in business.

This discussion seems to suggest that such a good or service would not be provided at all, but there is an alternative. Like a circuit-riding preacher on the American frontier, the function can rotate through a series of centers, with each center providing the good or service one day in every three, four, seven, or some other interval. Such a system is usually called a *periodic market*. When several periodic markets meet the same consumer demands, they arrange their market areas like larger central places. In such a case,

FIGURE 7.12 (cont'd.)
(c) obtaining barber service; and (d) shopping for furniture.

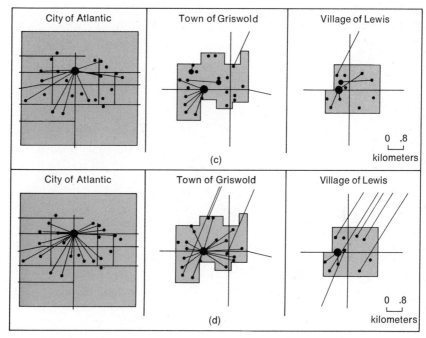

the frequent overlaps between market areas of towns and cities show up as occasional interlocking systems where, for example, one traveling merchant arrives Tuesdays, another on Saturdays.

7.3.8 An Alternative Model

So far in this chapter, we have been considering elaborations of the Christaller/Lösch model of how central place hierarchies arrange themselves in space. But there are other models. James Vance, for example, has studied the historical role of wholesalers in international trade and has concluded that classic central place theory does not correspond very well with what actually happened. And he has proposed a "mercantile" model as an alternative.

Central place theory is focused on the relationship between a node and the consumers in the area near it. Connections are internal within the market area. The nodes, however, get many of their goods from places farther away. What if the location that is best for the local market area is not best for the external connections? The external links may be the deciding factor.

In North America, central places developed to meet the consumer demands of Europe. The main objective was to collect, store, and transport goods for external markets, not to serve local markets. The number and spacing of the nodes depended heavily on the size of the European demand and the convenience of the traders. Even-

FIGURE 7.13
Trade Areas: (a) one town
in Indiana; [continued on
next page]

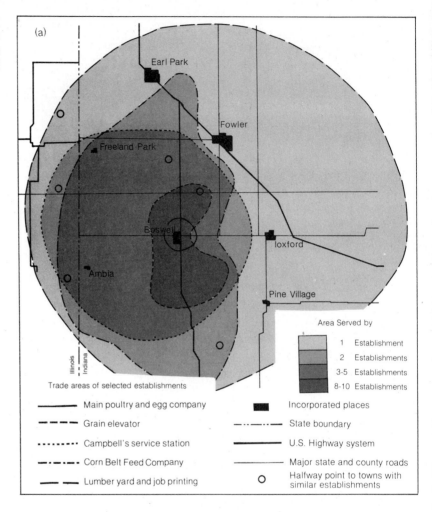

(a)

Earl Park

Fowler

Freeland Park

Boswell

Ambia

Ioxford

Pine Village

Illinois
Indiana

Trade areas of selected establishments

——————— Main poultry and egg company

– – – – – Grain elevator

·············· Campbell's service station

–··–··– Corn Belt Feed Company

— — — Lumber yard and job printing

Area Served by

	1	Establishment
	2	Establishments
	3-5	Establishments
	8-10	Establishments

 Incorporated places

–··–··– State boundary

——————— U.S. Highway system

——————— Major state and county roads

○ Halfway point to towns with
similar establishments

tually some of these nodes—especially seaports where goods were transferred from land transportation to ships—grew large enough to become important markets themselves. This *mercantile* central place pattern, together with its network of connections, became the skeleton for the pattern that evolved later on.

7.4 *EXAMPLES*

At least partly because our cities and towns are in fact arranged less evenly than central place theory seems to predict, the ideas dis-

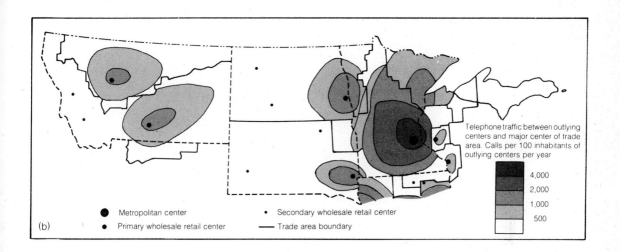

Telephone traffic between outlying centers and major center of trade area. Calls per 100 inhabitants of outlying centers per year

4,000
2,000
1,000
500

● Metropolitan center   · Secondary wholesale retail center
(b)
• Primary wholesale retail center   —— Trade area boundary

FIGURE 7.13 (cont'd.)
(b) wholesale-retail trade areas in the Upper Midwest.

cussed in this chapter have been studied with a lot of vigor for several decades. Some investigators, persuaded by the logic of Christaller and Lösch, have been motivated by an interest in showing that the concepts are valid. Others, such as Vance, have believed that central place theory has little relation to the rich and complex processes of human settlement, and they have sought evidence to support their belief. From the dialog between these two kinds of people has come an increased emphasis on the kinds of issues introduced in Section 7.3. Some examples will help show why the concepts are considered worth learning.

7.4.1   *The Arrangement and Functions of Places*

Where in the United States can an investigator find a relatively flat and environmentally homogeneous study area? In the summer of 1960 a research team gathered a great deal of data in western Iowa about the shopping behavior of the people and the functions of the central places. As the theory predicts, the study showed that the market areas for localized goods such as food were smaller than those for more specialized goods such as clothing (see Figure 7.12). And it provided support for the idea that central places group into several hierarchically related categories.[1]

This information extends a picture earlier sketched out for the United States by Brush and Philbrick, and it has been further extended by the investigations by Borchert and others of major wholesale and retail trade areas in the upper Midwest (see Figure 7.13). Borchert found that this part of the country was dominated by the Minneapolis-St. Paul metropolitan area. At such a regional level of service, he has suggested that the United States is divided

FIGURE 7.14

Trade Areas in the United States: (a) as they appear on a map; and (b) as they appear if population density is held roughly constant.

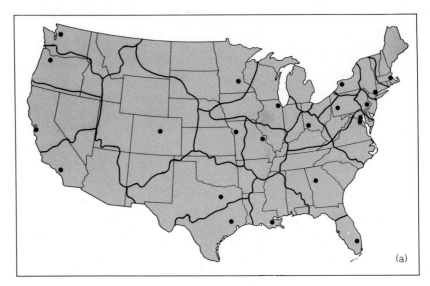

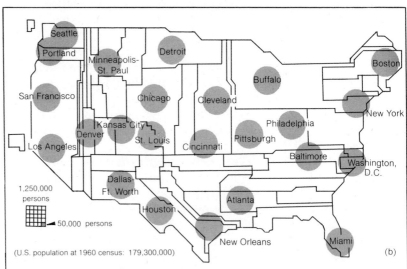

into the trade areas shown in Figure 7.14(a). The irregular pattern seems to contradict the theoretical expectation. But central place theory assumes that consumers are evenly distributed; if the map of trade centers and their market areas is stretched so that the population density is roughly the same everywhere (enlarging the dense areas, condensing the sparsely populated ones), the trade centers turn out to be much more regularly spaced, as shown in Figure 7.14(b).

TABLE 7.2
The Spacing of Trade
Centers in Indiana

	142 Hamlets	73 Villages	19 Towns
Theoretical distance, in miles (if equally spaced with hexagonal trade areas)	5.6	10.0	19.8
Average of actual straight-line distances between centers, in miles	5.5	9.9	21.2
Range of variation, in miles	1.0–12.0	3.5–18.5	7.0–38.0

SOURCE: Brush, J. E. "The Hierarchy of Central Places in Southwestern Wisconsin." *Geographical Review,* vol. 43:1953, pp. 380–402.

In general, the pattern of market areas resembles the honeycomb pattern most closely for smaller trade centers. Figure 3.4(b) illustrated the similarity for small villages in the flat Gangetic Plain of India, for instance. And G. W. Skinner has shown that parts of rural Szechwan, China, fit two of the three types of honeycomb patterns remarkably well (one example is shown in Figure 7.15). Market areas, however, may vary for different cultural groups within the population; average figures often hide important aspects of the variation around the average (see Figure 7.16).

Another way to investigate a possible correspondence between our observations of the world and our theories is to compare measures of the patterns. For example, Brush found that Indiana trade centers, on the average, were spaced almost exactly as far apart as hexagonal trade areas would require (see Table 7.2). And several investigators, working in different countries, have found that the most common number of sides to an administrative area is six (although the most common angle between adjacent sides is 90 degrees, which suggests that the norm may be a shape like New Mexico's instead of a beehive's hexagon).

As a central place system evolves, we might expect at least two things to happen in the right circumstances: (1) new centers would probably emerge near the boundaries between earlier market areas, and some research in Sweden bears this out[‡]; and (2) as many towns thrive and grow, some others will disappear, especially if they are close to more successful places. The remaining places will be fewer, larger, and more widely spaced. And, again, there is supporting evidence, this time from Saskatchewan (see Tables 7.3 and 7.4, page 142).

[‡]   S. Godlund, "The Function and Growth of Bus Traffic within the Sphere of Urban Influence," *Lund Studies in Geography,* Series B, no. 18, 1956.

FIGURE   7.15
Actual and Generalized
Patterns of Market Centers
in Rural Szechwan: (a) a
portion of Szechwan near
Changtu; (b) first
abstraction of (a);
[continued on next page]

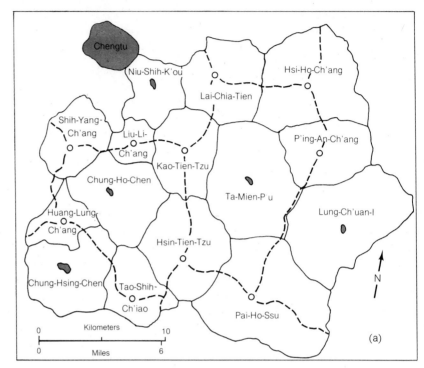

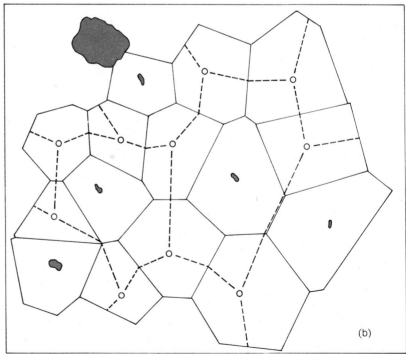

FIGURE 7.15 (cont'd.) (c) the 3:1 central place arrangement. A similar study in another part of Szechwan showed a close resemblance to the 4:1 arrangement.

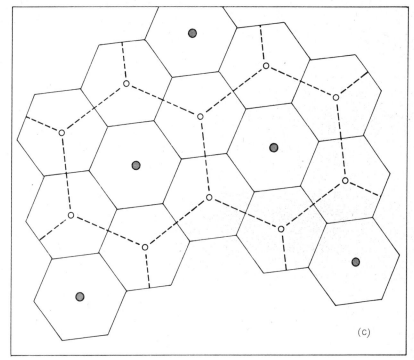

(c)

FIGURE 7.16 Cultural Differences in Shopping Behavior: (a) old order Mennonite travel for clothing and yard goods; and (b) "modern" Canadian travel to buy clothing and yard goods.

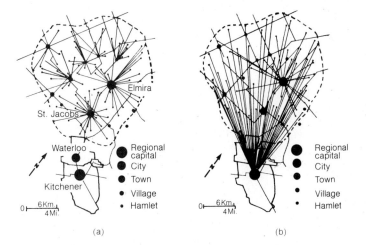

7.4.2 *The Arrangement of Activities*

We have said that the equilibrium arrangement of an activity depends on a balance between the push influence of transportation costs and the pull influences of agglomeration economies. Dispersed activities are familiar ones: grocery stores, barber shops, dry cleaning establishments, and fast-food outlets. They must be close

TABLE 7.3

Changes in the Average
Spacing of Towns in
Saskatchewan,
1941–1961

Classification	Number in 1961	Average Spacing, in miles	
		1941	1961
Hamlet	404	9.1	9.6
Village	150	10.3	13.5
Small town	100	15.4	19.8
Town	85	25.9	22.5
City	29	40.4	39.5
Regional city	9	119.8	67.5
Regional capital	2	144.0	144.0

SOURCE: Hodge, Gerald. "The Prediction of Trade Center Viability in the Great Plains" (Ph.D. thesis, Massachusetts Institute of Technology, 1965).

TABLE 7.4

Changes in the Density of
Small Trade Centers near
Large Centers in
Saskatchewan,
1941–1961

Distance Zone	Number per 1,000 Square Miles		Percentage Change, 1941–1961
	1941	1961	
Within 10 miles	5.2	4.0	−23.1
10–15 miles	7.6	6.3	−17.1
15–20 miles	8.2	7.2	−11.0
Provincial average All small centers	7.2	6.2	−16.7

SOURCE: (Same as Table 7.3.)

to their customers to survive; thus they exist in small central places and most urban neighborhoods.

The importance of the economies that lead activities to cluster is less familiar. In analyzing data from the 1954 Census of Manufacturing, R. M. Lichtenberg found that many industries were highly clustered in the New York City metropolitan area. Table 7.5 lists 6 of 87 categories of firms that were relatively concentrated in the area. Many of these industries are characterized by small, often one-plant firms—needing a cluster of colleagues to support necessary supply, marketing, and service activities.

On a more local level, activities often cluster because of the way most people like to shop: taking care of several errands at the same time (bank, drugstore, grocery store), often comparing prices and products from store to store (antique stores, retail clothing stores, shoe stores). Multipurpose clusters become central places in their own right. Single-activity clusters simply show that in those

Industry	Percentage of Total U.S. Employment
Hatter's fur	99.9
Lapidary work	99.5
Artists' materials	91.9
Fur goods	90.4
Dolls	87.4
Hat and cap materials	85.7
Handbags and purses	75.6
Tobacco pipes	75.3

SOURCE: Lichtenberg, R. M. *One-Tenth of a Nation*. Cambridge,
Mass.: Harvard University Press, 1960, pp. 265–268.

cases the advantages of locating close to similar activities outweigh
those of being closer to customers; but, even here, each cluster is
separated from other clusters in a way that follows the principles of
central place theory.

7.5 A RECONSIDERATION

We have now considered three components of location theory: (1)
the best activity for a location (following von Thünen); (2) the best
location for an activity (after Weber and others); and (3) systems of
locations and activities. As the examples have indicated, the
theories were developed from different emphases: von Thünen was
concerned mainly with agriculture, Weber with industry, and
Christaller and Lösch with retail and wholesale activity. But the
models have been found to be useful for other purposes as well (for
example, the von Thünen theory for modeling urban land values).
All three are still based on thin evidence from the "real world," and
all three are continuing to grow and change, usually because ob-
servant persons continue to point out ways that the theories are in-
adequate. In the meantime, they survive because decision makers
find them useful collections of concepts.

The trade area concept, for instance, is especially valuable in
marketing studies. Is there a market for a new apartment building
or a new supermarket in Rochester, New York? What would be the
trade area of the proposed activity? How many people live in the
area? What proportion of them are likely customers? Is this a large
enough market to make the activity profitable?

MAJOR CONCEPTS AND TERMS

For definitions, see the Glossary.

Agglomeration
  economies
Central place theory
Central places
Economies of scale
Equilibrium spacing

Hexagonal pattern
Hierarchy
Market area
Mercantile model of
  settlement
Periodic market

Range of a good or
  service
Rank-size rule
Threshold for a good
  or service

Footnote for Chapter 7

1.   The results of the study are summarized in Berry, B. J. L. *Geography of Market Centers and Retail Distribution.* Englewood Cliffs, NJ: Prentice-Hall, 1967, Chapters 1 and 2.

PART IV

LOCATIONAL ADVANTAGE

*C*hapter 3 showed us that economic well-being differs from place to place, and Chapter 4 hinted that these differences are related somehow to our preferences as decision makers for some locations over others. Consequently, in Chapters 5, 6, and 7, we considered the logic by which economic location decisions are made.

With this background, we are ready now to see why these decisions give some areas advantages over others—why some places end up offering more opportunities and benefits than other places. In the next three chapters we will consider a place as a sort of island in a "sea of everywhere else." Chapter 8 will consider the basis of a regional economy: the kinds of activities that serve as the foundation for all the rest. Chapter 9 will explore the significance for this of the environments that characterize a place. And Chapter 10 will outline the various reasons why a geography of locational advantage results.

CHAPTER 8

THE BASIS OF LOCATIONAL WELL-BEING

*T*hink how advantage reinforces itself. A dense population allows ice cream parlors to be clustered close together, which gives us a greater choice of banana splits and hot fudge sundaes—and employs more people to live in the area to support more laundries and grocery stores and garbage collectors. A large population, which usually means more purchasing power, spreads the von Thünen rings of land use farther out from the center, raising the value of land. It exerts more of a pull on the locational decisions of manufacturers, increasing the likelihood that new employers will locate there. And these industries offer agglomeration economies to other decision makers choosing a location.

Where does it all start? What gets the process going?

8.1 SITUATIONS

8.1.1 The Interstate Highways
You grew up in a midwestern town, the oldest child of the owner and operator of a hardware store on the town square. A major U.S. highway ran through the center of town. Some small local industries were important customers, and their employees meant important business as well. As a child, you thought that someday the store would be yours, and you have continued to think about it ever since.

But in the early 1960s, after considerable political maneuvering, a new limited-access interstate highway was routed away from the town so that it passed through another town 20 miles distant. Although the effect was not immediate, the hardware store has not done as well since then. One of the local industries has relocated to a city several hundred miles away, and another has gone out of business. Several new industrial plants have come to the larger region in the past ten years—one to the nearby town on the interstate. But no one seems interested in your town.

In the meantime, business volume at the store is declining, and the population of the town is slowly shrinking and becoming older as the young people leave. Your parents have asked your advice. What can they do to improve their business? Is it their fault? Or is it just a reflection of what has been happening to the town as a whole since the new highway bypassed it?

8.1.2 *The Bowling Alley*

You are the manager of a small 24-lane bowling alley in a small city with a population less than 100,000. Although you like the job and would hate to trade it for a desk in a big office, business has been pretty poor. You are having to offer cut rates in order to have more than a few lanes in use during working hours on weekdays, and only three nights a week are heavily booked by leagues. Your salary has been the same for three years, and the owner says that it cannot be increased unless revenue improves—a lot. In the meantime, the finances of the bowling alley are so tight that you can afford to pay for very little advertising. It's hardly worth the long hours.

Three years later: a couple of months after the previous low point, a metal fabricating firm decided to locate a large new factory in your city, making use of several vacant but solid buildings that were available. About a year ago, the factory went into operation, employing more than four hundred people, many new to the city. Since then, six new bowling leagues have been formed, at least three composed exclusively of factory employees or their spouses. Your weekly revenues are up 40 percent over last year. You have gotten a raise. The owner of the bowling alley is talking about adding another 24 alleys, and you have had some preliminary discussions with a local television station about a live local bowling show, to be sponsored partly by local merchants who have found the big factory to be a good customer.

And there are reports that several other companies are planning to locate manufacturing plants in your city, where they can work on a day-to-day basis with the metal fabricating factory. Two of the prospects would base their production on metal fabricating machinery and replacement parts for the machines.

Things are looking up for the bowling business.

8.1.3   *The Young Dentist*

Suppose that you are graduating from dental school. You have been advised to get started by borrowing a very large amount of money and using it to buy a practice from a retiring dentist somewhere. But you are stubborn enough to want to build a practice on your own, and you dislike the idea of being so deeply in debt. Your preference would be to "hang out a shingle": rent an office, borrow just enough money to buy your equipment and to pay for food and lodging for a while, join some local organizations to let people know that you are there, and let matters take their course. Obviously, there is a possibility that you will end up sitting in lonely isolation in your office, but you believe that there must be someplace you can go to make a good living.

The key, you think, is to find a place where a lot of new people, especially families, are moving in—people without a long-time local family dentist. Generally, this is understood to mean suburban locations in general and in the South and West in particular. But you have heard that since the 1970 U.S. Census was taken, there is some question whether all of these trends are continuing. Basing your decision on somebody else's analysis of migration trends seems too risky to a cautious person like you.

You decide to spend a few weeks in the library of the business school at your university, looking for information about where new manufacturing and other business is locating. In some of the most recent material you find that a particular city is mentioned several times: two new manufacturing plants and a large relocated company headquarters have selected it as their future location. Just to be sure, you get a copy of the city's telephone directory, count the number of dentists listed in the Yellow Pages, and compare the ratio of dentists to city population with similar counts of dentists for several other cities of about the same size. You find no significant difference.

Clearly, the city will need new dentists to serve the people who will move there to work in the new activities. You will be one of them.

8.2   *BASIC IDEAS*

The question is: what is the basis of the economy of a place? What is its *economic base*? And what difference does it make: why are some places bigger than others? Why are some growing while others decline? Let's begin by dividing the economic activities of a place into two types: *basic* and *nonbasic*.

1. **Basic activities.** These bring money into a place from outside it. Examples are steel mills, which sell steel to a large market area, and soybeans, high-fashion dresses, tourist attractions, and major universities.

2. **Nonbasic activities.** Once money is brought into the place, these circulate the money within it. Examples are local bakeries, lawyers, and automobile repair shops.

In Section 4.3.3 we viewed the production of goods and services as a combination of various factors, or kinds of inputs, such as land, labor, capital, and technology. Maybe we can account for the output of a place by adding up the amounts of things like capital, labor, land, and technology that are invested there.

One of the reasons that this total output figure is important is that it has a direct relationship with the total income of the place. National income is equal to the total national production, or Gross National Product (GNP), less the part of the output that is used to replace capital that gets used up (old machines and buildings are examples). Although total income does not indicate how the income is distributed among the people, the relationship does suggest that the basic way to improve incomes in a place is to increase its production of the goods and services that someone wants.

Think of what happens when a consumer from outside the area buys something from inside it. For example, a tourist buys a meal in a restaurant. With the money earned from a lot of tourists, the restaurant owner decides to order new menus from a local printer. With the money from that job, the printer buys a new desk from the local furniture store. With the commission from the sale, the salesperson eats at the restaurant the next week. And the new income for the town has become much more than just the sum paid by the tourist. A dollar of new money, received in exchange for goods and services, has turned into more than a dollar's worth of new economic activity for the place.

The ratio between the economy's total new income and the initial new income is called a *multiplier*. As explained in Box 8.1, this ratio is related to the tendency of people in an area to spend rather than save, a factor that presents a dilemma for a growth-oriented, self-contained economy. It wants to increase its total income, which is done by increasing the value of the new income multiplied by the multiplier. The way it gets new income is by increasing savings, which are invested in income-producing activities. But this reduces spending, which reduces the multiplier. Clearly, then, the challenge is to find new income from *outside* the system: new consumers, new technology, new resources, new aid or gifts (and this is the basis of a theory of regional development). In simplest terms, one dollar's worth of basic activity also means some dollars' worth of nonbasic activity, because basic activity means new money; and the new money gets passed around several times before it heads out in exchange for something that is being brought in from outside. Basic activity is the foundation of the economy of a place.

Its effect on an area depends on the multiplier for the area.

BOX 8.1 THE MULTIPLIER

An autonomous change in an economy that increases the level of investment in the economy without reducing local spending usually causes an even larger increase in the total level of economic activity. The simplest way to express this is:

$$\Delta Y = k\ (\Delta I)$$

where

Δ stands for "a small change in . . ."

k is called a "multiplier": a value that indicates how much the initial change is magnified by the way the various parts of the economy are linked.

In this case, we are considering an income multiplier, which relates to how much of the people's incomes is put into the economy instead of being hidden in a box under the bed. The relationship is expressed this way:

$$k = \frac{1}{1 - MPC} = \frac{1}{MPS}$$

where

MPC is the marginal propensity to consume: the likelihood that the next unit of income will be spent rather than saved (note that this is not the same as an *average* propensity to consume)

MPS is the "marginal propensity to save," where MPC + MPS = 1.0

	MPC	*MPS*	*k*
1	0.2	0.8	1.25
2	0.5	0.5	2.0
3	0.8	0.2	5.0

Therefore, the greater proportion of any new income that is spent (on the average) by people in the place, the larger is the increase in total income as a consequence of an increase in new income from external sources.

Clearly, this is a highly oversimplified example. MPC, for instance, is hard to measure, may vary widely between people, and may change through time. And the relation between an income multiplier and a place's overall economy can be very complex. The concept, however, has been a useful one.

Predictably, a larger multiplier means a greater impact. For example, if a new factory that is a completely basic activity will employ 300 people, with an annual payroll of $3 million and the local multiplier is 3.0, then the effect on the total income of the area is the $3 million plus another $6 million in income earned by people employed in nonbasic activities—totaling $9 million. A lot of people share in the consequences (see Box 8.2). This same reasoning works in reverse if a place loses a basic industry.

In this way, the population and income of a community or a larger region are related directly to the size of the community's collection of basic activities. In general, the more basic activities it has, the more total economic activity it will have: jobs and income. Therefore a basic activity, like a manufacturing plant or the Mayo Clinic, is an area builder, while a nonbasic activity, like a coin-operated laundry, is an area supporter. An area grows economically by attracting or generating basic activities. It declines if it loses them.

BOX 8.2 ECONOMIC BASE AND POPULATION GROWTH

The concept of economic base, together with the concept of the multiplier, can be used to estimate the effect of a new basic activity on a place's population. In this case, the focus is on new employment rather than on new income. A much simplified version of the procedure is this:

1. Estimate new nonbasic employment by dividing new nonbasic income by the average income of employed persons in nonbasic activities. For example, $6,000,000 ÷ $10,000 = 600.

2. Add this to the new basic employment to estimate total new employment: 600 + 300 = 900.

3. Divide total population by the number of employed persons. For example, suppose that the answer is 2.0, meaning that on the average one employed person supports one person who is not employed—a child, a spouse, and so on.

4. Multiply total new employment by this number: 900 × 2.0 = 1,800. Under these conditions, a new factory employing 300 people will probably lead to a population increase of 1,800.

Actually, step 1 may be improved by considering the wages in selected nonbasic activities that will receive more of the impact of the new basic employer (see Chapter 10), and it is a good idea to assess the possibility that wage rates will rise because of increased demands for labor. Also, step 3 may overestimate the effect if some of the newly employed persons were already present in the place but unemployed. But the concept is straightforward: new basic activity means not only more nonbasic activity but a still larger number of people supported as a result.

8.3   ELABORATING THE BASIC IDEAS

What could be simpler than the concept of an economic base? Regrettably, as usual, the concept is simpler than the world it describes. There are several important ways in which these complications should make us revise our thinking a little.

8.3.1   Export Theories of Growth

Most of the prominent examples of basic activities (steel plants, crop plantations, mineral extraction, and so on) bring money into their area by *exporting* a product to buyers outside, and one measure of the net advantage of an area is a comparison of its exports and its imports. If exports have a greater value, the area should have a surplus of money to be used internally to support nonbasic activities, to invest in facilities that will attract more basic activity, and to import additional things that businesses and people want. If imports exceed exports, the area faces deficits and, in a sense, is undersupplied with basic activities.

This situation has led some individuals to say that the true basis of a lively, growing economy is an export surplus: regional growth follows—and is a consequence of—a net growth in exports. Although this is certainly one factor among many, it is not very satisfactory as the only explanation, as Section 8.3.2 hints and Section 8.3.4 elaborates.

8.3.2   Partly Basic Activities

A difficulty with the distinction between basic and nonbasic ways of making a living is that a lot of activities are partly basic and partly nonbasic. For example, some of the trailers manufactured by a local steel fabricating firm may be sold to people in other states, while some are sold in the vicinity of the plant to local people.

Consequently, in identifying an area's economic base, there is a need to figure out how much of the output of a partly basic activity is basic output. This point has a very logical connection with the size of the area involved. Suppose that we are talking about a large public university. From the point of view of a small university city, most of the output is basic. Some tuition and state taxes are paid by local residents, but most of the money received and spent locally by the university comes from elsewhere. The wages of the professor, secretary, and plumber who live in the city are paid mainly by outside money. But from the point of view of the state as a whole, the university is much less basic. Most of the students and taxpayers come from within the state, so that the impact of the university as a basic activity is likely to be much smaller on the state than on the city.

Generally, then, the larger the area we are considering, the smaller will be the part of the activity that is actually basic (see Box 8.3). But a larger area will have more internal transactions; the new money will usually pass through more hands. Therefore larger and more diverse areas often have larger multipliers. Although a single new basic activity—new both to a small city and a large region—bring more basic income to the city than to the region, each dollar of basic income supports more nonbasic activity in the larger area.

8.3.3 *The Distribution of Benefits within a Place*

As we have noted before, simply increasing the amount of income in an area will not necessarily improve the lives of very many

---

BOX 8.3 LOCATION QUOTIENT

One way to partition an activity into basic and nonbasic categories is to calculate a *location quotient:* a formula that compares a local situation with a national situation. For example, if income is a good indication of consumption of the product of the activity:

$$\frac{\text{Output of Activity } X \text{ in Location } I}{\text{Total National Output of } X} \div \frac{\text{Total Personal Income in Location } I}{\text{Total National Personal Income}} = \text{Location Quotient}$$

If the location quotient is greater than 1, location *I* is probably an exporter of *X*. If it is less than one, *I* is probably an importer of *X*.

Consider a shoe factory. Let's say that region *I* (southern Appalachia or the upper Great Plains) makes 5 percent of the shoes in the United States, as measured by the wholesale price of output. And *I* has 2.5 percent of the personal income in the country. The location quotient would be 2.0: the region's proportion of shoe production is twice its proportion of consumption. Therefore, on the average, about half of the shoes are exported from the region, and only about half of the income and employment of a shoe manufacturing plant should be considered basic.

Note two cautions, though. For some products or services, income is not the best indicator of demand, and something else should be used in its place. And, since the location quotient is a way to estimate *net* exports for the whole region, it may be a poor characterization of a single plant. The particular plant being studied might, for example, be making high-fashion shoes for a single department store chain in another region—and exporting all its product. Or it might be making cowboy boots for local western clothing stores, with no significant exports.

The alternative to using a location quotient is to get detailed information about actual movements of money into and out of the area. This requires a comprehensive survey of transactions, to see what parts of income and expenditures are linked with buyers and sellers who are not local residents.

people. The true impact of an increase in basic activity depends on what happens to the new income. Is it circulated as wages for employees or spent outside the area to buy new machines? How much of it is saved rather than spent? Often, these decisions are made by a very few people, and what is best for them may not be what is best for others in the place.

Some of the dimensions of this are geographic. Consider three examples:

1.   A large new manufacturing plant locates in the central city of a region. The city does not have enough labor available to do all of the jobs, and a consequence is the movement of people from rural communities to the city to take the higher paying new jobs. This affects both the city and the rural areas in a wide variety of ways (see Chapter 13).

2.   The new plant is big and basic, but it is also noisy and produces large amounts of heavy smoke, and black dust settles on everything the smoke passes over. Clearly, some of the region gets income and employment benefits from the plant—higher prices for houses, more business in shopping centers—but is far enough away to be spared the noise and is upwind often enough to miss most of the smoke. Other parts of the area pay heavy costs in cleaning bills and even hearing losses.

3.   Two brothers operate lunch counters in two different parts of the city, one near the new plant and the other all the way across town. The business of one triples; the other changes very little.

The distribution of benefits thus relates not only to a person's position in the economic and social structure of the region. It also depends in many cases on the person's physical location with respect to the new activity.

8.3.4   *A Flaw in the Theory*

We have said that the economic growth of an area is the result of increases in basic activity, which bring in money from outside the area. But we know that the world economy grows, even though all the economic transactions at that scale are internal, nonbasic. There must, then, be some other ways that a community or region or country can grow by pulling itself up by its own bootstraps, by serving its own consumers.

One explanation of the fact that nonbasic (local-oriented) production often contributes to growth is that the local production can help to reduce imports, thus improving a new export balance; but this does not explain the case of the world as a whole. In fact, growing regions usually show increases in imports, not decreases. Historically, seafaring European countries boomed by stressing imports of raw materials from Asia, Africa, and South and Central America, implying perhaps that an area with a big import surplus might be the one to grow fastest.

It is not easy to reconcile all the things we observe in our world, and this case of contradictory evidence is one of the biggest challenges in economic geography and related fields. Our theories emphasize exports as a basis for economic growth, but our observations note that imports play a prominent role.

Although we are not yet ready to deal with all of the factors that affect regional income,* let's briefly consider two ideas as alternatives to an export-base theory of regional growth. One is to emphasize the role of supply rather than the role of demand. We have been assuming that the driving force is demands by consumers. Whatever is demanded will be supplied; the key factor is the balance between demands for exports versus imports. An alternative is to assume that whatever is produced (regardless of how much) will be sold, and that the wealth of an area depends simply on how much it is able to produce. The key factors here are the capacity of the area to produce and its ability to get the inputs it needs for production. If I want to manufacture cars that I know I can sell, I need to find steel, glass, plastic, and other materials to make the cars. Exporting cars may well require importing steel.

It is fairly obvious that both demand and supply are important. A lack of either can limit a city's or region's level of economic activity. An economy based on rubber plantations is hurt by the development of synthetic rubber for tires because demand is reduced. An economy based on power consumption is hurt by a shortage of energy (for example, a shortage of gas fuels), a supply constraint. Both demand and supply are needed to maintain a high level of economic activity.

A second alternative is to say that the places that have grown the most in the past will continue to grow the most in the future. Just as in the biblical parable, them that have are usually them that get. Agglomeration economies and scale economies mean that the rich places will often get richer, regardless whether they are exporters or importers. This possibility will be explored a little more in Section 10.3.2 and in Chapter 16.[†]

---

*   See Chapters 10 and 16.

[†]   Chapters 13 and 16–18 will also consider the possibility that what happens to a place depends more on what other people do than on what its own people do.

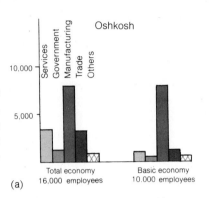

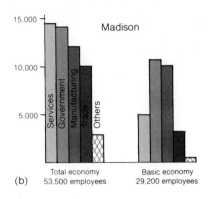

FIGURE 8.1
Basic Employment in Two Wisconsin Cities: (a) Oshkosh; and (b) Madison. Note that government is the largest sector of basic employment in the state capital, while it is relative unimportant in Oshkosh.

8.3.5 *Agglomeration Economies and New Basic Activities*

One further comment. A multiplier and a location quotient may allow us to anticipate the effect of a new basic activity on the economy of a place. But there is often an additional long-term contribution to regional growth as well, because the new activity may help to attract still others. Because a steel plant arrives, metal fabricating plants may follow. Because a new road is built to serve the steel plant, someone may locate a new warehouse on land that was previously inaccessible. Such repercussions may continue for some time, each effect causing further effects.

8.4 *EXAMPLES*

Perhaps the best way to illustrate the importance of basic economic activities is to see if any cities or regions are getting along without them. Can we imagine a city with no manufacturing activity, wholesale trade, or service activities that serve a larger area? For instance, in an atlas compare the geographic distribution of population in the United States with the pattern of manufacturing; the similarity is obvious.

Actually, however, one city or region may differ a great deal from another in the specific nature of its basic activities. Figure 8.1, for example, shows how government is a basic activity for a state capital (in this case Madison, Wisconsin), with an effect on the local economy very much like that of overalls and other products of manufacturing for Oshkosh.

Consequently, the interesting question is not what kinds of activities are basic, because the answer is usually either trite or highly localized. It is this: how much of a particular category of basic activity *must* a city or region have in order to sustain a par-

FIGURE 8.2
Minimum Proportions of the Labor Force Employed in 14 Sectors of the Economy, as They Relate to City Size. The sum of the minima for each size class can be interpreted as the bare minimum nonbasic employment needed to support a city of that size. Note that the vertical axis is measured on a logarithmic scale, which makes it possible to show the relationships as straight lines.

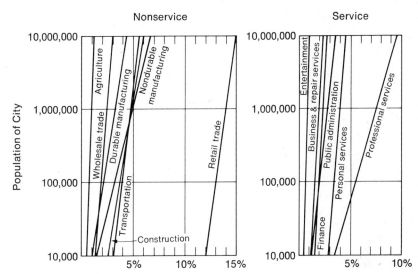

ticular level of overall economic activity? What is the minimum nonbasic employment in each sector? The sum of these minima should represent the barebones nonbasic requirements of the area, and the difference between actual employment and nonbasic needs should be an approximation of basic employment (or perhaps basic employment plus "redundant" nonbasic employment).

Careful studies of employment by economic sector in cities have shown that nonbasic needs increase with the size of the city (see Figure 8.2; also see the final paragraph in Section 8.3.2). There is further evidence that nonbasic needs also vary between regions in a country. But detailed investigations of basic and nonbasic employment have generally been directed toward informing decision makers rather than toward building theory. There are probably two reasons for this: (1) it is so hard to partition employment figures or other measures of economic activity into basic and nonbasic parts; and (2) the concept of an economic base is most useful as a simple one: it appears to gain very little from sophisticated analysis.

One of the kinds of information that are often called for is an estimate of the future levels of population and incomes in an area. For instance, if the United States increases its purchases of energy from western states by buying coal, oil shale, and uranium ore, how much will the populations and incomes of these states grow? Part of the answer lies in the size of the new mines and other production facilities: how many people they employ and what wages they pay. But another part has to do with the multiplier effect of this

TABLE 8.1

Secondary/Basic Employment Multipliers and Population/Employee Multiplier for Operation Employment

Year	Ratio of New Secondary Employment to New Basic Employment[a]	Ratio of New Population to New Employment
1980	0.4	3
1985	0.8	3
1990	0.8	3
2000	1.0	3

SOURCE: White, Irvin L., and others. *Energy from the West.* Washington: U.S. Environmental Protection Agency, July 1977.

[a] The multipliers increase over time as the regional economy becomes more diverse and internally self-stimulating: Crawford, A. G., Fullerton, H. H., and Lewis, W. C. *Socio-Economic Impact Study at Oil Shale Development in the Uintah Basin, for White River Shale Project.* Providence, Utah: Western Environmental Associates, 1975, pp. 147–158.

TABLE 8.2

Overall (Construction Plus Operation) Expected Population Increases After 1975 Due to Energy Development in Eight-State Region

	Assumed Level of Energy Development		
Year	Nominal Case (Most Likely)	Low Demand Case (Less Development)	Low Nuclear Availability Case (Special Case)
1980	95,500	60,900	86,800
1985	218,300	147,900	235,900
1990	280,900	192,900	289,200
2000	1,247,600	768,300	1,133,100

SOURCE: (Same as Table 8.1.)

NOTE: The 1975 estimated population for the eight states was 9,551,000 according to the U.S. Department of Commerce, Bureau of the Census, "Estimates of the Population of States, By Age: July 1, 1974 and 1975 Advanced Report." *Current Population Reports,* Series P-25, No. 619, January 1976.

increase on basic activity. Table 8.1 lists some multipliers used in an attempt to answer the question (for eight western states), and Table 8.2 shows the resulting population projections. It is important to remember that such future population estimates are heavily influenced by the multipliers that are used. Similarly, the research team was able to arrive at estimates of the addition to incomes on the western states as a result of new energy development (Table 8.3).

8.5 A RECONSIDERATION

If the foundation of an area's economy is basic activity, together with the inputs to support it, the central question for growth is how

TABLE 8.3
Changes in Annual Personal Income, Six Western States, Nominal Case Energy Development

Additions to Aggregate Income Above 1975 Levels, in Millions of 1975 Dollars

State	1980	1985	1990	2000
Colorado	16	383	478	3,414
New Mexico	318	217	215	572
Utah	86	88	124	482
Montana	164	497	618	2,374
North Dakota	119	258	379	2,165
Wyoming	185	286	321	1,632
Six-state total	**888**	**1,729**	**2,135**	**10,639**

Effect of Energy Development on Statewide Per Capita Incomes, in Constant 1975 Dollars

State	1974	1980	1985	1990	2000
Colorado	5,970	5,970	6,020	6,020	6,380
New Mexico	4,620	4,770	4,690	4,690	4,830
Utah	4,970	5,010	5,000	5,010	5,140
Montana	5,330	5,410	5,520	5,540	6,100
North Dakota	6,200	6,260	6,290	6,330	6,900
Wyoming	5,760	5,890	5,920	5,890	6,570
Six-state total	**5,475**	**5,550**	**5,575**	**5,580**	**5,986**

SOURCE: (Same as Table 8.1.)
NOTE: The estimated error range is ±20 percent.

to get that basic activity. We know that the challenge is to convince a decision maker that the area offers economic advantages. Until we get to Chapter 12 we can consider these advantages to be essentially of two types:

1. **Economies of agglomeration.** The area's economy is big enough and vigorous enough so that a new activity can find markets, inputs, and other desirable things there.

2. **Economies of environment.** The area is distinctive in some respect—the presence of plentiful cheap raw materials or labor, for example—that is attractive for a particular activity.

In historical terms, these two kinds of advantages are related: environmental advantages help to create economies of agglomeration, and the scale of an economy helps to sharpen the people's focus on the potentials of their environments. To consider this matter of environmental advantages, we go on to the next Chapter.

MAJOR CONCEPTS AND TERMS

For definitions, see the Glossary.

Basic activities	Export theory of	Multiplier
Economic base	growth	Nonbasic activities
Employment sector	Location quotient	
minimum		

CHAPTER 9

ENVIRONMENTS AND LOCATIONAL DISTINCTIVENESS

*T*he economy of a place affects—and is affected by—many other things about that place: its physical resources and surroundings, its society, its political system, and its level of technology. Since these environments of the local economy are a key to the locational advantages it has, both in the total amount of advantages and in their specific types, and since the environments also influence what is done with the advantages, they have a great deal to do with the well-being of the people who live there.

Environment is a term that once was used to mean physical surroundings: mineral resources, land surface, climate, plants and animals. But to us as economic decision makers, our surroundings are much more diverse than this, and the environmental factors that are most important may vary according to our objectives.

9.1 SITUATIONS

9.1.1 The Job-Seeking Engineer

In a few months you will graduate from a leading engineering school as one of their top electrical engineers, and you would like to find a good job in the research and development division of a major corporation. Because of your record, you have been able to get a lot of job offers, but you have narrowed the choice down to two attractive possibilities.

One of the R & D facilities is near Portland, Oregon; the other is in a large, industrial eastern city. The eastern job would pay a higher salary, but your responsibilities would be about the same in either position. You have visited both places, and you liked the people equally well.

As you see it, if both positions paid the same salary, the Oregon job would be the choice, because the area is so attractive to you; you like the scenery and the recreation opportunities. But how much is that scenery worth: $2,000 a year, $5,000? How much money are you willing to forego in order to live in Oregon?

In the end, you decide to take the Oregon job, even though it will pay you less.

9.1.2 The New Professor

Again, you are an academic superstar, this time with a Ph.D. in economics and an interest in teaching at the university level. And again, you have a half dozen good job offers, all in the same general salary range and all from public institutions. The jobs are in six different states.

In comparing the options, you find yourself asking some questions about what a salary level means in one state versus another. Income taxes, sales taxes, and property taxes are lower in Oklahoma than in New York, which means that more of your pay would be yours to spend; but New York provides much more in the way of state-supported services. Taxes are higher in Illinois than in New Hampshire; but the higher education system gets more financial support from the state government and citizens in Illinois, which means that your salary might rise faster there. Although the trade-offs between states are hard to weigh, it is clear that the social and economic policies of the state governments will affect your economic well-being.

Your final decision, by the way, is to go the state with the strongest demonstrated commitment to support higher education over the years, even though taxes are higher there than in several of the other states. You figure that this will be the most important factor in determining your economic status five or ten years from now.

9.1.3 The Marketing Director

As marketing director for a company selling a patented new kind of swimming pool nationwide, part of your job is to screen the graduates of your sales training program and assign them territories. In his or her area, the salesperson is expected to develop a system of local representatives, each of whom will arrange for newspaper and other advertising, respond to inquiries, and show prospective customers a sample pool. The key to an effective sales effort in a territory, you have found, is the ability of your salesperson to communicate with the local representatives: finding interested people, choosing effective ones, training them, and giving them support. Since you get a small percentage of the income from every pool sold, you have a very strong interest in finding the best possible fit between salesperson and sales territory.

The best sales prospect in the current class of trainees is a woman who has been a lifetime resident of the New York City area, and you have in front of you eight folders, each representing an important territory. First, you eliminate the territories in which a New York accent and manner would be a disadvantage; after ten years in the marketing business, you have made enough mistakes to know which these are. From the remaining folders, after some thought, you pick the one with the best market potential: it has a climate that allows outdoor swimming six to eight months out of each year (the ten-to-twelve-month places are already heavily supplied with swimming pools), and it has a lot of upwardly mobile young families living in homes without pools.

Now, you turn to your file on another trainee, a native of Mississippi and also a strong prospect . . .

9.2 *BASIC IDEAS*

It is clear that a map of places as locations for economic activity overlaps maps of many other kinds. There may be maps of social connections, political jurisdictions, cultural groups, mineral resources, climate, and other characteristics that interact with a local economy. The way economic systems are usually defined, these are not part of the system itself. Nature is used by an economic system as a source of raw materials, and the system returns a lot of garbage to it; but nature is not a *part* of the economy. In the same way, political institutions, culture, and technology are environments for a regional economic system.

We are familiar with many of the ways environments relate to locational advantages:

1. **physical environments.** Kuwait's oil, fish off the coast of Iceland, California's Napa Valley for growing grapes, the flat plains of Kansas for harvesting wheat with big machines, the sun of California's Imperial Valley for vegetables, bananas in Central America, the beaches of Florida

FIGURE 9.1

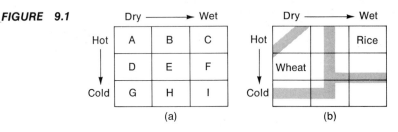

(a)   (b)

2. **social and cultural environments.** Japanese industrial productivity, American socioeconomic mobility, Swiss watchmakers, the media and the arts in New York City

3. **political environments.** Singapore's incentives for industry, corporation tax advantages in the Bahamas, labor productivity in Yugoslavia, import restrictions in New Zealand, environmental standards in Oregon

4. **technology environments.** American computers, Japanese optics, Indian handicrafts, the reflection of low technology levels in low wage rates

Some of the effects of environmental differences have already been introduced: distortions of von Thünen rings, irregular patterns of isotims, and disruptions of an idealized pattern of hexagons. We know that "noneconomic" things are not equal from place to place, however convenient the assumption may be for economic theory building. The land surface is rougher here than there—or the history different, the political system divergent, or the people looking for different things from life.

More generally, the question is how to evaluate the economic importance to people and places of all this. Consider the simple physical environmental situation shown in Figure 9.1(a). Suppose that the decision is whether to grow wheat or rice. At any particular level of technology, we can identify the effect of environmental variation on each option (see Table 9.1). Some conditions will be impossible, some ideal, and most somewhere in between (see Figure 9.2).

Evaluating the relative advantages of the nine regions in Figure 9.1(a), we can anticipate that the decisions will be resolved so that a pattern like that in Figure 9.1(b) is the result. In the same way, we could assess the environmental advantages of the regions for a metal fabricating industry or for homebuilding (see Table 9.2); or we could define environmental variation in a totally different way (for instance, think about a figure such as 9.1, where one dimension is the political economy—laissez faire versus centrally

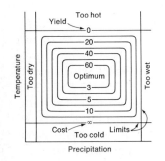

FIGURE 9.2

A Diagram Illustrating that for Any Crop There Is an Optimal Combination of Moisture and Temperature. Conditions that are less than optimal result in lower yields; beyond certain limits, yields become zero.

TABLE 9.1
Environmental Variation
and the Costs of Crop
Alternatives

Climate	Crop	
	Wheat	*Rice*
Too dry	No crop without irrigation	No crop without irri-irrigation, takes more irrigation than wheat
Too wet	Poor-quality harvest; crop diseases, competition from other species	Drainage control and cultivation more difficult
Too hot	Crop will burn up	Cultivation more difficult
Too cold	Crop will not grow	Crop will not grow, threshold temperature higher than for wheat
Locational preference, no irrigation	E	F or C
Locational preference, with irrigation	D	E or B

TABLE 9.2
Environmental Variation
and the Costs of Nonagri-
cultural Activities

Climate	Industry	
	Metal Fabricating	*Homebuilding*
Too dry	Depends on the metal; cooling water scarcer	Landscaping, waste disposal more difficult; domestic water scarcer
Too wet	Storage of parts and products may be more difficult	Materials deteriorate faster
Too hot	Metal difficult to handle; work more difficult without air-conditioning	Air-conditioning needed
Too cold	Metal difficult to handle; work more difficult without heating	Heating and insulation needed

directed—and the other dimension is a characteristic of the social system—such as highly mobile versus highly stratified.

For dealing with environmental variation, the most basic concept is that of *regionalizing*: identifying areas within which there is relatively little variation. Such an area may be defined by a single feature, such as coal mining, or by many features, such as a particular combination of agricultural activities. Regardless of whether it is large or small, if it is approximately the same in some respect, it is what professional geographers mean when they use the term *region* (see Box 9.1).

Sameness (or homogeneity) can refer to either of two kinds of cases. One is a situation in which a characteristic is pretty much the same throughout the area: flat terrain, or the political jurisdiction of Costa Rica, or the raising of wheat as the main land use, or most of the people professing the religion of Islam. This can be called a *uniform region*. It is defined by a comparison with other areas—looking for where the sameness ends. The other case involves a situation in which places in an area share a common structural relationship of some sort: the area drained by the Arkansas River or served by the Oklahoma City *Daily Oklahoman*. This is called a *nodal region* when the structure is focused on a node; otherwise, it is called a *functional region*. It is defined by connections within the area.

There is nothing more intrinsically geographic than making sense of a kaleidoscopic world by subdividing a large space into smaller areas so that most of the variation occurs across boundaries rather than within them. Some people have gone so far as to say:

BOX 9.1   THE MEANING OF "REGION"

Region is a confusing term because different people use it to mean different things. The most common definitions are these:

1. an area larger than a city but smaller than a large country, such as the Great Plains

2. a grouping of countries from the same part of the world having common interests, such as the Benelux countries or the Central American countries (for example, "regional cooperation")

3. an area of any size that is approximately the same in some respect, as described in Section 9.2

In this book, we are essentially combining #1 and #3, so that region means an area of an intermediate size that is approximately the same in some respect; #2 is a special case of this.

There are other related terms as well. *Regionalism* refers to a feeling of distinctiveness shared by people who live in a particular area. *Regionalization* is a task of drawing boundaries between regions.

The face of the earth can be marked off into areas of distinctive character; and the complex patterns and associations of phenomena in particular places possess a legible meaning as an ensemble, which, added to the meanings derived from a study of all the parts and processes separately, provides additional perspective and additional depth of understanding.

P. E. JAMES[1]

This view led people to try to define regions of the world or of the United States—taking everything into account.

The problem is that the regions most useful to a manufacturer may not be the same as the ones that would interest a farmer or an advertiser. Most often, therefore, regions are areas that people have identified for a specific purpose, taking into account the kinds of variation most important for that purpose.

Defining a group of regions is not a simple matter. It requires information about a great many places, and it requires some rules for deciding how similar is "similar" and how different is "different" (see Box 9.2).

BOX 9.2   REGIONALIZING

This is a map of sixteen small areas, with a number in each telling something about it:

35	26	18	12
31	24	15	11
24	19	18	13
14	16	23	10

How would you divide it into regions, so that each region has roughly similar numbers within it?

The fact is that regionalizing is not easy. Think of the judgments that must be made: how many regions to define (anywhere from 2–15 are possible), whether or not to draw regional boundaries that divide individual areas on the map, how to handle anomalies (23), how to resolve gradual transitions.

And this example involves just one kind of variation. What if there were 6 kinds—or 30? First of all, regionalizing requires a set of decisions about how to handle the judgment cases. And then, for most cases, it requires the use of specialized analytic techniques that have been developed to handle complex classification problems.

9.3 ELABORATING THE BASIC IDEAS

Defining environmental regions does not answer questions about the effects of environmental variation on economic activity. It simply makes it easier to make general judgments about advantages and disadvantages. For a deeper understanding of a connection, it is necessary to inquire into the particular kind of environment that is involved. This is a hazardous process, however, because few things are as simple as they seem. In this section, we will consider the economic meaning of environmental differences a little further, note a classification of resources that is especially timely in today's world, and briefly introduce some applications of the regional concept in economic planning.

9.3.1 Environmental Influences

Environmental Determinism   We know that a certain kind of mixed farming is characteristic of parts of western Europe and North America that have similar climates—a high-value blend of grain cultivation, livestock raising, and vegetable growing. The land use is not rice paddies or banana plantations or reindeer herding. Does this mean that the mixed farming has happened *because* of the physical environment? Obviously not, since the land uses were in fact very different in the year 1600. Other factors are involved.

On the other hand, a more crowded world is one that may be more dependent on certain kinds of resources, such as water and energy sources, and some places are better endowed than others at any particular time. We can see some correspondence between a map of world population densities and some maps of physical environmental variation. For example, areas with sparse rainfall (say, an average of less than 20 inches of rain per year) are seldom the same as those with dense population, and population density seems to show some relationship with soil characteristics. Clearly, we are aware that oil-rich countries have distinct economic advantages these days. Physical environments do affect the patterns of scarcity of things that we value, although they do not determine them.

What makes things complicated is that there are usually several ways to take care of the same need. We can make automobile tires from Indonesian rubber or from synthetic rubber derived mainly from crude oil. We can assure ourselves an acceptable ambient air temperature by living in a comfortable climate or by creating one artificially inside an enclosure. We can find water where we are or transport it to us. Consequently, the locational advantage of a place because of its environmental endowments depends on the kinds of things we considered in Section 4.3.2: the availability of substitutes, for example (also see Section 10.3.1). A well-known case of this is Chile, the world's best source of natural sodium nitrate. Nitrates are in demand for fertilizers and explosives. For more than half a century, Chile exported huge quantities of this resource; in fact, it reached the point where nitrate exports provided two-thirds of the revenues of the country's government. Then someone found another way to produce nitrates. Chile still had a lot of sodium nitrate, but it no longer had such an advantage because of it.

As the technology explosion of the twentieth century has progressed, our physical environments have become more and more a product of human creation and modification, so that maps of the land surface, drainage systems for water, the temperatures at which people live and work, and perhaps even the climate are a reflection of culture and technology as well as of nature. This fact illustrates how each of our environments, itself very complex, is intricately tied not only to a regional economy, but to other environments. It is probably fruitless to try to generalize for all times and places about how environments "cause" locational advantage. But for any single time and place, the environments of a local economy are an important element of the costs and benefits of doing business there.

The Carrying Capacity Concept   In talking about human life and development, ecologists have been interested in the fact that animal populations seem to regulate their size according to the characteristics of their environment: the size of the area, the materials available, and other factors. A population grows until it reaches some density, at which it usually stabilizes (although there are some cases in which the population drops sharply instead of becoming constant in size).

A familiar example is a cattle ranch. A rancher knows that some pastures will fatten 10 cattle per hectare. In other pastures, that many cattle will result in skinny animals and perhaps even in the appearance of bare spots without grass. The ranch is in fact a mosaic of 1-animal-per-hectare pastures, 5-animal pastures—and 10, 20, and 50. A sound ranching operation depends on a careful evaluation of the *carrying capacity* of pastureland available.

Some people believe that it is desirable to define the carrying capacities of land areas for people (see Box 9.3). Maps of "overpopulation" and "underpopulation" could then be developed, and a population redistribution program could be organized. For example, in the early 1960s a Belgian geographer proposed that Black Africa could support ten times as many people without a change in agricultural technology. Estimation of land potential is an attractive idea; note the resource endowment distinction in Figure 9.3. But there are serious problems involved in trying to put it to work, because it is so difficult to separate potentials from preconceived attitudes (see Box 9.4) and because the carrying capacity of an area with a specified physical resource endowment depends on so many other things:

BOX 9.3 POTENTIAL PRODUCTIVITY

A concept related to carrying capacity but applied at a more detailed scale is *potential productivity*. Suppose that an issue in a developing country is that urban dwellers are paying most of the taxes to support the country's economic development programs, but most of the people are rural dwellers—and even a larger proportion of the land area is nonurban. Is there a way to get rural people and areas to bear more of the fiscal burden of the development effort?

Perhaps there is, if some of the rural land is underutilized—if it is being used in a way that is less productive than is possible, given available technology and resources. To give a rather dramatic example, potentially excellent farmland may be serving as a private hunting preserve. An approach to remedying this is to set up a system of land taxes based on what parcels of land *can* produce, rather than on what they are now producing. A landowner can still choose to use the land in other ways than the most productive ones, but he or she pays the same taxes as if the land were used more productively. In theory, this gives landowners powerful incentives to use the land in the way that contributes most to economic growth, and it avoids some of the penalties to the country as a whole from land use decisions based on other criteria.

The main criticism of this idea has been that it is impossible to carry out. Most people agree that it would be very helpful to be able to compare a pattern of actual land use with potential land use, but they argue that the survey requirements are time-consuming and expensive, the valuations of potential are hard to make, and the process is susceptible to corruption and political pressure. With modern data system technology, however, the possibilities are improving. Aerial surveys, together with computerized data storage and analysis, can be converted into broad classifications of potential agricultural productivity, if the value of crops per hectare can be associated for a given level of technology with measures of physical characteristics (such as the capacity of the soil to retain water). And these classifications can be further refined by incorporating measures of accessibility and the market capacities for particular crops.

1.   **Technology makes a difference.** A society with advanced technology can exist more densely than a society with primitive technology. There is, for example, a clear positive relationship between agricultural intensity and population densities in rural areas.

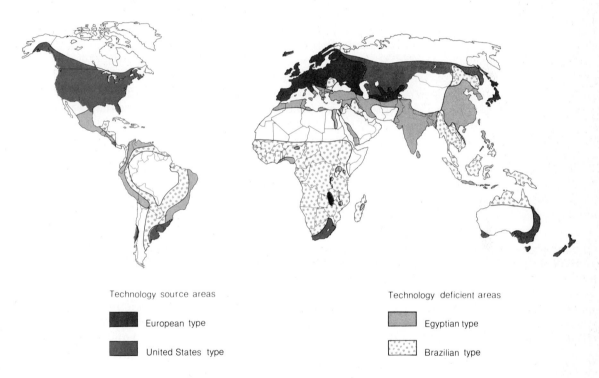

Technology source areas

■ European type

■ United States type

Technology deficient areas

▨ Egyptian type

⬚ Brazilian type

FIGURE 9.3

Technology/Resource Regions of the World (as of 1966). Resource endowment per person is interpreted as a measure of population pressure on available resources. Technology source areas are those which export technology; technology deficient areas are importers. Four types of regions are indicated: (1) technology exporters with limited resources (such as much of Europe); (2) technology exporters with relatively abundant resources (such as the United States); (3) technology importers with limited resources (such as Egypt or India); and (4) technology importers with relatively abundant resources (such as Brazil). Today, many people would reconsider the classification of such areas as Iran, Saudi Arabia—and perhaps the United States.

2. **Culture makes a difference.** What kind of population density represents "overcrowding" to the point that human beings feel stress? The answer for a wheat farmer in Saskatchewan is so different from the response of a lifetime resident of New York City that it is dangerous to generalize.

3. **Land use makes a difference.** Some kinds of people-supporting activities, such as legal practice and medical care, require a lot less space than others, such as farming or most types of mining. The carrying capacity of a location depends on the activities that are concentrated there—and also on the activities to which the location is accessible.

4. **Exploration makes a difference.** The carrying capacity concept assumes that the characteristics of an area are known and constant. For example, a map of world resources shows a particular pattern of minerals, arable land, and other desirable things; and this map would be a basis for arriving at a pattern of acceptable population densities. But a resource map prepared in 1940 would show no petroleum resources in Nigeria or Indonesia, and uranium would probably not appear at all. In fact, resource endowments are largely a matter of what people look for and how hard they look. An oil-rich country such as Saudi Arabia is well advised to use a lot of the revenues from

---

BOX 9.4   PHYSICAL ENVIRONMENTS AND OVERCROWDING

A natural resource is a physical material *that people know how to use.* As recently as the nineteenth century in the United States, an individual looking at crude oil saw an unpleasant, heavy liquid of little or no apparent use, and not very many sources were known. At that time, a place with a lot of petroleum would not have been able to support any more people than a place with no petroleum. Clearly, this is no longer true (although we can ask what will happen to a densely populated area, where many livelihoods are based on petroleum, when the oil gets used up).

Suppose that you were asked to compare the capability of a tropical rain forest to support population for an indefinitely long time with the situation of a hilly area in the middle latitudes. What would you say? If your mental pictures are of the Appalachian states in the United States and the forests of Southeast Asia, you might say that the rain forest can support a higher density. But if your thoughts are of China and northern Brazil, your impression would be just the opposite.

This illustrates both the role of culture in environmental effects and the limitations of simple questions about these effects.

a depletable resource—oil—to identify other resources, such as the potential for solar energy production and deposits of valuable minerals. A resource endowment also reflects the further fact that what is regarded as a resource is a changeable thing. Substitutes may be developed for rubber, glass, coal, or cotton. A material such as uranium, once without much value, may become important. And all these developments affect a measure of carrying capacity. Remember, by the way, that exploration makes a difference in defining human resources as well as physical resources.

9.3.2 *The Renewability of Resources*

A key distinction in thinking about physical resources is between those that are renewable and those that are nonrenewable. *Renewable resources* are replenished just about as quickly as they are used (although the rate of renewal may vary from time to time). Examples include direct solar energy and cultivated plants. *Nonrenewable resources* are replenished so slowly that, from the perspective of a few human generations, what we have now is all we will ever have. Examples include coal, oil, iron ore, and gold.

Some resources that are renewable in theory are depletable in practice. For instance, water can be withdrawn from underground aquifers by wells so fast that, eventually, water is exhausted in the zone close enough to the surface to be affordable. (It is expensive to pump water from very deep wells, and a farmer who needs irrigation water can only pay a limited amount for it; otherwise, the farm loses money). In this sense, water can be mined like coal; the aquifers may recharge themselves with time—but much more slowly than the water is being used. As another example, the nutrients in soil needed for a commercial crop are used up in a very few years of cultivation unless specific, deliberate action is taken to replace them. Agricultural production without declining yields requires either using fertilizers, selecting crop mixes that return nutrients to the soil, or allowing a particular plot a number of years to recover after it is cultivated.

This adds a further dimension to locational advantages that result from local physical resources, such as mineral ores or rich soils. Not only may the advantage be affected by substitution and other market forces elsewhere, but it may be limited in terms of the region itself. In some cases, the resource is essentially finite in amount; the main question is how fast to use it up. In others, the resource is renewable only if it is used at a judicious rate, recognizing the realities of the replacement process.

Whether or not such distinctions have some meaning for other environments than physical ones has been investigated very little as a question for economic geography.

9.3.3 *Applications of the Regional Concept in Economic Planning* *

The technical concept of the region and the task of regionalizing are widely used in economic planning. Generally, there are two related sorts of applications: (1) identifying patterns in economic activities because they are useful information; and (2) identifying bounded areas where the conditions for economic activity are important enough and similar enough to deserve special treatment.

9.3.3.1 *Economic Regions*

There are many reasons for identifying areas where economic activities are similar (for example, farming areas or manufacturing areas) or where they are oriented to the same central location. This is an effective way to communicate information, to gain insight, to organize marketing campaigns, and even to prepare to gather information (see Chapter 3 if you need a reminder of this). Consider Figure 9.4, for instance, which shows an example: the corn belt agricultural region of the United States—an area that is distinguished by a particular combination of agricultural and industrial activities.

For a country like the United States, one of the conclusions that a person usually reaches is that such economic regions have very little to do with internal political boundaries such as state lines or city limits. The New York City nodal region, by almost any criterion, spills out of New York state into New Jersey and Connecticut. The economies of Chicago and Cincinnati show the same disrespect for state boundaries, and Washington, D.C. moves indistinguishably from the district to state territory. Except for relatively rare cases in which political environments intervene, corn or wheat or coal mining or the manufacture of clothing shows a regional pattern that relates very little to political jurisdictions.

Such regions are usually answers to specific questions by decision makers: where is cotton being grown? Where are large groups of people who can do highly skilled labor in a plant manufacturing electronics equipment? Where are the unemployed people who want to work?

But there are also times when there is a need to study regional economies as integrated wholes, in which various kinds of activity are linked together in significant ways (the next chapter will get

---

* Also see Chapter 16.

FIGURE 9.4
An Economic Region: (a) the Corn Belt agricultural region of the United States, where the production of corn, hogs, and other compatible agricultural goods is concentrated; and (b) the location of the food-processing industry of the United States. Note how the Corn Belt region is reflected in the pattern of this kind of industrial activity as well as patterns of crops and livestock. Note also how it relates to the population distribution in Figure 2.1.

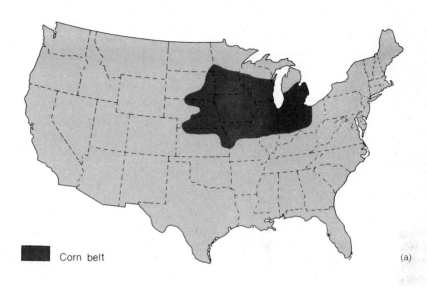

Corn belt

(a)

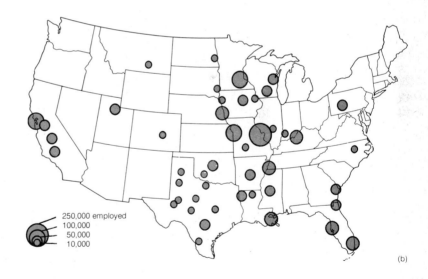

250,000 employed
100,000
50,000
10,000

(b)

into this). This need—which relates to data gathering, the application of research tools, and the search for an understanding of relationships—often leads to the division of a country, state, or province into economic areas that serve a multitude of purposes. It is sometimes hard to keep in mind that boundaries that began as expedients need to be continually reexamined. For instance, who

FIGURE 9.5
An Example of Reconciling Uniform and Nodal Regions in a Single Set of Planning Regions: (a) uniform regions of New York state; (b) nodal regions; and [continued on next page]

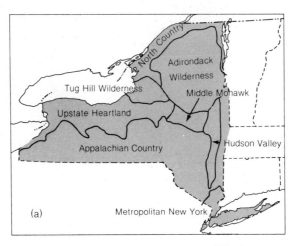

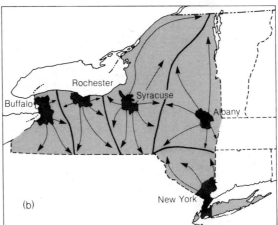

ever heard of a region that lacked one side—was open-ended? Try dividing a state into economic areas. Some of the boundaries will be easy to spot. Others will be impossible to determine with any confidence. But once the boundary lines are on the map, the lines all look the same. Will somebody else who uses your map be able to tell which lines you are uncertain about?

9.3.3.2   ***Planning Regions***   There are many times when it is useful to divide a large area into smaller parts so that the special problems of similar localities can be handled more efficiently. For example, the New York City area differs from the Adirondack Mountain area in

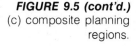

FIGURE 9.5 (cont'd.)
(c) composite planning
regions.

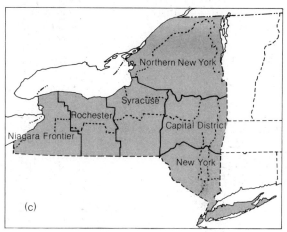

northern New York State in population density, economic activities, cultural diversity, and many other ways. Both areas have
economic problems that call for coordination among local decision
makers, and both are part of a continuing effort to plan for a better
future. But a plan for New York City will have little in common
with a plan for the Adirondacks, and the planning process may be
simplified by developing a separate plan for each.

Both uniform regions and nodal regions play a role in this.
Figure 9.5 is an example of an attempt to take both into account,
with the suggested composite planning regions oriented to nodes
because they will be administered from headquarters in the nodal
cities. But subdivisions of regions having similar concerns, such as
the southern tier of the Rochester and Syracuse regions (which can
be considered part of the same uniform region), might occasionally
meet as an entity to coordinate their actions and reinforce their
common concerns.

There are many cases of planning regions based on functional
regions, and many based on uniform regions. The Tennessee Valley
Authority and other efforts to develop riverine water resources in
a coordinated manner had to start by defining the area involved: the
area contributing surface water runoff to the river system (and
thus involved in watershed management). The result is a functional
planning region. Or a group of states or counties with the same
problems may join together to plan what to do. For instance, the
Federation of Rocky Mountain States, a nonprofit private firm directed by the governors of five American states, helps the states

coordinate and strengthen their planning as it relates to common concerns (such as natural resources, transportation, and economic growth). In some respects, the five states constitute a uniform planning region.

Chapters 14, 15, and 16 will discuss planning regions in more detail as instruments of governments. But private individuals and firms use them as well. A sales territory is one example. If the area is relatively homogeneous, it is easier to train the salesperson. The company has to pay for fewer samples because some of its products are of little interest in that particular territory. Or consider a carefully prepared, generously budgeted advertising campaign, which uses slightly different messages (and accents in the TV commercials?) in different market areas. Or a large firm operating in 33 countries that wants to divide its international division into three to five subdivisions.

9.4 EXAMPLES

Several generations ago there was a great deal of study of the relationships between environments (especially physical factors) and human activity, but this kind of work came to be discredited by its frequent use of extravagant generalizations and inappropriate examples (see Box 9.5). It was followed by a period in which a great deal of time was devoted to mapping regions of various kinds, in many cases without inquiring very deeply about their causes or their significance. But one of the most basic perspectives of geography is identifying a pattern of regional variation in one thing and observing whether or not other things vary in a similar way, and there are many interesting examples of this kind of relationship.

9.4.1 A Potpourri of Environmental Influences

Some kinds of environmental effects are quite obvious. In a developing country like India, for example, the major source of water for farming is rainfall. Most of the rain falls during the summer monsoon, which advances from east to west and then retreats—leaving areas in the west with less water than areas in the east. Figure 9.6(a) shows this pattern, which is a major reason why wheat is the staple food in the west but rice does the job in the east—see Figure 9.6(b). Some other associations are shown in Figures 9.7–9.9.

But these examples should not be taken to indicate that physical environmental factors are always (or even usually) dominant.

Wine making in the United States cannot be related simply to a "Mediterranean" climate: New York State? The main factor was probably that immigrants who had experience with raising grapes and making wine from them settled in these places, and this early cultural environmental advantage helped them to establish a reputation that other areas find hard to match. Or in an atlas look at the map of aircraft manufacturing. It makes sense that this activity would seek clear skies and other conditions that are attractive for test-flying aircraft, and Southern California and Kansas seem to qualify. But Seattle?

Many important economic insights are contained in a pattern like that shown in Figure 9.10: culture regions, technology regions, political regions. As an example of an economic effect of such "noneconomic" regions, a study of the growth of per capita income

BOX 9.5   ENVIRONMENTAL DETERMINISM

Environmental determinism is a concept stating that differences in human activities and characteristics are caused by differences in physical environments. Although it is a little unfair to the authors to take their remarks out of context, it is instructive to see why environmental determinism was discredited. Consider these statements:

> *Among mountain as among desert peoples, robbery tends to become a virtue; environment dictates their ethical code.*
>
> ELLEN CHURCHILL SEMPLE, INFLUENCES OF GEOGRAPHIC ENVIRONMENT

> *The population of rugged regions is scanty, poor, and backward but mountaineers generally have better health and more energy than lowlanders.*
>
> ELLSWORTH HUNTINGTON, F. E. WILLIAMS, S. VANVALKENBERG, ECONOMIC AND SOCIAL GEOGRAPHY

> *In cold or dry areas which cannot be cultivated, . . . highly civilized people are there mainly as intruders. . . . If any*
> *are willing permanently to endure the uncultivated, unattractive conditions which prevail among the sparse and untutored native populations, they generally revert toward the native culture. For example, . . . the southern part of Alaska . . . is the only portion where there seems as yet to be much assurance that a permanent white population will ever take root.*
>
> ELLSWORTH HUNTINGTON, THE HUMAN HABITAT

Critics have had a field day with such statements, and an unfortunate consequence was to scare scholars (especially in geography) away from asking questions about the significance of environmental differences. More recently work has resumed, with two somewhat different emphases: (1) stressing the impact of humanity on our physical environments, rather than the other way around; and (2) interpreting "environment" in a much broader way, for example, speaking of a neighborhood environment.

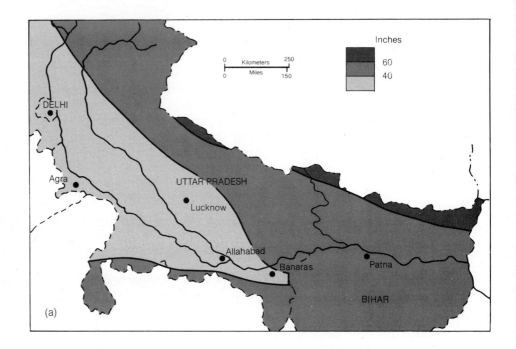

FIGURE 9.6
Rainfall and Crop Choice
in the Central Gangetic
Plain, India: (a) average
rainfall and [continued on
next page]

in some Appalachian counties from 1950 to 1960 showed that the increase was consistently less than a regional expectation for rural, nonmining counties in eastern Kentucky, while it was more than expected for similar counties in southern West Virginia. The reason was probably a difference during that period in the state-level political environment for economic assistance.

9.4.2 *The Impact of Environmental Change*

We are well aware that where environmental characteristics are important conditions for human activities, a change in a characteristic can have a powerful impact. On the semi-arid southern margin of the Sahara in central Africa, for example, a relatively small change in annual rainfall between 1968 and 1975 (coupled with human and animal overpopulation) reduced food production, causing mass starvation in 1973 and 1974 (see Figure 9.11). On the positive side, the introduction of irrigation, the development of a new religion, the coming of the Industrial Revolution—such environmental modifications can make a very real difference.

To get some idea about the magnitude and complexity of impacts, consider an arid seacoast in a developing country: sparsely populated, perhaps with a few small fishing villages along the coast

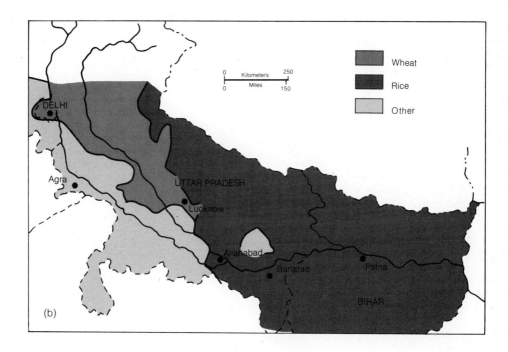

FIGURE 9.6 (cont'd.)
(b) first-ranking crop by district.

and a few nomads and small-scale mining activities in the interior. Suppose that it becomes feasible to locate a "nuplex" somewhere along the coast—a very large nuclear power plant using the abundant energy to desalinize sea water, with the water used to irrigate the desert, and much of the agricultural production then used by an industrial complex also powered by the nuclear plant. Remember that arid seacoasts are common around the world: North and Northwest Africa, around the Persian/Arabian Gulf and the eastern Mediterranean, the south of Pakistan and west of India, the west of Mexico and parts of the west coast of South America, and even some coastal areas in Australia and the United States.

A nuplex would make for a remarkable change in the environmental conditions of an area and would affect its ability to support population and produce useful goods and services. We can imagine some of the repercussions: people—managers, industrial laborers, farmers, providers of urban services—would have to be attracted to an area that has been considered undesirable (where would they come from?), new skills would have to be developed, social and political structure modified and infrastructure provided (roads, housing, sanitation, power, schools, communication—and in what sequence?). Problems would have to be faced: finding mar-

FIGURE 9.7
Cotton Cultivation and Rainfall: (a) cotton acreage in 1879, before drainage in the Mississippi valley and irrigation in Texas (and transportation) changed the pattern; and (b) average annual precipitation in the United States.

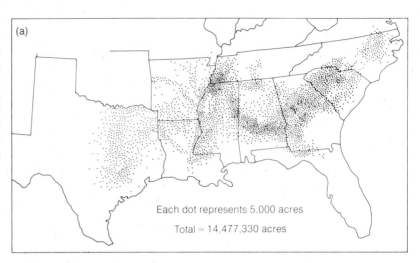

(a)

Each dot represents 5,000 acres

Total = 14,477,330 acres

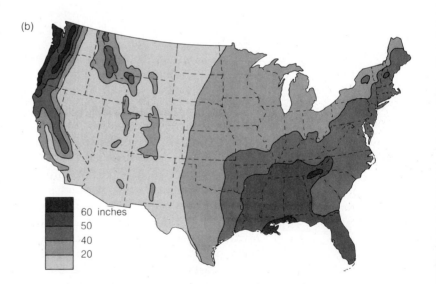

(b)

60 inches
50
40
20

kets for the agricultural and industrial goods, dealing with the soil salinity that often results from irrigating desert land, figuring out where the nuclear technology would come from, locating supplies of fertilizer, dealing with the fact that available farmers may be inexperienced in raising the kinds of crops that the planners think would be best, responding to worries about the safety of the nuclear power plant, anticipating political problems as a previously weak political unit becomes strong and affluent.

Each of these issues suggests a way that environmental variation is important.

FIGURE   9.8
(a) Forest Land and
(b) Wood Processing in
the United States.

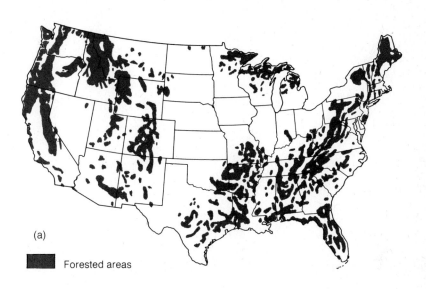

(a)

■ Forested areas

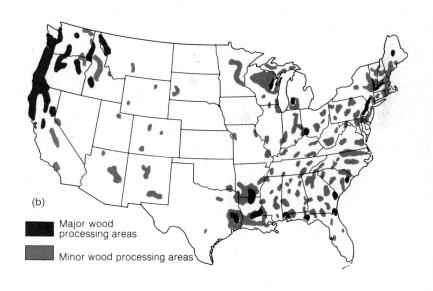

(b)

■ Major wood
processing areas

▨ Minor wood processing areas

9.5   *A RECONSIDERATION*

In considering environmental variation, we are trying to focus on
what makes a place distinctive, because this distinctiveness offers
the place a chance to specialize in economic activities that it can do

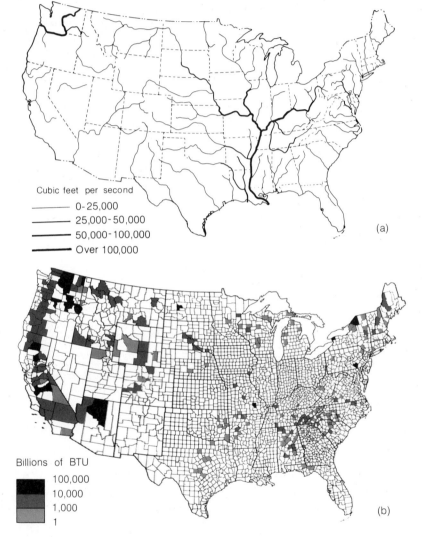

FIGURE   9.9
(a) River Flow and (b) Hydroelectric Power in the United States.

Cubic feet per second
—— 0-25,000
—— 25,000-50,000
—— 50,000-100,000
—— Over 100,000

(a)

Billions of BTU
100,000
10,000
1,000
1

(b)

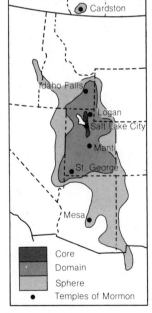

FIGURE   9.10
An Example of a Culture Region: the Mormon Culture Region.

better or more cheaply than other places. It indicates how a place has a cómpetitive advantage in supplying the needs of consumers there and elsewhere—and a place with more advantages usually gets more benefits. The environments of a local or regional economy are thus an important component of its locational advantages.

But environments are changeable things, and their importance for economic activity is always complex and often subtle. For this reason, locational advantage is often affected as much by the perceptiveness of people defining the environmental advantages of a place as it is by the environmental variation itself.

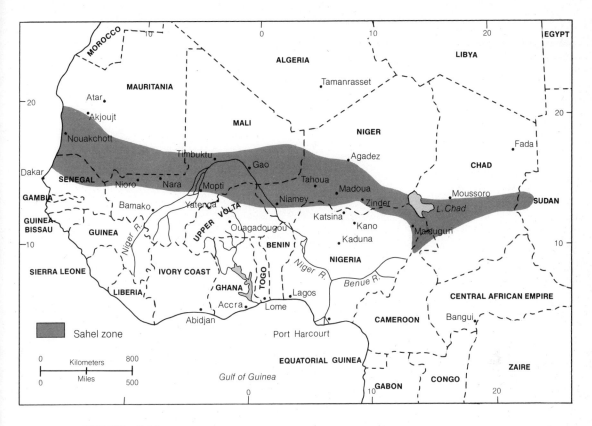

FIGURE 9.11

The "Sahel" Zone in Africa. In a year of normal moisture, the zone is the home of more than 20 million farmers and nomadic herders, living precariously but successfully between the dependably well-watered area to the south and the desert to the north. An extended dry period, however, combined with increasingly intense use of the land, means that the desert marches southward across the zone, and people die.

MAJOR CONCEPTS AND TERMS

For definitions see the Glossary.

Carrying capacity
Environment
Environmental
  advantage
Environmental
  determinism

Functional region
Nodal region
Nonrenewable
  resources
Potential
  productivity

Region
Regionalizing
Renewable resources
Uniform region

Footnote for Chapter 9

1. James, P. E. "Toward a Further Understanding of the Regional Concept." *Annals, Association of American Geographers,* vol. 42 (1952), p. 195.

CHAPTER 10

THE GEOGRAPHY OF LOCATIONAL ADVANTAGE

*C*hapters 8 and 9 told us (1) that an area gets economic advantages from some of the ways its environments are distinctive; and (2) that the foundation of the economy of the area is a basic activity or activities. It is time now to try to connect these two ideas and to see what "economic advantages" mean.

10.1 SITUATIONS

10.1.1 Another Entrepreneur

After fifteen years of hard work, you have saved enough money to start your own business, and you decide that it is time to take the plunge. After a month hiking in the mountains to sort out your thoughts, you believe you have a good idea.

Countless small items are made of plastic, from containers to tiny parts in machines and gadgets. But the cost of plastic items is rising along with the cost of the hydrocarbon feedstocks—oil and gas—for manufacturing plastics, and there is likely to be a shift in many cases to other substances (paper, metal, wood, glass) as the alternatives, once more expensive, become relatively cheaper. You decide to build a small manufacturing plant to produce lightweight but strong ceramic items to do some of the jobs presently being done by plastic items. A six-month product development and marketability study is highly encouraging; you know now what the items will be, where the markets are, what constitutes a competitive price, and the size and design of the plant to make all this possible.

But where to locate it? That's another question. The only way the plant will be economically competitive is if you can find an area that provides a combination of factors: the right kinds of clay, some skilled and experienced labor at reasonable wage rates, and available buildings that can be modified for your use. You decide to look carefully at some places that were once centers for the manufacture of glass and pottery products (before plastics arrived) but have declined more recently.

10.1.2 *The Country Capitalist*

With a lot of knowledge about how agricultural prices are determined (and a lot of luck), you made a killing on the commodity market a few years ago, and since then you have used the money to gain control of a number of companies. You are now heavily involved in arranging and rearranging corporate mergers, and your flagship company has grown impressively in worth and responsibility.

While doing all this, you have continued to live in your old family home on a farm near Ithaca, New York, and the center of your operations has been at Ithaca. Increasingly, though, you find this inconvenient. As your operations have expanded, you have needed more and more lawyers, accountants, bankers, economic analysts, and other specialists to assist you. Although telephone service is fine and other communication services are available as well, many of these people need to be right at hand, because often decisions must be evaluated and made very quickly. And, besides, you like to be able to communicate face-to-face with your advisors. You have built your own office building in Ithaca, but more and more you find yourself spending time and money flying to New York City to look after day-to-day business. There, instead of trying to handle all your needs for services with full-time employees of your own, you can hire large law firms, accounting firms, brokerage firms, and banks to provide those professional services at no extra cost—but with much greater depth and balance (and you can simply change firms if you do not like the results).

Regretfully, you have decided that, as much as you like rural upstate New York, an Ithaca location for your headquarters is a kind of bottleneck for your aspirations. The parent company will have to relocate to New York or some other large city, and the family farm will have to become an occasional place for rest and rejuvenation.

10.2 BASIC IDEAS

Both of these situations suggest that locational advantage might be related not so much to single characteristics of places but to combinations of characteristics: both ceramic clay and skilled labor; assemblages of complementary service activities, together with large office buildings, apartment buildings, and transportation systems to support them; and so on. Combinations of activities remind us of the concept of *agglomeration economies*, introduced in Chapter 6. But here we are extending our interest beyond the overall size of the combination, because it is also important how the activities are linked with each other.

First, we will consider this matter of linkages. Then we will survey some of the ways that environmental characteristics join with these linkages to define locational advantage, and we will note how these advantages shape our maps of economic activity.

10.2.1 Economic Linkages Within a Place

The economy of a place is a little like an organism—composed of different parts that depend on each other for their mutual survival. Adding or subtracting a major part has the effect of changing the other parts as well.

Going beyond a simple distinction between basic and nonbasic activities, let's look more carefully at how economic activities relate to each other. A steel mill, for example, is certainly connected with many parts of an economy: coal and iron ore mines that supply raw materials, automobile manufacturing companies that buy steel, and others. If we know what these linkages are, we ought to be able to estimate the effects on the entire economic "organism" of an increase in the level of steel production. How much more iron ore would be needed? How many additional workers? How much more energy, glass for windows in an extension of the plant building, legal services for the company, vending machines for the new employees, and other goods and services? The more of such linkages that can be provided by a place, the more attractive it will be as a site for the increased production.

A useful way of visualizing these linkages is an *input-output* table. Table 10.1 is a very simple one, which groups all productive economic activities into three sectors: agriculture, industry, and services. The numbers in the table indicate the value of exchanges between sectors in a given period of time (often a year). In this example, $1 million worth of goods and services were provided by

TABLE 10.1   An Example of an Input-Output Table.

Output from Sector, in Millions of Dollars	Inputs in Millions of Dollars				
	Agriculture	Industry	Services	Household Consumers	Total Production
Agriculture	1	2.25	0.2	1.55	5.0
Industry	2	6	1	16	25.0
Services	0.2	3	1.8	15	20.0
Total consumption	3.2	11.25	3.0	32.55	50.0

SOURCE: Theil, Boot, and Kloek, *Operations Research and Quantitative Economics.* New York: McGraw-Hill, 1965, p. 54.

agricultural activities to other agricultural activities, $2.25 million to industrial activities, $200,000 to service activities, and $1.55 million to households (for instance, as food). Adding up these numbers, the total agricultural production was worth $5 million. Along with the agricultural raw materials they purchased, industries received industrial goods, a variety of services, labor from a household sector, and certain items from outside the area; in this table, the total consumption of the industrial sector had a value of $11.25 million. In this simplified case, the production totals add up to the same value as the consumption totals: the "gross regional product," which is a measure of the overall level of economic activity in the place.

As a whole the table summarizes the characteristic structure of this particular economy. Not only would a second place be different if it had a larger gross regional production, but its character would also depend on where the large numbers are in the table. Agricultural production in that place might be larger than industrial production, or household consumption might be 40 percent of the regional product instead of the 65 percent indicated by Table 10.1.

But what can the table tell us about the impact of a change in the economy? What if the conditions that lie behind one of the numbers change: for example, industrial production increases or household demands for agricultural commodities grow? How much will the other numbers need to change in order to support this new situation? Are all of these needed changes going to be possible?

For simplicity, let's adopt an assumption of *proportionality*. Essentially, this means that the structure of the economy is the same after the change as it was before. If we want agricultural production to increase by 20 percent, then all of the inputs to the agricultural sector will have to increase by 20 percent to make this possible. But this is only the beginning. Some of these additional inputs, for example, are from industry, which must therefore increase its production, requiring all of its inputs to be increased. And so the effects spread through the economy (see Box 10.1).

It is not usually very helpful to construct input-output tables that identify only 3 or 4 sectors because a heading like "services" is too broad to tell us much. Measuring interactions among 30 or 40 sectors gives a much better appreciation of a region's economic structure, and a pioneering effort for Philadelphia, Pennsylvania went far beyond this to consider more than 400 sectors.

10.2.2 *Environments, Linkages, and Locational Advantage*

An input-output table is a dramatic indication of how widespread and important linkages are for economic activities (for some examples, see Section 10.4.1). It indicates that we should expand our view of the relationship between the distinctiveness of a place and its advantages as a location for economic activity. Along with a particular combination of weather and culture, a place has a characteristic economic structure. Present environments are reflected in this structure, but so are past environments and the uses people have made of them.

BOX 10.1   TECHNICAL COEFFICIENTS

The proportionality assumption allows us to build a different kind of input-output table, one that makes it easier to see the effects of a change in a level of production. If we divide the input amounts for agriculture ($1 million, $2 million, and $0.2 million from agriculture, industry, and services) by the amount of agricultural production ($5 million), we get three proportions: 0.2, 0.4, and 0.04. For every additional dollar of agricultural goods produced, we will need an average of 20 cents' worth of agricultural inputs. As long as proportionality is assumed, these proportions are the same regardless of where or how much production changes.

Consequently, a table of these ratios can be constructed:

Outputs From Sectors	Inputs to Sectors		
	Agriculture	Industry	Services
Agriculture	0.2	0.09	0.01
Industry	0.4	0.24	0.05
Services	0.04	0.12	0.09

These numbers are often called *technical coefficients*, and they are used to calculate the effect of one change in production or demand on the levels of activity of all the sectors (see 10.6).

We already know from the concept of agglomeration economies that this structure influences the attractiveness of a place to a prospective new activity. And we can imagine that, in this and other ways as well, it affects the opportunities for people at that place to improve their economic well-being.

There are still other economic advantages of agglomeration. For instance, the larger concentrations of economic activity are often where most of the new economic and technological ideas pop up, and there are advantages to getting a head start on using your new ideas.* And in bigger agglomerations, the chance is better that a regional import can be reduced by finding something locally that can substitute for it.

Agglomeration economies (whose value depends on linkages within an area as well as the size of the concentration) are thus at least as important in evaluating future prospects of well-being as is the present balance between regional imports and exports. And there are other factors, too. Let's briefly catalog the characteristics of a place that are believed to help it improve the average income of its residents:

1. its supply of factors of production: labor, capital, physical resources, and technology (see Box 10.2).

2. its economic structure, especially as it relates to (a) the locational preferences of outside economic decision-makers,[†] and (b) the efficient use of those factors—getting as much output as possible per unit of input.

3. the demand for its goods and services, in terms of both (a) the size of the local market and (b) the volume of exports to consumers elsewhere[†]

4. its capability to respond favorably to changes in market conditions (such as the declining value of a resource or product because of technological change)

A place has a *comparative advantage* if it looks good to an economic decision maker in these ways. But the various environmental and structural characteristics are evaluated differently by a firm that wishes to mill uranium ore than by a firm that specializes in repairing teletype machines. And they are evaluated differently by a single-function, single-location firm than the very large and

---

*   This idea will be discussed further in Chapter 17.

†   These are only two of many ways that economic well-being at a particular location is affected by conditions, activities, and decision in other locations. See Chapters 11–18.

diverse firms that account for so much of the economic activity in industrial countries.

It is clear that the locational advantages of a place are a complicated combination of things it probably cannot determine (such

---

BOX 10.2   FACTORS OF PRODUCTION

Providing goods or services that people want can require many different kinds of inputs: raw materials, component parts, machines, people, office space, telephones, and countless others. An area that is richly endowed with an important input for an activity has an advantage in trying to convince that activity to locate there. But what effect does a change in an input have on an activity? What effect does a change in the level of activity have on the input: buying more land? Hiring more workers? Buying another machine for the factory or office?

It is sometimes helpful to be able to talk in simplified terms about *factors of production,* such as land, labor, and capital. Generally, it is possible to do a job in a number of different ways, combining the factors in different proportions. You can make more trivets either by buying another machine or by hiring more workers. You can raise more corn either by buying more fertilizer or by buying more land. You can get the benefits of "closeness" either by spending money to locate close or by spending money for a fancy communication system. Each location is different from most others in the trade-offs it offers among the various factors of production, and places are evaluated by economic decision makers with these trade-offs in mind.

The easiest way to look at the importance of one factor is to create a simple model where that factor varies but all the other factors stay the same. For example, think of agricultural production as having two kinds of

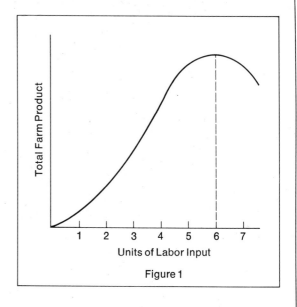

Figure 1

inputs: land and labor. Suppose that the amount of land is fixed, at least in the short run, and we want to consider the consequences of increasing labor inputs by adding a hired hand. In effect, we would create a graph such as Figure 1. When the farm has fewer than six workers, the addition of another one will increase production. (Note that the graph would probably be different for a location with different physical, economic, or technological characteristics).

More realistically, though, we could spend the additional money either to hire another worker or to lease additional land. Either might increase production. Studying this possibility calls for a graph such as Fig-as the weather), things it may be able to determine (such as labor skills, transportation facilities, and social mobility), and things it often can determine (such as localized economic costs: taxes, power rates, and similar items). Many of the important determinations are

BOX 10.2   (cont'd.)

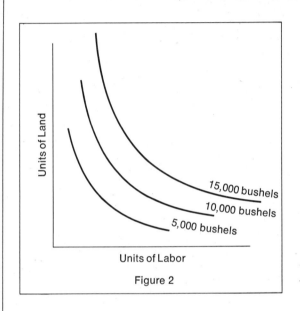

Figure 2

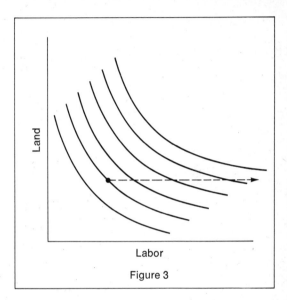

Figure 3

ure 2, the equational version of which is known as *production function.* Each curve on the graph indicates the various combinations of land and labor that will give a certain level of production. The present situation of a farm—a production level, an amount of land, and an amount of labor—shows up on the graph as a dot, and the challenge is to find the best path from that point to a higher level of production: the best combination of new inputs. Finding a precise solution requires concepts that we will not deal with here, but it is not usually too difficult, given good information about the costs of inputs and their profiles (by graphs such as Figure 3).

As an activity grows, it traces out an *expansion path* on the graph of its production function. When the curves in the production function are convex, as Figure 3 shows (and is usually the case), this suggests an important idea. What happens if a farm keeps on adding more and more hired hands? This is represented on the production function graph as a horizontal line, indicating that the added production (the movement toward higher level lines) becomes less and less, and eventually there is very little addition at all. This is the law of *diminishing returns,* which says that no factor of production is completely, endlessly substitutable for another.

inherited from earlier generations. Even though some of them relate to environmental conditions that no longer exist, they have insinuated themselves into an economic structure that is itself now a part of locational advantage—a structure that carries with it a kind of momentum of its own.

10.2.3 *Advantage and Specialization*

But what does it mean to a place to have a "locational advantage"? The concept is so complex, mixing so many different kinds of attractions, that advantages are much easier to identify by observing what individual decision makers actually do than by some kind of objective judgment of what they ought to do.

The basic concept, however, is a simple one, related to the reasoning of Chapter 5. Suppose that there is only a large enough market for an activity to support one location for it. It will locate in the place that offers the most locational advantages for it, combining desirable environmental characteristics, the needed linkages in the local economic structure (agglomeration economies), and other attractions. If that same location is the most advantageous for two activities but can only handle one, the more profitable one will be the preferred one (the highest and best use), and the loser will seek its second-best location.

This kind of logic usually leads a locational decision maker to focus on a few places—the same few that would be chosen by other people locating in the same sort of activity. Consequently, the forestry people will end up locating the same several areas, and the park people will pick the same as each other—but different ones from the forestry people.

The result is that a place becomes economically *specialized*. Some activities locate there but others do not. Some activities can be conducted there cheaply and effectively enough to compete successfully with other would-be suppliers. Others cannot.

We can still go one step farther. We know that environments are often regionalized, and a characterization of the economic structure of a place is also based on a definition of the "place" that usually covers a fairly large area. A decision maker often finds that if the most desirable location is not available, a nearby place is nearly as good because its characteristics are similar. Because differences in locational advantage tend to be grouped into regions, economic specialization is likely to be regionalized as well, and this tendency is reinforced by economies of scale in production and marketing.

A map of the geographic distribution of economic activities is therefore a reflection of locational qualities: characteristics of places that influence hard-nosed decisions about how best to compete for the privilege of supplying specific goods and services to consumers. In a very basic sense, places differ in the things they have to offer, such as a lot of labor, a lot of wood, or good transportation facilities. Economic activities differ in the things that they need. A place will usually end up specializing in those activities that most need what that place is best prepared to provide (see Box 10.3).

10.3   ELABORATING THE BASIC IDEAS

Because it is so far-reaching in its implications, the concept of locational advantage has been elaborated, qualified, and otherwise massaged at great length. Many of the important points will be introduced in the next six chapters, where advantages that result from *outside* conditions will be considered. But there are several issues that we need to deal with here.

10.3.1   The Transiency of Advantage

As Chapter 9 suggested, a characteristic of a place that amounts to a locational advantage at one time may be unimportant at another time. Advantages can be fleeting, for three basic reasons:

1. **Substitutability:** someone may develop a substitute for your raw material or labor skill: synthetic rubber for rubber trees, plastic for glass, machines for people, or tax subsidies in place of low wage rates.

BOX 10.3   THE HECKSCHER-OHLIN THEOREM

For which kinds of activities does a particular location have advantages over others? A Swedish economist named Ohlin, drawing upon the ideas of another economist named Heckscher, noted that areas differ in the prices of their factors of production, such as labor, natural resources, or capital; and he suggested that an area has an advantage when it can make intensive use of its most abundant (least expensive) factors. The resulting products can out-compete similar products made in other places because they can be made more cheaply. Of course, as these products are made and sold in larger and larger numbers, the abundant factor gets scarcer, and its price rises. Eventually, then, trade reduces the difference between areas in the prices of factors of production.

This idea became known as "the Heckscher-Ohlin Theorem," and it was later extended by the American economist Paul Samuelson. Although the idea is a useful one, however, it describes only one of many aspects of economic relationships between places. (Also see Section 10.3.2, Chapters 11–13, and Chapters 16–18.)

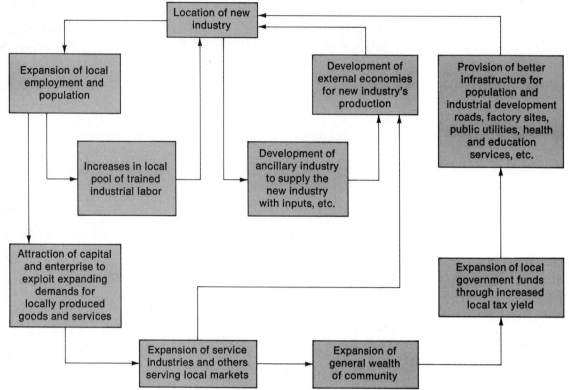

FIGURE 10.1
A Simplified Illustration of
Myrdal's Process of
Cumulative Causation.

2. **Renewability:** some advantages can be used up. Mineral resources can be exhausted. Underground water can be withdrawn faster than it is replaced, as can soil nutrients. Even low wage rates can be "used up," in the sense that the more activity they attract, the greater will be demand for the available labor—driving wages up.

3. **Technological and cultural change:** in addition to creating substitutes for inputs and particular purposes, changes in the level of technology can modify the purposes themselves. Buggy whip manufacturing, wood as fuel, cyclamate production, child labor—such things are replaced by new kinds of demands. In the same way, cultural preferences and rules change. In an automobile age, nearness to a market may become less important than the variety of products offered there. A physical environment well suited for growing marijuana may change from a social problem to an economic opportunity because of a single piece of legislation.

Consequently, a part of judging locational advantages is anticipating future needs, not just measuring current ones. As Section

10.4 illustrates, there are a great many examples of major shifts of economic activity from one general area to another. And it is better to be the first person to get the word than the last.

10.3.2   *Cumulative Causation*

Even if a few factories move from one area to another to find lower wage rates, we know that once a place gets a good start, its economic scale and structure will assure it of some advantages. As Chapter 8 indicated, agglomeration economies are often the most important of all attractions, regardless what the other locational advantages turn out to be.

A Swedish economist, Gunnar Myrdal, has argued persuasively that places with the advantage of past economic prosperity and growth are likely to be the prosperous places of the future, and vice versa. Advantage (or disadvantage) is *cumulative* because of the kinds of linkages depicted in Figure 10.1.

Clearly, this common sense observation—that advantages perpetuate themselves—diverges from what the preceding section concluded: that locational advantages may change with time (Chapter 16 will return to this paradox). The world of the decision maker includes both the inertia of a stable pattern of established advantages and the flux of a shifting pattern of temporary and changing advantages. And places can be classified as to whether they must rely on one kind or another, or can offer both.

10.3.3   *Sectoral Evolution*

Locational advantages can also be judged as to the long-term prospects of the kinds of activities they favor. Economic history indicates that the balance of employment in the primary, secondary, and tertiary sectors of a country has usually evolved as shown in Figure 10.2. If Place A has advantages over other places only when the question is where to locate a primary activity, its long-term prospects are poor unless it can convert its primary production into other assets. If Place B is a focus of secondary activity, its economic growth is likely to level off eventually unless it devotes its attention to new tertiary activity, because services are the true national growth sector (if history is our guide).

It is important to note that this does not mean that Place A must go through an industrial phase before it gets to a stage where its economy emphasizes tertiary activities. (There are other limitations of Figure 10.2 as well; for example, in what sector do we put a person who grows flowers and also sells them? And what does it mean for a very large company operating in all three sec-

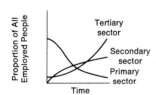

FIGURE   10.2
The General Historical Trend in the Distribution of Employment Between Sectors of a National Economy.

tors?) What this kind of *sectoral transformation* means, instead, is that a place without compelling agglomeration advantages can sometimes turn underutilized factors of production (land, labor, or capital) into locational advantages, to its economic benefit. It is not just a matter of the resources a place has; it is also a matter of how those resources are used.

The standard example is people who are making a relatively small contribution to the economic output of a town, city, or region. Consider a farm hand or a janitor. If he or she changes status, taking a factory job at little increase in salary, the output of the factory may increase more than the output of the previous employer drops. In a strictly economic sense, the resources of the place are being used more efficiently. If a lot of this kind of occupational mobility is possible, the place has an advantage in attracting industries looking for inexpensive labor; new industries arrive; and the total income of the place increases. If, however, the goods or services of the low-productivity sector are important to the place, even if they are not very remunerative to the people there (for instance, food supplies), the addition of capital investment in the growing high-productivity sector needs to be accompanied by capital additions in the supplying sector (for instance, mechanical cotton pickers in place of humans, or waste disposal chutes in place of wastebaskets).

10.3.4   *An Objective of No Growth*

So far we have been thinking in terms of growth, expansion, and attraction. But an increasing number of places are deciding that it is time to stop growing—perhaps even that they are too large already.

It is important to note that everything we have considered in Chapters 8, 9, and 10 can be used in reverse as the basis of a no-growth strategy. Locational advantages for basic activities, once identified, can be countered by artificial disadvantages: taxes, constraints, bureaucratic complexities. Limitations (on, for example, transportation facilities and power supplies) can be protected against the urge to make additions.

But the first step in stopping growth is to understand how and why it occurs: why a location is judged to be attractive, to whom it is attractive, and what kinds of negative incentives will have an impact on the comparisons these people will make between locations. Just as it often takes more skill for an ice skater or high-wire artist to act unskilled than to do his or her job with grace, it is usually harder for a place with real locational advantage to discourage growth than to induce it.

10.4 EXAMPLES

The concepts in this chapter play an important role in determining what places are like, what people there do for a living, and how these characteristics change from time to time. A few examples will help to illustrate this.

10.4.1 Internal Linkages

The most complete study of the linkages between economic activities in a region has been the Philadelphia input-output table, developed by Walter Isard and his associates. This table has been used for more than a decade to answer questions about the Philadelphia economy. For example, what if in 1968 the Vietnam war had not been going on? Would Philadelphia have been worse or better off economically? Clearly, an activity such as its Naval Shipyard would have been spending less money (an estimated $40 million less), reducing the purchases of machinery, power, and labor in Philadelphia (1700 fewer workers would have had jobs in the impacted sectors, according to the input-output study). But if the $40 million had been spent instead by the federal government on housing construction and education, total employment and consumer demands would have remained stable (again, according to the input-output study). A local utility company, in trying to anticipate the effect of any new trend or event, is vitally concerned with linkages in the regional economy—but so is the machinist, lawyer, and printer.

A different kind of linkage question concerns the location of a new activity. In seeking a source of jobs for Puerto Rico during the late 1950s, Isard and others decided (as had experts studying the reconstruction of Eastern Europe after World War II) that no single activity, inserted into the economy by itself, had very good prospects. Too many linkages would be absent, and too much locational advantage would be lost as a consequence. Rather, the approach should be to identify a *complex* of related industrial activities that would benefit from being located together. They recommended a petrochemical complex, focused on an oil refinery; Figure 10.3 is an example. It appears to have been good advice. Isard reports that by 1973, 7,000 Puerto Ricans were filling jobs in the petrochemical sector (see also Chapter 18).[1]

Or consider a need to expand an activity very rapidly. Where are the possible bottlenecks and how can they be avoided? For example, when World War II began the United States needed to

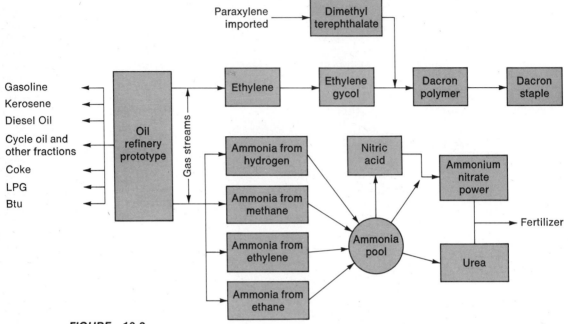

FIGURE 10.3

The Design of an Industrial Complex for Puerto Rico: a petrochemical complex, which not only produces gasoline and other refinery products but produces fertilizer and synthetic fibers from gas byproducts of the refinery.

build ships. Suppose that a particular shipyard had enough labor available to build a ship; so it began construction. But ships are built largely of steel, and supplying the steel at that time took coal. Assume that the coal mines were short of labor. Because the labor was not there to mine the additional coal, the coal was not there to support increased production from the iron and steel works, and the steel could not be delivered to finish the ship. Maybe it would have been a better idea to try to convince some of the shipyard workers to make a little wartime contribution in the coal mines, because the labor supply for coal mining was acting as a bottleneck for expanding the shipbuilding effort.[2] Input-output analysis is especially well suited to identifying such situations.

10.4.2　*The Impact of Locational Advantage*

Determinants of Locational Advantage　An indication of the advantages of a place, as they are evaluated by a host of decision makers, is its economic growth compared to other places.[‡] In 1967 a careful study of the experience of eight European countries and the United States was published, assessing the factors that con-

---

[‡] From the point of view of a nongrowing place, rather than that of a mobile economic decision maker, this may be seen as rather discouraging. But Chapters 16–18 suggest some remedial courses of action.

tributed to economic growth between 1950 and 1962 (note that, as usual, the comparisons were based on information about entire countries rather than regions within a country).[3] The study (together with a later evaluation of Canada) indicated that economic growth was based on both an increase in inputs and an improvement in the efficiency with which inputs were used.

In these relatively highly developed countries, the most important new inputs were labor, both quantity and quality, accounting for more than 70 percent of national incomes. The contributions of capital and land were surprisingly small, perhaps partly because the data counted some of their impact as increases in the quality of labor. The most important advances in efficiency were the utilization of new technologies, labor shifts from agriculture to other sectors, and growing economies of scale.

Illustrating that there are alternative pathways to economic growth, about 60 percent of North America's growth during the 1950–1962 period resulted from new inputs, with the quality of the labor force (as indicated by education) especially important. Europe by contrast, achieved 60 percent of its growth by using its inputs more efficiently—allocating more of its labor to high-productivity sectors and realizing greater economies of scale. This does not mean, however, that Canada and the United States were being relatively inefficient. Because they were economically much more efficient than Europe in 1950, they had less room for improvement. Europe was in fact closing the gap.

Changes in Locational Advantage The environments of a place join with its internal economic structure to make it a logical place for some kinds of activities but a poorly suited location for others. As we have seen, however, a pattern of advantage is a changeable thing, and the shifts are as much a part of understanding locational advantage as is the pattern at any particular time.

Some kinds of advantages are hard to move or replace. The need for uranium has boosted the mining industry in the American Southwest because that is where the best deposits in the country are located. Test areas for guided missiles for national defense are located where there are large expanses of sparsely populated area: desert or water. Rockets continue to be launched from the NASA complex in Florida (and from a military installation in California) because it would be too expensive to duplicate the launch pads, storage facilities, and control rooms anywhere else. For theater in the United States, Broadway is still the dream.

But none of these situations has been in existence for very long. Each one of them is an example of a fairly recent economic or political need, technological development, or cultural preference.

FIGURE 10.4
The Changing Location of
Cotton Production in the
United States: (a) 1879;
(b) 1909; and
[continued on next page]

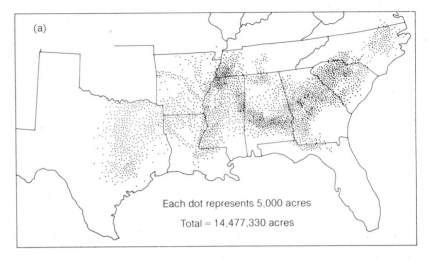

(a)

Each dot represents 5,000 acres

Total = 14,477,330 acres

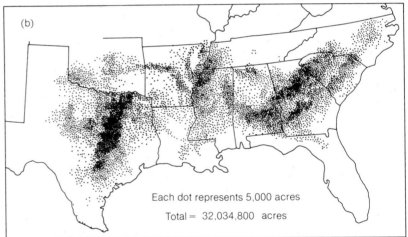

(b)

Each dot represents 5,000 acres

Total = 32,034,800 acres

Even though all of them are important to particular places now, there are people alive who can remember when none of them was very important.

It is perhaps more interesting to look at instances where locational advantages have changed: major regional shifts in the location of a kind of activity and major displacements of one kind of activity by another. The classic case is the movement of textile manufacturing plants from New England to the South Atlantic states during the first half of the twentieth century. As labor costs rose in New England (and labor became better organized), the original locational advantages there—cheap power and nearness to markets—started to be offset by the lower wage levels that other places could offer. And when the time came for a manufacturer to

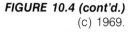

FIGURE 10.4 (cont'd.)
(c) 1969.

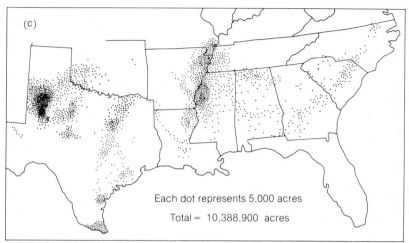

Each dot represents 5,000 acres

Total = 10,388,900 acres

replace an obsolescent plant with a new one, a state like North Carolina looked more attractive than the prospects of rebuilding in Massachusetts: cheaper labor, weaker labor unions, often lower construction costs, in general simpler, less disputatious conditions for work—and closer to where cotton was being produced.

A more gradual shift has been the pattern of cotton production in the United States, following the expansion of irrigation westward in search of more sun, cheaper land, and larger parcels of land that could be handled efficiently with a high degree of mechanization (see Figure 10.4). Since the western margin of the main area of production is using water from the wells faster than it is being returned to water-bearing formations underground, the direction of movement of the boundary is likely to reverse itself before long. In these marginal areas, cotton growing is more like a form of mining—based on the extraction of a depletable resource over a limited period of time—than our usual conception of agriculture as a long-term land use.

Other changes are simply a response to shifts in market preferences. The von Thünen model in Chapter 5 showed how an increase in demand or a change in price could affect boundaries between land uses. An example in the United States is the spread of soybean cultivation since World War II, when it was advocated as a protein-rich substitute for meat. Partly because of a steady increase in their use in the United States, but even more because of growing demands from other countries (notably Japan, where it is a food staple), soybeans have become a profitable crop to grow in areas that had once raised wheat, corn, and other crops (Figure 10.5). And this raises the question of where the displaced wheat and corn production have located.

FIGURE 10.5
Soybean Production in the
United States: (a) 1954
[continued on next page]

☐ Less than 1,000 bushels	▦ 25 million-50 million bushels
▧ 1,000-5 million bushels	▨ 50 million-75 million bushels
⠿ 5 million-15 million bushels	▩ 75 million-100 million bushels
▨ 15 million-25 million bushels	■ More than 100 million bushels

Similar kinds of shifts occur for services, although the transfers are more often between cities than between regions. An example is the movement in the 1960s of many corporate headquarters and research activities from the Northeast to Texas, Colorado, California, and other locations in the West and South. With improved communications technology, it was less important to be close to eastern markets (which were often declining in relative importance); and space rental costs, taxes, and other economic differences made it easier to justify a decision that may have been based more on a belief that family life and recreational opportunities were better in these new locations.

10.5 A RECONSIDERATION

This whole discussion has emphasized how the economic linkages and noneconomic environments of a place put it at an advantage or disadvantage as a location for a particular economic activity in a competitive world. But we have been overlooking a key factor.

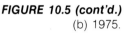

FIGURE 10.5 (cont'd.)
(b) 1975.

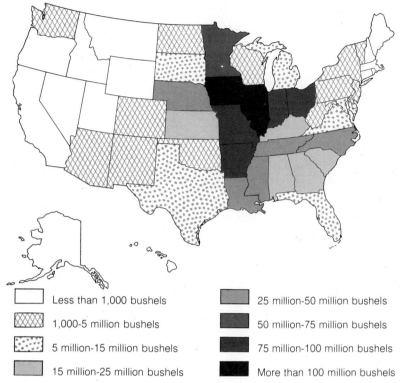

Less than 1,000 bushels	25 million-50 million bushels
1,000-5 million bushels	50 million-75 million bushels
5 million-15 million bushels	75 million-100 million bushels
15 million-25 million bushels	More than 100 million bushels

Along with such characteristics as labor costs and skills, important attributes of a place include a factor that appeared prominently in Chapters 5–7: facilities for transportation and communication. Historically, some places have thrived very largely as locations where people and things get together, with places a premium on movement systems. Little Phoenecia bought and sold items that never came close to home shores. Switzerland as a money market, New York as a stock market, Chicago as a commodity market—all of these are examples of a locational advantage built on an economic structure that is especially well suited to handle exchanges. Even the contribution of ocean shipping to the Greek economy can be considered an example of this.

This kind of advantage—a *marketing* advantage—depends partly on communication facilities, and it depends in important ways on cultural and political environments—the experience and aptitudes of the people. But it also depends on where the place is located with respect to other places that need a market, which is the starting point for the next chapter.

10.6   *TOWARD GREATER PRECISION*

Input-output analysis, as an approach to studying an economy, has developed for over thirty years until it is now a powerful, sophisticated tool (see Box 10.4). Input-output tables are maintained for most states and many other areas as well, and they are uniquely suited for assessing the impact on an area of some kinds of change in the economic system. The long series of reverberations through the linkages in the economy, far too tedious to trace by ordinary arithmetic, can be handled by linear algebra in modern computers, producing *general equations* that allow an immediate calculation of the effects of any change. For example, the general equation for the textile sector tells us the way its level of production is related to levels of demand from all the sectors. If any of the demands increases, textile production will have to increase. Consequently the impact of an increase in automobile production can be estimated quickly by substituting the new demands from the automobile manufacturing sector into all the general equations. And these new production levels can be scrutinized to see whether or not they are feasible.

BOX 10.4   INPUT-OUTPUT ANALYSIS

Input-output analysis developed from studies of transactions between sectors of the economy of the United States by Wassily W. Leontief, whose pioneering book *The Structure of American Economy, 1919–1939* was first published in 1941. In 1973, Leontief received the Nobel Prize in economics for this work and the further investigations that followed it.

During the 1950s, Walter Isard and his colleagues at the University of Pennsylvania began to explore the input-output approach as a way to understand *regional* economies as well as national economies. Although the data problems were often severe, they found that input-output analysis was very useful in answering questions about the economic impact of a new activity on a region, the effects of the loss of an economic activity, and the best location for a large new manufacturing plant that would benefit from having a wide range of related activities nearby. The technique was featured in Isard's book *Methods of Regional Analysis: An Introduction to Regional Science* (1960), and was developed in remarkable detail for the Philadelphia metropolitan area. Several other books have followed, including one that incorporates transactions between economic sectors and the physical environment, and input-output analysis is now accepted as one of the basic tools of regional economics, regional science, and economic geography.

It is important, though, to note that input-output analysis has limitations. Three are especially significant. First, the table format requires that every unit of activity (company or plant) be identified in only one sector. Since, for instance, one manufacturing plant may produce all sorts of things (and in fact most important firms operate in more than one sector), this is a serious problem. A frequent practice, although it is not a solution, is to adopt someone else's classification scheme, such as the U.S. Census of Manufacturing. A second limitation is that an input-output analysis is only as good as the numbers it starts with—the input-output table. But it is often difficult to determine how reliable these numbers are, because they usually depend on the cooperation of business firms that have little reason to worry about assuring that the figures are completely accurate. In fact, firms are characteristically reticent about giving detailed information of this kind. The third limitation is the traditional assumption of proportionality, which is fundamentally flawed but is by far the simplest way to get a solution from the analysis. In general, most people suggest that the assumption gives reasonably good approximations of the real economy as long as predictions are limited to a short span of time—maybe five years. For longer-range predictions, it is necessary to revise the transaction table from time to time and make corrections as the proportions change with each new set of measurements.

MAJOR CONCEPTS AND TERMS

For definitions, see the Glossary.

Agglomeration economies

Comparative advantage

Cumulative causation

Economic efficiency

Factors of production

Industrial complex

Input-output analysis

Locational specialization

Production function

Sectoral transformation

Technical coefficients

Footnotes for Chapter 10

1. Isard, Walter. *Introduction to Regional Science*. Englewood Cliffs, N.J.: Prentice-Hall, 1975, p. 456.

2. Adapted from Theil, Boot, and Kloek, *Operations Research and Quantitative Economics*. N.Y.: McGraw-Hill, 1965, p. 70.

3. Denison, E. F. with J. P. Poullier. *Why Growth Rates Differ*. Washington: Brookings Institution, 1967.

PART V

INTERACTION AND DEPENDENCE

Chapters 8, 9, and 10 considered some of the reasons places differ in their comparative advantages. But they limited their attention to individual places relating to the rest of the world as a kind of amorphous, homogeneous, equidistant haze.

We know that a place is in fact connected with other places of different sizes at different distances, and with different characteristics. We also know from our introduction to how economic decision makers think about locations (Chapters 5, 6, and 7) that these differences are important. They shape the opportunities that particular locations offer.

The next three chapters will examine the relationship of (1) the interaction between places and (2) the locational advantages of places. Chapter 11 will summarize some ideas about the role of distance in interaction. In Chapter 12 the advantages of this interaction will be outlined; and Chapter 13 will look at some of the disadvantages.

In general, we will continue with the theme that in a competitive world decision makers at a particular place will specialize in doing those things that can be done cheaper and better there than in other places. But if the people at a wide range of different places, specializing in different things, want pretty much the same goods and services, this requires that they do a lot of trading. The consequence is interaction between the places, which is affected by the distance between them.

CHAPTER 11

THE LOCATIONAL ENVIRONMENT

*J*ust as a local economy operates in partnership with physical, cultural, and political environments, it has a kind of "locational environment." It is but one piece of a mosaic of local economies, and it affects and is affected by many of these other localities. Is this web of connections entirely accidental and unsystematic, or are there things about it that are predictable, efficient? Can we make sense out of it?

We have one clue already: the relationship between distance and movement costs that was central to Chapters 5, 6, and 7. Building from this idea, this chapter will develop a fuller conception of the role of distance in defining locational advantage.

11.1 SITUATIONS

11.1.1 The Short Vacation

Because next Monday will be a national holiday, you have a three-day weekend ahead of you, and you decide that you want to turn it into a vacation. The question is where to go.

You consider the alternatives. You know that you want a little camping and hiking. There is a nearby state park that is attractive but unexciting, and you have been there several times before. There are other state parks farther away, but they are not much more exciting and the longer drive will give you less time there. Or there is a national park that you could reach in one very long day's drive: two long days on the road for one day of hiking. Alternatively, you could fly to California and take a bus or rented car to Yosemite, which you have always wanted to visit; but that would be pretty expensive for such a short stay.

Considering the time, the holiday traffic, and the travel costs, you decide to drive to the nearest state park that you haven't visited before. It's not ideal, but time and money are short.

11.1.2   The Shopping Trip

You have put it off long enough. It's time to go shopping for a variety of little things that you need: transistor batteries, underwear, a shoe tree, a screwdriver, a road atlas, and a birthday present. Because of the variety of the things you want, you'd like to be able to visit several stores, which means going downtown, to a neighborhood shopping area, or to a suburban shopping center.

You get into your car, with the shopping list in your pocket. There are 14 different centers that you know about in your metropolitan area. Which one will be your destination? Your neighborhood shopping street is close, but the stores there don't carry your favorite brand of underwear, and the selection of birthday presents is limited. A huge new shopping center would have everything, but it is 45 minutes away, across town. The downtown stores would have everything, too, but you don't like to drive in downtown traffic, and you are afraid you might have to pay to park.

After shuffling the possibilities quickly in your mind, you head off to the suburban shopping center that you believe you can reach most quickly.

11.1.3   The Theme Amusement Park

You have had a lifelong dream: to own and operate a theme amusement park like Disneyland, Six Flags over Texas, or King's Island. Besides the fact that they can be successful businesses, you have always been an avid seeker of bigger and better roller coasters and arcades, and you are fascinated with the idea that a new amusement park could be designed as an experiment in the use of technology, with an objective of solving some kinds of urban problems (such as waste disposal).

With this in mind, you have worked for twelve years as a rising executive in the business, and you believe that your credentials are now solid enough so that you can get a bank, investment company, or someone else to loan you the money to create a new park. But the loan will have to be a very large one, which means that the plan will have to be a very good one.

Your research tells you that there are 29 theme parks operating in the United States, about half of them in the northeastern quadrant of the country. Other concentrations are in Southern California, the Dallas-Fort Worth metropolitan area, and central Florida. Obviously, you tell yourself, such a park needs a large local population (for employees—especially seasonal ones—and a regular clientele), and it benefits from an influx of vacationers. Where can you find such a volume of people?

First, you eliminate areas that are already close to a park, because it would be hard to convince the people there to forget the facility that is already familiar to them. As a preliminary screening technique, you look for a location that is (1) within one hour's drive of 1.5 million people but more than three hours' drive from an existing park; and (2) on an interstate highway that carries more than 10 million out-of-state tourists a year. Although the information only allows you to do this approximately, you arrive at several candidate locations.

Referring to projections of population trends in the United States between now and the year 2000, you decide to concentrate on the southwestern margin of the northeastern quadrant (got that?), and you go looking for more specific information about the cost of land between Tulsa and Oklahoma City, Oklahoma—in the vicinity of Stroud, on interstate highway 44.

11.2 BASIC IDEAS

No city or region exists in isolation. Even the remotest island in the Pacific Ocean is touched by the rest of the world: a bit of radioactive fallout from nuclear test explosions, ecologists on research grants doing esoteric studies, an occasional boat with a trader offering to buy or sell something, a machine, a missionary, a germ.

Although all of these contacts are important, economic geography focuses on those that relate to exchanges of things of material value (see Section 4.2). As we have said, because locational advantages for producing such things vary from place to place, individual location decisions lead to a kind of locational specialization that is only possible with interaction: a specialized place can only provide itself with a variety of goods and services by interacting with other places that specialize in other things.

This kind of interaction means movement. Chapters 5, 6, and 7 introduced us to the truism that movement is costly. It is a matter of time, trouble, funds, and other kinds of expenses. Nonetheless, movement is a part of all our lives. People move. Things move.

Information moves. The question is: why and how does movement take place? In this chapter, we will investigate the how.

Our experience tells us that most moves are short ones. It seldom makes sense to go a mile to get a 15-cent cup of coffee if one is available in the next room. When we shop each week, we usually travel a shorter distance than we do for an annual vacation. Even trucks and trains and airplanes make more short trips than long ones (as long as "short" is not too short).

Physical distance—in meters or miles—is a convenient, easily measured approximation of the effort it takes to move from one place to another. Because going farther usually calls for more effort (money, time), we usually choose not to do so. Or, to put the idea into more professional language, interaction with a place is usually less frequent or less intense if that place is farther away. The likelihood of contact decreases with distance.

But there is another factor as well. We often find that there are advantages to coordinating our movements with others. If six of us need a forklift to unload our trucks and a warehouse to store our cargoes, it is easier and cheaper for us all to use a single central truck terminal. In choosing a route for an automobile trip, it is easier and cheaper to follow a public highway than to negotiate the right to move across private property along a line that is uniquely ours. Even air travel is often a series of steps between navigational beacons.

Consequently, our movements tend to be affected by distance, but they are also affected by a pattern of movement facilities: places of frequent departure and arrival and well-defined lines of travel along which a lot of movement occurs. These facilities take geographic form as networks (see Chapter 2), except for relatively rare cases such as radio transmissions and open-water routes between marinas.

Movement, therefore, involves two kinds of *transfer costs*: (1) variable costs—expenditures of time, money, and energy that differ with the scope of the transfer; and (2) fixed costs—minimum costs for using the facilities that are most appropriate regardless of the scope of the transfer (see Box 11.1). The total costs can depend on the distance of the transfer (a variable cost), the method of the transfer (partly a fixed cost), the size of the job, any special requirements of the move (such as refrigeration), and a long list of other factors: for example, the competition between movement services, the direction of the move (will the carrier have to return empty?), and the value of time.

As least-effort beings, we try to minimize these costs for a particular movement requirement, and a result is that the world around us shows some distinctive geographical regularities. Densities of all kinds decrease with distance from a focus (see Box 11.2); movement networks imprint themselves on our impressions of places until they become the skeletons for our mental maps; and locational advantage comes to be a matter of ease of access as well as the kinds of things we discussed in Chapters 8, 9, and 10.

11.3   *ELABORATING THE BASIC IDEAS*

Because movement between locations is central to developing ideas in economic geography, a major concern has been to get a better appreciation of the kinds of regularities that our behavior demonstrates.

11.3.1   *Regularities and the Individual*

It is one thing to observe the shopping behavior of ten thousand people and say: 85 percent of the people choose to travel shorter

---

BOX 11.1   TRANSFER COSTS

Because transfer costs include both fixed expenses and variable expenses, longer trips usually cost less per mile or kilometer. Consider, for example, a trip in a rented automobile with the following costs:

1.   fixed: $15 a day, which repays the rental firm for buying the car (plus a profit)

2.   variable: 20 cents a mile, including maintenance and gasoline

We can display the cost of two-day trips of various lengths on a graph:

This tells us that the trip expenses would be: for 100 miles, $50 (or 50 cents a mile); for 300 miles, $90 (or 30 cents a mile); for 500 miles, $130 (or 26 cents a mile). The average cost per mile decreases as the length of the trip increases because the fixed costs are being spread over more distance. Whenever fixed costs are a factor, this is usually the case, al-

though the contrast is sharper for some comparisons (such as 100 versus 300 miles) than others (300 versus 500 miles).

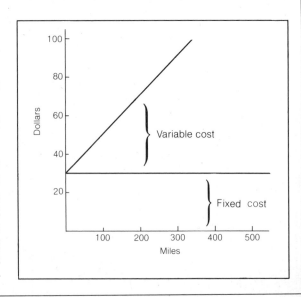

distances rather than longer ones. It is quite another thing to say: because most people minimize least effort, I predict that Mr. Hector I. Smith, in his next trip to the grocery store, will go to the store closest to his residence. To predict Mr. Smith's behavior, we need to know a great deal more: about the things he wants to buy, his long-time shopping habits, any other stops he plans to make, and even his knowledge of the relative nearness of different stores.

In generalizing about movement behavior in this book, we are drawing upon a research literature concerned mainly about groups, not individuals. This does not mean that individual behavior is not important, and we need to remember the limitations of the evidence. But it is useful to know what most people do when they make least-effort movement decisions; and it is much easier to get information from available sources about aggregate transfers—for example, numbers of long truck hauls versus short ones.

For individuals, the main value of the perspective is its clear sense of a relationship between distance and time. Opportunities exist at locations, whether they are opportunities to buy, sell, or make contact with specific people. Because some of the locations are distant, and it takes time to overcome distance, some of them are simply not available in a short span of time. Moreover, deciding to spend a lot of time getting to one of the locations means that there is less time for other opportunities. The main limitation of the

---

BOX 11.2   LEAST EFFORT AND SPATIAL INTERACTION

We see regularities and symmetrical patterns all around us. When we see an undisturbed ant hill straddling a crack in the sidewalk in the summertime, we are struck by its symmetry. The ants carry grains of sand out and drop them, carrying them no farther than necessary to prevent them from rolling backwards into the nest. The grains are distributed over an area that is almost perfectly circular. The depth profile resembles that of the density of litter deposited away from each edge of a highway. It is reliably reported that the railway line from Adelaide to Perth, Australia, is lined with beer cans for 1,600 kilometers and on a sunny day the route is visible from the air by the light reflected from the ribbon of shiny cans. Because of the principle of least effort, a beer can, cigarette wrapper, or junked car is seldom more than a few feet beyond the edge of the road. In each case the process is waste disposal away from a point or a line source. In each case a symmetrical density profile is the result because structure follows process and the process operates under a simple rule or principle called least effort.

ABLER, ADAMS, AND GOULD, SPATIAL
ORGANIZATION, p. 237.

perspective is that it overlooks the way a particular movement is affected by what the person was doing before—and what he or she plans to do afterward. Least effort involves a much broader context than the distance of a single trip alone.

11.3.2   *Distance-Decay Processes*

Distance is the measure that turns least effort into a subject that geographers can investigate. The concept of *distance decay*—the idea that frequency of contact declines with distance—is the foundation of most of this investigation.

In the nineteenth century, people studying migrations between cities (and regions) noticed that more migration took place between nearby places than distant ones—with one qualification. The size of the cities made a difference. More migrants left and arrived at big cities than small ones, if the distance of travel was the same. Attraction, therefore, could be said to be greater if a place were larger and less if a place were more distant.

Several centuries before, Sir Isaac Newton had defined a "law of universal gravitation" that sounded very much like the same sort of thing: the attraction between two bodies is proportional to the product of their masses and inversely proportional to the square of the distance between them. In 1929 W. J. Reilly suggested a Newtonian kind of formula as a way to understand the size of market areas—a particular kind of migration. The formula turned out to have some utility, and a *gravity model* of interaction between places was given intensive study in the 1940s and 1950s. The general form of the model is this:

$$F_{12} = k \; \frac{P_1 P_2}{d_{12}^{\,b}}$$

where

F_{12} is the measure of the interaction between places 1 and 2

P_1 and P_2 are measures of the sizes of the places

d_{12} is the distance between them

b is an exponent (2.0 in Newton's gravity model)

and k is a constant number that is characteristic of the particular type, time frame, and setting of interaction referred to (usually defined by observing a lot of examples of it).

This kind of formula is very helpful, but it is still rather ambiguous because so many terms need to be defined in order to arrive at a number for F (for example, a predicted volume of truck freight between Toronto and Ottawa). P is often approximated by the population of a city. However, population may be measured by the city itself, its urbanized area, or its larger metropolitan area. Furthermore, measures of economic activity, such as the average income, affect "attractiveness"; and other factors as well might enter into a definition of the "size" of a city or region. One may measure d as straight-line distance, shortest highway or rail distance, the time of travel, the cost of travel, or some combination of these. And b may be assumed to be 2 (the "gravity model" proper) or 1 (which seems to describe many kinds of social interaction in the United States); or it may need some further study for a particular case. It is likely, for instance, that the exponent—which indicates the degree to which distance inhibits contact—is smaller in countries that have a higher level of transportation and communication technology (see Box 11.3).

As the box shows, this approach is easily applied in a world that consists of single uninterrupted connections between each pair of locations (see Box 11.4). But we know that—as usual—things are not this simple. For example, in the box, the interaction between cities 3 and 5 is probably less with City 4 between them than if the path were clear. We are more likely to go 8 miles to a shopping center if there is none closer than if we pass another shopping center along the way. Consequently, *intervening opportunities* have the same effect as an addition of distance; in fact, when intervening opportunities are densely clustered, distance can be approximated simply by counting them. Where there are many traffic lights and stop signs along a route, their number may be a better indication of distance than a physical measure such as kilometers or miles.

A true measure of the locational advantage of a place is not just its interaction with *one* other place but its potential for interacting with *all* other places. It can be useful to calculate an F for Minneapolis with all other North American cities and add them to get a total interaction potential; then repeat the process for each of the other cities, and examine the resulting map of potentials. An example derived in approximately this way is shown in Figure 11.1; seen in this case as a pattern of access to purchasing power, it emphasizes the attractiveness of the Northeast as a marketing center. Similarly, it might be possible to evaluate the agglomeration potential of a location.[1]

11.3.3   *Modal Choice*

Although it is generally true that interaction decreases with distance, because the cost of movement increases with distance, we know from our experience that the relationship is different for a bicycle than for an airplane. When we contemplate moving something—ourselves, a box, a message—we consider different ways, or "modes," of getting the job done.

Each of the modes has its own characteristic relationship be-

BOX 11.3   ESTIMATING SPATIAL INTERACTION

The way to use a gravity-type model to estimate spatial interaction is: (1) collect information about P, F, and d for similar cases of interaction; and (2) use this information to estimate the values of k and b (unless one of them is assumed, in which case only one has to be estimated).

For example, suppose that our interest—as forward-looking owners of a trucking company—is in anticipating the movement of a certain class of commodities between cities ten years from now. For a formula in which b is assumed to be 1, please refer to the art and tables below. From these data, we conclude that 3.0 is a reasonable estimate of k.

Next, we consult population projections for the five cities for the next ten-year period, and we find that City 2 is expected to grow to 80,000 and City 3 to 600,000. We predict the freight flow between them ten years from

now by:

$$k \cdot \frac{P_2 P_3}{d} = 3.0 \frac{(80{,}000)\,(600{,}000)}{200} = 720{,}000 \text{ tons per month}$$

If both k and b are unknown, the procedure is a little more complicated, but it is well within the grasp of any person who has completed a couple of years of high school mathematics.

Note that this application assumes that the relationship between F and P will stay the same for the next ten years as it was during the last five. A more careful procedure would be to look at trends in this relationship and, if they show a steady change, to project the change ten years forward.

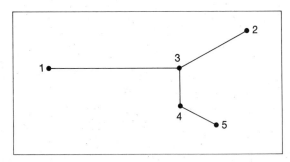

City	1	2	3	4	5
Population	100,000	50,000	500,000	200,000	50,000

Link	City 1: $P_1 P_2 \div$ 1,000,000	City 2: d	City 3: $P_1 P_2 / d$ (rounded)	City 4: Actual F, in 1,000 tons per month	Estimated K (4 ÷ 3)
1–3	50	300	170	500	2.9
2–3	25	200	125	400	3.2
3–4	100	150	665	1900	3.0
4–5	10	100	100	280	2.8

FIGURE 11.1

Population Potential in the United States, 1960. The "contour" lines show equal access to the total population of the United States. A value of 600 means that people at that location, with the same amount of effort, have the potential of twice as many contacts with other people as people at a location with a value of 300. This concept was first illustrated by William Warntz.

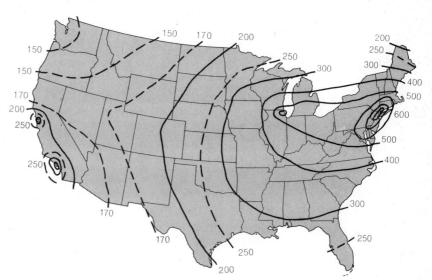

tween cost and distance; and for a particular job and distance one mode usually has an advantage. Figure 11.2 shows how this works; the same thing applies to such detailed comparisons as between types and sizes of trucks (see Box 11.5).

But technological change and other factors can cause competitive advantage to change through time. One of the most dramatic shifts in the United States during the first half of the twentieth century was the replacement of trains and trolley cars by the automobile as a people mover. More recently, trucks have grown in importance as commodity movers, and it is possible that the movement of pulverized coal (mixed with water or another liquid) in pipelines will compete with rail transport in the last quarter of the century.

BOX 11.4   ESTIMATING TRADE AREA BOUNDARIES

An application of the gravity-model approach has been to estimate the location of the marketing watershed between two cities. On one side of the boundary, individuals trade with one city; on the other side, they trade with the second city.

If the cities are equal in size, the boundary is obviously halfway between them. But what if one is larger than the other? In Box 11.3, the population of City 4 was 200,000 and of City 5, 50,000; they were 100 kilometers apart. The break-point is calculated in this way:

$$\text{Distance from 4} = \frac{d}{1 + \sqrt{P_5/P_4}}$$

$$= \frac{100}{1 + \sqrt{50,000/200,000}} = \frac{100}{1\frac{1}{2}} = 66.7$$

The trade area of the larger city, therefore, extends two-thirds of the way to the smaller city.

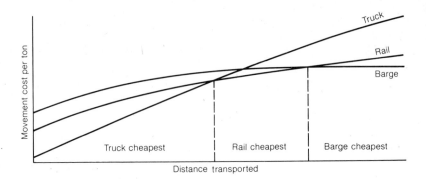

FIGURE 11.2
Modal Choice. In this way, the best transportation mode for a purpose may depend on the distance to be traveled. Note also how particular modes fill niches in a spectrum of needs.

An increasingly important option is communication as a substitute for physical movement. Telephones can replace trips or letters. Improved communication and transportation systems can make it easier to centralize storage facilities. For example, instead of shipping spare parts to 20 regional centers where some of them will sit unused (and eventually have to be shipped back or transferred to another center), an improved communications system, using teletypes and computers, might make it possible to work from two centers. Eventually we might be able to shop for groceries without leaving our houses: by tapping catalog orders into a household computer, along with a credit card number, and awaiting delivery. In such directions lies the future.

11.3.4   *Movement Network Design*

Obviously, some movement networks serve us better than others (try coping with the local bus system in a strange city), and there are some general perspectives that can be helpful in understanding the differences.

Suppose that we had before us an uncharted new land—unknown territory. How would we organize our movement to learn

BOX 11.5   ALTERNATIVE MOVEMENT SERVICES

We have suggested that for a particular job and distance, one mode usually has an advantage, but this implies that a potential user has a wide range of choice. Often, the actual alternatives are relatively few. Rail transportation may be the cheapest in theory, but this means very little to a person who cannot get rail service at his or her location.

In general, a person has more alternatives at a location close to large transfer terminals, where different modes meet and exchange whatever they carry. And since these terminals are often in big cities, this adds to the agglomeration economies that such places offer.

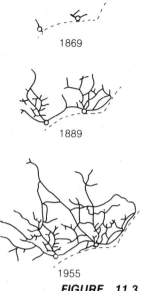

1869

1889

1955

FIGURE   11.3
The Growth of the Railway
Network in Southeastern
Brazil.

as much about the area as possible in a time? A spare treelike system of paths might develop first, later to be supplemented by a finer pattern of local paths extending out into the more promising areas that are located nearby. Figures 11.3 and 11.5 show such a sequence, illustrating two points: there is a tendency for the empty spaces to fill with additional paths, and there is an increasing difference between the main, high-volume paths and the local ones.

Movement networks are typically hierarchical, just as central places are. A familiar example is our system of roads, which includes limited-access highways, intercity highways with more intervening obstacles, and local farm-to-market roads. Both theory and experience tell us that there is a relationship between movement hierarchies and central place hierarchies, with high volume links connecting the largest places and the larger places serving as junction points for links of all sizes.

But the form of each level of a movement hierarchy is itself a kind of compromise between the advantages of having as many connections as possible (making it cheaper for a user to get from any one place to any other) and the advantages of having as few connections as possible (making it cheaper to construct and maintain the network of facilities). Figure 11.4 shows two very different

BOX 11.6   THE TRAVELING SALESMAN PROBLEM

To the user of a transportation network, the form of the network is not an issue. It is there. The question is how to use it in the most efficient way. A classic problem of this sort is how to figure the shortest path for reaching a series of places: the dilemma of a traveling salesman who wants to leave home, visit customers at different locations, and return home.

Computer programs have been developed to solve problems of this type, even taking into account the fact that some routes are easier to travel than others. It is especially feasible to get a very good "approximate" solution. The figure shows an example of such a solution for a traveling salesman who needs to visit 23 towns in southern Ghana.

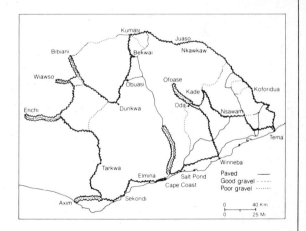

The Shortest Path for Visiting 23 Towns
in Southern Ghana, considering Route Length
and Road Quality.

ways to connect the same places (also see Box 11.6). As Figure 11.5 shows, a system often evolves from the treelike form toward a circuitlike form. As one level in a movement network becomes more circuitlike with increased usage, the pressure increases for a more treelike higher level to develop because it is costly to distribute the volume of the movement through so many channels with limited capacities. In this sense the interstate highway network in the United States was probably an inevitable development.

11.3.5 *Factor Movements*

Although it is difficult to move some kinds of natural resources (for instance, sunlight or petroleum reservoirs), labor and capital move all the time from place to place, and technology moves as well (also see Section 12.3.3). One of the reasons for these flows of factors of production is that the prices of the factors vary from place to place. Just as this situation encourages flows of commodities from low-production-cost areas to high-cost ones, it can stimulate movements of the factors themselves (if they are mobile).

The general idea is that labor and capital flow from low-benefit locations to high-benefit ones. Workers—especially those with high levels of skill or with special capabilities for management—move to areas where the wages are higher. Capital moves to places where a higher return is offered (such as a higher interest rate on invested money). Over a period of time these movements tend to reduce the differences in benefit levels; for example, the more abundant labor in high-wage areas will push wages down, while the increasing labor scarcity in low-wage areas will push salaries up.

Higher benefit levels are therefore an important "pull" in explaining movements between places. But the simplicity of this idea straddles a lot of complications. A high wage rate may reflect a higher cost of living, not a higher level of well-being. Labor mobility is also affected by locational preference, information about other places, the cost of moving, and the time required to make movement decisions. And moving from a secure job near long-time friends may mean some serious "social costs," regardless of the economic benefits. A higher interest rate may reflect a higher degree of risk in a region; capital mobility is influenced by differences in risk and uncertainty as well as by momentary differences in interest rates. In addition, investment money is often tied up in big projects, making it difficult to shift large amounts of capital back and forth between places as rates of return change. Both labor and capital mobility can be affected by commodity movements, which in some cases can serve as a kind of substitute for factor movements

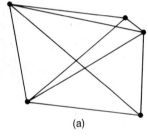

(a)

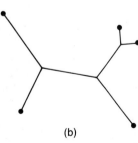

(b)

FIGURE 11.4
Alternative Ways to Connect Five Places: (a) maximizing connections; and (b) minimizing route length.

in reducing differences in factor prices. And the relationship be-tween mobility and wages or interest rates is not always as direct as it may seem. For instance, both wage differences and labor move-ments may be a response to differences in employment op-portunities, rather than to each other. Finally, and maybe most important, geographic flows of factors of production are affected by political institutions and policies (see Chapters 14 and 15).

11.3.6 *Spatial Pricing*

Factor movement is only one of many ways that price differences between places affect economic decisions. As the preceding para-graph suggested, commodities also tend to move from low-price areas to high-price areas, reducing geographic differences in the prices. Consider what you would do if you were a marketing execu-tive for a national chain of grocery stores. In Atlanta, people are buying a new line of frozen foods at the regular price. In In-dianapolis, they are buying the new products—but only at the spe-cial low price that was used to introduce the line. Indianapolis stores want a supply of the frozen foods, but they want a break on the wholesale price so that their profits do not suffer. Where do you ship frozen foods? Mostly to Atlanta, where you can get the full price without complaint. After a while, maybe, the product will become scarce enough in Indianapolis that it will sell at the regular price. Of course, it may become so abundant in Atlanta stores that they will have to start putting it on sale.

In such a way, a *spatial price equilibrium* is eventually reached (in theory). The price of a commodity or a factor of produc-tion is the same everywhere, except for differences in transporta-tion costs. And the movements of factors or commodities stabilize so that the equilibrium stays that way.

But the role of movement costs in spatial pricing is not always simple to figure out. Chapter 5 introduced the idea that prices might be higher with increasing distance from a center of produc-tion or marketing, and this is indeed one strategy. The price is set at the center, and the customer pays the movement costs. Au-tomobiles are a familiar example. Sometimes, to simplify the busi-ness of pricing, uniform rates are used over a range of distances (for example, the same addition to price for customers 500–700 miles from the production point); mail order catalogs often use this ap-proach. Other strategies are commonly used as well. For instance, when a product is advertised on national television at $5.99, it usu-ally means that transportation costs are being averaged for all con-sumers. People near the production point are paying more than the actual costs, distant people less.

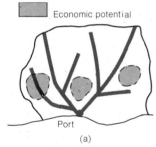

Economic potential

Port

(a)

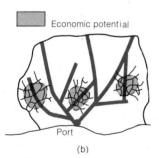

Economic potential

Port

(b)

FIGURE 11.5

The Evolution of a Road Network Penetrating an Underdeveloped Area: (a) space searching and (b) exploitation of economic potential.

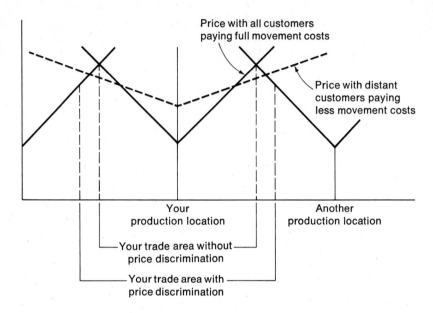

FIGURE 11.6
An Illustration of How a
Producer Can Increase
the Market Area by Redis-
tributing Charges for
Movement Costs.

Price with all customers
paying full movement costs

Price with distant
customers paying
less movement costs

Your
production location

Another
production location

Your trade area without
price discrimination

Your trade area with
price discrimination

The practice of discriminating in favor of more distant customers in setting prices is in fact a classic way to try to extend one's
market area. Presumably, a person at an in-between place will buy
from the marketer offering the lower price. The market area will be
bounded by the intersection of one's "price funnel" (see Section
5.5) with those of surrounding marketers (see Figure 11.6).

This may be one of the reasons that prices are generally high
not only at *very* distant places (such as Alaska or Hawaii) but also
at centers of production and marketing.* In fact, prices often decline away from the center more slowly than do the opportunities
for earning income. This makes the periphery of a high-price center
a frequent locus of economic disadvantage.

11.4   EXAMPLES

Locational environments are indicated dramatically by maps of
movement networks, which course through our areas like capil-
laries carrying oxygen from the lungs to the body. In general, they
resemble the map of population density, both because they serve
that population's needs and because the opportunities presented by

---

*   Another reason for relatively high prices at centers of economic activity is the high
cost of using land in an area where competition has made it expensive.

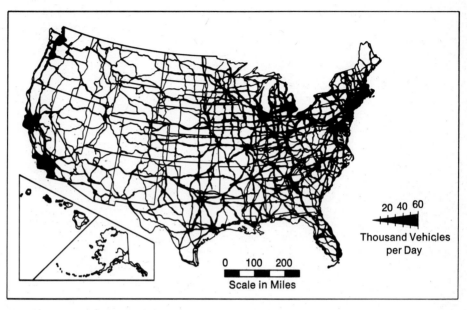

FIGURE 11.7
An Example of a Movement Network in the United States: highway traffic flows. Compare the densities in this pattern with the population distribution shown in Figure 2.1.

accessibility to movement networks usually attract more people and activities.

A careful look at Figure 11.7 will show how the traffic flowing along American roads thins out as it gets farther away from the urban centers. We have seen this distance-decay effect before. In Chapter 5 von Thünen's model of agricultural land revolved around the cost of moving products to market; the crops involving the most movement per acre or hectare were located closest to the market town. In Chapter 6 we constructed isodapanes of equal transportation cost in order to choose a location for a new industry; the dominant concern was with the way a greater distance from the location of a resource or market meant greater operating costs for the industry. In Chapter 7 we found that the pattern of many activities of the same type depends on the trade-offs between movement costs and economies of scale and agglomeration. The idea is a familiar one—and a basic one.

Consider, for example, the common practice in East Asia of using human wastes, or "night soil," as fertilizer:

> An important tie between countryside and city is the fertilizer which the latter provides. Since the amount of night soil is most abundant in the vicinity of cities and large towns it is the land closest to the urban centers which is most heavily fertilized and yields the largest returns. Thorp writes: "Every large city and town which I have observed in China is surrounded by a more or less irregular ring of very fertile soils

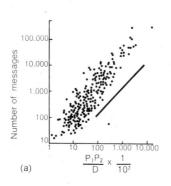
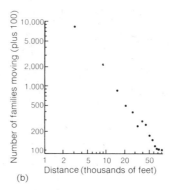
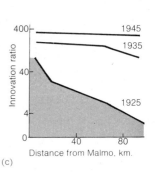

(a)   (b)   (c)

FIGURE 11.8

Examples of "Distance Decay" Effects: (a) telephone messages between 311 pairs of cities in the U.S. in 1940; (b) family migration between locations in Cleveland, 1933–1935; and (c) the adoption of an innovation (radio receivers) in southern Sweden, related to distance from the source of the innovation, the city of Malmo.

A long trip

A moderate trip

A quick trip

FIGURE 11.9

Lines of Equal Travel Time in Seattle.

which usually extends at least as far as a man may walk and return in one day." The fertility rings round the city walls where market gardens occupy much of the land. Here the soils are as black and rich as typical chernozems. On the North China Plain one can often tell when he is approaching a city by the improved appearance of the crops. Thorp suggests, as a rule of thumb, that for the first few kilometers around each city the fertility of the soil roughly varies inversely with the distance, or perhaps the square of the distance from the city.

TREWARTHA, GLEN, "CHINESE CITIES: ORIGINS AND FUNCTIONS."[2]

This kind of distance effect seems to apply to a very wide range of kinds of human activity—freight movements, migration, telephone traffic, retail shopping preference, the spread of new ideas, and many other things that are a part of our everyday lives. Figure 11.8 displays just a few of the many examples that are available. It is especially worth noting Figure 11.8(c), which shows that distance has some effect on how our lives change as new ideas and products are discovered.

But we know that distance is usually measured in our own minds by the time or cost of movement, not by a measuring tape stretched out on the ground. Figure 11.9, for instance, shows how, in peak-hour traffic in a city, lines of equal travel time from the center of the city are much more irregular than the concentric circles of actual straight-line distance.

And those of us who have rented trailers for cross-country trips know that, although the base rental rate is higher for longer distances, the total rate sometimes reflects other factors. For instance, in 1975 a trailer destined for Texas from Baltimore in late August involved a sizeable surcharge because Texas was oversupplied with rental trailers. Too many were arriving; too few were leaving. The total rental rate, therefore, would have been less for a longer trip to an area that had a shortage of trailers.

11.5 A RECONSIDERATION

This chapter has emphasized kinds of moves that are from one well-defined location to another—point to point. But this is misleadingly simple. Origins or destinations of movements may be at points, along lines, or in extensive areas. Table 11.1 displays the possibilities, with an example of each. Selecting a least-effort path is a different kind of problem for each of the nine cases, but distance is a useful surrogate of effort in every one of them.

It should be recognized, too, that the gravity model does a better job of explaining movement behavior in a stable, "business as usual" situation than in a time of social upheaval: economic crises, wars, famines. It has been said that the model fits best when people "are not doing anything interesting and are squinted at from afar."[3] When major events change the direction of economies or societies (and these are the causes of most instances of large-scale international migration), it is hard to anticipate what "attractiveness" will mean.

TABLE 11.1
Types of Moves

Origin	Destination		
	Point	*Line*	*Area*
Point	Individual trip from home to work	Sewage flow from a home to a sanitation line	Radio broadcast to a listening area
Line	Natural gas from a distribution system to a home	A freeway interchange	A canal irrigation system
Area	Timber from logging area to a sawmill	Commuters from a suburb to a highway	The expansion of a trade area

MAJOR CONCEPTS AND TERMS

For definitions, see the Glossary.

Distance decay	Interaction potential	Spatial symmetry
Factor mobility	Modal choice	Transfer costs
Gravity model	Spatial price equilibrium	

Footnotes for Chapter 11

1. Richardson, H. W. "Agglomeration Potential," *Journal of Regional Science*, vol. 14: 1974.

2. Trewartha, Glen. "Chinese Cities: Origins and Functions," *Annals of the Association of American Geographers*, vol 42: 1952, p. 86.

3. O'Sullivan, P. "On Gravity and Eruptions," *The Professional Geographers*, vol. 29: 1977, p. 185.

CHAPTER 12

LINKAGES AND WELL-BEING

Why does economic interaction take place? Most basically, because people at one place find that they can get things that they want more cheaply and easily from somewhere else. This frees money and time for other things that they want as well. As a result, interaction makes a contribution to their standard of living. The potential to interact with other places—by means of linkages with them—thus represents a very substantial kind of opportunity, and the linkages themselves become valued items.

12.1 SITUATIONS

12.1.1 Snowbound

It seemed like a good idea at the time. Your family's vacation home in the Finger Lakes country in central New York state. Wintertime. Nearby ski slopes. A big fireplace. No telephone. Peace and quiet.

But the third day after you arrived for a one-week stay, it snowed heavily. You called off that day's skiing jaunt, put another log on the fireplace, and got out a couple of good paperbacks. No problem. You could ski tomorrow.

On the fourth day, it was still snowing heavily. And on the fifth day. By then, you were running short on bread, beer, and reading material; so you decided to head into town and restock. But after spending nearly an hour cleaning snow and ice off your car, you realized that the little road to the main highway nearly a mile away was blocked by snow drifts, some of them nearly 10 feet deep. Back to the cabin to put on another log.

The sixth day. Still snowing. Your food is running out. The water pipes have frozen. The electric power went out last night; you don't know why. You are out of clean underwear. It's getting pretty important for you to get in contact with the rest of the world.

You decide to walk out to the main highway, although you didn't bring any outdoor clothes except for ski clothes. It's a long way, and it takes you more than an hour to get there. You find the highway covered with snow. Not even any tracks. Obviously no one has been along that way for some time. The nearest town is 6 miles away. As far as you know, the cabins between here and there are all vacant for the winter. It's too far to try to walk.

Discouraged and more than a little uneasy, you trudge back to your cabin. Your first move is to turn on the radio to find a weather report. The batteries are dead. You are alone.

12.1.2   *The New Interstate Highways*

Your family owns a restaurant in Cobleskill, New York, a small town west of Albany. Although you are proud of the good food it serves, you have never been able to see much future in it for you. The town has been off the beaten track, and you are looking for a job that offers possibilities for growth and expansion.

But after a long and uncertain period of political maneuvering, it has been announced that a new interstate highway is to be built, connecting Binghamton and Albany (see Figure 12.1). As you look at the map, you see that the new highway will pass near Cobleskill, and it seems to you that a lot of people driving between northern New England and the West and South in the United States may use this route to bypass the New York and Philadelphia metropolitan areas. Besides that, it will put Cobleskill within 30 or 40 minutes of the Albany-Schenectady area, which has 300,000 or so permanent residents.

All of a sudden, Cobleskill doesn't look so bad. You start talking to your parents about buying some land east of town, near the caverns that may be a tourist attraction for people on their way through on the new interstate. You see a country restaurant as part of a larger roadside complex—a specialty food store, gifts, a landscaped play and picnic area. At least three stars in the Mobil travel guide. A favorite spot for people from the Albany area. The best eating place between Pennsylvania and Massachusetts for interstate highway travelers. Now, this is more like the kind of future you want.

FIGURE   12.1

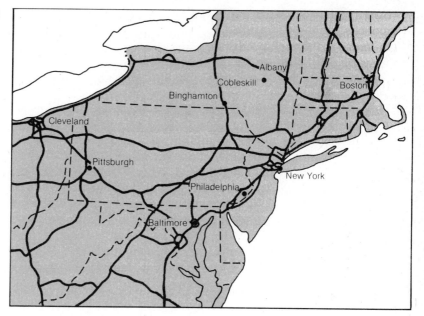

12.1.3   *The New Frontier*

Alaska has always had oil. Quite a while ago, in fact, the U.S. Navy set aside a sizeable part of it as a petroleum reserve, just in case of an emergency. But Alaska didn't need much oil, and there was no way to get the oil to where the consumers were: in the "lower 48" states. Now, the Alyeska pipeline has been built, connecting the north slope oil fields with the southwestern Alaskan coast, where tankers can pick up oil year-round.

As a student of the old West, you have always thought you would like a frontier situation—excitement, opportunity, rewards for flexibility and quick thinking. For several years, you considered taking off for Australia; but you weren't too eager to become an opal miner or hired labor on a sheep-raising "station."

Maybe Alaska is a possibility. Everything you read indicates that the pipeline construction activities and oil royalties will mean a lot of money in a state with not very many people, and a gas pipeline and gas royalties seem sure to follow. The future is uncertain, but it seems ripe for an entrepreneur.

Off you go to Alaska. Your first idea is to import Mexican food items for the Texans and Oklahomans maintaining the Alyeska pipeline and getting ready to build another pipeline south from the Naval Petroleum Reservoir on the north slope. With the help of a local bank, you soon have three thriving restaurants and a contract to supply chili and other items for the company that will build the second pipeline. And you are already getting ready for the day the new pipeline is finished. Working with a couple of engineers from a major oil company, you have come up with a way to carry large quantities of nonperishable consumer goods on oil tankers that would otherwise be returning empty to Alaska, where people are willing to pay very high prices for food, clothing, beverages, and other items. As you know from your studies, the people who made money with minimal risk in the old West were the storekeepers, not the miners or the cowboys.

12.2   BASIC IDEAS

We can divide our ideas about the advantages of interaction into two categories: (1) the benefits themselves, wherever interaction takes place; and (2) the factors that give a particular place an advantage in reaping the benefits.

The primary benefit from interaction (in an economic sense) is that it allows a place to become more specialized in doing those things that it can do best. For example, a farm town in Kentucky need not raise its own lettuce, because it can concentrate on tobacco, some of which will end up in the pipes of Californians. In theory, this kind of division of labor provides all the things that people want at the lowest possible prices. A product or service would not be provided from the lowest-cost area of production only when the cost of interaction with buyers is too high (for the consumer, the price reflects production prices, not production costs, but competition makes prices proportional to costs.) At any rate, in a competitive situation,* in theory the activity will concentrate at the location from which it can undersell anyone else, and consumers will be rewarded by relatively low prices for the things they want. The greater the variation from place to place in the conditions of production (such as natural resources and labor skills), the greater will be the savings to the buyers from this kind of specialization.

This causes a pattern of exchange to develop,† in which each partner is not only benefiting from the higher level of consumption allowed by the lower prices; it is also profiting from the chance to develop economies of scale and other advantages of specialization

---

* Meaning that new providers can enter the competition without difficulty and that consumers have full information about their options (as you know by now).

† See sections 4.3 and 8.3.1, especially Figure 4.1.

in its area. This pattern enhances the area's comparative advantages and makes it more difficult for new areas to become competitive.‡

In Chapters 8 and 10 we found that there is a further benefit as a corollary of these advantages: a relationship between trade and the economic growth of a place (although the relationship is a complex one). Trade is essential to an "economic base." In addition, it helps to create a local demand for new products and services that may eventually be supplied by local entrepreneurs. And it assures that the items needed for local production activities are supplied and that the results of the activities have access to a wide range of markets.

These substantial benefits are more available to some locations than to others. One factor, clearly, is the nature and degree of the *comparative advantage* a place has, as discussed in Chapter 10. More comparative advantages improve the chances for interaction. But there are two other important conditions as well. One is *complementarity*. Remember that the most basic economic meaning of interaction is trade—and *trade* is a word with a very clear meaning. A person who wants to trade comic books or bubblegum cards looks for someone else who has some different cards that he or she wants. Each trading partner must *want* something that the other has to offer, and each must *have* enough to offer so that an agreement can be worked out. Consequently, whether the trade is books for rice, computers for cars, or recreation for clothes, a place is better off if its comparative advantage provides it with exactly those goods or services that are desired by other places offering the things that the local area lacks. It is not much help to have plenty of something that nobody wants any more, or that is wanted only by places or people that have little to offer in return. Supposedly, the use of money instead of barter reduces the importance of complementarity a little because it facilitates the arrangement of very complex multipartner trades. But the concept continues to be a useful way to explain many of the exchange patterns that we can observe in our world: they show a marked degree of reciprocity.

The other condition that helps a place to realize the benefits of interaction is *relative location*. We know from Chapter 11 that interaction is easier between places that are near each other—in space, time, movement costs. And we learned even earlier, in Chapter 5, that comparative advantage is related to *where* one place is

---

‡ When, as in the real world, competition is less than perfect, economic decision makers may respond to other influences on their well-being than minimizing prices for consumers. Specialization, for instance, may reflect attempts in places that are not least-cost sites to inhibit competition from other places that would produce lower cost items if they could just get a start (see Chapter 13).

with respect to others: for example, the nearness of a farm to the market town.

For convenience, let's refer to this concept of the nearness—or proximity or connectiveness—of a place to "where the action is" as its *accessibility*. An accessible place usually has more opportunities for interaction than an inaccessible place because the effort required for interaction is less. But accessibility is a relative concept, not an absolute one. It has meaning only when several things are clear: accessible to/from what? For what purpose? For whom? For what time period? Accessibility may refer to the ease of getting to a movie theater from home, the time it takes to get to or from an airport or an office, or the cost of distributing products from a factory to retail stores. It may be focused on one point of origin and one point of destination, or it can refer to many. It may mean convenience in using a communication or transportation system that connects with many places. But once it is defined, having more accessibility generally increases the chances of interaction—and thus of getting its benefits (also see Box 12.1).

BOX 12.1   REASONS FOR COMMODITY FLOWS

Edward L. Ullman, an American geographer, spent many years studying the movement of freight between regions in the United States. He concluded that three conditions were the major ones in explaining the pattern of interaction between places (when that interaction involves commodities):

1. **Complementarity:** movements are stimulated by a fortuitous combination of a surplus in one region and a deficit in another: wood or steel, for example.

2. **Intervening opportunity:** complementarity is a reason for a commodity movement between two regions only if there is no intervening region with a deficit (to serve as the destination) or with a surplus (to supply the deficit region from a shorter distance). An intervening opportunity is a kind of "spatial sponge, soaking up potential interaction between complementary places."*

3. **Transferability:** some commodities are more cumbersome or expensive to move than others. Since this difficulty gets translated into transportation cost, a flow of freight will probably be less if the commodity is less easily transferable; the cost to consumers at the destination point will be high enough to encourage a search for substitutes.

These conditions are reflected repeatedly in patterns of trade, but it is worth noting that if intervening opportunities are arranged with a certain amount of spatial regularity, they may encourage interaction by causing networks of shorter links to develop. And such a network—for instance, a railroad system—can help to reduce the impact of transferability as a constraint.

* Abler, Adams, and Gould. *Spatial Organization,* p. 194.

12.3 ELABORATING THE BASIC IDEAS

12.3.1 Factors Influencing Trade

The preceding section mentioned three factors as the keys to establishing and maintaining economic linkages between places: comparative advantage, complementarity, and accessibility. Although the concepts are simple enough, applying them to real-world decision making is considerably more complicated, and some of the extensions are worth thinking about.

Comparative Advantage In economic theory, comparative advantage is often illustrated by the productivity of labor. If a typical worker in Transylvania can make 50 percent more refrigerators a day than a typical worker in Atlantis, Transylvania has a comparative advantage in producing refrigerators, and the best way of organizing an economy (from the point of view of efficiency and low prices) is for the Transylvanians to be the refrigerator makers. This way of judging comparative advantage, however, is too limited to be a trustworthy predictor, for several reasons. For example, the wages of a typical worker may not be the same in both places—even if they are equally productive—which has an effect on comparisons of the production cost of a refrigerator; the workers in Transylvania might be better able than those in Atlantis to produce other things than refrigerators; and Transylvania might be a lot farther away from the markets for refrigerators than Atlantis is.

This last qualification indicates that accessibility can be a part of a location's comparative advantage. For some port cities, transport junctions, and other favored spots, it can in fact be enough of an advantage to support the local economy by itself. Similarly, complementarity affects the benefits from comparative advantage. Having special advantages in supplying such precious items as oil and brain power means a great deal more to a place economically than being well endowed with gravel or horsemanship.

Complementarity The intricate reciprocity of trade in a world where currency is more acceptable than most commodities can be described by an expanded version of the input-output tables discussed in Chapter 10. Table 12.1 suggests how an understanding of *interregional* input-output relationships can be developed. Linkages exist not only between one place and another, or between agriculture and industry in one place. They exist between one sector in one place and a sector in a second place (for example, agriculture in Iowa to household consumers in New York).

TABLE 12.1 Interregional Input-Output Linkages

		Area 1				Area 2				Area 3				Area 4			
		Agr.	*Ind.*	*Ser.*	*Hshld.*	*Agr.*	*Ind.*	*Ser.*	*Hshld.*	*Agr.*	*Ind.*	*Ser.*	*Hshld.*	*Agr.*	*Ind.*	*Ser.*	*Hshld.*
Area 1	Agr.																
	Ind.																
	Serv.																
Area 2	Agr.																
	Ind.																
	Serv.																
Area 3	Agr.																
	Ind.																
	Serv.																
Area 4	Agr.																
	Ind.																
	Serv.																

Seen in this way, the concept of an economic base becomes a part of an input-output framework that recognizes different *places* as well as different sectors of production and consumption. We can observe the extent to which agriculture, industry, or services in Area 1 are destined for consumers in other areas, and we can identify complementarities in the specialized activities of different places. With this as a starting point, we can go on to estimate the economic effects of a change at one place on other locations. For instance, a new factory in a small town in one area may call for an increase in the number of bankers and lawyers in a large city in a neighboring region (see Section 12.3.4).

Accessibility It is obvious that if it cannot afford delivery trucks with warming ovens, a pizza delivery service needs to be close to a lot of potential customers, because delivering cold pizzas is not a very good way to build business. In other words, the location where the pizzas are made needs to be accessible to the market for the pizzas. From the point of view of the person driving the delivery car, closeness means a short time of travel, and this has two dimensions: distance and the nature of the transportation system (if an entrance to a freeway is only one minute away, hot pizza may be able to be delivered much farther away than if the surroundings are stop-lights and congested streets).

In Chapter 11 we considered the distance dimension, and we are already familiar with the idea that economic activities (from pizza parlors to steel plants) often choose meeting points of transportation links as their locations.[§] But the concept of a network as a "graph" (see Box 12.2) is a powerful one—and not so obvious. Each place is enmeshed in a pattern of linkages, and its location in the web affects its opportunities for interaction: central versus peripheral, on a main route or "out in the sticks," tied directly to several networks versus limited to one.

"Centrality" of location, though very important, is thus not always immediately obvious. We know that the place that is the exact center of a land area—a country or a continent—is seldom the center of a market (remember Figure 11.1), a communication network, or the other things that interest us in this book. The potential for interaction involves a gravitational pull (complementarity is an example) as well as the cost and inconvenience of overcoming distance.

12.3.2   *The Evolution of Linkage Systems*

If movement networks are so important a part of the advantages available to a decision maker at a particular location, how do they develop? The best-known model, based on a careful study of the history of Ghana and analogous to the "stages of growth" suggested by W. W. Rostow in 1960,[1] was proposed by Taaffe, Morrill, and Gould.[2] It suggests four stages (see Figure 12.2):

1.   Initially a few scattered nodes have little contact with each other, simply interacting for short distances with their immediate surroundings.

2.   As the more vigorous of these nodes extend their search for trade (or political control), links develop between them and more distant nodes, and the more successful of the initial centers become larger.

3.   As interaction continues to develop, the terminal centers continue to grow, intermediate centers appear, and lateral connections also appear, linking nodes that had previously been out of contact.

4.   As lateral connections proliferate, some of the linkages are upgraded to carry especially heavy traffic.

[§]   See, for example, Section 6.3.2.

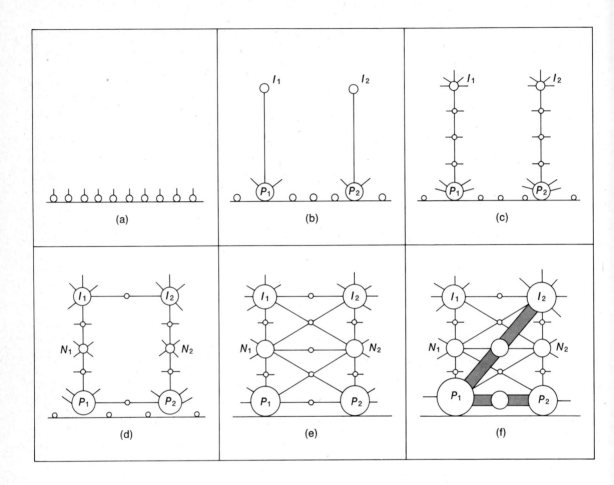

FIGURE 12.2
A Model of the Development of a System of Linkages: (a) scattered ports; (b) penetration lines and port communication; (c) development of feeders; (d) beginnings of interconnection; (e) complete interconnection; and (f) emergence of high-priority main routes.

There are serious questions about whether any kind of development always takes place in discrete stages, and the evolution of a network does not always proceed as an extension inland from coastal nodes; but the concepts imbedded in the model are very useful. First, new links develop as a response to a search by someone for benefits from interaction. Second, there is a great deal of inertia to a pattern of linkages once it is established. The skeleton provided by the early stages of a network has a strong influence on the morphology of the "mature" network. Third, the network develops different categories of links—from a few with a very large capacity to a great many with a very small capacity to carry traffic (see Section 11.3.4; note especially the similarity between Figure 12.2 and Figure 11.3).

From the point of view of an economic decision maker, this means several important things. For example, new links are valuable items, both because they facilitate interaction and because they influence the form of the network as it evolves thereafter. The fortunes of many towns have risen or fallen with decisions about the path of a new rail line or interstate highway. And the model emphasizes the fact that networks are changing things, not static ones. We can be certain that any network we observe now will be different in significant ways twenty years from now. Anticipating these changes is an important part of making good long-range locational decisions.

12.3.3   *Noncommodity Movements*

As Section 11.3.5 suggested, because freight movements are such handy examples of economic interaction—tangible, measurable, and with market values attached—it is easy to forget that linkages of other kinds are important as well. Movements of people, for instance, are critical; a modern business executive can hardly afford to live at a location that is hours away from a major airport (in fact, access to linkages is usually essential in attracting top managerial talent to a location). Sales representatives circulate through their territories. Consumers travel to shopping areas. Harvesting equipment follows the wheat harvest in the Great Plains of the United States (see Box 12.3). A little less obviously, money moves from place to place, often in a direction that is the reverse of the orientation of flows of goods and people—money from wages, purchases, profits.

And messages move, too. Since communication systems such as telephones, the postal service, radio, and television are so universally available in the United States, differences in accessibility to messages are relatively small (faster mail service, more telephone lines, variations in the quality of the local media).[II] But they can be significant. Suppose, for example, that a bit of information reported in *The New York Times* has the potential to stimulate a new economic idea: a new product or service or activity. The few people who will take advantage of this opportunity will have to act quickly. Who has the advantage: the person who gets the paper delivered at 11 PM the night before at the apartment in New York City and reads it during the TV news or the person on a small, remote Hawaiian island who either waits for the paper to come by mail or has to depend on a local newspaper to reprint the item? Access to networks that carry messages is important because information and ideas have value.

[II]   This is so unless face-to-face contact is essential for communicating effectively, which is sometimes the case.

In general, since transportation and communication are to some degree substitutable, it is possible to compensate for inaccessibility to transportation networks (which may offer advantages such as quiet, scenery, and innocence) by assuring access to communication networks. An international hotel reservation service that operates by telephone can be as efficiently located in Tennessee as in New York, for instance. The key is to realize that for some activities communication is more important than transportation, although for others it is the reverse. And, for a precious few, such as writing poetry or novels, neither may be essential.

BOX 12.2 A NETWORK AS A GRAPH

It is sometimes useful to reduce a transportation or communication network to its sparest form: a pattern of nodes and links—dots and lines. Two dots are either directly connected or they are not. And in a surprisingly large number of instances, it is useful to measure the distance between two nodes as the smallest number of links that can be traversed between them: the minimum number of stretches between traffic lights in getting from one city apartment building to another, the minimum number of stops on a subway, the minimum number of stops on an airplane from one city to another (see Section 11.3.2).

In such a case, we can measure accessibility in two ways that seem too simple to be at all respectable. Consider the little network—four nodes and four links—illustrated by Figure 1.

(1) We can simply count the least number of links between each pair of nodes (the shortest path distance): or

	1	2	3	4
From 1	0	1	1	2
2	1	0	1	2
3	1	1	0	1
4	2	2	1	0

(2) We can even more simply note whether two nodes are directly connected or not, showing a connection as a 1 and a lack by a 0:

	1	2	3	4
From 1	0	1	1	0
2	1	0	1	0
3	1	1	0	1
4	0	0	1	0

By adding up the numbers in the rows or columns of the shortest path "matrix," we can arrive at an inaccessibility score for each node. The smallest score means the most accessible place (#3). The second table of numbers, a "connectivity matrix," tells us the number of ways we can get from any one node to any other *in one step*. By using matrix algebra to multiply this matrix by itself (like squaring a number), we can arrive at the number of alternative paths in two steps. With another multiplication, we find out the three-step possibilities. And so on. This provides a way to identify indirect connections as well as direct ones, and it can be converted

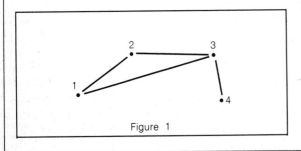

Figure 1

The locations that have the advantage of unusual accessibility to transportation networks are most likely to get the benefits from the kinds of interaction that depend on transportation facilities. But places that are at a disadvantage in this respect can still have locational advantages for interaction with people and ideas.

12.3.4 *Linkages and Economic Growth*

It is clear that what happens in one economic activity affects others: an increase in its level of operation or a decrease. Input-output analysis was developed primarily to trace these kinds of effects. It

---

BOX 12.2 (cont'd.)

into a powerful accessibility index (see Section 12.6).

For example, the highway network in a hilly part of southeastern Oklahoma is approximately as shown in Figure 2 (solid lines):

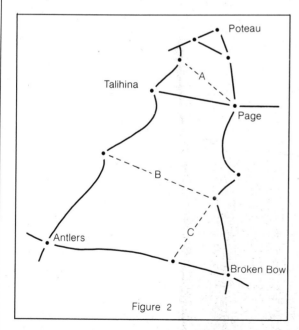

Figure 2

Suppose that the state government, concerned about the relative inaccessibility of

the towns to each other, proposes to build one new state highway in a particular four-year period. Three routes are suggested: *A*, *B*, and *C*. Which contributes the most to reducing inaccessibility, and which nodes benefit the most from each of the alternatives? Displaying the road network as a shortest path matrix, finding the inaccessibility scores for each node and adding them to get an overall index of inaccessibility, it turns out that *B* reduces inaccessibility the most (about 6 percent). *A* and *C*, which cut the network into sections of less equal size, have less of an impact. As might be expected, in all three cases the nodes that serve as the origin and destination of the new link show the biggest improvement in accessibility.

This illustrates the very real importance of linkages between nodes in establishing locational advantage. With *B*, Talihina is the most accessible place to the other nodes shown. With no new road or with *A* or *C*, Page is the most accessible.

This kind of study can be made more realistic by weighting the nodes or links rather than by keeping them constant in size. And it is possible for links to be "one-way" rather than the two-way connections considered here.

makes sense, then, that economic growth might be efficiently brought about by investing in a key activity that will spread the benefits to others—by buying more of their products, for example. The problem is to pick the right target. Such an activity (or sector, such as the manufacture of durable goods) is called a *growth pole*.

In the same way, as interregional input-output analysis shows, places are linked to each other, and an attractive alternative for improving an economy in a large area might be to invest in a key place that will spread the benefits. Such a place is called a *growth center*. Again, the problem is to identify the place.

This indicates an important kind of benefit that results from a linkage of places. Anything good that happens to one will often help the others as well. But there is still a great deal of uncertainty

---

BOX 12.3   MOVEMENTS OF PEOPLE

Movements of people usually occur because the people want to enhance their well-being. Our own movements include many examples of this:

the journey from home to work

the journeys from home to places where we buy goods and services

interaction with friends and relatives

business trips

vacation trips

migration to accept a job somewhere else

migration after retirement to a pleasant place to live

Some of these movements are temporary, and some are permanent. Some are repeated movements; some happen only once.

In general, the concepts we have considered about the best activity for a location (Chapter 5) and systems of activities at systems of locations (Chapter 7) are concerned with recurring temporary movements. Our concepts about the best location for an activity (Chapter 6) combine the permanent move of an activity with subsequent recurring moves of resources, products, and—at a local scale—labor from home to work. In all these cases, a kind of gravitational effect can be said to apply: attractive, highly valued locations exert a pull; but distance usually reduces that pull.

There are several special cases, however, that are not fully accounted for by such a simple summary:

1. **Transient movements:** movement itself is a central part of many people's lives. Migrant labor, for instance, follows the harvest season northward in the spring and summer. Truck drivers, airline stewardesses, and traveling salespersons also move to make a living. And many career tracks, from military service to employment in a large corporation, include an expectation of relocation from time to time.

how this process works, how many benefits are distributed, how far they spread and to whom, and how the benefits that flow through the linkages compare with the negative effects. Some of this uncertainty may mean that growth center effects vary for different kinds of areas: developed, developing, developed but lagging, or pioneer regions.

In considering growth centers, the usual focus is on a region that has economic problems: unemployment, low incomes, and so on. The idea is that rather than spreading scarce development money to so many cities, counties, and towns that it will have little impact, the investment should be concentrated at one or a few growth centers, selected by studying the kinds of linkages identified in input-output tables and central place studies. Developing

---

BOX 12.3 (cont'd.)

2. **The transiency of locational opportunity:** many locational opportunities are temporary. For example, the construction industry moves from one project to another. Oil exploration shifts from one promising area to another. People with certain kinds of skills and personal predilections spend a lot of their lives hopping from one opportunity to another, even when large distances are involved. This is perhaps especially characteristic of a frontier situation, where advantages are fluid, information is uncertain, and people are opportunistic.

3. **The appeal of distance:** as least-effort beings, we generally act to travel short distances rather than long ones. Paradoxically, however, we often attribute special merit to long trips, at least partly *because* they require greater effort and are therefore more unusual. A vacation trip to a far-off place contributes to social status. A long religious pilgrimage is a demonstration of special piety. A long journey to a family reunion or a college homecoming gets more attention than a short one.

4. **A "push" stimulus for moving:** movement may be the result of a push rather than a pull. Population migrations due to famine or war, for example (or movement of investment money to escape a new tax law), are sometimes affected very little by the cost of overcoming distance.

5. **Differences between people:** some kinds of people are more sensitive to the costs of distance than others. A careful understanding of movement behavior might require a different model for each category of the population (young versus old, one cultural group versus another, high income versus low, family-oriented versus wanderlust-inclined, and so on).

agglomeration economies with this kind of help, these centers will be able to compete with locations outside the region for new economic activities that will provide jobs, income, and an increased demand within the region for the goods and services it generates.

There seems little doubt that an aggressive growth-center strategy can cause economic growth in the growth centers themselves, but the *spread effects* on other places in the region are less certain. There are two main reasons for this. First, the growth centers may in fact hurt their surrounding areas economically by increasing their own relative advantages (making it harder for a town that is not a growth center to compete). For instance, as wages rise in the favored centers, high-quality labor in the region may be drawn there as if by a magnet (see Section 11.3.5). This is sometimes called a *backwash effect*. Second, each growth center is linked economically with other centers outside the region, and many of the benefits may flow along these lines—laterally or up the central place hierarchy rather than down it. A study of the spread of industrial employment/unemployment in the United States, for example, showed that a change in Pittsburgh was more quickly felt in Detroit than in nearby Morgantown.[3]

12.4   *EXAMPLES*

12.4.1   *An Isolated City*

It is difficult to realize how much a city depends on links with other places to meet its needs unless that city is suddenly cut off from those other places. After World War II, Berlin—the prewar capitol of Germany—was divided into four sectors for occupation by representatives of the United States, Great Britain, France, and the Soviet Union. The rest of Germany was similarly divided, with Berlin ending up deep in the Soviet zone of occupation. On June 24, 1948, the three sectors of Berlin that later became West Berlin were sealed off by the Soviet Union from road or rail contact with Western Europe or the surrounding Soviet zone. The options were three: capitulate to the political demands of the Soviet Union; do without any items that could not be provided from within the beseiged sectors; or find another way to supply the city's needs.

It was immediately clear that the Western sectors could not get along without supplies from outside Berlin. The 2.5 million residents could produce only a very small part of their own food and fuel. By wintertime, in an area where winters are bitterly cold, the situation would be impossible. Logistics experts estimated that by fall the sectors would have a minimum daily requirement of more than 4,000 tons of coal, food, and other essentials (such as medicines). This would include a bare minimum of 1,200–1,400 tons of food per day (about one pound of food per person) and allow *no* fuel for heating private homes and almost nothing in the way of industrial raw materials. 4,500 tons a day would provide Berliners with a few briquettes of coal a day for warmth (it was estimated that 700 tons of coal a day for domestic use would allow each household a total of 340 pounds to last the entire winter).

The American, British, and French governments decided that the only alternative was air supply, although in 1948 the job seemed virtually impossible. Using the cargo planes available then (one kind having 3 tons of freight capacity and the other 10 tons), it would be necessary for a plane to take off or land from one of West Berlin's two airports about once every minute, 24 hours a day, for as long as the blockade lasted—just to meet minimum requirements. These planes would have to move in and out of Berlin in a 20-mile-wide corridor without running into each other. And the supply levels on good weather days would have to be high enough to compensate for problems when the weather was bad.

By September 1948, the airlift was operating smoothly and meeting the minimum needs. On the best day, 896 airplanes brought in nearly 7,000 tons of coal, food, and other supplies— with a takeoff or landing every 48 seconds. On May 12, 1949, after the western sectors survived the fall, winter, and spring, the blockade was lifted. But West Berlin, still cut off from free interaction with the area around it that would normally provide food, fuel, and raw materials, remains heavily dependent on the expensive transport of basic needs from a hundred or more miles away.

12.4.2 *The Pattern of Trade Flows*

Most often in the "real world," flows of commodities are heaviest between: (1) places with more highly developed economies; (2) places with complementary relative advantages; and (3) places that are relatively close to each other.

For instance, even considering oil exports from the Middle East, the major importers and exporters in international trade are the United States, Japan, and countries in Western Europe, usually trading with each other. The share of international trade represented by exports from less-developed countries, not including oil, has steadily declined. For several decades, international trade has increasingly emphasized manufactured goods, exchanged among specialized countries with a high level of economic development, rather than movements of raw materials from resource-rich less-developed countries to manufacturing centers elsewhere.

And even the flows of raw materials and agricultural commodities are often the greatest between more affluent countries. An example is the traditional relationship between the United States and Canada—close together, with no intervening opportunities for international trade. As the United States has consumed its own supplies of industrial raw materials, it has turned to Canada—rich in ores, fuels, and wood products—to supply many of its needs. Similarly, the United States has become a food supplier to countries such as Japan and the Soviet Union.

Within a country, the effect of distance on trade is often marked, especially when the economy is focused on a core of activity. The major exceptions are commodities such as California lettuce and wine that are produced in highly specialized locales and that bring a high enough price to pay for movement costs.

Internationally (and sometimes internally), this effect is modified by the kinds of boundary effects already discussed, and it is also conditioned by the frequent use of sea transport for bulk commodities (which is very slow but very inexpensive). If distance is measured by freight rates rather than by miles or hours, countries

---

BOX 12.4   IN THE MULTINATIONAL FIRM

When we think about linkages between countries, we usually visualize one company in, let's say, Canada and another company in the Netherlands. But many important kinds of international economic interaction take place between affiliates of the same company: a *multinational* corporation. Many firms, such as International Telephone and Telegraph (ITT) and Unilever, operate in several countries through subsidiary and affiliated companies.

With production costs and tax rates varying from country to country, this offers the parent firm some significant economic advantages. A product can be manufactured in the country where the costs are lowest. Then, showing transfers within the company in the most advantageous way, many of the profits can be reported in the country where the taxes are the lowest.

Since some of these multinational firms are very large (with annual sales larger than the gross national product of most countries), their decisions can have a major effect on the countries in which they choose to operate; and some observers have been critical of their political and economic influence, which can be expected to be oriented toward what is good for the company and not necessarily what is good for a country. Consequently, some kind of international regulation of their activity is likely to develop, but their role in international trade will almost certainly continue to grow.

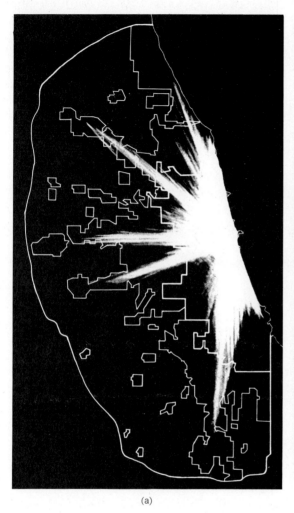 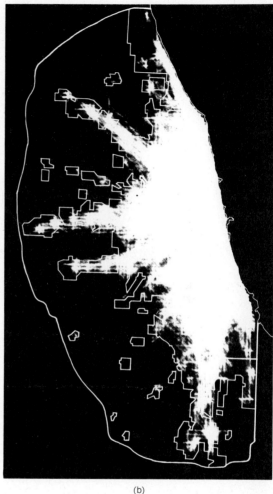

(a)   (b)

FIGURE 12.3

Travel "Desire Lines" in Chicago: (a) by mass transit and (b) by automobile. Each line connects a traveler's trip origin directly with the destination. Note that the pattern is "spikier" for mass transit trips, where travelers have less flexibility in choosing trip end points.

separated by 3,000 miles of ocean may in fact be closer together than if they were separated by 500 miles of land, crossed by several national boundaries.

An important trend is the replacement of commodity movements by foreign investment (factor movement). For instance, German exports of Volkswagens to the United States have dropped because the relatively high purchase prices, raised by currency revaluations, have hurt sales. The response has been to invest German money in a plant in Pennsylvania to assemble Volkswagens for the American market. Even when production costs are not a factor, such foreign investment is often a way to avoid tariffs on manufactured products (see also Box 12.4).

FIGURE 12.4
Commuting fields in
Washington.

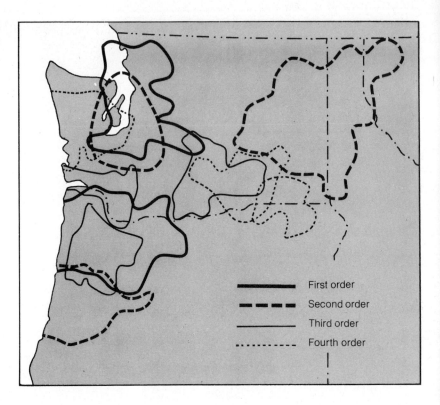

First order
Second order
Third order
Fourth order

12.4.3 *The Pattern of People Flows#*

People movement contributes to well-being in a variety of ways, from vacations to job-related moves across the country, but the most fully documented examples are cases of home-to-work commuting. A detailed study of the Chicago area in 1956, for instance, produced dramatic evidence of a distance-decay effect, together with the impact of major transportation radials out of the city (see Figure 12.3, page 249). In this sense, every economic activity—and every central place—is the focus of a commuting field or "labor shed," a very special kind of trade area (Figure 12.4).

As for the relocation of people, the general trend in most countries is for people to move from rural areas to urban areas. Within the urban areas, at least in the developed countries, there is frequently a trend toward a shift of the population in the direction of the urban periphery. And, in some countries, a net shift is

Also see Section 2.2.1.

taking place between regions as well. In the United States, as has been widely reported, the growth areas are in the West and South.

12.4.4 *The Evolution of Linkage Networks*

Clearly, the flows of trade and people are related to existing networks of transportation facilities. But an existing network is like a snapshot of a running horse: it is a moment in a process of change. Figures 12.5 and 12.6 illustrate the interaction between transportation and settlement in the history of the United States, as trails gave way to railroads and then to an interstate highway network and air routes (try a comparison with Figure 12.2). The extension of new lines into pioneer areas was a means of land development as well as a way to get from here to there.

12.5 *A RECONSIDERATION*

Let's reflect first on the way linkages are built into the basic fabric of human systems, and then reflect on the benefits of travel for its own sake.

During the 1960s, a Greek planner named Doxiadis suggested a theory of *ekistics*: a science of human settlements. He proposed that all human settlements are part of a complex system involving nature, society, people, the structures we build, and the networks that connect us. Within this system, we seek to do five things:

1. maximize contacts with other parts of the system—elements of nature, other people, human artifacts

2. minimize the effort required to make and maintain this contact

3. optimize "protective space"—to maintain contacts while, at the same time, keeping the objects of the contact at enough of a distance to avoid discomfort

4. optimize the quality of our relationships with our environments—including nature, society, structure, and our contact networks

5. optimize the combination of these four goals

As our patterns of settlement evolve in response to these motives, the basic factor is "the distance man wants to go or can go in the course of his daily life."[4] The distance—and the range of contacts and choices opened up by it—is greatest along certain paths, and thus these paths impose a kind of geographic structure on our

***FIGURE* 12.5**
Transportation and Settlement in the United States. Transportation systems are shown in the form of a network, including air travel paths in 1976. Population density is shown as a surface. (a) 1776; (b) 1876; and [continued on next page]

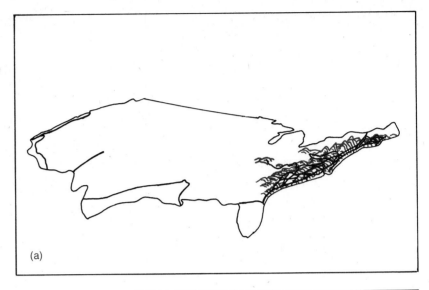

(a)

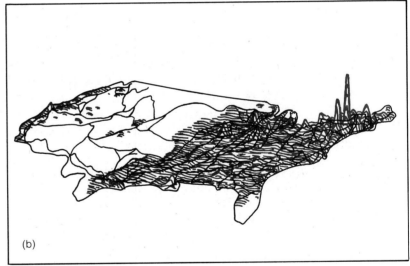

(b)

history of settlement (see Figure 12.7). Although this process operates differently in small spaces than large ones because the relation between distance and choice is more direct for large areal units, it certainly seems to be a part of the way we live, act, and arrange ourselves.

But merely seeing linkage/contact/movement as an expedient or a behavioral imperative is only a part of its meaning for most of

FIGURE 12.5 (cont'd.)
(c) 1976.

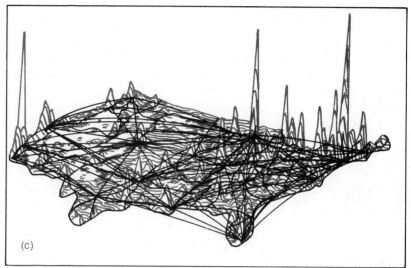

(c)

us. What about "Sunday drives," scenic routes, ocean cruises, the "joys of the open road"? Some of the time (perhaps not often enough), we travel for the sheer pleasure of it—seeing new things, immersing ourselves in new settings, stimulating our curiosity, challenging our preconceptions, shrugging off the social and psychological pressures of familiar places. We travel not so much to get somewhere as to enjoy the process of getting there—the experience of a passenger train or a ship, the quiet country road, the little hotel or restaurant that no tourist guide has yet discovered.

In improving our personal well-being, linkages are an important kind of means, to be sure, but they can also be ends in themselves.

12.6 *TOWARD GREATER PRECISION*

Accessibility—the ease with which a place can interact with other places—is a concept that can be used in two ways. In a broad, qualitative sense, it is a robust idea that gives us many insights into human behavior. But to be used as a basis for precise prediction or specific decisions, it needs to be converted into something more concrete. We need to be able to measure it, so that we can determine if A is more accessible than B—and, if so, how much more.

FIGURE 12.6
(on the right)
Transportation and Land
Development.

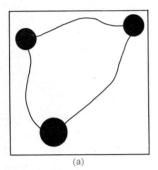

(a)

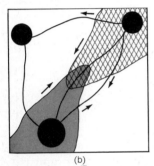

(b)

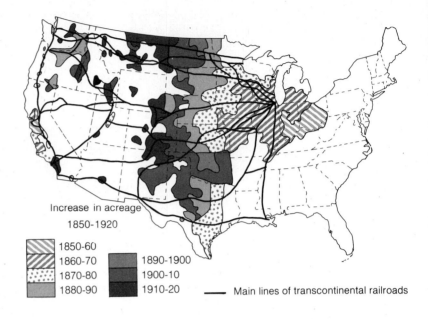

Increase in acreage
1850-1920

▨ 1850-60		
▧ 1860-70	▦ 1890-1900	
⣿ 1870-80	▩ 1900-10	
▩ 1880-90	▩ 1910-20	

—— Main lines of transcontinental railroads

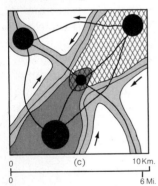

(c)

0   10 Km.
├─────────────────────┤
0   6 Mi.
├─────────────────────┤

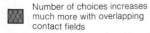

● Inhabited built-up areas

— Paved roads

→ Directions of easier traffic and therefore increased number of choices

▨ Number of choices increases much more with overlapping contact fields

• A new center is created in the area of increased choices

As a rule, indexes of accessibility are based on a numerical measurement of movement effort from a place to other places. For example, adapting the gravity-model type of formula, the accessibility of a location might be expressed as:

$$A_i = \sum_{j=1}^{n} a_j d_{ij}^{-c}$$

where

a_j is a measure of the opportunities at place j to which i wants access

d_{ij} is a measure of the movement effort between i and j (such as distance, time of travel, cost of travel, or minimum number of links)

c is an expression of the degree to which movement cost impedes interaction

Viewed as an "average cost of reaching opportunities,"[5] accessibility is a behavioral concept in which a_j involves *probabilities* of

FIGURE 12.7 (on the left)
Growth of a Settlement System: (a) contact on foot; (b) contact during early development of mechanical movement; and (c) full development of contact with a variety of available modes.

interacting with other places and *probabilities* that opportunities will be available at destinations, aside from the effects of distance. Trip objectives vary, and the opportunities at other places are less than certain (for example, the store may have sold all its copies of the new Stevie Wonder album).

The key steps in measuring accessibility are usually those that prepare numbers to be inserted into the index: conceptualizing and measuring a_j, d_{ij}, c, and so on. For instance, how important is a_j (opportunity) compared with d_{ij}^{-c} (impedance)? Because these operational decisions are resolved by different people in so many different ways, an accessibility map based on one measure will often show a pattern that is not the same as a map based on some other measure. If a person wants to make careful predictions from an accessibility map, this poses obvious problems. And if the predictions turn out to be poor, it is hard to tell whether it was because the index was inappropriate or accessibility was relatively unimportant in that case. This suggests that the link between accessibility as a broad concept and accessibility as a precisely measurable attribute of places is not yet as good as it needs to be.

MAJOR CONCEPTS AND TERMS

For definitions, see the Glossary.

Accessibility	Ekistics	Locational specialization
Backwash effects	Growth center	Multinational firm
Comparative advantage	Growth pole	Relative location
Complementarity	Interregional input-output analysis	Spread effects

Footnotes for Chapter 12

1. *Stages of Economic Growth* (Cambridge, 1960).

2. Taaffe, E. J., R. L. Morrill, and P. R. Gould. "Transport Expansion in Underdeveloped Countries: A Comparative Analysis." *Geographical Review*, vol. 53: 1963, pp. 503–529.

3. Jeffrey, D., E. Casetti, and L. King. "Economic Fluctuations in a Multiregional Setting." *Journal of Regional Science*, vol. 9: 1969, p. 397.

4. Doxiades, C. *Science*, vol. 170: October 23, 1970, p. 395.

5. Harris, Britton. "Notes on Accessibility." Mimeographed discussion paper. Philadelphia: University of Pennsylvania Institute for Environmental Studies, 1966.

CHAPTER 13

LINKAGE AND VULNERABILITY

*W*hen we considered the concept of a growth center in Chapter 10, we caught a glimpse of a darker side of the interaction between locations—an undesirable "backwash" effect on some places which reduces the opportunities of people who live there. This, in fact, is only one of several ways that linkages can create *disadvantages* for some economic decision makers and areas. Whether a high degree of interaction and specialization is a contribution to a person's well-being can depend on that person's point of view.

13.1 *SITUATIONS*

13.1.1 *The Textile Worker*

For more than thirty years (ever since you graduated from high school), you have worked in a large textile mill in North Carolina, making cloth from cotton and synthetic fibers for products such as shirts, sheets, and dresses. During this time you have developed special skills, and your hourly wage is now up to a level that provides you and your family a comfortable living. You are proud of your work, and you like your job.

When you go to the local discount store or chain department store, you have formed a habit of checking the items that are made from the kind of cloth that you help to manufacture. You look at labels and try to determine whether that cloth came from your mill. Partly, it is because you like to feel that you had a hand in creating something attractive and useful; but you are also concerned about reports that the sales of your plant are dropping, and you want to know more about the competition.

Increasingly, you notice that the children's clothes and other items have labels that show they were made in such places as Korea and Romania. You know it's not your cloth. When you ask the store manager why, you are told that items manufactured abroad using cloth also manufactured abroad are much cheaper.

The manager asks, "Wouldn't you rather pay $15.00 for your little girl's dress than $25.00?"

"If our plant's business gets any worse, I'll lose my job; and then I won't even be able to pay $5.00," you mumble.

At the next meeting of your local labor union organization, the topic of discussion is a new contract with the company that owns your plant. The union is seeking a major pay increase to offset rises in the cost of living, which you believe is only fair. The management negotiator is arguing that higher wages will require higher prices for the cloth, which will reduce their sales competitiveness with foreign manufacturers. Your observation tells you that this is probably true. Either way, you fear, you are going to lose in the end.

13.1.2   *The Price of Bread*

You are coming out of the grocery store, grumbling about the way prices have gone up. You are especially irritated at the way the price of bread has increased twice in the past six months, because you eat a lot of bread—and you think of it as a staple that is important to the diet of many poor people. Outside the store, you see a place to buy a newspaper, and you casually take a look at today's front page. The big headline announces another massive sale of wheat to overseas buyers.

Now, your exposure to economics tells you that one cause of a price rise can be a shortage of the product, and you wonder if there might be some connection between the price of bread in your supermarket and the headline in the newspaper. Maybe so much wheat is being exported that it has become scarce enough *inside* the country to make wheat more expensive, which would drive up the prices of bread and other products made from wheat.

You think, "Why should I pay more for bread in order that those people overseas can get some of our wheat?" and you go home and write to your representative to Congress.

13.1.3   *An Oil Embargo*

International relations don't interest you very much. Your life revolves around your job (in an office in the center of a city in the southwestern part of the United States) and your home, where your family is comfortably situated in an impressive house in a spacious new development about 40 miles from the city by interstate highway. You drive to work because in your area there is no real alternative. Bus service is infrequent and inconvenient. There is no commuter train. Most of your neighbors who work in the city have jobs on the outskirts, not in the center; so it's hard even to arrange a car pool. Since your family has only one car, this is sometimes a problem, but the house payments are too high for you to be able to afford a second one.

When you hear on the TV news that oil producing countries have announced that oil shipments to your country have been stopped for an indefinite period, it makes you angry because the action seems unfriendly; but you don't expect it to affect your own life. Your country has plenty of oil from its own resources, you believe.

Two months later. Your neighborhood service station has closed on Sundays and the last several days of every month because it can't get enough gasoline to be open every day. Instead of gassing up a couple of mornings a week on the way to work, you have to wait in long lines on the way home, tired and impatient. And gas prices are up by nearly two-thirds, which adds a lot to the cost of living of someone who drives 1,700 miles a month going to and from work.

But what really worries you is a gasoline rationing plan that the government says it will have to adopt if the embargo continues. Because the country had been importing one-half of the oil it was using, and these imports have stopped, in another month there will not be enough gasoline for unrestricted purchases. The plan now being discussed would limit each private automobile to 50 gallons of gasoline a month. You use 100 just to get to work, not counting any weekend or evening driving.

What are these foreign oil producers doing to you? Making you move to the city? Trade in your car on a smaller one that will get 40 miles to the gallon? Buy ration stamps at an inflated price from people who don't need all of theirs?

How could your country let this kind of thing happen?

13.2   *BASIC IDEAS*

If all the effects of economic linkages were desirable, there would be every reason to develop and rely on the links as much as possible. Yet we hear terms such as *energy independence* and *national self-sufficiency*, which imply that somehow, for some reason, external interaction should be reduced, not increased. Apparently, interaction is (or has the potential of) decreasing the well-being of people in a particular area.

As we know, linkages allow and encourage the development of locational specialization. This kind of specialization is often economically efficient for the world as a whole (at least given certain assumptions). But consider the effect of the invention of the automobile on a center of buggy whip manufacturing. . . .

Specialization means efficiency, but it can also mean vulnerability. People in a highly specialized place depend in important ways on the actions of people elsewhere: suppliers, buyers, inventors, decision makers reacting to conditions that are beyond local control.

One important case of vulnerability is the dependence of a local economy on a key import or export. The United States, for example, has become increasingly dependent on imports of crude oil to meet its energy needs. Without this oil, most vehicle traffic would stop. Home heating costs would skyrocket in many areas because fuel oil is being used to generate their electricity. In many such ways, the economic impact of an end to imports would be dramatically disruptive. Consequently the current health of the American economy depends very heavily on the actions of petroleum exporting countries—actions over which the United States has little control. Most American policy makers are trying to increase the country's energy self-sufficiency so that this vulnerability will be lessened.

Dependence on a particular export can be equally unsettling. Suppose that a small developing country, seeking to build its economy by increasing exports, finds that it can sell cocoa beans on international markets. It converts two-thirds of its agricultural land to produce cocoa, and the foreign money starts rolling in. But one year, the big buyers of cocoa beans in Europe and North America find that their sales have dropped a little. As a result, they still have a lot of cocoa in their warehouses, and they will only be buying a little this year. The cocoa price drops because cocoa is suddenly overabundant rather than scarce. The producing country, with its crop planted, can do little but sell cocoa at a loss and suffer. Governments have fallen for less reason than this (see Box 13.1).

A more insidious disadvantage of interaction is the fact that the benefits are often distributed unequally among the partners. Suppose, for example, that a vast new wilderness area is discovered, rich in minerals, furs, and other resources. It is inhabited only by scattered primitive tribes. Before long, development begins, and raw materials begin to flow to manufacturing centers where they are turned into fur coats, jewelry, and expensive metal alloys. Clearly, investment and production linkages have been expanded, and many people are benefiting. But these benefits are probably concentrated in the centers of manufacturing, wholesale and retail sales, and consumption. The tribal people in the newly developed area might provide some unskilled labor, but they receive no stock dividends from the companies handling the exploration and development. In fact, the difference between the economic well-being of the tribal people and the city people is almost surely *increased* by the new links.

Because economic linkages between places do not necessarily mean that the residents of all of the places share the benefits (business profits, for instance), interaction can be a disadvantage for some of the people who are affected by it. As the example above suggests, it has been more common in world history for linkages to sharpen differences in well-being than to lessen them. This can occur for two reasons. First, in what can be called relative deprivation, the richer partner gets a lot more benefits than the poorer one. As a result, the gap widens between their levels of well-being. Second, some of the activities located in the area occupied by the poorer people may have serious negative effects: environmental pollution, landscape disruption, social and cultural shock, labor

---

BOX 13.1 THE DIVERSIFIED PORTFOLIO

When a person first goes to talk to an investment broker about buying stocks, he or she is advised that diversified investments are less risky than concentrated ones. A person who owns stock in a hundred companies will benefit if any one of them does well—and will only be hurt a little if any of the companies has an especially bad year. Concentrating on one company, a person rises or falls with the fortunes of that one firm. The risk is much greater, unless the person has special knowledge that other investors lack. Consequently, the less the person can afford to lose, the more important is diversification. For this reason, people with only a small amount of money to invest are often advised to consider mutual funds, which offer group participation in a diversified portfolio.

A similar logic can be applied to places. Specialization offers the chance of impressive benefits, but it can mean risks as well. Diversification may reduce the likelihood of a major jump in benefits, but it can reduce risks. In certain cases, regional economic cooperation can provide some of the advantages of a diversified economy—but only if the partners add up to a balanced and complementary group of specializations.

shortages in traditional sectors, and others. Not only are most of the benefits going to the richer areas, but the poorer ones are bearing most of the indirect costs.

Consequently, people at a particular place may find interaction to be a disadvantage for them if they are vulnerable to external control either because their economy is highly specialized or because the interaction is so heavily controlled by outsiders that most of the benefits flow away with the exports. Place characteristics such as accessibility and the complementarity of environmental assets, usually considered to be desirable, can bring about a lower level of economic well-being for some of the people involved.

13.3 *ELABORATING THE BASIC IDEAS*

It is sobering—and a little perplexing—to realize that economic linkages between places may actually diminish the well-being of people in some of the places. From an economic point of view, this means either that (1) what makes sense in the short run does not lead to what makes sense in the long run; or (2) for reasons that are difficult to incorporate into economic theory, the interests of a small area are not quite the same as the general interests of the larger area. Some further discussion will illustrate these points.

13.3.1 *Reasons for Restricting Interaction*

For the moment, let us assume that unrestrained interaction between locations has an important benefit for society as a whole. It leads to a pattern of activity that provides goods and services at the lowest possible cost to the "typical" consumer. Why, then, might there be a reason to restrict this interaction?

1. **To reduce vulnerability.** If interaction—and the specialization encouraged by it—makes people's livelihoods susceptible to unpredictable or uncontrollable actions of others (or the physical environment), the costs may be greater than the benefits. For instance, many American advocates of reducing oil imports to the United States cite "national security" as the reason. A one-export country or region may opt for less efficient economic diversity in order to avoid large year-to-year changes in the health of the economy. A farming region that booms or busts according to the yearly rainfall may decide to look for other crops and vocations as supplements.

2. **To negotiate for a redistribution of benefits from interaction.** If Islandia and Atlantis are linked by shipments of wheat from Islandia to Atlantis, but Islandia is not getting a fair share of the benefits from the interaction (because, for instance, the purchase prices of wheat in Islandia are too low and the harvesting in Islandia is being done by organizations from Atlantis), Islandia might decide to limit or stop the shipments until new marketing arrangements are made. Clearly, this strategy will only work if Atlantis has become dependent on the shipments—if it is vulnerable because other suppliers at a comparable price are unavailable. But it is a logical extension of standard marketing principles: unless you will offer me enough mangoes for my chicken, I won't sell it.

This rationale has become a prominent factor in world trade, as countries exporting scarce raw materials (such as crude oil or rare metals) or staple foods realize that the dependence of their trading partners on imports makes it difficult for the importers to refuse a change in the terms of trade. In some cases, this has helped formerly poor and weak countries to correct trade relationships that were unfair to them.

Unless it is applied sensitively, however, such a strategy can cause problems in the long run, because price rises that result from the restricted interaction can encourage competitors to enter the market or substitutes to be developed. For example, limitations on the flow of oil to the United States from the Middle East would have two certain consequences: increased exploration and drilling activity in other parts of the world, such as Southeast Asia, and increased efforts to develop other sources of energy to meet American needs.

3. **To develop comparative advantages.** Consider the case of a developing country that has a comparative advantage for producing widgets: raw materials, unit labor costs, access to markets. But it has no widget factories, no marketing organization, no management and labor experience. The world demand for widgets (including needs in the developing country itself) is being met by industries in economically more developed countries. How can the local industry get started? The first few years will be expensive and uncertain. The products will have to develop a reputation for quality. The current suppliers may cut prices for a while to keep a strong competitor from getting started.

One answer is to protect the "infant industry" by restricting imports of widgets. This can assure the local factories that their products will be in demand in local markets while the industry grows to a point where it can compete on its own. Although such a policy will lead to higher local prices for widgets in the short run, it may offer lower prices and other local economic benefits in the long run.

4. **To guard against the loss of scarce resources.** In developing comparative advantages, a particular problem can be a continuing loss of resources as a result of interaction between places. Linkages tend to reflect geographic differences as they are (and have been), not as they could be. Consequently, a place with low wage rates and a lot of skilled labor—a comparative advantage—may lose much of the skilled labor to other places that offer higher wages. Similarly, instead of being invested locally, money may flow to other locations where it will buy or earn more; and a material or product that has become scarce locally may continue to leave for other areas where prices are higher.

It is common, as a result, for exports to be restricted. From time to time the United States considers limiting exports of wheat, soybeans, and other agricultural products because a shortage within the country would lead to higher food prices there. Many countries limit the amount of local currency that a tourist can "export," thus encouraging tourism within the country and reducing the outward flow of money. And a number of countries make it very difficult for skilled labor to emigrate (even, in one extreme case, raising a wall to stop it).

5. **To protect noncompetitive economic activities.** Economic theory implies that the factors of production are highly mobile. If the United States loses a comparative advantage in textile manufacturing, the labor, machines, and buildings can very quickly be switched to another activity that is more competitive internationally. Actually, however, the adjustment is often slow and painful. A person who has operated a machine in a textile mill cannot immediately begin to make components for digital computers.

From the point of view of the employees in the newly noncompetitive sector—and of others who depend on it as a basic activity for their economy—it is as important to protect this "aging" activity as it is to protect an infant industry.

These reasons help to account for the fact that economic linkages, especially between countries, are often limited rather than free. But it should be recognized that their limitations are usually intended as temporary measures—protective devices adopted during a period of transition because the current competitive situation will make it difficult to reach longer range goals. Because they impose costs, in the sense of higher prices for consumers, they can be difficult to sustain indefinitely.

13.3.2   Linkage and Backwardness

Chapter 12 suggested that there is a close relationship between linkages and economic well-being, but several of the ideas of this chapter show that linkages can perpetuate economic disadvantages as well. There is a great deal of inertia to an established economic pattern (remember cumulative causation), and people tied to less remunerative parts of the pattern can find it difficult to change. For example, suppose that bananas from Central America are exchanged for radios from North America. The wage rates for the radio makers are much higher, but the Central American workers may have little prospect of ever becoming radio makers (because so many other countries have already developed research and production capabilities in the electronics industry). From a worldwide point of view, perhaps, the regional specialization is economically rational, but from the point of view of a poorly paid Central American head of a family, that is little consolation.

In part, the problem is that a worldwide system of linkages has helped a few suppliers of radios to cover the world. But in part, it reflects the fact that there is a geography to the linkages themselves, giving some people and places more access to advantages than others (see Box 13.2). And this geography is hard to change very rapidly.

In describing developing countries, it is quite common to mention dualistic development, which refers to the side-by-side existence of (1) cities and regions that resemble those of developed countries, and (2) areas that have changed very little for hundreds of years. In many ways, the advantaged areas depend on the rest for raw materials, food, and cheap labor; but they return little to their "hinterlands." On a much different scale, this situation has some parallels with the relationship between developed and developing countries.

Such economic dualism is the result of geographic interaction, and its continuing existence often depends on a system of links and flows between advantaged and disadvantaged areas. Unless the system changes, the well-being of some people will be limited. But if the system changes, the well-being of others will be affected. As a result, economic linkages are not only complex in their consequences; they can generate controversy regarding what to do about the consequences.

13.3.3 *Economies of Geographic Scale and Configuration*

There is a connection between the vulnerability of an economy to harmful effects from interaction and the geographical extent of the economy—its size and configuration. Most directly, a larger area is simply more likely to contain a larger variety of environments, thus a larger collection of comparative advantages, thus a more diverse group of specializations. Because of this variety, any event that harms one activity will have less of an effect on the economy as a whole. For example, it is difficult to conceive of a country as large as the United States or the Soviet Union specializing in just a few kinds of economic activity. Even when a large country is dependent on an import such as oil, it is likely to have a wider range of energy resources to turn to as substitutes.

Since size is usually an advantage in diversifying an economy in a competitive world, smaller countries have logically turned to regional cooperation: loose economic confederations of neighbors, seeking the efficient development of complementary activities by the participating countries (see Box 13.3).

The configuration and geographic orientation of a country can be important as well as its size. For instance, if a country is long

---

BOX 13.2 SHADOW EFFECTS

In most developed countries there are regions with economic problems: unemployment, the emigration of skilled labor, an aging labor force, and others. Some of these regions are in remote areas, to be sure, but many of them are found at the fringes of the most active and prosperous regions. It is almost as if the tall figures of these growth areas cast a shadow on their immediate surroundings.

It is not hard to figure out why this could be. For instance, an activity that wants to locate somewhere in the general area of higher production and wealth would find more agglomeration economies closer to where the action is. Skilled labor in the surrounding areas would tend to move to the jobs, salaries, and excitement—with a back-wash effect on the areas left behind. Because of the hierarchical nature of transportation and communication systems, being at the periphery of the growth center might offer little advantage over being located in another growth center farther away, with access to high-order movement facilities between the centers.

If a person cannot locate quite close enough to a center of prosperity to share its benefits, it is sometimes easier to be well separated from it—more distant from day-to-day competition for labor and capital. And, because nearness often means environmental similarity, separation may increase the chances of identifying competitive advantages over the thriving region.

and narrow, it has a relatively long border for an area of its size. Even with some filtering of interaction by international boundaries, it is likely to have more external trade than a country of the same size and economic characteristics but a more compact shape. And, at least for agricultural production, it may make a difference whether the long, narrow country extends from north to south or east to west. Because a north-south orientation is likely to mean a greater variety of climates, it lends itself to a greater degree of crop diversification.

13.4   *EXAMPLES*

Because the idea of interaction as a *disadvantage* is important but often overlooked, some cases of such disadvantages may be illuminating. First, we will consider the point of view of the destination area; then we will take a look at problems for the area of origin.

13.4.1   *Dependent Consumers*

The Energy Crisis   On October 17, 1973, the petroleum exporting Arab countries decided to stop shipments to many of the large importers. One of the embargoed countries was the United States.

There was little immediate impact from the stoppage, because American energy companies had a great deal of crude oil in storage and because oil tankers that had been loaded before the embargo continued to arrive afterward. And, after all, imports from the Arab countries were only a relatively small part of the energy picture of the United States: oil represented about 46 percent of total energy consumption; about 32 percent of it was imported, and only about 12 percent of the imports were from the boycotting countries. Less than 2 percent of the nation's energy supply was directly affected (although forecasts at that time indicated that this proportion would grow steadily in the next decade).

By December, however, the United States government was reporting a domestic shortage of 2–3 million barrels of oil a day as a result of the Arab boycott, and if the boycott had continued indefinitely the impacts would have been dramatic. The National Petroleum Council, for instance, estimated that future oil shortages would reduce the Gross National Product by $48 billion a year and increase unemployment by more than 50 percent. The most direct effects of the boycott were on transportation, which consumed more than half the oil. Highway speed limits were cut. Service stations had limits placed on the amount of gasoline they could sell: as a result most were closed by the end of each month, and many decided to close on Sundays. Motels and roadside restaurants showed dips of up to 50 percent in their weekend revenues. Ski resorts and other weekend recreation spots were hurt. Second home purchases slowed down. Plants manufacturing large automobiles were shut down. In addition, airlines could get less fuel, which meant slower speeds, fewer flights, laid-off pilots and other employees. Private aviation was hurt even more. Urban mass transit and intercity trucks and buses were operating on a day-to-day basis. Agricultural equipment needed to plant crops in the Southwest and

BOX 13.3   REGIONAL ECONOMIC COOPERATION

Relatively small countries can join together to get some of the economies of scale and size that are usually only available to large countries. In essence, a number of countries, generally neighbors, agree to act as if they were one country (at least for some economic matters). The key agreement is to let most types of goods move within the group just as freely as they move between states of the United States. In some cases, capital and labor move freely as well.

The best known example of this kind of cooperation is in Western Europe: the European Economic Community (EEC), also called the European Common Market. In the rebuilding period after World War II, the Netherlands, Belgium, and Luxembourg agreed to drop tariff barriers to the flow of goods between them. Because "Benelux" and other later experiments with cooperation were successful, in 1957 three countries—West Germany, France, and Italy—joined the original three to create the EEC. In 1973, they were joined by the United Kingdom, Denmark, and Ireland. In addition to providing for free trade among the members, the Common Mar-

ket attempts to integrate economic policy and planning within the group. Other (peripheral?) West European countries—Switzerland, Austria, Sweden, Norway, Finland, Iceland, and Portugal—belong to the less far-reaching European Free Trade Association (EFTA), which trades some goods freely with the EEC.

The experience of the EEC has borne out many of the optimistic predictions for it. Regional economic cooperation has encouraged economic growth, interregional specialization, and trade between the countries; and it has also facilitated social and political cooperation.

With this kind of record, it is not surprising that the idea is being tried in other parts of the world, too. For example, the Central American Common Market (CACM) joins five countries located between Mexico and South America; Comecon integrates the economies of the Soviet Union, most of Eastern Europe, and Mongolia; and the New Zealand-Australia Free Trade Agreement (NAFTA) may be the beginning of a more general free trade area in the South Pacific.

harvest crops in California was stalled for lack of fuel. Commercial fishing fleets were idle. Even more serious, some drilling rigs searching for new oil within the United States lacked the diesel fuel to operate, and towboats and tugboats needed to help deliver fuel oil by river and sea (and diesel trains needed to deliver oil and coal by rail) were seriously short of fuel.

Another impact was on electricity generation, since many generating plants had been built to use fuel oil as their source of energy. Although few of these effects actually became widespread before the boycott ended, it was expected that store and school hours would become shorter, with some schools even closing for a while during the winter (and planning to make up the work in the summer). Power brownouts or blackouts would be frequent. Energy for home use would be rationed (allocation formulas were in fact put into operation for propane, an important fuel for home heating in rural areas). Commercial lighting would be cut drastically—not only neon signs but lighting levels in corridors, lobbies, and rest-rooms.

Other effects extended to industries that used liquid fuel for process heat (for example, plywood mills using propane to produce heat to dry wood) and to industries that used petroleum as a source of chemical feedstocks (such as for plastics manufacturing). The average price of gasoline in the United States in 1972 was about 36 cents; a year after the boycott, it was up more than 50 percent.

The list of effects could continue for pages and pages. And there was very little the United States could do about the situation. New energy sources would take five or ten years to develop. Until the Arab countries decided to lift the boycott (establishing a price for oil of their own choosing), the effects would persist.

For countries such as the United States, Canada, Japan, and those in Western Europe, it was a sobering reminder of how dependent they had become on other countries whose decisions they could not control. Almost a kind of bondage.

Japan   If the impact of the Arab oil boycott, involving 2 percent of the nation's energy supply, was significant for the United States, consider the case of Japan: 75 percent of its energy consumption was based on oil, nearly all imported—and 80 percent of the imports came from the Middle East. In 1973, the supply of oil from the Arab countries to Japan was reduced by one-quarter, or nearly 15 percent of Japan's total energy supply.

This is only one of many examples of the dependency of Japan on imports, since it is a country with very limited natural resources (given current technology) to support its population and economy.

1973 was a bad year for Japan. Earlier that year (in June), the United States had imposed export controls on soybeans because their price in commodity markets was rising too rapidly; and President Nixon had proposed limiting exports of other commodities such as wheat, corn, and feed grains.

Japan protested vociferously, because the nutrition of its citizens was directly involved. Imports of wheat and soybeans—a key part of the Japanese diet—and maize and sorghum as livestock feed amounted (in weight) to 50 percent more than all the rice produced in Japan. More than 80 percent of the imports were from the United States (88 percent of the soybeans), and the imports represented about half of all the consumption in the country. A long-term embargo on exports of American soybeans would mean hunger in Japan.

Japan also imports 85 percent of its shellfish, 58 percent of its timber, 92 percent of its iron ore, 59 percent of its coal, 100 percent of its bauxite (for aluminum), and 73 percent of its copper. It is no wonder that their foreign policy has traditionally been concerned with assuring the supply of key inputs.[1]

Autarky   It is clear that if a country wishes to be entirely its own master, it must have the capacity to be self-sufficient. Under Stalin, the Soviet Union made national self-sufficiency or "autarky" a national goal—partly as a reflection of deepseated Russian nationalism, partly as an aid to ideological purity. By the 1950s, except for some trade with Eastern Europe and China, it was a remarkably self-contained economy. Everything from steel to oil, wheat, tea, and oranges came from within.

Some of this independence was bought at a high cost, however, and it is perhaps significant that the 1970s have seen an increasing flow of international trade to and from the Soviet Union. Some of the trade (for example, purchases of sugar from Cuba) is motivated by political considerations rather than economic ones, but other imports (for instance, machinery and grain) indicate a willingness to accept trade as an alternative to bearing all the costs of meeting every domestic need by domestic production.

13.4.2   *Disadvantaged Providers*

The Brain Drain   According to the National Science Foundation, in 1967 12,500 scientists and engineers were granted immigrant status in the United States, along with 3,300 physicians. More of these were from Asia than from Europe. Although the numbers began to drop in 1968, when immigration policies were revised, there continues to be a steady flow of skilled people from poor nations to rich ones, especially in the health professions. In some cases it appears that the United States may in fact get more monetary value from these individuals than it returns to their countries in foreign aid.[2]

This kind of "brain drain," which also occurs between regions in a country, often widens the economic gap between areas by making it difficult for less developed areas to create a scientific and technical establishment that can compete with the more affluent countries. The reasons for it are not difficult to understand: higher salaries, higher status, greater professional opportunity, better facilities, perhaps a lack of receptivity to change in the home areas. As these factors change, the highly mobile professionals may return—as many European and Japanese scientists and engineers have recently done. But these changes in conditions happen more slowly in the less developed countries. A study published in 1968 noted that "France takes pride in her aid to former colonies, yet the new state of Togo has sent more physicians and professors to France than France has sent to Togo. . . . There are more American-trained Iranian doctors in New York alone than in the whole of Iran."[3] An estimated 20 percent of students who come from less developed countries to study in the United States end up staying.

The brain drain is highly selective in occupation and source area, but it is a serious problem for a country losing its human resources. A United Nations report, for instance, has estimated that 5 to 10 percent of India's high-level manpower leaves the country. Pakistan and the Philippines have similar problems. In many cases, from the point of view of the country, this stems from overspecialization in the training process; excess Indian brain surgeons stay in Boston while India has too few general practitioners. Economics Ph.D.s join American consulting firms while Indian states and cities suffer from a shortage of able public administrators. Once specialized, a person finds it difficult to forego the use of his or her special skills. The most obvious alternative is also unpleasant—a coercive limitation of opportunities for able individuals—but the long-term implications (perhaps even genetically) of a steady loss of 10 percent of an area's best young people every year are certainly very serious.

International Trade and Hunger Less developed countries have a great many hungry people, but their economies often depend heavily on exports of agricultural products. This is a disturbing paradox, especially when some of the more advanced countries that are the buyers are at the same time restricting their own crop production in order to stabilize food prices.

Let's look at the role of less developed countries in world trade. In general, they represent only a small—and declining—part of it. Most of the trade flows from one advanced country to another. Of the exports of the less developed countries, some move to each other, but an important segment of trade involves an exchange with advanced countries. This exchange follows a characteristic pattern: the less developed country importing capital equipment and machinery, while it exports primary commodities (agricultural goods, minerals, fossil fuels).

Although such trade is often well established along lines that were once colonial, the less developed countries are in many ways stuck with the less desirable end of the deal (unless their product is oil). Their primary commodities are the more susceptible to price fluctuations and substitution. Their demand rises slowly; production is often slow; and they bring lower prices than the imported items, which tends to cause balance of payment problems (more paid out to international partners than is received back). Such problems, in turn, lead to import restrictions, which can slow development and lessen the quality of life: and they also encourage an increased emphasis on exports, which can aggravate internal scarcity.

Consequently, most of the Peruvian fish crop ends up (as fish oil or fish meal) in North America and Europe. Thailand sends maize to Japan; the Philippines ships sugar to the United States, and Cuba ships it to the Soviet Union. Bananas are exported from Central America to North America and Europe. Peanuts move from Africa to Europe, and meat from South America to Europe and North America. In every one of these cases, food is moving from a hungrier area to an area where most people are much better fed. The pattern is economically efficient, in the sense that the products are moving from lower price market areas to higher price ones and the food production is usually located in areas where production costs are relatively low. But, especially considering recent evidence of a relationship between nutrition and mental ability, this linkage may present real problems to a less developed country trying to develop its human resources.

13.5 *A RECONSIDERATION*

An emphasis on self-sufficiency usually means that at a particular time things cost more than in a world of free interaction. But other considerations, including long-term economic ones, may be even more important. In particular, it should be recognized that the free trade idea makes most sense when a truly free competitive market exists. But our world is not like that. Economic interaction decisions are shaped by political alignments, the vested interests of large institutions, and economic, social, and technological gaps between areas. Consequently, unrestrained linkages often mean vulnerability and disadvantage.

Whether or not this is the case depends on two related questions: who controls the interaction, and who benefits from it? A new mine, factory, or resort hotel in a less developed area may be of slight benefit to the area if the decisions are made elsewhere and the profits flow to owners in the more affluent area that consumes the goods and services. Well-being is not simply a matter of comparative advantage, accessibility, and complementarity. It is also a matter of political and economic influence.

MAJOR CONCEPTS AND TERMS

For definitions, see the Glossary.

Autarky	*Export/import*	*Locational*
Brain drain	*restrictions*	*vulnerability*
Dualistic	*Infant industry*	*Relative deprivation*
development		*Shadow effects*

Footnotes for Chapter 13

1. Okita, Saburo. "Natural Resource Dependency and Japanese Foreign Policy." *Foreign Affairs*, January 1970, pp. 348–372.

2. U.S. Congress. House Foreign Affairs Committee. *Brain Drain: A Study of the Persistent Issue of International Scientific Mobility.* Washington: Government Printing Office, 1974.

3. Adams, Walter, ed. *The Brain Drain.* New York: Macmillan, 1968, p. 2.

PART VI

PUBLIC POLICY AND ECONOMIC PATTERNS

*A*t this point, we have reached the end of our review of the concepts that are central to economic geography as it is usually defined. But, with only a few exceptions, we have been acting as if all the decision makers in an economy were private firms and individuals, acting and interacting without any kind of special incentives or constraints. The largest economic institution in most countries, however, is the central government, and governments often make decisions differently than private firms. In addition, governments plan, legislate, regulate, and take other actions that are intended to influence private economic decision making.

This section will consider how governments influence economic-geographic systems: the location and distribution of activities and the pattern of movements among them. Chapter 14 will examine governments as providers and consumers, and Chapter 15 will consider governments as shapers of private decisions.

CHAPTER 14

GOVERNMENT AS AN ACTOR IN AN ECONOMIC–GEOGRAPHIC SYSTEM

*T*he action in a drama is brought to life by actors working within a stage setting. It is sometimes useful to think of an economy in similar terms, made up of decision-making actors operating in a setting made up of various kinds of environments—physical, cultural, and locational.

Generally, governments are considered part of the setting rather than part of the cast of performers. But about a third of the gross national product of the United States is purchased by government bodies in the form of goods, services, and labor. One dollar of every three spent in the United States is spent by governments; the federal government is by far the biggest consumer in the country. In 1972, total tax receipts by governments at all levels amounted to 31.7 percent of the gross national product, which makes governments the biggest repository of savings in the country (as well as the biggest debtor). Government is also one of the largest providers in the country. In the fiscal year that overlapped 1971 and 1972, about $10 billion was spent providing mail service in the United States, about $70 billion for education, $40 billion for highways, $24 billion for public assistance, $17 billion for health care, $14 billion for natural resources (such as national parks), $5 billion for housing, and about $23 billion in interest on debts. No private firm in the world provides such diverse goods and services on such a large scale. Governments are leading actors indeed.

Although this is interesting for its own sake, it would not affect our discussion of ideas in economic geography if the concepts that describe private decision making were just as valid for describing the decisions that governments make as economic actors. But they are not. The idea of measuring profits at the ballot box rather than at the bank has not been a part of our perspective yet. Even though it is not possible yet to lay out a precise theory about how governments in countries such as Canada and the United States make economic-geographic decisions, we need to become aware of some of the major issues and influences. Maybe one of you readers will become the person to develop the first truly satisfactory theory. . . .

14.1   SITUATIONS

14.1.1   The Old Army Camp

Not too far away from where you live there is a very large wooded area that is owned by the federal government. It was used during World War II as a training base for Army units, and it is still used for a few months each summer by Army Reserve and National Guard groups. Most of the time, though, little goes on there. Hunters and hikers make occasional illegal forays into the area. Once an independent movie company shot some film for a war movie there. It has been alleged that there are a few stills in the area.

But to the towns around the old Army camp, it is simply land that is of little value to them. Lumber companies can't cut trees there. Livestock raisers can't let their stock forage there. No taxes are paid for the land.

But one day, the Pentagon decides to activate the base. A large training unit will be stationed there. New permanent buildings will replace the ramshackle World War II prefabs. With a regular contingent of 1,000 and a trainee capacity of 10,000, the new activity will transform a sleepy relic into a bustling center.

Quickly, before others get the idea too, you get together with some acquaintances at a nearby bank and organize a real estate firm. With a loan from the bank, you purchase 50 acres of land at the edge of the town nearest the main gate of the old camp. After subdividing the land into 1/4 acre plots, you hire a contractor to build homes in the $40,000–$60,000 price range, planning to sell some of them and rent others.

Two years later, your subdivision (MacArthur Park) is complete. About 90 percent of the units have been bought or rented. The bank loan is nearly repaid in full. And your firm is now building a small shopping center nearby.

14.1.2 *Where the Jobs Are*

Your high school class has decided to hold a reunion, and against your better judgment you have been persuaded to be a member of the committee to organize it. The problem is that you have never been able to learn to keep your mouth shut, and this usually leads to work. History repeats itself. Incautiously, you wonder about the "big picture" of your group—where they are and what they are doing. Before you know it, you have been assigned to write a report.

Grumbling all the while, you send out a questionnaire to all the graduates at their last known addresses. Three months, a lot of postage, and a number of telephone calls later, you have a response from 80 percent of the people, and you start to sort through the results. First, you make stacks according to the categories of professional, other self-employed, small business, big business, government, and not employed—planning later to make a map of each category. But to your surprise the government stack soon becomes so high that it keeps toppling over.

Interested, you look through the questionnaires (surely government hasn't become *that* big!). The people include teachers, members of police departments and fire departments, military personnel, doctors and nurses in municipal hospitals, employees of city transit companies and state recreation departments, office workers, a couple of elected officials, two social workers, a planner, and many other jobs.

You think, "You know, if anybody had asked, I would have said that I don't know many people who work for the government."

14.1.3 *The Drug Treatment Center*

Drug use is a problem in your area, and so is the incidence of robbery and burglary. You believe that there is a connection, and you have worked hard to help elect a new mayor who has promised to set up methadone treatment centers to help heroin users break their habits. You are convinced that this is a very high-priority need in your city, and you are impatient to see the centers put into operation.

In your neighborhood (in fact, in the next block), there is a vacant office in a small building on a business street. It is across the street from the neighborhood movie theater. In the same block is a drug store/cafe where the neighborhood teenagers gather in the afternoons and evenings. It is a lively, busy block—a social focus for a much larger area around it.

When the plan for drug treatment centers is announced, you find that the south-side location will be that vacant office nearby. Suddenly, you are besieged with calls from parents and business people in the neighborhood: "You know this mayor. Tell her that we don't want that center here! We won't stand for it!"

Parents are concerned that heroin addicts will be mixing with their children. Businesses fear that families will begin to go somewhere else to shop, that young people will be encouraged to gather somewhere else. Along with all of them, you are concerned that the center may mean the decline of one of the city's most successful neighborhood shopping areas, together with the loss of a valuable sense of neighborhood identity.

When you contact the mayor's assistant, he says: "Hey, nobody wanted treatment centers more than you, and they have to go *somewhere*. You mean you only like them if they are located in somebody else's neighborhood?"

14.2 BASIC IDEAS

Situations 1 and 3 hint at the geographic impact of government agencies as economic actors, and situation 2 indicates just how many different kinds of agencies are involved. How, then, are "public" location and movement decisions different from the decisions of private firms and private individual entrepreneurs?

When governments make economic decisions, their concern is not with maximizing economic profits—the difference between costs and revenues. Their primary interest is in maximizing services or, perhaps, maximizing political support or influence. Consider, for example, a decision about where to locate a controversial public facility, such as a minimum-security prison. In economic terms, the lowest cost location would be the one at which land prices, construction materials, and wage rates add up to the smallest bill. But this is often given a lower priority than finding the place whose residents complain least or have the least clout in trying to avoid the facility. Likewise, desirable facilities may be located in a way that wins votes or rewards political supporters rather than one that maximizes economic benefits to the government agency.

The same motives are often at work when a government body decides the best use for a piece of publicly owned land (and the federal government is the largest single landowner in the United States, as well as the biggest single owner of many kinds of resources, including coal and petroleum). A politically sensitive example is the so-called school lands in most western states. When land in the Great Plains was first surveyed in preparation for selling it, one section in each township was reserved for the support of schools, while all the land around it was sold to individuals, railroads, and others. Most of these parcels ended up as state-owned land open to a variety of uses, generally leased or rented to private users, with the revenue going into state school funds. It would stand to reason that, from the point of view of state taxpayers and users of the school system, the state should be seeking to assure the highest and best use of this land, to generate as much revenue as possible for supporting the public school system. In some states, however, the school lands are simply leased for long terms at low rates to large landowners (such as ranchers and farmers) whose lands border the parcels. One explanation is that the administrative cost of a continuing reexamination of every parcel would exceed the added revenues. Another is that the political support of the large landowners is more important to government bodies than realizing the true economic rent of the state lands.

These examples illustrate the complex nature of economic decisions by government. On the one hand, they often seek to reflect the larger concerns of society, as expressed by political support or opposition. They take into account needs, regardless of ability to pay. They consider such hard-to-value factors as environmental quality and local community self-determination; and they respond to the preference of people with limited economic resources. On the other hand, the economic decisions of governments can be susceptible to the exaggerated influence of people and groups with money, organizations, and other special capabilities for putting pressure on public decision makers. This is especially true when there is no way to hold elected officials directly accountable at the ballot box for decisions by officials of public agencies.

In part, this complexity results from the difficulty of evaluating many of the goods and services provided by governments. The utility of an apple, a radio, or a football game is easily enough measured by observing people's preferences. If an apple and an orange are 20 cents apiece at the local store, and you can afford to buy only one, which do you buy? If it is the orange, how much cheaper would the apple have to be before you would buy it instead? But how can we evaluate the utility of fire protection? Strictly in economic terms, we might consider the cost of an additional fire station (which would put fire protection nearer to many people),

FIGURE 14.1
Government as a Locational Decision Maker: facilities to be located so as to serve the population.

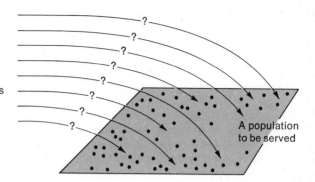

Hospitals
Schools
Birth control clinics
Fire stations
Voting booths
Administrative centers
Branch campuses
Playgrounds
Etc.

A population to be served

together with its personnel and equipment, and compare its benefits—the estimated monetary damage from fires that would be prevented as a result (see the discussion of cost-benefit analysis in Section 18.3.2). But what is the monetary value of one life saved? Similarly, it is difficult to make decisions about national or city parks, mental health facilities, school lunch programs, or government research for cures for cancer solely on the basis of economic definitions of the highest and best use of land and money. Too many activities of general value to society would be excluded. In theory, then, the emphasis is on maximizing *social welfare* rather than *economic well-being*.

These ideas are not geographical in themselves, but they take on spatial meaning because every economic decision by government means different things for some locations than others. Facilities must be put *somewhere* (see Figure 14.1). Purchases of materials or services benefit the areas that have the basic activities to supply them: they are procured from *somewhere*. Public lands are unevenly distributed from place to place. Employees of federal and state governments spend most of their wages in the vicinity of the capital city, not at the locations the elected officials represent. Every economic decision by a government body is a locational decision.

It is particularly important to recognize that government and the public facilities supported by it are often very powerful basic activities. They draw in money from elsewhere and circulate it locally. They are dependable—and omnivorous—employers. They build buildings and use energy (see Box 14.1). And many of them, such as educational and health care systems, are hierarchically arranged central place functions, with their own market areas and sets of linkages.

The framework of thought introduced in Chapters 5–13 is therefore very much a part of examining the *effects* of economic actions by government bodies, and it is a source of insights about what the actions should be. But it is a much less certain predictor of public decisions than private decisions.

14.3 ELABORATING THE BASIC IDEAS

This has been a very spare introduction to a subject that fills scores of books by itself. To understand it a little better, we need more information about the functions of government as an economic actor and the way these functions take on comprehensible spatial patterns. Sections 14.3.1–14.3.3 will summarize the functions; 14.3.4 the ways they are expressed in economic patterns; and 14.3.5 some opportunities that are presented for private locational decision makers.

BOX 14.1 NASA'S MANNED SPACECRAFT CENTER AS A BASIC ACTIVITY

In 1961, as a key element of Project Apollo, NASA decided to locate a Manned Spacecraft Center in Houston, Texas. It was expected that the facility would have a significant impact on the Houston area: over 200,000 new residents, over $400 million in additional personal income, $180 million in new bank deposits, $140 million in increased annual property taxes, and $245 million in increased retail sales per year. And its impact did turn out to be great. Within three years after the center opened, more than 100 aerospace firms established offices in Houston, and 92 percent of the 1,150 scientists and engineers at the space center itself moved to Houston from other locations.

Other sites considered for the Manned Spacecraft Center were Boston, St. Louis, Jacksonville, Tampa, four sites in Louisiana, eight in Texas, and six in California. What if the center had been located in Bogalusa, Louisiana?

The reasons for selecting Houston included its substantial industrial community and university resources, its large work force, its deep channel and port facilities, a central location for a program whose contractors were spread nationwide, and the donation at no cost to the federal government of land for the site. Some observers thought it was also significant that the Vice-President, the Speaker of the House of Representatives, and four key members of Congress were Texans.

By 1967, however, NASA expenditures began to decline. Because the earliest budget reductions were in the construction of facilities and equipment, the initial economic impact was felt more strongly in Mississippi and Alabama than in Houston, but a less drastic "boom and bust" syndrome was a reality in the Houston area by the early 1970s.

SOURCE: Murphy, Thomas P. *Science, Geopolitics, and Federal Spending.* Lexington, Mass: Heath, 1971, Chapters 7 and 12.

14.3.1   *Government as a Pluralistic Decision Maker*

There is an almost irresistible tendency to talk about government as if it were a single, unified entity. But government is usually as diverse and pluralistic as the society it represents. In the United States, for example, three formal levels of government operate: federal (national), state, and local. The federal and state governments include separate executive, legislative, and judicial branches. At any level, the judiciary includes judges with different interpretations of the law, legislators with diverse views of priorities, and executive agencies competing with each other for influence. Interspersed among these levels are multistate regional commissions and compacts, multilocal districts, and other governmental entities that can make economic decisions (see Box 14.2).

BOX 14.2   ECONOMIC ROLES OF REGIONAL GOVERNMENTS

These are some examples of regional governments in the United States that are economic actors:[a]

Entity	Activity	Entity	Activity
Substate or Interstate Metropolitan Region		*Multistate Region*	
		Appalachian Regional Commission	Plans and provides financial support for highways, health, housing, and vocational education
Association of Bay Area Governments (ABAG), California	Regional planning—for example, reviewing proposals for programs that would receive federal aid		
Port of New York Authority	Operates transportation and trade facilities	Western Interstate Commission for Higher Education	Research, higher education training programs, student placement
Lower Savannah Regional Planning and Development Commission, South Carolina	Regional and urban planning	Interstate Palisades Park Commission	Operates amusement park and other recreational facilities
LENOWISCO Planning District Commission, Virginia	Solid waste disposal and small stream maintenance	Delaware River Basin Commission	Water resource planning and regulation
Brockton Water District, Massachusetts	Domestic water supply, reservoir maintenance		
Central New York Transportation Authority (CENTRO), New York	Operates transportation facilities		

[a] A number of cases are summarized in *Multistate Regionalism* (1972) and *Regional Governance: Promise and Performance,* Substate Regionalism and the Federal System, vol. II, 1973, issued by the Advisory Commission on Intergovernmental Relations, Washington, D.C.

Consequently, there are federal prisons, state prisons, and county and city jails. We can buy U.S. savings bonds or municipal bonds. We can identify federal lands, state lands, and city property—sometimes in the same county. Locational decisions by "government" are not necessarily coordinated or even consistent, because the political constituencies and points of view of the different levels of government may not be the same. In fact, different bodies or branches of government may even see each other as adversaries. But a decision by one unit usually affects the others, which means that economic effects of the decision must be traced through political linkages as well as economic ones.

14.3.2   *Economic Activities of Government as a Provider*

The economic decisions assigned by a society to its governments are a reflection of that society's cultural background, historical ex-

---

BOX 14.3   POLITICAL ENVIRONMENTS AND GOVERNMENT FUNCTIONS

The same environments—cultural, technological, physical—that affect private economic activity also affect government activity. They shape its institutions and influence its priorities. Consequently, the roles of state and local government as economic actors usually depend more on these environments, together with the regional economic situation, than on party politics.

Many political scientists and economists have found that government policies and expenditures depend heavily on measures of economic activity, as well as vice versa. This makes intuitive sense. An area with a healthier economy pays more taxes and can thus spend more on services such as education, transportation, and health care.

But economic measures alone do not explain many important differences in policies, such as the degree of reliance on real property taxes, the centralization or decentralization of state government, or expenditures on vocational education. These and others show a clear regional pattern; for example, southeastern states differ consistently from northeastern states.

In a book entitled *American Federalism: A View from the States*, Daniel J. Elazar attributes this pattern to the "geology" of political culture in the United States—distinctively different cultural environments for political decision making, spreading across the country by migration from source regions in the east. These environments have a great

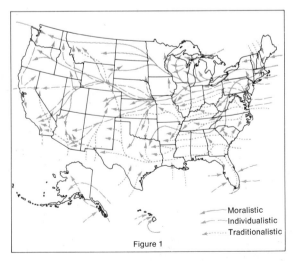

Figure 1

SOURCE: Murphy, Thomas P. *Science, Geopolitics, and Federal Spending.* Lexington, Mass: Heath, 1971, Chapters 7 and 12.

perience, and political viewpoints (see Box 14.3). At a minimum, government functions usually include the ownership and use of some property, the provision of goods and services for which profit making is not socially acceptable, the provision of goods and services that are needed by society but are too risky or too unprofitable to attract private decision makers, and the provision of goods and services that are of such general value that the provider has a hard time collecting direct payments from all those who benefit. But the specific definition of, for instance, socially acceptable profit making can vary considerably from country to country.

Even in the United States, where the government role is viewed more restrictively than in most places in the world, a great many goods and services are provided by the "public sector"— units of government (see Table 14.1). Consider these cases:

BOX 14.3 (cont'd.)

deal more influence on government decisions than the political party of a governor or the political composition of a state legislature. The following maps show (a) the pattern of spread, according to Elazar—a *moralistic* approach from the "Yankee" Northeast, an *in-dividualistic* point of view from the middle Atlantic states, and a *traditionalistic* culture from the South (Figure 1); (b) the regional distribution of these political cultures in the 1960s (Figure 2); and (c) the dominant political culture by state (Figure 3).

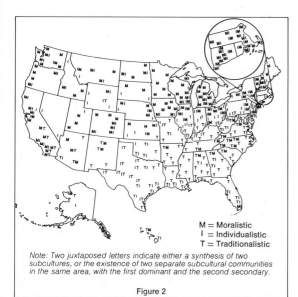

M = Moralistic
I = Individualistic
T = Traditionalistic

Note: Two juxtaposed letters indicate either a synthesis of two subcultures, or the existence of two separate subcultural communities in the same area, with the first dominant and the second secondary.

Figure 2

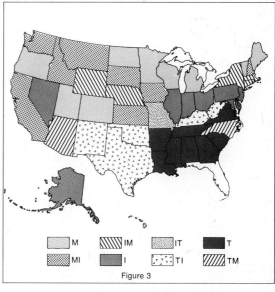

M   IM   IT   T
MI   I   TI   TM

Figure 3

1. **Public lands and resources.** Federal or state ownership of land includes parks, military reservations, wildlife refuges, highway rights of way, hospitals, prisons, and schools. It also includes substantial natural resources in these areas. For example, the federal government owns more than 50 percent of the total fossil energy resources in the United States (37 percent of the petroleum, 43 percent of the natural gas, 50 percent of the coal, and 81 percent of the oil shale). It also

TABLE 14.1

Summary of General Expenditures (Direct and Intergovernmental), by Function, by Level of Government, 1971–1972

Function	Amount (millions of dollars)				Percentage			
	All Govt.	Federal Govts.	State Govts.	Local Govts.	All Govt.	Federal Govts.	State Govts.	Local Govts.
All Functions	321,389	188,100	98,810	105,393	100.0	100.0	100.0	100.0
Direct	321,389	154,516	62,051	104,822	100.0	82.1	62.7	99.5
Intergovernmental	a	33,584[b]	36,759	571	a	17.9	37.2	0.5
National Defense and International Relations[c]	79,258	79,258	0	0	24.7	42.1	0	0
Postal Service	9,366	9,366	0	0	2.9	5.0	0	0
Space Research and Technology	3,369	3,369	0	0	1.1	1.8	0	0
Education	69,990	13,045	38,348	47,786	21.8	6.9	38.8	45.3
Direct	69,990	5,104	17,153	47,734	21.8	2.7	17.4	45.3
Intergovernmental	a	7,941	21,195	53	a	42.0	21.5	0.1
Highways	19,442	5,540	15,380	6,303	6.0	2.9	15.6	6.0
Direct	19,442	432	12,747	6,263	6.0	0.2	12.9	5.9
Intergovernmental	a	5,108	2,633	40	a	2.7	2.7	0
Public Welfare	23,558	15,739	19,191	9,012	7.3	8.4	19.4	8.6
Direct	23,558	2,488	12,247	8,822	7.3	1.3	12.4	1.4
Intergovernmental	a	13,251	6,944	190	a	7.0	7.0	0.2
Health and Hospitals	17,033	5,478	6,963	6,983	5.3	2.9	7.0	6.6
Direct	17,033	4,166	6,008	6,858	5.3	2.2	6.1	6.5
Intergovernmental	a	1,312	955	125	a	0.7	1.0	0.1
Natural Resources	14,215	11,729	2,595	649	4.4	6.2	2.6	0.6
Direct	14,215	11,105	2,470	640	4.4	5.9	2.5	0.6
Intergovernmental	a	624	125	9	a	0.3	0.1	0

owns about 50 percent of the geothermal and uranium re-sources.[1] Decisions about public property and resources are made by public officials who are often allowed considerable discretion in making choices.

2. **Public assumption of economic risk.** Federal and state governments are providers of things that are economically too risky for private industry, especially when the risk is com-

TABLE   14.1 (cont'd.)

Function	Amount (millions of dollars)				Percentage			
	All Govt.	Federal Govts.	State Govts.	Local Govts.	All Govt.	Federal Govts.	State Govts.	Local Govts.
Housing and Urban Renewal	5,411	4,611	149	2,748	1.7	2.5	0.2	2.6
Direct	5,411	2,630	34	2,747	1.7	1.4	0	2.6
Intergovernmental	a	1,981	115	1	a	1.1	0.1	0
Air Transportation	3,575	2,538	178	1,013	1.1	1.3	0.2	1.0
Direct	3,575	2,419	144	1,012	1.1	1.3	0.1	1.0
Intergovernmental	p06a	119	34	1	a	0.1	0	0
Social Insurance Administration	2,291	1,911	1,133	3	0.7	1.0	1.1	0
Direct	2,291	1,155	1,133	3	0.7	0.6	1.1	0
Intergovernmental	a	756	0	0	a	0.4	0	0
Interest on General Debt[c]	23,077	17,114	2,135	3,287	7.2	9.1	2.2	3.6
Other and Combined	50,805	18,402	12,738	27,068	15.8	9.8	12.9	25.7
Direct	50,805	15,910	7,979	26,916	15.8	8.9	8.1	25.5
Intergovernmental	a	2,492	4,758	152	a	1.3	4.8	0.1

SOURCE: U.S. Bureau of the Census, *Governmental Finances in 1971–1972*. Washington: Government Printing Office.

NOTE: Because of rounding, detail may not add to totals. Local government amounts are estimates subject to sampling variations.

[a] Duplicative transactions between levels of government are excluded.

[b] Entirely to states except for $6,104 million paid directly to local governments, including $1,712 million for education, $1,926 million for housing and urban renewal, $60 million for airports, $411 million for waste treatment facilities, and $171 million federal lump-sum contribution to the District of Columbia.

[c] Entirely direct expenditure.

bined with great expense. For instance, urban public housing, rail passenger transportation, solar thermal electricity generation, and educational television stations are considered poor prospects for private profits; therefore, if society wants them, it must ask the public sector to take the responsibility.

3. **Socially defined nonprofit activities.** A pharmaceutical company knows that it is socially acceptable to maximize profits on aspirin or vitamin C, but it is socially unacceptable to increase company dividends by adding as large a profit margin as possible to the sales price of a cure for cancer. Profits for helping people feel good are viewed differently than profits for saving lives. Generally, therefore, cancer research must be provided as a result of public investment. A major distinction between political-economic systems in the world is in the degree to which this reasoning is extended to other economic activities, such as transportation, steel production, insurance, or food production. But it is especially likely to happen where scale economies make it difficult for private competitors to coexist, leading to a monopolistic situation—with the potential of socially and politically high prices as a result.

4. **Goods and services of general utility.** There are not very many "private" highways because it is too hard to restrict the benefits of a highway to paying customers of a private company. For instance, how does the company get a fair return from all the landowners whose property values rise because of the new road? Unless the firm simply must have a new road in order to make profits from another activity, it will normally use its money in other ways. Likewise, it is hard to place a precise economic value on elementary education, emergency medical care, national defense, or law enforcement (the value strictly of the protection of property is easier to measure). There are many such "nonmarketable" services and facilities that are needed and used by nearly everyone—but that usually require public support. And these activities, in turn, can lead to other, more conventional economic activities by government agencies (see Box 14.4).

14.3.3 *Economic Activities of Government as a Consumer*

In order to carry on its activities, economic and otherwise, a government must find the necessary resources: money, people, materials. And because the supply side is so massive, so are the demands of governments as consumers. For instance, the federal

BOX 14.4 THE U.S. FEDERAL GOVERNMENT AS AN ADVERTISER

When it comes to advertising, Uncle Sam isn't about to take a back seat to J. Walter Thompson.

A like amount of money was spent last year promoting the U.S. Air Force and Head & Shoulders shampoo. The bill for selling all America's defense forces approximated Proctor & Gamble's 76 million outlay for its detergents, soaps, laundry and household products alone.

For the third year in a row, the U.S. government places tenth on the list of the 100 largest national advertisers in the country, according to Advertising Age's annual survey. The federal ad budget for 1975, totaling an estimated $113.4 million, surpassed those of commercial giants such as Colgate-Palmolive, American Tel-Tel, General Mills, Chrysler and Ford.

Uncle Sam spent almost the same amount of money to recruit military personnel, stimulate railroad passenger traffic and encourage use of change of address forms as R. J. Reynolds did to sell cigarettes. . . .

The federal government increased its ad budget by only 2 percent in 1975, whereas the industry as a whole raised its post-recession promotion investment by 6.7 percent to a record $6.4 billion. Most military services' budgets actually declined last year, a trend that is due to continue in the upcoming fiscal year. Much of the 2 percent increase went to Amtrak, up from $3 million in 1975. Its directors have requested a $9 million ad budget in fiscal 1977.

The largest federal publicity seeker

is still the U.S. Army, which spent about $33 million on recruiting ads in 1975, a mere 10 percent more than Bristol Myers put into Clairol hair ads. Slightly more was spent promoting Preparation H than the U.S. Marines ($8 million), while the U.S. Postal Service's ad expenses were on a par with those for Tide detergent.

This year, the Postal Service is testing a campaign to encourage Americans to write personal letters. If approved, it would cost $5 million annually, or just 10 per cent more than General Foods spent last year to encourage Americans to eat Raisin Bran.

The USPS campaign is intended as a direct confrontation to AT&T's long-distance telephone promotion. One pilot, prepared by Young & Rubicam, features a mother and small daughter receiving a letter from a distant friend. Daughter: "But couldn't she call?" Mother: "Of course, but when I get a letter from her, I guess I feel like you do when you get a gift."

In the case of the federal government, more than twice as much. . . was spent on unmeasured as measured advertising last year. The unmeasured included posters, brochures, displays and outdoor material appearing on military installations, college campuses and public institutions, as well as inserts in Social Security mailing and free public service announcements.

SOURCE: From Nancy L. Ross, *The Washington Post*, Fall, 1976. (*Norman Transcript*, September 6, 1976, p. 5).

government consumes about 3 percent of all the energy supplied in the United States each year (the largest part of this goes to the Department of Defense, for whom special energy reserves are maintained). As a supporter and user of research and development activities, the federal government spent an estimated $21.6 billion in 1976—some of this for work by government agencies themselves, some for work by private contractors and grantees. And governments at all levels are employers; in fact, federal, state, and city governments are becoming the major source of new jobs in many areas (see Box 14.5).

To pay these bills, governments must generate revenues, with taxes as the predominant source. In 1972, for instance, governments in the United States received $361 billion in taxes, contributions, and other income; $275 billion of this was in taxes on income, property, sales, gasoline, cigarettes, liquor, and other items. In many cases, the need for revenue is greater than the funds available, and governments borrow—U.S. savings bonds and municipal bonds are familiar examples. In 1972, governments in the United States paid more than $23 billion in interest on their debts: local governments alone owed more than $120 billion.

In seeking such loans, as in employing secretaries and buying electricity, governments are actually in competition with private decision makers. And they have some special advantages that they can use to offset a more cumbersome set of procedures for making decisions (what private firm could declare interest earned on bonds to be tax-free?).

14.3.4 *Patterns of Government Economic Decisions*

It is generally easier to illustrate the consequences of government decisions than to identify in a precise way some concepts that will predict the decisions. But this section will provide a starting point for thinking about such concepts. Remember that every decision by a government to allocate money or other resources is a *locational* decision, because it affects some places more than others.

The Best Place for an Activity If we could express the figures in Chapter 5 in terms of political costs and benefits instead of dollars, we could approach a set of concepts for government locational decisions. But it is difficult for an outsider to estimate the value of political currency in any other way than watching what government decision makers do.

For many locational decisions by government, certain factors are the same as for a private firm. A "market" can often be defined (for instance, school children or riders of an urban mass transportation system). There are costs to overcoming distance, including some social and political effects. As an example, a psychologist in England found that young children who travel farther to school have a more difficult time adjusting to it. And land rent is usually important, because taxpayers dislike seeing more money spent for land acquisition than necessary. Consequently, locational efficiency and economies of scale often lead to a pattern of activity that differs very little from what a private provider would select. But governmental decisions are sometimes made without much certainty about locational alternatives. Even when they include the same information that a private decision maker would seek, a least-distance solution may lead to a politically or socially undesirable result,

BOX 14.5   GOVERNMENTS AS CONSUMERS OF LABOR

Few employment sectors have grown as steadily as government. The following graph shows government employment in the

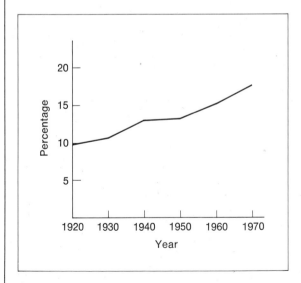

Governments as Consumers of Labor. The vertical axis shows U.S. government employment as a percentage of all employment in nonagricultural establishments (not including armed forces).

United States as a percentage of all employment in nonagricultural establishments (not including the armed forces). More than 8 million people in the United States are employed in federal, state, or local government—more than the total population of Sweden and Switzerland. And for more than fifty years government employment has expanded more rapidly than total employment.

Although the numbers and types of jobs vary a good bit from place to place, the message is pretty much the same everywhere (barring dramatic political and cultural change). In fact, if recent trends in some states were to continue, before the end of this century 100 percent of their employed people would be working for a government agency.

It is worth noting that government employment sometimes provides important kinds of job training. In military service, for instance, high school graduates often acquire skills that they use to get jobs afterwards. Similarly, police officers may become private detectives, district attorneys may become defense lawyers, public school teachers may set up private schools, and government managers may move into private industry.

such as leaving a particular constituency without nearby services or creating a racially imbalanced school system.

As a result, economic patterns that result from decisions by governments as providers and consumers may take on a distinctive form. The political attractiveness of giving each locality a desirable facility, for instance, often leads to a more dispersed pattern of facilities than economic factors alone would call for. And the number of public facilities named for important political figures (which itself has a geographic pattern) is not unrelated to the influence of those individuals on locational decisions. In this sense, the key factor in locating a new military installation can be the seniority of a committee chairperson in a legislature. When the proposed facility is a "noxious" one, viewed as undesirable by some of the people who would be near it (such as a sewage treatment plant, a mental-health-care outpatient clinic, or a nuclear power plant), political power becomes a repelling force rather than an attraction. Consequently, many such activities are located in areas occupied by people with little political power, near boundaries between different cohesive groups, or in peripheral places.

In general, the effect of these noneconomic influences is felt most strongly on decisions about specific sites: will the new road be built across *this* piece of property or *that*? It has less effect on comparisons of regional situations, where an economically irrational decision is likely to be more visible—and thus politically less acceptable. But even at this scale, it tends to turn an indifference curve into a much thicker band of economic equivalency (see Chapter 4).

It is also worth noting that governments sometimes have the power to modify locational conditions (Chapter 15). For example, in extreme cases they can use their "right of eminent domain" to remove from a private land owner the power to define the rent by bargaining with all possible buyers.

The Best Activity for a Place   Likewise, governments operate in a different world in deciding the best use of a particular location. They are accountable to voters and political supporters rather than to stockholders, generally acting to use places in ways that realize less than the theoretical land rent but meet social needs that would otherwise be neglected.

Many examples of this are quite clear-cut. An acre of New Mexico forestland would probably earn more as a source of lumber than as a national forest, but it would be politically impossible— and in the view of most people, socially and environmentally undesirable—to convert it to timberlands. Other cases are more complex. What is the "rent" of a parcel of ocean bottom far out on the outer continental shelf? There may be oil or gas under it, but no one has drilled a hole yet to find out. Before allowing the drilling to take place (assuming that environmental impacts are judged to be acceptable), the federal government wants to be sure that the public will be fairly compensated for any discoveries that a private firm may make. But if it sets the rate of compensation too high, no developers will be interested, and the public will get no compensation—and no new oil and gas. Assessing the *public interest* is much more tenuous than determining private economic benefit.

Since governments make decisions about acquiring land as well as using the areas they own, this is a constant challenge. "Open space" may be assured by land purchases. Unspoiled natural settings may be acquired so that they can be preserved. Parts of cities may be appropriated and redeveloped (urban renewal). Rights of way for highways may be purchased.

This means that the economic patterns around us reflect an intricate mixture of different processes. In part, we can see the relationships discussed in Chapters 5 and 6, such as distance decay in land rents. But the pattern is interrupted by enclaves and bands of *publicly owned land*, for which the explanations relate to different institutions and values. Interspersed in the pattern are economic activities of government that are not strictly comparable to private activities because they pay no taxes and please a broader constituency.

It is difficult to generalize about the spatial pattern of these public land uses except to say that they are often found in areas that, at a particular time in history, were relatively unattractive to private decision makers. Federal lands in the United States, for instance, are obviously concentrated in hard-to-farm parts of the West (see Figure 14.2). Museums, parks, civic office buildings, and public housing have filled many of the areas cleared for urban renewal. It is politically much easier for a government to implement a socially beneficial land use at a particular location if the result is not a sharp reduction in the economic benefits being realized from the location.

Systems of Activities at Systems of Places Market area patterns for private activities are a consequence of movement costs and economies of scale (see Chapter 7). Since many public activities are also subject to these kinds of costs and economies, it is not surprising that functions such as schools and the postal service are "central place activities." It makes sense for health-care clinics and recreation centers to be spaced with care. They serve market areas defined by a maximum range for the service and a minimum threshold size for the activity. They reflect a continuing debate about the

FIGURE 14.2
Federal Lands in the
United States.

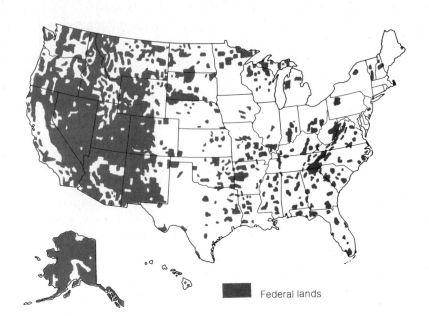

Federal lands

relative merits of a larger number of smaller units that are closer to consumers and fewer, perhaps more efficient or better equipped larger units (as in neighborhood schools versus consolidation). They are organized hierarchically (for example, elementary schools, junior high schools, and high schools). Their service areas are usually clearly defined. What is different is their marketplace: how decisions are made about what to do and what to change (also see Box 14.6).

BOX 14.6 NONECONOMIC LOCATION DECISIONS

Just as the concepts in Chapter 7 apply to many government activities, they often work for location decisions by private groups that are motivated mainly by noneconomic factors. For example, in a growing metropolitan area, a great deal of planning goes into the acquisition of property for churches. The planners—usually a consortium of people from a particular religious denomination—consider the location and size of the activity (the minimum size for a self-sustaining church), economies of scale (the ability of a larger church to support a larger staff and offer more services), and the "competition" (the location, sizes, and "market penetration" of other churches, existing and planned). Sometimes, similar denominations even enter into agreements not to duplicate their "market coverage."

Clearly, government functions are as diverse as the actions of private decision makers. Just as the retail sale of clothing is more likely to be organized in a geographically predictable way than the writing of paperback novels, school systems are better described as central place activities than are government data storage facilities. In particular, there is a difference in the impact of movement costs on spatial arrangement. In addition, public economic activities vary widely in how precisely the market's location can be identified (for instance, an elementary school district compared with an Army basic training facility). There may be a distinction between activities that meet pressing social needs, as opposed to those that offer more specialized conveniences. And, when the objective is to assure social welfare, the resulting pattern may be different than if the goal is simply to provide public goods, because the area of need becomes the geographic focus for locating service facilities.

There is an inherent complexity to organizing systems of activities at systems of places because there are so many questions to be answered: how many units should there be? what should be their capacities? will their capacities be fixed or varying? what are the candidate locations? what will be the sequence of implementation (since it is seldom possible to establish all the units at the same time)? A change in the answer to any one of these questions may affect all the others. Given the location of the residences of school children and the number of elementary schools to be provided, for instance, it is quite possible to define school district boundaries that minimize the distance traveled by students. For an example, see Figure 14.3(b). For a variety of historical and social reasons, the actual boundaries always differ, as shown in Figures 14.3(a) and (c), and minimizing distance is not always the primary objective. But even if it were, the solution could be affected by every move of a family into or out of a district, and it would be substantially affected by a decision to build a new school.

Government activities are often distinctive in the specificity (and rigidity) with which these "market area" boundaries are defined. A private firm that decides to shift its Oklahoma City territory from its Kansas City office to its Dallas office can simply make that decision, responding to changes in conditions. But such frameworks as Federal Reserve Bank district boundaries tend to create nodal regions that become difficult to change, and many other services have their jurisdictions defined by preexisting political boundaries (for example, courts, public safety, county schools, and state health care programs). In addition, because the multiplicity of government activities makes coordination difficult, as seen in

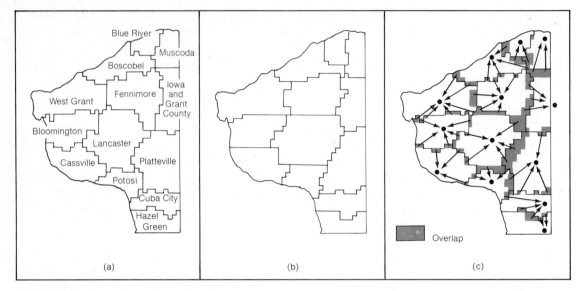

FIGURE 14.3

High School Districts in Grant County, Wisconsin, 1961: (a) actual districts; (b) spatially efficient districts; and (c) the difference between the two. In (c), arrows indicate a school that is nearer to to place of residence than to the district school.

Figure 14.4 (a), common service regions are sometimes defined for a group of services that would individually call for different boundary systems, as shown by Figure 14.4 (b). Generally, these politically determined boundaries mean greater transfer costs, which must eventually be absorbed by the provider or consumer; but other considerations may be judged more important (see Box 14.7).

Government Activities and an Economic Base   In addition to taking on a pattern themselves, economic activities of government influence other patterns (see Box 14.1). Two kinds of effects are especially important:

1.   **Infrastructure.** As providers of basic services such as transportation and education, governments provide for key needs of private economic decision makers. The Interstate Highway System in the United States, for example, has facilitated the movement of freight by truck and has enhanced the locational advantages of cities at junctions of major limited access highways. Schools and other public services are central elements of the *amenities* offered by locations to prospective new economic activities; if two places are roughly equal economically, a decision maker will usually opt for the one with the best schools, recreational attractions, and cultural opportunities.

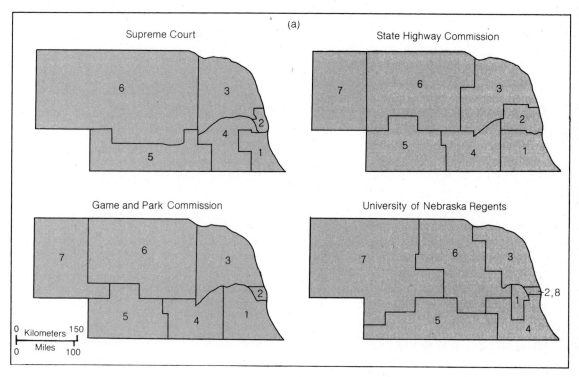

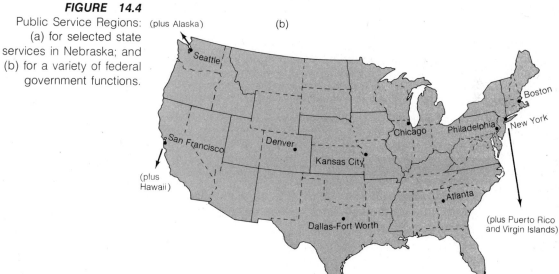

FIGURE 14.4

Public Service Regions: (a) for selected state services in Nebraska; and (b) for a variety of federal government functions.

2. **Government as a basic activity.** Whether the activity is a state university or a centralized welfare agency employing hundreds of managers and clerks, the area where the facility is located usually receives more (in wages spent and purchases made) than it loses (in taxes to pay for the activity and in property taxes foregone). The inflow of tax money activates an economic multiplier in the local area, as discussed in Chapter 8. In addition, the government activities offer agglomeration economies to private individuals and firms, ranging from lobbyists to office supply firms, telephone servicing centers, and consulting firms. Government is nearly always good business for its site.

14.3.5 *Government Providers and Consumers as Economic Opportunities*

If a private economic decision maker understands how government as a provider and consumer makes decisions, opportunities can

---

BOX 14.7 FISCAL FEDERALISM

According to one body of theory, the most efficient way to provide public services is to arrange them in a particular geographical pattern, so that the political domain of decision making is the same as the geographical extent of an area that receives the benefits *and* pays the bills. This suggests a kind of *fiscal federalism*, where each area that receives benefits from a public facility is delimited. Then the revenue needed for the facility is raised from within that area. And that area decides on its own level of services and payment.

C. M. Tiebout, who developed this theory, noted that it identifies an optimal distribution of government functions that is similar to what central place theory would identify for the private sector.

In practice, there are a number of problems that make it difficult to convert fiscal federalism from theory into policy. For example, each particular government function has benefits that spread over an area of a distinct size and shape (compare a municipal hospital with a city park). But it is awkward to define a different revenue-raising district for each individual service; in fact, four or five levels of government are the most that are usually encountered. This means that there are cases in which beneficiaries do not pay, in which people getting no benefits do pay, and in which the power to make political decisions may have little relation to either benefits or fiscal responsibility. It would be nice to be able to say that the "geographic spill-overs" balance themselves out—that spill-outs are usually about the same as spill-ins. But this is not always the case.

Consequently, for administrative convenience, we make our governmental decisions at a very small number of different geographic scales. The price is a loss of efficiency and, in some cases, a reduction in the level of self-determination.

often be identified. A familiar example is the increase in property values that follows a decision to build a new highway near a person's land. But many of the possibilities are less obvious than this—and more open to individual initiative. Most governmental units are obligated to announce beforehand that they plan to buy something: new police cars, spools of copper wire, tons of stationery. This allows potential suppliers to identify themselves, so that the public agency can get the best deal possible. In general, a governmental activity as a consumer operates more publicly, with its plans and the rules of the game spelled out for all to see. Private entrepreneurs who know the plans and understand the rules can avail themselves of a very big customer.

This kind of opportunity tends to have a spatial pattern, partly because the purchased items have to be moved to the consumer—but more fundamentally because an understanding of the opportunities depends on information. For instance, when the federal government decides to "buy" a big piece of research, it is usually required to notify potential contractors of its plans. Packets of information are sent to groups that are known to be prospects, and an announcement is published in the *Commerce and Business Daily*, which is mailed to subscribers. But people who are in Washington frequently have several advantages. For example, they often hear about the need well before distant people get something in their mail, which is a major benefit in meeting what are sometimes very tight deadlines for proposals; and they have a chance to get to know agency personnel better, which can help when proposals from unknown people are being compared with known quantities. Remember, though, that governments are ubiquitous, and city and county governments spend money, too.

A further kind of opportunity in our increasingly specialized world is helping businesses in their relations with government. One example is specializing in preparing offers for competitive sealed bidding on government construction projects. Another is information and public relations, both in communicating the interests of the private sector to governments and in helping businesses interpret the mass of laws and regulations that apply to them.

A special opening for private enterprise in some situations is taking on functions that government is asked to perform but prefers not to do itself. Some communities, for instance, have found that it is more efficient to hire a private company to provide fire protection services than to maintain a fire department. An advantage is that periodically the performance of the contractor can be evaluated, and if it is not as good as other bidders could provide, the contractor can be changed. Another advantage is that if a government function can be terminated, the decision is not complicated by the

FIGURE   14.5
Federal Grants-in-Aid to
States, 1970 Program
Levels, in Dollars per
Capita: (a) per capita
grants; (b) public
assistance; and
[continued on next page]

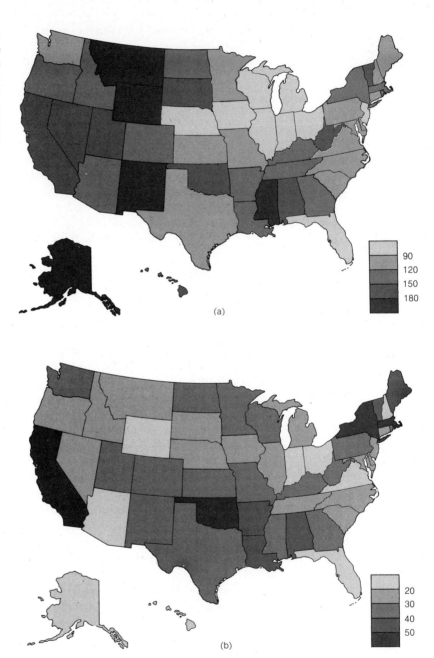

(a)

(b)

internal pressures of a part of the institution trying to survive.
These opportunities, of course, are geographically just as specific as
if the government were continuing to be the actor.

FIGURE   14.5 (cont'd.)
(c) education. (Also see
Figures 14.8 and 14.11.)

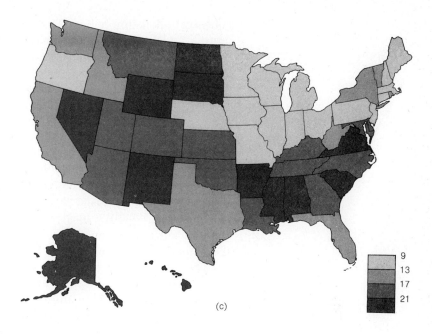

(c)

14.4   EXAMPLES

The preceding sections have included a lot of examples of how
governments act as economic decision makers. To add some additional images to the picture, this section will describe how the federal government in the United States operates as a provider in the
fields of energy and income, and it will offer a few indications of
how uneven the economic actions of governments are from place to
place.

14.4.1   Examples of the U.S. Federal Government as a Provider

Energy   For a variety of reasons, the federal government of the
United States has decided that the country needs to supply more of
its energy needs from domestic sources. Along with a large number
of indirect actions (see Chapter 15), it is serving directly as a provider in ways that include these:

1.   It supports research, development, and demonstration activities intended to create new or better energy supply and

conservation technologies. The fiscal 1976 budget called for more than $1.8 billion in obligations for energy research and development (R & D), plus an additional $0.5 billion for supporting programs studying environmental health effects and engaged in basic research. In large part, this is a continuation of a long involvement with nuclear power technologies and with information about natural resources. It includes the development of technologies that are offered for sale to private industry (sometimes competing with privately developed technologies), the provision of facilities to support privately operated nuclear power plants, and the generation of information to aid in evaluating environmental impacts and policy needs. Many sensitive locational decisions are required.

2. It owns substantial energy resources. As mentioned earlier, the federal government is the owner of immense quantities of resources. This includes offshore and Alaskan oil and gas and most of the coal, oil shale, and uranium in the western part of the United States. Using these resources is presently a very uncertain business because the decisions are scrutinized by a public with diverse views about the "public interest." Because these resources are regionally concentrated—offshore from coastal areas, in the West, and in Alaska—the policies of the federal government as a provider have a distinct geographic pattern, which is affected in turn by the policies of governments of the states that contain federal land. For instance, concerns about environmental preservation in the state of Colorado have added to uncertainties about the use of oil shale resources on federal lands in the state. And the regional impact of natural gas from Alaska is believed to differ substantially according to the transportation system: liquified natural gas tankers delivering supplies to the West Coast or a trans-Canada pipeline making deliveries to the upper Midwest.

Income   In addition to being a provider of wages to its employees, the federal government is a distributor of income supplements and substitutes. When this happens, it reflects the view of society that private economic markets, acting alone, are defective; they fail to meet some needs. For example, federal old age survivors and disability insurance (Social Security) results in payments to individuals throughout the United States. Though payment levels are the same regardless of the location of the recipient, there are more recipients at some places than at others (popular retirement areas, for instance—but also aging small towns and some parts of large cities).

FIGURE 14.6
Revenue sharing in
1972–1973: (a) total share
per capita, (b) local share
per urban resident.

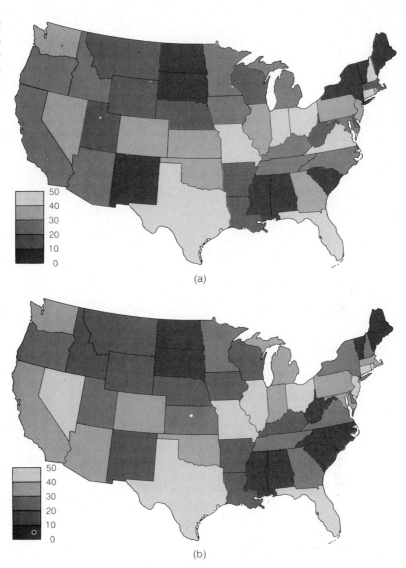

(a)

(b)

Other programs allow localities to establish their own standards,
which can result in striking regional differences in support levels.

In some cases, rather than distributing money directly, the
federal government disburses income substitutes. An example is
food, in the form of food stamps and school lunch programs. Public
health care, transportation, and subsidized public housing are other
examples, as are educational and housing benefits for veterans of
military service.

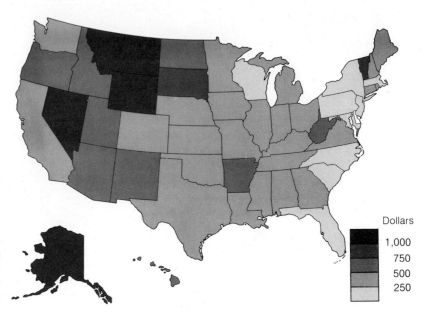

FIGURE 14.7
Total Federal Expenditure on Domestic Transportation by State, 1957–1971, per capita. Although a great many factors influenced this pattern, a comparison with Figure 2.1 shows that the less densely populated areas generally received higher per capita expenditures. Partly, this reflects the fact that movement distances per person are often greater in sparsely populated states (also compare with Figure 2.4). It may also indicate that in many such areas a substantial part of the traffic is meeting national rather than intrastate needs; the facilities will not be provided if the decision is left up to the states themselves, because most of the benefits will be for out-of-state residents.

Dollars
1,000
750
500
250

An alternative to direct federal action is the channeling of federal money to states and smaller units of government. This aid may take the form of conditional grants for particular activities (based on a formula for eligibility—such as population size—or on local matching funds or the need to demonstrate a new program somewhere), or it may allow the locality to use the money as it chooses. Figure 14.5 (page 300) shows how distribution of conditional grants can vary geographically (note the differences in the patterns, as Chapter 3 suggested). Unconditional grants also show a pattern, because they are usually based on a formula that considers other factors besides population size. For instance, the payments to state and local governments under the General Revenue Sharing Program consider income levels and the state tax effort as well as population size. In the first year of the program the formula resulted in the complex patterns shown in Figure 14.6 (page 303).

Other possible programs are proposed from time to time. One suggestion, intended to simplify the system of welfare aid to low-income people, has been a "guaranteed annual income" (see Box 14.8).

14.4.2 *Patterns of Government Service and Consumption*
In serving as economic providers and consumers, governments almost invariably create uneven patterns of benefits and burdens. In

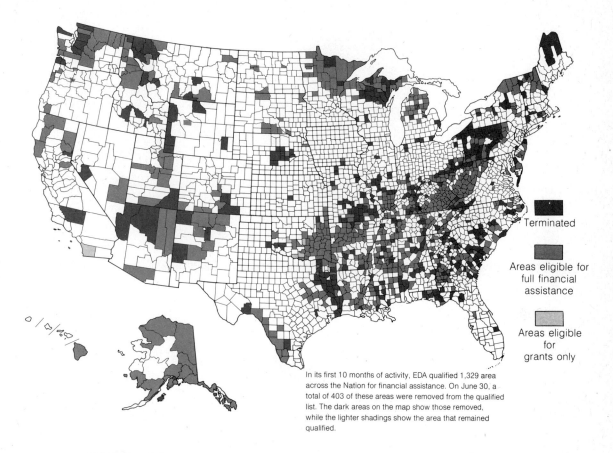

Terminated

Areas eligible for
full financial
assistance

Areas eligible
for
grants only

In its first 10 months of activity, EDA qualified 1,329 area
across the Nation for financial assistance. On June 30, a
total of 403 of these areas were removed from the qualified
list. The dark areas on the map show those removed,
while the lighter shadings show the area that remained
qualified.

FIGURE 14.8

Areas Eligible for Federal
Economic Development
Administration Financial
Assistance, FY 1966.

some cases, the unevenness is intentional (for the kinds of reasons
discussed in Chapters 15 and 16); in others, it is unintended. But in
either case it influences private economic decisions and affects the
well-being of people at particular places.

To get a sense of the immense variety of geographic differences in government services, tax collections, and other economic
activities, consider Figures 14.7–14.13. Figure 14.7 shows how federal expenditures on national infrastructure (in this case, transportation) vary from state to state over a 15-year period. In certain cases, federal expenditures are limited to specified areas with
particular needs (Figure 14.8 is an example). In other cases, a federal system for spending money to meet a social need is im-
plemented by individual state programs, and important variations
arise from the latitude allowed the states (for example, Figure 14.9).

Revenues, both in total effort and the source of the tax collections, also vary geographically (see Figures 14.10–14.12), and the

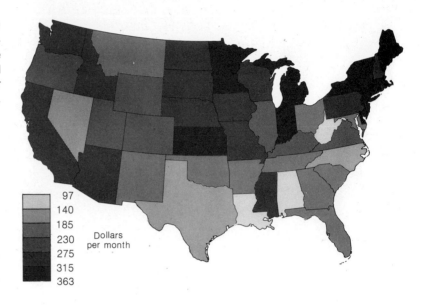

FIGURE 14.9
Aid to Families with Dependent Children: state variations in the standard for determining need for assistance.

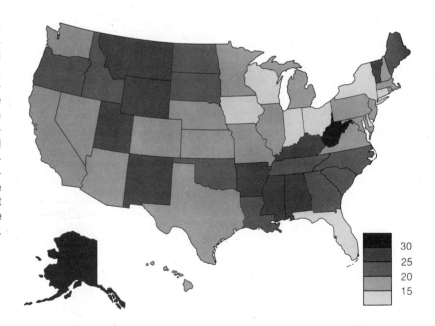

FIGURE 14.10
Federal Aid as a Proportion of Total State and Local General Revenue, by state, 1971. This illustrates how the role of the federal government can vary as a provider of revenue for state and local governments (but remember that the proportion is affected by state and local government contributions to revenue as well).

implications are significant. For instance, a state with a large sales tax but a low level of state and local property taxation probably benefits high-income people more than those with lower incomes, and vice versa.

FIGURE 14.11
Property Taxes as a Proportion of Total State and Local Tax Receipts, 1971. This is only one of several ways that taxes differ from place to place. A map of the variations in state personal income tax rates or local sales tax rates would show a different pattern.

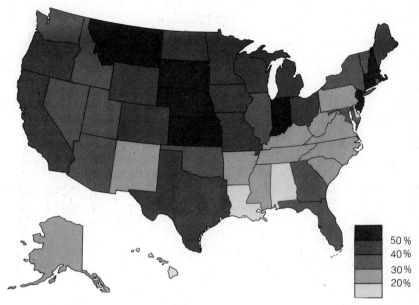

50 %
40 %
30 %
20 %

Finally, Figure 14.13 indicates one of the differences between states in their roles as economic actors: investors, bank depositors, and debtors.

Using your now well-developed perspective as a geographer, and remembering your own needs as a locational decision maker, it is worth spending some time studying these maps—and perhaps searching for information that will make it possible for you to make some other maps of your own. For example, what is the relationship between state and local tax effort and the quantity and quality of public services in an area?

14.5   A RECONSIDERATION

In viewing governments as economic decision makers, there are several key points to remember:

1. A government may decide on a course that a private decision maker would not choose, because governments respond to different "market" conditions.

2. These decisions have a geographic pattern of impact, just as they would if they were private decisions.

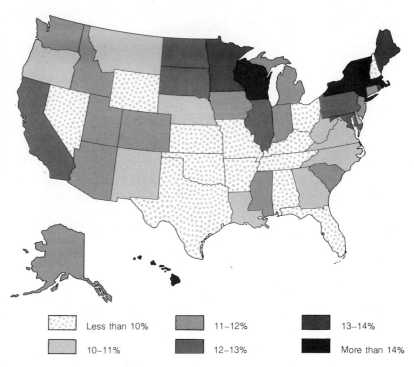

FIGURE 14.12
Relative Tax Effort in 1970, by State (estimated by total state and local tax collections as a percentage of adjusted personal income). This is an indicator of the willingness of a state to provide support for public services (compare with Box 14.3).

Less than 10%   11–12%   13–14%

10–11%   12–13%   More than 14%

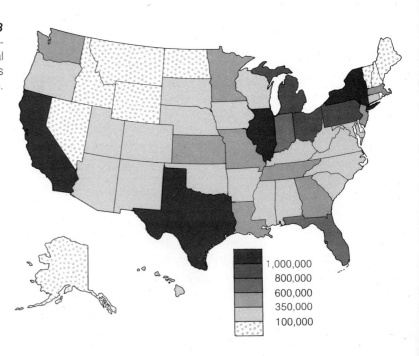

FIGURE 14.13
Cash and Security Holdings by State and Local Governments, in millions of dollars, 1962, by state.

1,000,000
800,000
600,000
350,000
100,000

3.   Even though the pattern may differ, the effects on the local areas involved are similar: a modification of the supply-demand balance, a regional multiplier, an addition or loss of opportunities and benefits.

4.   A pattern that diverges from the one that would be ideal from a purely economic perspective has the effect of adding some economic costs. Locating a government office in a remote area, for example, might be a highly desirable social action to boost the economy in that area; but it could require higher transportation and communication costs, along with the construction of a new building at the site compared with the use of avail-

BOX 14.8   THE REGIONAL IMPACT OF A GUARANTEED ANNUAL INCOME

Guaranteed annual income is one term (an unfortunate one for political proponents) for a particular approach to assuring the welfare of unemployed and very low-income people. Such an income maintenance program calls for an annual federal payment of a set amount ($2,400, $4,000, $6,500, or another number) to a family of a certain size with no income. Families with very low income are eligible for payments on a decreasing scale until their incomes reach a ceiling level. With this kind of program, it is believed possible to do away with a variety of federal, state, and local public assistance programs that are awkward and expensive to administer.

Clearly, a locality with a large number of people eligible for such benefits would receive a lot of money from it. Figure 1 shows the regional pattern of benefits from a plan introduced to the U.S. Congress in 1971. Note that, although the largest total amounts would go to the most populous states (such as New York and California), the greatest benefit per person would be concentrated in the southern and border states, with an outlier in the Dakotas.

Surprisingly, for a variety of reasons the states that stood to receive higher levels of payments turned out to be opponents of it, and the income maintenance idea has not yet had much political success in the United States.

$101.39	$171.56
$ 83.85	$154.02
$ 66.30	$136.47
$ 48.76	$118.93
	$101.39

Payments Per Capita from a Proposed Family Assistance Plan.

able office space at a state capital. Consequently, in considering different options for assuring social welfare, it is useful to compare them according to economic criteria as well as social ones, so that decision makers are informed about the whole range of effects.

5.   Government decisions are intricately related to private economic activities. Although the specific relationship varies geographically, a person at any location who understands it better than other people has a significant economic advantage.

MAJOR CONCEPTS AND TERMS

For definitions, see the Glossary.

Amenities	*Infrastructure*	*Public interest*
Fiscal federalism	*Locational conflict*	*Public lands*
Governmental	*resolution*	*Public sector*
jurisdiction	*Public facilities*	*Social welfare*

Footnote for Chapter 14

1.   Ford Foundation. *A Time to Choose.* 1974, p. 271; and U.S. Congress, Committee on Interior and Insular Affairs. Washington: 1972, p. 197.

CHAPTER 15

GOVERNMENT AS A SHAPER OF AN ECONOMIC-GEOGRAPHIC SYSTEM

As important as government is in its role as an economic-geographic "actor," its effect is even more widespread as a shaper of private location decisions. Governments at all levels establish conditions, set limits, and otherwise cause us to act differently than some of us might otherwise act. As a result, we often choose different locations for our economic activities, different activities for our locations, and different routes and destinations for our movements.

Just as in Chapter 14, this shaping of our economic geography reflects a particular definition of "public interest." We can agree that certain human activities are socially undesirable, such as murder or child labor. It is in the public interest to exclude murder and child labor as *permissible activities*; therefore they are defined as illegal, and severe penalties are imposed on those who break the law. In a similar way, we may agree that certain land uses are socially undesirable—and prohibit them. Because such limits affect an individual's range of choice, it can affect the pattern of land use that develops.

Often, though, such outright prohibitions (on, for example, certain land uses) are themselves seen as socially undesirable, both because freedom of choice is viewed as important for its own sake, and because the entire range of effects of a prohibition is hard to anticipate. An alternative is to affect the bases of economic decision making more subtly. For instance, governments have a variety of ways to make certain activities, locations, or destinations more (or less) expensive than they would otherwise be. And this can have a profound impact on the decisions of an economically rational private individual or group.

15.1 *SITUATION: THE AVERAGE DAY*

ALLENTOWN, PA. (AP) — At 7:45 A.M., Nancy Ruddell sits down for her first cup of morning coffee, adding an artificial sweetener containing saccharin.

"Contains no cyclamate" reads the little packet of Shop Rite Superior Quality Sweetener. Cyclamate lacks saccharin's bitter aftertaste, but it cannot be sold for human consumption because of a U.S. Food and Drug Administration (FDA) ruling in 1969.

This day that started at 6:15 A.M. is a mostly unexceptional one for Tom and Nancy Ruddell. They take their two children to school: Tom goes to work at Pennsylvania Power and Light; Nancy makes two shopping trips; and they give a small party.

But throughout this day, and every other day, the Ruddells' lives—and those of every American—are shaped by federal regulations.

The effects of most regulations slip by unnoticed—like U.S. Department of Agriculture's fat content for the choice beef sold at the local supermarket.

Others are not so hidden—like the required seat belt ignition interlock on Nancy's red Volvo station wagon which she calls a constant pain in the neck.

. . . This is a look at the regulations in a day in the life of one American family in this city of 109,000 in the rolling hills of eastern Pennsylvania.

6:15 A.M.—A burst from the alarm clock reads that particular time because Congress decreed Daylight Savings Time ended when October did.

6:25 A.M.—Geoffrey, age 5, slips out of his pajamas that are flame retardant because the Consumer Product Safety Commission requires sleepwear for children to be so treated.

6:50 A.M.—Three quarts of Abbotts homogenized milk deposited earlier in the morning outside the back door are brought in by Geoffrey. Nancy makes a mix of the milk and reconstituted Shop Rite Instant Non-fat Dry Milk, cutting the drink's calories and cholesterol. But the resulting mixture is also cheaper than ordinary skim milk because the U.S. Department of Agriculture sets a higher support price for skim milk than whole milk.

7:37 A.M.—Jennifer, 10, and Geoffrey take the Hess's brand of fruit-flavored chewable multiple vitamins. A bit later Tom and Nancy both take a multivitamin made by the Treasury Drug Co. for the J.C. Penney Co.

The manufacture and labeling of vitamins are now regulated by the Food and Drug Administration, but Sen. William Proxmire, D-Wis., is sponsoring a bill to prohibit the FDA from regulating the potency of such diet supplements. This would mean consumers would be able to buy massive doses of various vitamins, whether or not the FDA concludes such doses have a medical benefit.

7:50 A.M.—Tom starts for work. The federally mandated seat belt alarm on his Audi sedan doesn't make a shrill buzz when he turns the ignition key. It's been disconnected. It's my way of protesting the system, he says.

7:55 A.M.—Driving to work, Tom recalls the story of how a federal safety inspector ordered the wearing of hardhats and installation of guardrails at the workshop of the Trolley Museum in Kennebunkport, Maine. During the family's summer vacations, Tom spends much of his time working as a volunteer in restoring old trolley cars.

They probably did us a favor, but my Lord, it makes you think. They've even gotten to trolley museums, he says.

8:14 A.M.—Nancy backs her Volvo station wagon out of the garage on the way to take Jennifer to school. She pulls a small greyish box out of the glove compartment, presses its button, and the garage door closes.

The box is a low-powered radio transmitter, a Wickes model 116-56, which was built according to meet Federal Communications Commission standards.

But FCC rules are just not something Nancy thinks about. She notices the label on the back of the transmitter for the first time: this label is required by FCC rules. Do not remove.

8:19 A.M.—Jennifer carries her homemade lunch of a ham and tomato sandwich into the Union Terrace School. Many other students at Jennifer's public school will eat a lunch prepared at the school cafeteria, federally subsidized at about 23 cents for each lunch.

The U.S. Department of Agriculture requires that, to qualify for the subsidy, the school must serve a Type A lunch, which the department specifies must contain 2 ounces of meat or a meat substitute, ¾ cup of at least two vegetables or fruits, bread, butter and a half pint of milk.

8:35 A.M.—The federal government is constantly looking over Nancy's shoulder as she buys the family groceries at the big, brilliantly illuminated Shop Rite supermarket.

Nancy picks up a two-pound jar of Skippy peanut butter, which the FDA says can be called peanut butter because it is 90 percent peanuts. Any less, the FDA says, and it must be called peanut spread.

The label on the can of sliced peaches lists the vitamins, minerals, and calories that each serving of the fruit contains. The FDA is again responsible.

The Department of Agriculture set the standard that determines that the eye-of-the-round roast Nancy buys is choice rather than prime. And it inspected the farm that was the source for the $1.87/pound beef.

These regulations are not on Nancy's mind as she shops.

I'm looking for food that I think is nutritional. I don't care what the government says is right, she explains. I don't listen to Ralph Nader either.

12:17 P.M.—As if to underline her statements, Nancy makes her second shopping stop of the day at the Allentown Farmers Market, where mostly Pennsylvania-grown produce is sold in stalls in the open-air market, largely free from federal control.

Nancy buys apples and cheese.

Both are sold by farmers under federal agricultural marketing orders, which are designed to control supply and allocate income among producers. The federal government also props up the price of cheese by keeping foreign cheese out of the country and by buying quantities of American cheese when prices fall.

Much of the produce available at the market avoids much federal regulation, for it is produced and sold inside Pennsylvania. For example, there is meat on sale that is not USDA inspected because it is not shipped across state lines and thus is not in interstate commerce.

1:10 P.M.—Tom goes over a report at his office. It shows, based on a poll of the company's supervisory officers, that 23 federal bodies either receive reports from Pennsylvania Power and Light or affect its business in some way. The Agriculture Department loans money for rural electric service, the Environmental Protection Agency controls smokestack pollutants at generating stations, the Federal Power Commission controls wholesale prices on interstate sales of electricity to other utilities, the Equal Employment Opportunity Commission wants to know about PP & L's minority-group employees . . . the list goes on.

So numerous are the government connections that PP & L has launched a project, in which Tom is involved, to consider whether to set up a new company department to handle all contacts with federal and state authorities.

1:25 P.M.—Nancy sits in the family room talking to a visitor about the EPA's ban on the insecticide DDT, which she blames for a plague of mosquitoes at their rented vacation home for the past few summers. They don't spray at the beach anymore, she says.

8:30 P.M.—Friends begin to arrive for a small holiday gathering. The children watch a Christmas special on television, the ads for which would be screened for misleading statements under Federal Trade Commission regulations. Tom pours drinks. The alcohol is measured and taxed by the Treasury Department.

Throughout this day and every day the Ruddells, like any other family in America, are affected by federal regulations when they sleep, eat, work, drive, shop or play.[1]

15.2   *BASIC CONCEPTS*

Although this familiar situation is not directly geographic, it reminds us how unrealistic it is to presume that very many of our location decisions are based on a truly free market. It is a fact of life that economic concepts operate within a public policy framework. The price of grain reflects the federal government's policy toward exports of food to other countries. The cost of an automobile is affected by legal requirements for vehicle safety and air pollution abatement. The possible uses of a piece of urban land usually depend in part on a city ordinance establishing *zones* of permissible land uses. Reflecting the concerns of society (as expressed by political support or opposition), this framework of laws, regulations, and institutions represents the *political environment* of economic decision making. Once, the dominant environment influencing economic geography was the physical environment. No longer. It is now this political environment. It is here that the competition between areas to offer comparative advantages is focused, here that the pattern of accessibility is shaped.

Although societies differ in how they define the need for governmental action, the most basic concern is with cases in which the economic "market," operating freely and without restriction, will lead to undesirable activities or patterns (for example, monopoly, child labor, or environmental degradation). As indicated earlier, the problem is to define the public interest. If unrestricted private activities will lead in other directions (see Figure 15.1), governments often act to bring economic rationality in line with social welfare.

For example, Figure 15.2(a) illustrates a simple locational decision for an industry with one raw material and one market. If

FIGURE 15.1
An Illustration of How Private Decisions and the Public Interest Might Diverge. Suppose that a private firm wants to choose the location that maximizes the difference between average revenue and average costs; it would choose a site in the growth zone (C). If the public at large is more concerned about the difference between social benefits and costs at alternative sites, it might prefer a site in the depressed area (A).

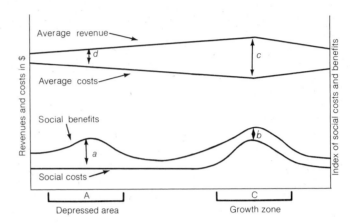

transport costs are the only major consideration, in this case the industry will locate at the market, where total transport costs are minimized. But suppose that this would create certain problems and fail to help with some others. The market city is already crowded and congested, and no more growth is wanted. Some intermediate locations are experiencing high levels of unemployment. And other factors add to this impression that another location might be socially more desirable. If a transfer tax were established, increasing the cost per mile of shipping the raw material, the isodapanes might then resemble Figure 15.2(b), which shows the least-cost location to be an intermediate point. Other policy options with much the same effect could include simply prohibiting the industry from the market and its vicinity (it would then locate at the boundary of the exclusionary zone), taxing the industry itself at some locations so that the tax *plus* transport costs would make a midpoint preferable, suspending taxes or reducing other costs in intermediate areas, and subsidizing (reducing) transport costs for the finished product. In any event, government action could influence a private decision about the best location for an activity.

As the example indicates, this action can take several forms:

1. **Defining limits for permissible activities.** For instance, heavy industry may be excluded from residentially zoned areas. Factories that emit too much sulfur dioxide from their smokestacks may be prohibited, or any new activity that will make the current level of air pollution any worse may be forbidden. These limits nearly always have a geographical impact, either because they have an identifiable pattern themselves (such as a zoning map) or because they change the

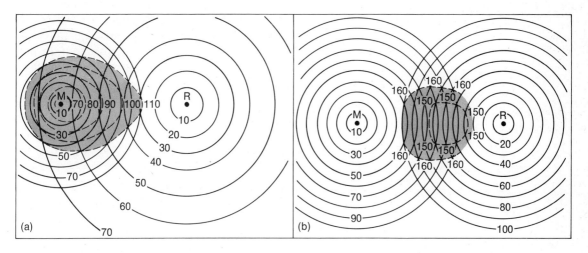

FIGURE 15.2
An Illustration of How
Government Action Can
Affect a Location Decision:
(a) isodapanes consider-
ing transport costs alone,
unregulated; solution:
market location, total cost
about 70; (b) isodapanes if
a transfer tax is applied to
shipments of the raw
material, increasing the
cost per mile for such
shipments (moving the
isotims closer together);
solution: intermediate location, total cost about 145.

pattern of comparative advantage in less direct ways (such as by giving a location just beyond the boundary of restricted activity a comparative advantage as a site for that kind of activity).

The definition of limits can take other forms as well. It can extend to regulating the way activities are conducted—putting limits on what is considered permissible conduct. Federal audits of "national banks" are an example, as are food quality standards. In these cases, the geographical meaning of government action is less clear.

2. **Modifying the map of site-specific costs and benefits.** Whenever taxes are higher at one place than another, the locational solution may be affected—just as if wage rates differed between the places. Conversely, a reduction in taxes or a similar inducement, such as the availability of guaranteed or low-interest loans, can make places attractive that would otherwise be at a disadvantage.

3. **Modifying the pattern of accessibility.** Whenever a government sets or regulates movement costs, or it taxes movement across a boundary, or it restricts the permissible amount of movement across a boundary, it is shaping accessibility as a location factor, and it is consequently shaping the pattern of trade—which responds to a map of prices and quantities rather than physical distances. Any governmental action that affects the economic meaning of distance has a fundamental geographic impact.

4. **Stabilizing production and prices.** In order to avoid uncomfortably large changes from year to year in production

levels—and thus prices—a government can establish regulations or offer incentives that seek a status quo. In essence, the attempt is to assure that a particular economic activity continues to be defined as the highest and best use for a place.

5. **Providing information.** By providing information about alternatives, a government can encourage mobility and change. By choosing not to disseminate information, it can do the opposite.

6. **Resolving conflicts.** Whenever different parts of society disagree about priorities and proper actions, a government is often put in the position of having to resolve the conflict (as, for example, between a utility company proposing a nuclear power plant to generate electricity and a citizen's group worried about plant safety and waste disposal). In arranging procedures, standards, and other mechanisms for seeking a social consensus, a government influences locational decisions in profound and sometimes contradictory ways.

These kinds of governmental functions give rise to distinctive institutions, such as the Interstate Commerce Commission in the United States. And in many countries they lead to a far-reaching centralized governmental effort in economic planning and development.

But the role of governments in shaping economic-geographic activity in a particular area is a direct reflection of the way the political system defines such terms as *social welfare* and *national interest*. At the state level in the United States, it often varies from region to region because (as Chapter 14 has pointed out) there are long-established differences in cultural values. Internationally, it varies even more—affected by culture, historical experience, economic level, and the spread and ebb of political ideology. Seen as a whole, the world turns out in some ways to be a living laboratory for attempts to identify the most appropriate roles and ways for governments to shape economic-geographic decisions.

15.3 *ELABORATING THE BASIC IDEAS*

In today's world, it is just as important for an economic decision maker to understand the political environment as it is to understand economic theory. This makes it useful to look a little more carefully at the way governments shape locational decisions for economic activities.

15.3.1   *The Legal Basis of Regulation*

The actions of governments in regulating economic activities are an extension of a broader conception of the appropriate role of government, outlined by a constitution or a body of legal precedents. As defined by the United States Constitution, for instance, the role of the federal government has come to include the direct federal administration of many things—such as a district court system and a National Park Service—which are reserved to states in many other federal systems (with the federal role focused on developing general statements of policy).

As a federal system, the American framework is distinctive in the size of the job allocated to the central government. This includes substantial regulatory powers (although they are not extended to some fields, such as police powers, in which the federal role is strong in some other countries). Most of these powers have developed because the Constitution assigned to the central government a role in interstate commerce (intended, for example, to avoid an attempt by Indiana to require people entering the state from Ohio to clear state customs and pay duty on valuable items in their luggage). Over the years, the power has extended far beyond air transportation systems, railroad systems, and pipelines—setting rates, deciding routes. It is the constitutional basis for establishing a national minimum wage, certain labor standards, and even some consumer protection legislation (such as the Wholesale Meat Act of 1967).

Other constitutional provisions involve the protection of individual rights (affirmative action policies), the regulation of monetary systems (the Federal Reserve Bank), postal systems, the military, and foreign affairs. Many of the specific governmental actions since the early days of the Constitution have depended on interpretations of the basic document by the Supreme Court—for example, in establishing national taxation.

In general, the trend in the first half of the twentieth century was a movement away from an emphasis on the federal ownership of property (a dominant concern with the advancing frontier in earlier decades) toward an emphasis on the federal collection and spending of money. More recently, the trend has been toward an expansion of the federal role in protecting the interests of individuals and groups that have limited economic and local political power.

This is only one case of the kind of evolving interpretation of the role of government that takes place continuously in all countries and at all levels of government. In order to anticipate future developments in the "rules of the game" for economic-geographic

FIGURE   15.3
Transport Rates for
Lumber (cost per 1,000
feet) from Washington and
Oregon. Although current
rates differ from these, the
overall pattern is similar.

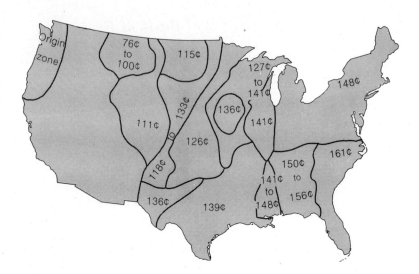

decisions, it is important to grasp the way those rules connect with
a legal framework that generally responds in predictable ways to
changes in social, economic, and ecological conditions. Easier to
say than to do. . . .

15.3.2   *How Governments Shape Spatial Organization*

The tools of government are often used to shape the pattern of
economic activity, both within the area that is governed and across
its boundaries. This section will consider internal effects; the next
will deal with boundary effects.

The Best Location for an Activity   In some countries government
agencies are directly involved in decisions about the location of
new economic activities. In others, governments act indirectly and
often indistinctly. But in either case the major options for shaping
the decisions are these:

1.   **Changing movement costs.**   Clearly, transportation costs can
be increased by adding taxes or setting rates at a higher level.
They can be decreased by rate setting, reducing taxes on
movement or on the transporters, or by the government's subsidizing movement by paying part of the costs itself.
     For example, Figure 15.3 shows transport rates for
lumber from Washington and Oregon to other parts of the
country (in 1966). Distance is reflected by higher rates, as
would be expected; but government regulation introduces
other factors as well, such as higher rates for shipments to the
Southeast, where competition from northwestern lumber

might put many southeastern lumber industry employees out of work. Similarly, it costs more to ship a ton of coal by rail from Oklahoma to California than from West Virginia, because for a variety of historical reasons the rate structure favors coal producers in Appalachia.

Less directly, a government can influence movement costs by providing better or shorter or lower cost transport connections. Traditionally in the United States, for instance, the use of streets and highways is subsidized by governments; users of highways pay for the construction and maintenance of the system only indirectly through taxes. By comparison, users of railroads and airplanes must pay a larger share of the cost in direct fees at the time of use. The fact that rail passenger transportation has suffered while truck freight has thrived is not coincidental. Other kinds of government actions might include traffic control to reduce congestion in the movement system, along with the public provision of attractive terminal facilities.

Even less directly, a government can act to reduce "social distance" rather than economic distance. When the mobility of people is involved, rather than commodities, a socially unfamiliar and/or unattractive destination is viewed as if it were very distant. The provision of amenities in the destination area—better schools or desirable recreational facilities, for example—is one way to deal with this kind of impediment.

2. **Changing characteristics of sites.**   As Chapter 6 pointed out, isodapanes were first developed to help evaluate the impact of site-specific factors on industrial location: for example, taxes, labor costs, energy costs, and land costs. A lower cost for one of these items can compensate for a higher level of transportation costs. Consequently, a government can often influence location decisions by lowering (or raising) taxes or land costs (for example, by renovating vacant structures to provide a low-cost industrial park).

The locational specificity of such an action often varies according to the jurisdiction of the government unit that adopts it. An example is water supply: a significant increase affects a service area larger than a particular industrial site. But specific items such as rail spurs and limited-period property tax exemptions are also used by localities as incentives for desirable new activity.

This process turns out to be a little less simple than it sounds. Low taxes are attractive—but so are high levels of public services, which require tax revenues. As a result, most new economic activities continue to locate in regions with relatively high tax rates. But the link between property taxes, local revenue, and the level of local services can cause economic differences between localities *within* these regions to increase (see Box 15.1).

3. **Making location decisions for private activities.** In many countries, when a new steel or fertilizer plant is proposed, the

---

BOX 15.1   FISCAL MERCANTILISM

For attracting desirable new economic activities—clean, aesthetically attractive, with congenial high-income employees—a place has an advantage if it can offer high levels of public services (such as schools and parks) but low levels of taxation (such as property taxes).

Consider two communities within a region; they have the same number of households. Community A has a lot of high-income people, not too many children, impressive streets and homes. Community B is mainly inhabited by poor people with large families. In order to raise $500,000 to support local schools, the poor town must tax its people more heavily than the affluent town. For example, see the following table. Since the poor town has more children, even this effort is insufficient to provide as small classes as in the schools in the affluent town.

The affluent town, therefore, is in a position to attract more of the kinds of people and activities that help it to keep its services up and its taxes down. Meanwhile, the poor town must impose high tax rates to support only adequate levels of service, which makes it even less attractive as a location for new residents.

This very common situation, which encourages localities to make land use decisions on the basis of local fiscal advantage, tends to increase differences between communities in the well-being of their residents. When local revenues are based heavily on local property taxes, and local services are based heavily on local revenues, the effect is especially strong. Consequently, since the early 1960s actions by the United States government and by state governments have gradually reduced the importance of property taxes as a source of local revenue and have increased the participation of nonlocal governments in the provision of services.

	No. of Households	Average Income per Household	Average Property Tax for Revenue of $500,000	Average Property Tax as a Percentage of Average Income
Community A	1,000	$20,000	$500	2.5%
Community B	1,000	8,000	500	6.3%

central government decides where it will be located. Elsewhere, the government role is more limited, but similar cases still arise. In the United States, for example, the route for the pipeline for Alaskan oil was in a sense decided in Washington, when the executive and legislative branches of the federal government chose to favor the Alyeska cross-Alaska pipeline/ocean tanker option over a trans-Canada pipeline. A similar question exists for transporting natural gas from Alaska: different consortia of private companies have proposed various alternatives, but the key decisions between them will be made by the government. When parts of society have more confidence in government decisions than private ones, such a situation is not necessarily opposed by industry. A case in point is the location of new electrical power generating plants in California. Under a law passed in 1975, a utility company proposes three possible sites to a state agency, which arranges public hearings and selects the site (or determines that none is acceptable). From the point of view of the utility, reaching agreement on a site is more important than which particular site is selected. One reason is that time delays may be more expensive than spatial economic inefficiencies.

4. **Using government activities as a location factor.**   In addition to providing public services at an attractive level and a reasonable cost, a government can influence location decisions by where it chooses to put its own facilities—for example, office complexes. As basic activities that offer agglomeration economies to certain kinds of private firms, government functions reduce for their locations the relative importance of other factors, such as distance or labor costs.

5. **Adopting general policies that favor some areas more than others.**   A government makes decisions on a very large number of issues. Examples are monetary policy, inflation or recession controls, income maintenance, price supports, and fuel allocation policies. Although these are seldom directed at particular locations, they usually have characteristic geographic patterns of impact. In Chapter 14, for instance, we saw that a particular income maintenance plan would inject more money into the local economies of the American Southeast, making that region more attractive as a location for retail and wholesale activities. Gasoline rationing could be expected to hurt parts of the country where people travel farther from home to work. A minimum wage law has more impact in areas where the cost of living is relatively low, just as an environ-

mental quality standard may have more impact on a traditional urban industrial area, with high current pollution levels, than other types of places. Recession usually hurts the economies of areas with substantial blue-collar employment faster than the white-collar areas. These kinds of geographic impacts of government policy are seldom identified very carefully, but they have the potential to be used to influence locational decisions as well as to solve problems of a nation as a whole.

Most governments use these kinds of tools in combination, usually with a specific geographic purpose such as the development of a lagging area (see Part VII). As might be expected, the government role is most explicit in the countries that have centrally planned economies (see Box 15.2).

The Best Activity for a Location   Obviously, the same tools affect the uses of locations as well as the locations of activities, because they shape the definition of the highest and best use of a place—by modified movement costs, taxes, subsidies, infrastructure, and other policy options. An especially dramatic example is the way public highway and transportation policies shape land use decisions. But three other alternatives deserve attention as well, because they are so widely used.

BOX 15.2   THE LOCATION OF INDUSTRY IN EASTERN EUROPE

In the socialist countries of Eastern Europe, economic decisions are based on (or at least coordinated with) an economic plan developed by the central government.[a] The location of large new industries is not only a part of the plan; it is an important tool in carrying out the general economic growth objectives of the country. In most cases, locational decisions are made by the government, which is itself the owner and operator of the facility. But the decisions are also influenced by the regulation of transportation rate structures and other factors.

In theory, these countries emphasize the location of new industry in less-developed regions as part of a broad-based plan to increase production by fully using the resources of all parts of a country (see Chapter 16). More processing facilities are located near the sources of raw materials than would perhaps be the case in a capitalist economy, and special attention is given to creating complexes of related activities in disadvantaged areas that lack enough agglomeration economies to attract one or two of the activities without the others.

[a] Yugoslavia is an exception to this practice.

1. **Constraints on permissible activities.**   When an unrestricted economic point of view may lead to an undesirable kind or level of activity, a government frequently establishes limits on what private decision makers can do. Some of these limits, such as prohibition of the private manufacture of agents of biological warfare, may apply everywhere—which means that their effect is on land uses at locations that would otherwise be the best ones for the prohibited activity. Other limits are geographically specific: defined on a map. In most cities, commercial activities are allowed in some places but not others, with substantial areas reserved for residential use; such restrictions are identified on "zoning maps." And certain constraints may be even more specific. For example, in Norman, Oklahoma, the entrance to a liquor store must be more than a specified number of feet from a public school.

   "Blanket" limitations apply throughout the *jurisdiction* of the government unit that adopts them. For instance, a state legislature might pass a law prohibiting the construction of new nuclear power plants until uncertainties about plant safety, materials safeguards, and waste disposal methods are reduced. This kind of action has a variety of consequences. Besides blocking one proposed use of some sites, it might (1) cause an increased demand for coal to fuel electricity-generating plants, increasing the likelihood of coal mining in areas with that resource: (2) cause more nuclear plants to be built in a neighboring state, with the electricity distributed through a network of power lines from there; and (3) reduce supplies of electricity in the state that passed the law, making it difficult to attract new activities that consume a lot of electricity. Often, a side effect that is viewed negatively by one part of society is seen positively by others, which makes exclusionary actions by governments a matter of controversy.

   Many of the most far-reaching constraints are the result of action by the central government. An important case is legislation to protect environmental quality, limiting air, water, and other types of pollution. The geographical ramifications are immense. For instance, activities that are in violation of the law are most often regionally concentrated, usually in areas where particular economic specializations are well established (heavy industry, urban concentrations, mining). Some areas can accept new urban/industrial development and still comply with environmental laws, but others cannot; and compliance with the regulations raises certain economic costs and prices, such as the price of automobiles with exhaust controls, which affects the comparison of alternative activities and locations. As a consequence, a firm may decide that an old factory would be too expensive to modify to meet the regulations; instead, it makes sense to build a new, modern factory somewhere else. Or private decision makers may find that it is economically undesirable to try to control emissions from smokestacks in small plants, because the controls are so expensive. As a result, a new kind of economy of scale leads to larger plants.

Another example of a central government action affecting decisions on the scale of activities is health and safety regulations. Standards for the quality of milk or meat generally make the minimum profitable size for a farm or meat packing operation larger. And further examples of regulations that shape private economic decisions are easy to imagine: for example, occupational health and safety standards and a 55 mile per hour speed limit.

Although these broad policies affect all our lives, the geographically specific kinds of constraints affect locational decisions in more tangible ways. Spatially, these controls can take several forms:

a. **Enclaves.** These are areas set aside for particular uses, such as national parks or industrial parks, surrounded by other areas without such constraints. A special case is the prohibition or permission of a particular activity at a specific site.

b. **Belts.** Because the activities in special-purpose enclaves are often affected by what goes on next to them, constraints may be placed on neighboring areas as well. A familiar example is the concept of a "green belt" (a zone around a city in which new construction is severely limited), widely used in Great Britain and elsewhere to try to keep open space within easy reach of city dwellers. These peripheral zones often take the approximate form of concentric rings around a focal area that has a different character (see Box 15.3).

c. **Sectors.** While an enclave is an enclosed cell and a belt is an area defined according to the periphery of an enclave, there is another possibility. It may be desirable to constrain or permit some kinds of land use in a "wedge" of area, surrounded on two or three sides by other uses but essentially open-ended in some direction. Examples are the special zoning of areas adjoining highways or rivers, and the preservation of open space in relatively undisturbed areas between radial highways.

The boundaries of such controlled land use areas may be set by some kind of process-related criterion; an

BOX 15.3   PROTECTING THE TRIGLAV REPUBLIC PARK

Since the early 1960s, the Yugoslav republic of Slovenia has been seeking a way to protect a scenic portion of the Julian Alps that contains Mount Triglav, a cultural symbol of the republic. At the same time, communities in and near the area have been seeking economic development opportunities (it should be noted that in Europe the creation of a national park nearly always involves an inhabited area). The challenge has been to reconcile the two aims.

In 1970, the Urban Institute of the Republic of Slovenia proposed a plan that would define two "core" areas of a park (N.P.) and identify zones of restricted land use nearby in order to protect the core areas from the impacts of activities in neighboring areas. The zones were roughly concentric around Mt. Triglav. The purposes of the plan were to protect the park area from "incompatible land uses in close proximity" and to encourage compatible development in the region.

The figure shows the plan. In the core areas, some sections were designated to be completely protected from change. Others would allow specific recreational construction, subject to strict conditions. The core areas would be surrounded by a general protection zone, in which all economic activities that damage the natural balance of the environment or landscape are prohibited. Tourist facilities and vacation home developments would be allowed in this zone, subject to environmental impact controls. An outer mixed

use zone would prohibit activities that would change the balance of the landscape or be incompatible with the activities of the inner zones, but urban development could continue subject to this constraint.

Since 1970, the plan has been repeatedly debated and modified by the Republic Assembly to meet the objections of a number of interest groups. In general, the changes have resulted in a contraction of the boundaries of the different zones, but the concentric zone approach has been preserved.

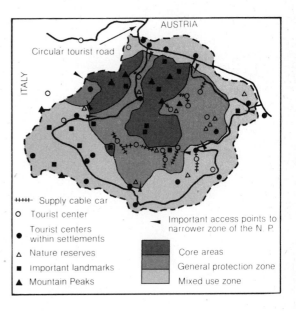

The Julian Alps Regional Plan.

example is the ecological range of an endangered species of animal or plant. But more often their precise delineation is determined by the boundary of a governmental jurisdiction, such as publicly owned land or a governmental unit.

2. **Financial and production controls.** Governments also shape decisions about the best activity for a place by attempting to stabilize markets. Consider a food production system—farmers, markets, household consumers. Because of the vagaries of climate and changing food preference, in some years the wheat crop is so big that the price of wheat drops below the break-even point for the farmer. Bread prices also drop, but some farmers have to sell their farms, and businesses in farming towns have to try to scrape by until their customers can find a way to pay long overdue bills. In other years, the wheat crop is very small. The price of wheat skyrockets; bread becomes very expensive; people with limited incomes find that their diet suffers. Clearly, there is some advantage in trying to assure that wheat production and prices stay within certain limits, so that both farmers and consumers are protected against problems caused by year-to-year instability. Milk and other commodities represent similar cases, as does the housing market.

The geographic impact of production controls is to reduce uncertainties about the best activity for a location or the best location for an activity. Decisions do not need to be changed as often, and decisions involving a large investment in a fixed installation are less risky. As a corollary, however, one might argue that when the controls themselves are changed, the impact on the geographic distribution of economic activity is likely to be especially great—because a stable pattern has been disrupted, rather than a pattern that has become accustomed to frequent but relatively gradual shifts.

In the United States the federal government offers loans to tide farmers over during hard times; and until 1973 it entered into agreements to purchase wheat (up to a specified amount) at a "support price," which means that the farmer is assured a price for the crop of no less than the support level. In order to be eligible for such supports, the farmer had to agree to restrict wheat acreage according to a formula derived by the Department of Agriculture. Price stabilization was thus linked with production stabilization (see Box 15.4).

Such a link, however, is less than perfect, because an acreage allotment challenges an enterprising farmer to identify the highest yielding acres and use them for wheat, and to find the highest yielding seeds for those acres. A result was that yields per acre rose, and wheat production generally continued to exceed national needs. In most years, land that would otherwise be planted in wheat was not, because of acreage restrictions, or land that would otherwise *not* be planted in wheat ended up growing wheat because of price supports.

In other fields, governments use their own spending to regulate unemployment, inflation, and the prices of some basic commodities. They can influence interest rates for savings, which affects the availability of money for new ventures. And they can encourage certain activities by establishing standards or loan programs. For example, the housing loan programs of the Federal Housing Administration (FHA) and the Veteran's Administration have historically favored single-family housing units, a factor that has probably had a significant impact on the look of American cities.

3. **Compulsory purchase and development.** In extreme cases, a government usually has the power of *eminent domain*, which allows it to acquire a piece of land at a price set outside the economic market mechanism and to do what it wants with the land. The most common example is the purchase of rights of way for highways and other transportation systems. The route is seldom set by old-fashioned bargaining between the government and individual landowners, because the resulting path might appear to have been traced by a weary drunk. For better or worse, the route is decided, and the land is acquired at a price determined by someone (usually a judge) to be fair. Another example of this process in American cities is urban

---

BOX 15.4 STABILIZATION ALTERNATIVES

Price supports and acreage limitations are one way to approach stabilization for basic agricultural commodities. But there are other alternatives—or supplements—that governments use as well. It is often possible to reduce year-to-year variations in the *conditions* of production that lie behind variations in the size of the crop. For example, erratic rainfall can result in erratic yields of wheat from a farm. An irrigation system providing a dependable supply of water can reduce this unpredictable variation, and governments around the world have actively promoted irrigation projects. Soil conservation practices sometimes help, too. And new varieties of the agricultural commodity may be developed that are more resistant to drought, pests, and other problems.

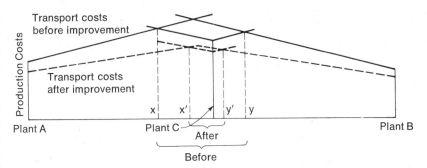

FIGURE 15.4
The Effect of An Improvement in Transportation on Market Areas. Firms A, B, and C are located along a transportation route. A firm's market area is bounded by the point where its delivered costs are equal to its neighbor's (farther away, the costs are greater; thus the competitor can undersell it). After an improvement that reduces transport costs, the larger plants, A and B, are able to expand their market areas because their larger size means lower unit production costs.

renewal; and national parks, military reservations, and wildlife refuges have been created or extended in the same way.

Systems of Activities for Systems of Locations   In terms of the central place theory outlined in Chapter 7, anything that increases the cost of overcoming distance to consumers leads to a more dispersed (or decentralized) pattern of activity. Anything that increases agglomeration or scale economies leads to a more concentrated (or centralized) arrangement. As we have seen, government actions can have either effect, thus reshaping the size and configuration of the market areas of activities—and changing their number and even their location. For instance, Figure 15.4 shows how an improvement in transportation facilities can squeeze the market area of a small activity located somewhere between two larger competitors.

In practice, government decisions are made by so many different agencies and at so many different levels that it is hard to sort out their overall effect. Suppose that 20 government actions favor a decentralized spatial arrangement of industrial production, while 17 favor a centralized pattern—with each of the 37 actions affecting some industries more than others. What does this add up to? Is the economic geographic impact of an air quality standard different from the impact of the Interstate Highway System? In fact, yes; but the total effect of both is harder to determine, especially over a period of many decades.

15.3.3 *Boundary Effects*

In addition to what they do internally, governments shape locational decisions by defining boundaries for themselves. A familiar example is a decision by a group of counties to prohibit the sale of alcohol within their territory. Before long, liquor stores and taverns begin to concentrate at a few points near the boundary of the "dry" area to meet the demands of the population within it.

FIGURE   15.5

The Effect of a Tariff on Trade Area Boundaries: I.

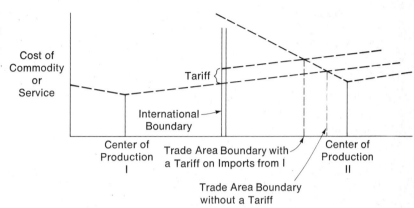

But for economic decision making the most powerful kind of boundary is a national boundary, because a country has a far-reaching power to decide what should be allowed to cross its boundary and under what conditions. The history of Europe, for example, was shaped for a century by the fact that Europe's best deposits of coal (in Westphalia) and one of its best deposits of iron ore (in Lorraine), only 200 miles apart, were separated by a traditional boundary between Germany and France. Decades of conflict were the result, making it practically impossible to arrange a sharing of resources for the benefit of both; and one effect was that Germany ended up buying iron ore from fields in Sweden more than 1,500 miles away.

More generally, as Chapter 13 pointed out, there are a number of reasons why unrestricted spatial interaction might be undesirable for a country. An excessive dependence on imports might be politically incautious, or it might drain money out of the country. Or a need may be to protect "infant" industries that are trying to get a start but are vulnerable to outside competition. Or trade restrictions may offer a way to raise government revenues.

The two most common approaches to regulating interaction across a border are limits on quantities (*quotas*) and additions to price (*tariffs*). Either may apply to inward or outward movements. Quotas, for instance, may limit immigration to a country or limit exports of grains to another country. Tariffs are a kind of tax levied by a government on items entering or leaving its territory. Like any tax, their overall effect is usually to raise prices and thus reduce demand (and the production level) for a commodity—and to generate revenue for the government. In either case, somebody has to know what crosses the border, which usually leads to a need to pick a limited number of border crossing points through which the movement is channeled (for example, customs offices).

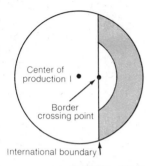

FIGURE 15.6

The Effect of a Tariff on Trade Area Boundaries: II.

FIGURE 15.7

A Classic Case of a Boundary Effect: the financial sphere of influence of El Paso, Texas. Each dot is a bank maintaining an account at an El Paso bank in 1914.

The geographic effect of a tariff is quite marked. Figure 15.5 shows how the added cost for an imported item (for which transport costs are important) reduces the size of its trade area across the boundary, and Figure 15.6 illustrates how this effect might appear on a map if the border can only be crossed at one point. Compare this with Figure 15.7.

But a tariff is only one of several "costs" that may be associated with crossing a border. For example, there may be a long wait even if no tariff is to be collected, or it may be necessary to go far out of one's way to reach a border crossing point. Since added time or added distance are costs, their spatial effect is similar to that of a tariff: they tend to reduce the amount and the reach of interaction. In a sense, then, a boundary is a kind of filter that increases the "behavioral distances" between places. The effect is especially dramatic when a boundary corresponds to a dividing line between different cultures or languages. For instance, a study of the interaction between Montreal and other Canadian cities (as indicated by the number of long-distance telephone calls) found that the contacts with cities in Quebec—the same province, where French is the dominant language—were about what was predicted by a gravity model. But the contacts with cities in Ontario—an adjoining province where English is dominant—were much less than the gravity model predicted (see Figure 15.8).

One of the consequences of this filter effect has been a distinctive shaping of transport networks. Note in Figure 15.9(a), for instance, the way the rail network—in a border area where terrain obstacles are not a factor—is affected by the small number of international gateways, and in Figure 15.9(b) the way a transport route skirts an international boundary for many miles rather than cross it (the two countries have a history of conflict).

A second consequence is the appearance of special kinds of economic activities in "frontier" areas. Suppose, for example, that Americans like to buy sweaters in Canada and Canadians prefer to buy shoes in the United States. A Canadian border town is likely to end up with more sweater stores than a town of its size could normally support. Other characteristic activities include banks handling currency exchange, branches of firms doing business on both sides of the border, and activities prohibited on the other side (for example, gambling).

15.3.4 Other Political Effects on Economic Patterns

It is hard to catalog all the possible effects of political decisions on the spatial organization of an economy, but a few more examples will help indicate their diversity.

FIGURE 15.8
The Impact of the
Quebec-Ontario Boundary
on Spatial Interaction.
From several cities in the
Provinces of Quebec and
Ontario, the number of actual telephone calls from
Montreal are plotted on a
graph in which the other
axis measures the number
of telephone calls pre-
dicted by a gravity model:
(a) calls to cities in
Quebec, (b) calls to cities
in Ontario. O = E indicates
that actual calls equal
predicted calls.

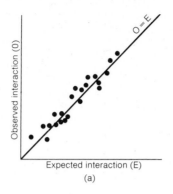

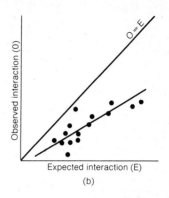

Generally, these effects are a consequence of the *aims* of government. If the philosophy, for instance, is to reduce differences between areas in the level of economic activity, governmental policy will try to disperse activities to correspond with that point of view. If the first priority is nationalism, the emphases may include such things as tariffs to protect local industry and the settlement and development of border areas whose status is in dispute. In a federal system of government, economic patterns may reflect differences in aims between units—and levels—of government. And trade patterns are heavily influenced by political relationships between the governments of different countries: by embargoes (trade prohibitions), "favored nation" status, free trade areas, and other kinds of governmental action.

The internal organization of space is influenced in more specific ways as well. In 1785, for example, the United States adopted a system of land survey that led to a rectangular grid of roads in many parts of the country, with main streets in most midwestern cities spaced a half-mile or a mile apart. A different kind of case is that of the Republic of South Africa, where an attempt is being made to maintain an apartheid economic system—enclaves of African settlement, with relatively traditional economies and relatively low standards of living, within a larger modern European-type economy.

Another kind of political effect is on the migration of people. The many centuries of Jewish migration, often involving the movement of impressive concentrations of skills, have affected the economies of many parts of the world, as have the migrations (for less clearly political reasons) of Chinese and Indian people in other parts of the world. The partition of South Asia into India and Pakistan in 1947 caused an estimated 17 million people to relocate, disrupting long-established economic roles and patterns of life. And slavery was a part of human experience for thousands of years.

FIGURE 15.9
The Effect of International Boundaries on Transport Networks: (a) the rail network along the Canada-United States border (from Lösch); (b) rail line in northwest Africa, avoiding a border crossing; the line moves iron ore, which provides most of Mauritania's exports.

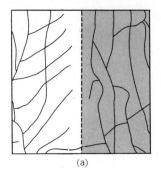

(a)

(b)

But the cause of migrations may be less directly coercive than in these instances. The sizeable movements of American blacks to cities outside the Southeast can be attributed at least partly to a history of limited opportunities for them in the Southeast—with the limitations tied closely to political processes there.

15.3.5 *Private Responses to Governments as Shapers*

Since governments have substantial power to influence private economic decisions—benefiting some people and places more than others—a common response of organizations and places has been to try to persuade governments to take particular kinds of actions. For instance, a single local department store might not be able to do much by itself, but it might have some influence as part of the National Alliance of Businessmen or the U.S. Chamber of Commerce. Consequently, trade associations and other representative groups, ranging from labor unions to the Sierra Club and the National Rifle Association, make a concerted effort to influence public policies that in turn influence economic patterns. At a given time, the *lobbying* activities of each group have an associated economic-geographic impact, although it is seldom identified very clearly.

15.3.6 *How Governments as Shapers Represent Economic Opportunities*

It has been estimated that 60 oil and gas organizations spend $10 million a year for lobbying payrolls in Washington, D.C., alone, in an attempt to influence governmental policies.[2] This is dramatic evidence that these policies are important for private economic decision makers. Note, for example, the strong concern of energy company executives (who tend generally to criticize government involvement in economic decisions) with the continuation of certain beneficial subsidies, allowances, and supports.

Someone who studies the role of governments as shapers of private decisions can often have an economic advantage over other individuals. In the United States there are countless governmental programs that offer subsidies, grants, loans, free information, and other incentives to those who qualify. Some apply to almost any activity and/or location. Others are quite restricted in the way eligibility is defined. But the first requirement is to know about the program. In the same sense, it is a challenge to find the least-cost way to comply with constraints on locational decisions, which depends heavily on understanding the constraints. A less direct but even more promising approach is to scrutinize government actions (and intentions) for their long-term economic effects. For instance, when they were first adopted, federal air quality regulations made it necessary for many electricity-generating plants powered by fuel oil to choose between installing expensive pollution control devices or buying low-sulfur fuel oil. A consequence was to raise the price of high-grade (low-sulfur) oil, enriching individuals who were prepared to market the low-sulfur oil.

A third approach, obviously, is to try to influence the political process. As the previous section indicated, there are perfectly legal ways to do this, but any one group's attempt will be competing with efforts by groups with other (sometimes directly contradictory) objectives.

15.4   EXAMPLE

As the situation described in Section 15.1 indicated, there are examples of governments as shapers of economic-geographic decisions everywhere we look—and many places we seldom look. To illustrate this a little further, let's look at U.S. federal government actions with respect to the supply of energy in the United States, as of the summer of 1977.

Actions Affecting the Best Location for Economic Activities
Many location decisions are affected by energy policies, even when those policies are not specifically focused on questions of geographic distribution and linkage. For example:

1.   **Policies that affect movement costs.**   Federal price regulation of oil and gas—both current and proposed—is based on the wellhead price (the price at the well rather than at the consumer's location); thus it does not itself shape movement costs. But federal policy determines where, when, and under what conditions wells can be drilled on federal lands and most of the Outer Continental Shelf. Natural gas from offshore

wells on the Atlantic coast would be cheaper for consumers in nearby states than if it were moved by pipeline from onshore wells more than 1,000 miles away. In addition, federal actions influence the location of terminal points where oil and gas enter the United States from other countries; an example is the government role in deciding the route for a gas pipeline from Alaska. And government-supported research on new technologies, such as for extracting natural gas from "tight" formations or producing pipeline quality gas from coal, may give many areas a chance to be closer to gas production sites.

Another group of impacts has to do with the movement of coal. Government policies that encourage or require a major increase in the use of coal by utilities and industry are certain to result in a heightened demand for rail transport facilities. Increased demand is likely to raise the price of railcars, and railroad congestion may cause shipping delays for other commodities. Rail beds will have to be improved. Moreover, firms replacing natural gas or fuel oil with coal will have to invest in coal storage and handling facilities, meaning additional fixed costs for energy movement. And small towns bisected by railroad tracks, whose traffic is interrupted when trains pass through, may exert pressure for new bypasses to be built.

2. **Policies that affect characteristics of sites.** The National Energy Plan of 1977 proposed, for newly produced natural gas, to eliminate the previous distinction between interstate and intrastate gas. The movement of gas from one state to another had been considered a federal matter, subject to price controls. But gas produced in northwestern Oklahoma and shipped by intrastate pipeline to Tulsa could be sold in a free and open market to the highest bidder. As a consequence, by early 1976 about half the natural gas produced in the United States was being sold within the state of origin, with wellhead prices rising three times as high as for interstate gas. As a result, in 1976 about 90 percent of the new gas produced in Oklahoma was for intrastate markets. Although this meant higher prices for new gas in these states, it also meant fewer worries about future gas shortages (except in a national emergency, when the federal government might intervene). Economic activities wishing an assured supply of natural gas as a clean fuel or a chemical feedstock found the gas producing states attractive places to locate.

A change in policy would remove this kind of location factor, perhaps redistributing gas supplies from the Southwest to the Midwest. This factor is one of several reasons why the 1977 National Energy Plan was strenuously opposed by representatives of such states as Texas, Oklahoma, and Louisiana.

Further examples of federal policies that affect the comparative evaluation of alternative locations include a wide range of environmental legislation. For instance, the Resource Conservation and Recovery Act of 1976 requires that certain solid wastes and sludges from power plants be handled as hazardous wastes. Assuring that trace elements, acids, and other materials will not escape from a land fill or settling pond is more expensive in some places than others—depending on such site characteristics as soil qualities and rainfall regime. The law does not change these characteristics of locations, but it changes their economic impact on location decisions for waste disposal sites (and the facilities that generate the waste).

No direct attempt has been made by the federal government to influence energy supply location decisions by tax policies, but some indirect effects can be seen. The National Energy Plan, for instance, proposes to allow an attractively high price for "new oil" (oil from wells first put into operation after a specified date). "Old oil" would be priced at one of two lower levels, depending on when it was first produced; but a federal tax would be imposed equal to the difference between the price of new oil and old oil. In theory, the higher price for new discoveries would encourage exploration, and the tax would encourage consumers to conserve energy without giving oil companies a massive increase in revenues. But new oil is defined as oil from a new well more than 2½ miles from an existing well or more than 1,000 feet deeper than a nearer existing well. Some people believe that this represents a tax on areas where wells are already clustered, in order to encourage exploration elsewhere.

Another category of taxation on energy resources is "severance taxes" on coal shipped out of a state. So far, the federal government has allowed states to make their own decisions on this, and current taxes range from 30 percent for Montana coal to 0.2625 percent for West Virginia coal. In this case, a federal policy of leaving taxation to the states has resulted in substantial variations. It should be noted, however, that there is no evidence as yet that location decisions for new coal mines have been affected by these variations.

3. **Government location decisions for private activities.** As has been mentioned, the federal government has played a specific role in setting the route of the Alaskan oil and gas pipelines, even though they are operated by private firms; and it is actively involved in decisions about the location of private activities, such as coal or oil shale mining and processing facilities, on federal lands. Most often, it asks firms to indicate their interest in particular areas under federal jurisdiction. Then it announces plans to lease tracts of land for private use, subject to certain conditions. The highest bidding firm or consortium is awarded the lease.

   In addition, the federal government is centrally involved in decisions about where to locate nuclear power plants, even when they are proposed by privately owned utilities. The federal role is focused on a decision to license the facility, which requires that the Nuclear Regulatory Commission be satisfied that the facility will be safe and will not harm the environment.

4. **Policies that favor certain areas more than others.** One of the most powerful geographic impacts of the 1977 National Energy Plan would come from its proposal to require the use of the "Best Available Control Technology" (BACT) wherever coal is burned. In effect, this would necessitate the installation of a flue-gas desulfurization device on every coal-fired power plant, regardless of the sulfur content of the coal that is burned. Since the main economic advantage of low-sulfur coal has been that it allows a utility to avoid the expense of such a device, the policy would favor coal mining in areas with higher sulfur coal.

   In the United States, a BACT requirement would boost coal mining in Appalachia and the lower Ohio Valley (Illinois, Indiana, western Kentucky) and perhaps slow coal development in such low-sulfur coal states as Wyoming and Montana. It appears, in fact, that the policy may have been specifically intended for this purpose, focusing accelerated coal development on areas with a more abundant labor force and a better developed infrastructure.

Actions Affecting the Best Activity for a Location

Likewise, there are countless examples of ways that federal policies shape decisions about what to do with specific locations. For instance:

1. **Policies that define permissible activities.** Most often, the federal government has narrowed the range of permissible ac-

FIGURE 15.10
Approximate locations of
critical habitats of en-
dangered animal and
plant species, 1978

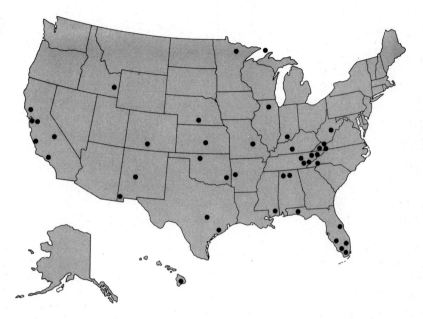

tivities at a place by establishing standards for protecting environment, health, and safety. Especially notable are the Wild
and Scenic Rivers Act of 1968, which protects certain rivers
from modification or interruption, and the Endangered
Species Preservation Act of 1973, which prohibits any activity
under federal jurisdiction that is likely to result in the disap-
pearance of a plant or animal species. The latter law may be
especially far-reaching in its effect. Figure 15.10 shows some
of the areas where endangered species have been identified;
others are found at a great many sites, since biotic subspecies
are nearly always highly localized. It is likely that American
society will eventually be faced with a decision between some
of its economic goals and the survival of some of its subspecies of plants and animals.

     In other cases, the land use restrictions are less direct.
They may be expressed in terms of the maximum allowable
concentration of a pollutant, the maximum allowable emission
rate for a pollutant, or standards for waste treatment and disposal. For instance, under the Clean Air Act, certain areas in
the United States are identified as having air that is so polluted that no addition from a point source (such as a new factory) will be permitted. In order to avoid an absolute prohibition on economic growth involving new construction in these
areas, an "emissions offset policy" has been adopted. A major
new facility is permitted if it includes the best available emis-

sion controls—*and* if emissions from other sources in the area are reduced enough to more than offset emissions from the new source.

Such laws and regulations often have an impact on location decisions, although most of them are still so new that the strength of the impact is not yet clear.

2. **Other policies.**   Other examples range from federal decisions about uses of federal lands (which may include a requirement that a private firm that is awarded a lease develop the activity according to an agreed schedule) to the government's use of its right of eminent domain to acquire land and the imposition by government of a limit on the rate of extraction from a well. Frequently, the roles of government are difficult to reconcile. For instance, at the same time that some federal agencies are seeking to develop offshore oil and gas resources, others are charged with protecting coastal environments. A result has been a Coastal Zone Management Act, which established procedures for resolving conflicts, including a fund to compensate coastal areas for damages that ensue from offshore energy development. At least potentially, the government role in conflict resolution is the most far-reaching of its powers to shape decisions about the best activity for a location.

Actions Shaping Boundary Effects   The United States government has immense powers to shape the flow of energy across its national boundaries. For many years, in order to assure the development of domestic petroleum resources, a quota was maintained on oil imports; one consequence has been a reduction in the amount of oil that remains on domestic reservoirs. Alaskan oil and gas resources have posed a different problem: whether or not to transport the energy through Canada, which is often technically simpler but politically more complicated. The decisions—shaped by the federal government through its review, permit, and rate setting processes—have been to ship the oil by tanker, bypassing Canada, but to ship the gas by pipeline through Canada. Although this suggests a certain inconsistency, it should be noted that a pipeline accident involving oil is usually more damaging to the environment than a gas leak.

The federal government also influences energy imports by negotiating with governments of other countries to set the price of imported fuel. For example, natural gas from Canada and Mexico is priced higher than the average price of gas from United States wells. And the government has the power to restrict exports of energy or energy technology. Except for metallurgical-quality coal, the United States exports very few energy resources, but it is an important exporter of enriched uranium fuel for nuclear power plants—and of the nuclear plant technology itself. Some countries fear that unless nuclear fuel reprocessing and enrichment are dispersed or internationalized, the increasing use of nuclear power may tempt the few countries that have the facilities to use quotas, prices, or embargoes to further their foreign policy objectives.

Summary   As an actor in energy supply, the federal government of the United States is an owner of resources, a developer of technologies, and in some cases a creator of institutions (such as TVA and the nuclear power industry). As a shaper, it regulates interstate shipments of energy materials and products, and in some cases it also regulates the prices of the items shipped. It often regulates imports. It sets environmental and safety standards that affect resource extraction and conversion into fuel forms. And it establishes regulations that apply to private industry in general, such as antitrust laws (which restrict cooperation between energy companies) and patent laws (which make private firms cautious about doing energy technology research jointly with government, because as a result they may be unable to retain certain patents).

In addition, state governments own resources, set environmental standards, approve rate structures, establish severance taxes on energy exported from the state, and become actively involved in assessing the economic and social impacts of proposed new energy facilities.

15.5   A RECONSIDERATION

It is unrealistic to view an economy as separate from government. The "market" never works quite as perfectly as theory must assume, and the objectives of individual participants in the economy do not always add up to the best interests of the group. Consequently governments play a role in economic decision making. In some countries the role is as a kind of balance wheel—a filler of gaps and a catalyst for compromises. In others, the role is much more comprehensive, more oriented toward acting than shaping.

But in either case governments affect economic geography. They have a spatial structure themselves: boundaries of jurisdictions, networks of linkages, distributions of facilities. Their decisions benefit some places more than others. And they not only define the national interest at the scale of the country as a whole;

they represent—and help to articulate—the interests of society as a whole at regional and local scales, and they work to reconcile these interests with those of private decision makers and other units of government. Perhaps it is no wonder that the job is not always done as well as we would like.

Finally, it is worth noting again that from a strictly economic point of view, any kind of regulation that interferes with the definition of the price of a good or a service in a free and competitive market involves a cost. Either the regulated price will be higher than necessary, or the level of supply will be less than is possible. In many cases, the social value of the regulation is more than sufficient to justify the cost. But even the most ideologically oriented countries find that some economic interaction is handled better by unregulated markets than by bureaucracies.

This returns us to the question why governments shape spatial organization. And more specifically, when they *know* that their actions will benefit some places more than others, what influence does this knowledge have on their definition of the national interest? The next section will begin with this concern.

MAJOR CONCEPTS AND TERMS

For definitions, see the Glossary.

Conflict resolution	Lobbying	Quotas
Eminent domain	Permissible	Stabilization
Government	activities	Tariffs
regulation	Planning	Zoning
Jurisdiction	Political	
	environment	

Footnotes for Chapter 15

1. *Norman (Oklahoma) Transcript*, March 16, 1976, p. 3. (This article is an Associated Press Newsfeature and is reprinted with AP permission.)

2. Freeman, S. David. *Energy: The New Era*. New York: Random House, 1974, p. 179.

PART VII

PLACE PLANNING AND WELL-BEING

*L*et's review what we have done so far. We started out by considering the perspective of economic geography: a perspective focused on questions of location and scarcity, and especially concerned with identifying the location of economic opportunities, benefits, and advantages. Then we looked at how opportunities and benefits actually vary from place to place—because if they did not, our perspective would be unnecessary. Next, we spent several chapters getting into the head of a hard-nosed business decision maker in order to see why advantages differ from place to place— why some places are determined to be more useful than others. We found that these kinds of judgments usually lead to some degree of areal specialization, because the characteristics that are most useful for some activities are not always the same as for others. Because of this specialization, a place must interact with other places to get all the things its residents want, even though this creates some dependence on the other places. In the last two chapters, we have considered how governments dominate many of these matters, both by making major economic decisions themselves and by shaping the decisions of others.

Now it is time to change our direction of concern. What if our interest is not only in our own direct economic well-being but in the cities and states and regions where we live—and in the well-being of the people who live there with us? Perhaps our first question is not: where can I go to improve my well-being the most? We are saying to ourselves: I want to live in Vermont or Oklahoma or South Carolina or Quebec. What can I do to improve my opportunities here? For some of us, the concern is not so much with finding the best location, wherever it may be, as with improving the local area enough to meet our minimum standards for well-being. We feel some loyalty to our home area, an identification with it, a feeling that it is worth supporting and taking care of. Whether this feeling is the most important consideration for us or simply a part of our collection of "nice to have's," a sense of place is an aspect of well-being for many people.

In this section, Chapter 16 will consider how an area fits into a national point of view about the best distribution of economic activities and benefits. Chapter 17 will take a look at how the prospects of a place can be evaluated. Because the prospects are not always what one would like, Chapter 18 discusses some ways that a place can change its prospects. Finally, Chapter 19 briefly addresses some of the limitations of planning for specific places.

CHAPTER 16

OBJECTIVES IN SPATIAL PLANNING

*I*n Chapters 14 and 15 we encountered the concept of national interest, which lies behind most of the involvement by government in economic decisions. In investigating how the level of economic well-being in a particular region can be improved—and especially how governments can contribute to this improvement—it makes sense to consider how the national interest might be related to what happens in that region. This chapter will introduce some ideas that often influence a national point of view about regional development.

16.1 *SITUATIONS*

16.1.1 *The Lonely Bureaucrat*
It is late in the evening, and you are still at your desk. Sometimes you wish you had not done so well in your fifteen years in the agency, because now the responsibilities are large and the decisions are difficult.

The current crisis is that day after tomorrow you must submit a budget for a $300 million program to help reduce unemployment in the United States. When you asked your boss for guidance last week, she said, "Do what's best for the country. Don't worry about politics; that's my job."

So there you sit, trying to decide what is best for the country, and knowing that many people are going to find fault with whatever you do.

You find that your thoughts keep returning to Los Angeles, the city where you grew up. You know that giving $6 million to each of the 50 states wouldn't help California very much, because the state is so large. You know that giving $30 million to each of the ten largest cities in the United States is politically unrealistic—and why ten? You suspect that Los Angeles might be helped most by simply spending the $300 million on aerospace equipment from companies in that area. But none of these options is your idea of what is "best for the country."

In fact, you don't really know what is. But you believe that the money should not be spread too thinly. Digging through the stacks of data on your desk, you go back to the figures on unemployment by state and by country. Where is the highest unemployment? Why is it that some of the higher figures are in high-income areas and some in low-income areas?

In the end, you decide that it will be necessary to base a county's eligibility at least partly on high unemployment. Now you must come up with a formula. How high must the unemployment level be? For how long? Should low-income areas get more help?

As you sit there running numbers through your calculator, you find that some formulas would help Los Angeles a good bit—but some would make it ineligible for anything. Your interpretation of the "national interest," converted into a dull-looking formula, will determine whether the recommended budget can provide any help for Los Angeles.

16.1.2   *The View from the Other End*

You are in the insurance business in a small city in the Northeast, and you think somebody ought to do something about all the vacant old industrial buildings in your city—and the 15 percent unemployment rate. It seems to you a real waste of resources. Surely, something useful can be done with these capabilities that are now lying idle.

When you go to the city government and the chamber of commerce, they say that they agree with you but that the firms they have talked to are not interested in the old buildings. It is simpler and (usually cheaper) for them to find some inexpensive land somewhere else and build new buildings there, specifically designed for their needs.

You think this works an unfair hardship on areas like yours that have "paid their dues," and you suggest to your representative in the U.S. Congress that a federal program to provide incentives for industry to use empty old structures would be a good idea. It might even save the country money, because it would take unemployed people off unemployment compensation and other welfare programs and make them productive again.

In a couple of weeks your representative writes back, saying that he has discussed your idea with officials in a number of federal agencies and staff members of several congressional committees. They advise him that, from a national point of view, there are better ways to use the money—ways that would employ more unemployed, and ways that would provide a greater increase in economic productivity. He thanks you for your interest and good citizenship.

Two years later, unemployment is at 20 percent, and you are absolutely convinced that the country should be paying more attention to the area's problems. Your friends and clients are starting to leave for other places. Many of those places are getting help of one sort or another from the federal government. Doesn't your city deserve some help, too?

You decide to support your congressman's opponent in the next election.

16.2   BASIC CONCEPTS

When national interest is associated with well-being, it usually takes the form of a concern with *productivity* or a concern with *inequality*.* Greater productivity means more income to distribute, more jobs to make available, more goods and services for consumers. Greater productivity is generally seen as desirable. Social or economic inequality means that some groups of people in the country have a notably higher level of well-being than others, which is considered by most to be undesirable both on moral and practical grounds. It indicates that human needs are not being met, and it is a source of very real stress to the political-economic system, especially when all people are well informed. The problem is that what one does to remedy low productivity is not necessarily what one does to reduce inequality, and it is not usually possible to tackle two different objectives effectively at the same time. Consequently, finding the right balance between the two concerns is a fundamen-

---

*   Other possible objectives include political stability and national political integration (see Chapter 1).

tal challenge to any country, and the balance is struck differently according to the political system and cultural history of the country involved.

In any case, the national articulation of an economic growth and development objective has an influence on each region of the country. Although the objective itself (for example, regional equality) may not itself be geographical, the policies and implementation strategies of public and private decision makers usually are, because there is an essential "where" to their investment decisions. An objective of productivity or equality, sooner or later, must be converted into the allocation of resources to this place or that.

This section will first take a look at the question of objectives, with special attention to reducing regional inequalities. It will then relate the objectives to the general idea that some kinds of spatial arrangements of economic activity are better than others.

16.2.1   *The Planning Target*

In planning in business or government, it is considered desirable to have a target to shoot for: a sales figure, an income level, or something else. Such a target helps in determining priorities, and it helps decision makers measure their success in achieving their goals. Let's consider the two objectives just mentioned—increased productivity and reduced inequality—as regional development targets.

Productivity   One possible objective is to get as much out of the economic system as possible, in the sense of maximizing the value of the goods and services that are produced. There are many motives that support such a target; from the perspective of individual and group well-being, the explanation is that increased productivity provides more total income and savings for the benefit of society as a whole. More jobs are created; more taxes are paid; wages rise along with rises in the productivity of individual workers.

Since an economic system at a given time has limited resources available to it, productivity as an objective means using these resources as efficiently as possible—getting the maximum benefit out of available inputs. A factory should be located where it will do its job at least cost to the economy. Facilities should be used to their capacity. Waste should be avoided.

This view of regional planning priorities normally leads to a concentration of both private and government investment at a few favored spots, taking advantage of agglomeration economies. As a result, it can mean considerable regional disparities in the level of economic activity and the benefits from it, at least for a while. A problem, however, is that the concentration of *capital* resources in a few places can result in the waste of *human resources* in others (and sometimes natural resources as well), if these other kinds of resources are less than completely mobile. This may lead to the creation of constraints on long-range productivity.

Productivity is usually measured by a country's gross national product, and targets may be set as a percentage of annual increase or an intended level at some future time. Related objectives include full employment and industrial production at capacity.

Equality In thinking about regional development, equality as an objective means an emphasis on attaining a material standard of living that differs very little from one area to another, assuring that no one is penalized economically because of where he or she chooses to live. Rather than trying to consider a whole range of inequalities, this effort is often focused on *income inequalities* as a convenient indicator of the standard of living, although there are dangers to taking such a short cut (see Box 16.1).

Because of problems in measuring incomes and in deciding on an ideal scale for identifying regions, the *equality* objective is usually transformed in practice to one of *equity*: a condition in which the standard of living of different regions is equivalent, even though a numerical average of money incomes may show considerable variation between regions. Equity, of course, is even harder to measure than equality, but it makes more sense in theory (and, probably more important to decision makers, it allows more flexibility in interpretation).

One way to view regional inequities is as a regrettable short-run condition—a lag in the adjustment of mobile factors of production (such as people) to changes in the location of optimum benefits. According to this view, investment should be made in low-benefit areas only if cost-benefit calculations show that such a location will pay off better. Because cost-benefit analysis gives very little value to long-term benefits (see 18.3.2), this does not happen very often.

Another view is that some action needs to be taken to help lagging areas—that cost-benefit analysis is blind to the long-term externalities from helping these areas reach their productive potential (and perhaps to the social value of helping the people there live at a decent and dignified level of well-being). Here, the course of action is focused on bringing the standard of living in disadvantaged areas up to the level of the more affluent areas. There are three basic options for this:

1. **Raise per capita income (or another measure of well-being) in a problem region without raising *total* regional income.** For example, even though money income stays constant, free or

---

BOX 16.1 REGIONAL INCOME AVERAGES AND THE STANDARD OF LIVING

What does it mean to say "regional income equality"? Most simply, it means that the numerical average of the incomes in every region is the same. The average money income per person is the same in every area being considered. But such figures, drawn from a census or some other kind of survey, can be very misleading as indicators of the local standard of living. The reasons include these:

1. **Unmeasured income.** Not all income is necessarily money income. We can imagine a remote farm family that raises its own food and makes most of the other things it needs, trading food or handicrafts (or moonshine) for things it is unable to make for itself. They might live quite well with little or no money income. If in 1977 they choose to sell some extra moonshine in order to buy a new stew pot, their money income increases compared with 1976, but their standard of living is not affected very much. This is the difference between money income as it usually appears in census publications and the theoretical concept of "real income," which is the value of everything received as a result of productive activity (even if it never passes through a market to be valued as "money income").

2. **Cost of living.** A unit of currency can buy more some places than others, so that a high per capita income figure may just mean higher prices, not a high standard of living. Easily the highest median family income in the United States is in Alaska ($12,441 in 1969); but the material standard of living is probably not as high as in Texas, where the same measure of income was only 68 percent as high in 1969 ($8,486).

3. **Income substitutes.** Public services can often vary in their abundance and quality from place to place, so that people in one place are paying some of their income for services that people elsewhere are being provided at no cost, or at a lower cost or with a lower tax rate.

4. **Noneconomic assets.** "Standard of living," interpreted broadly as about the same as "quality of life," includes many things that are as important as some amount of income but are not reflected in income figures (for instance, scenery or peace or opportunity).

5. **Within-region income distribution.** As will be discussed in Chapter 19, improving the average income of a region does not necessarily mean that very many individuals have benefited. Raising a few individual incomes substantially has the same effect on an average figure as raising a lot of individual incomes a little, but the impact on well-being in the region is not at all the same.

low-cost public services (such as education and health care) can be introduced, augmenting incomes and freeing money for other purposes. Another approach is to induce a reduction in population size (or a reduction in the rate of increase in population growth) without changing total income very much.

2. **Redistribute income between regions.** Even if the existing pattern of economic production changes very little, the resulting income can be redistributed so that all regions get an equivalent level of benefit anyway. One approach is to tax the more affluent regions and allocate the funds to the less affluent regions. Theoretically, in this way investments and production can concentrate at efficient locations, but no region is penalized because of it. In practice, the political obstacles are formidable. In addition, the resources of the lagging regions would not necessarily be developed, and some people would argue that rewarding a *lack* of productivity would dampen the motivation of the more productive areas.

3. **Change the pattern of economic activity.** Activity in the lagging regions can be increased in order to raise incomes there. This is the focus of most of the study of regional development problems and will be considered further in Chapters 17 and 18 (there are two fundamental questions involved: what to do to help a region, and how to make it happen).

16.2.2 *The Geographic Response to a Target*

According to the ideas we encountered in Chapters 5–13 (underlain by other ideas introduced in Chapters 2 and 4), spatial order is economically more desirable than disorder. There is a clear and definite geographic structure to economic activities if they are arranged in the most efficient way. Because of environmental variations and boundaries in our real world of decision making, this structure is distorted and interrupted, but the ideas are important enough that we can still improve our well-being by understanding and applying them. This is true regardless of the planning target, although the resulting pattern may differ according to the target (see Box 16.2).

The geography of an economic system most clearly shows its propensity for order by evolving toward a regular spacing of activities in "behavioral space." On a flat, unbounded, undifferentiated plain, this structure would take the form of a symmetrical

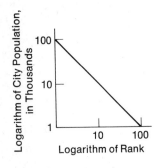

FIGURE 16.1

One Representation of a Balanced Central Place System.

geometry, regardless of an element of chance in the early history of the area:

A good analogy is the scattering of certain types of seeds by the wind. These seeds may be carried for miles before finally coming to rest and nothing makes them select spots particularly favorable for germination. Some fall in good places and get a quick vigorous start; others fall in sterile or overcrowded spots and die. Because of the survival of those which happen to be well located, the resulting distribution of such plants from generation follows closely the distribution of favorable growing conditions. So in the location of economic activities it is not strictly necessary to have both competition and wise business planning in order to have a somewhat rational location pattern emerge: either alone will work in that direction.[1]

The actual form of the geometry, of course, reflects the current environmental mosaic, as well as the economic regularities of the past and the present. And it reflects the fact that human behavior

---

BOX 16.2 SPATIAL ORDER: STRUCTURE AND PROCESS

Although the traditional concepts and methods of economic geography are focused on spatial structure—the relative location of and connections between elements of an economy—the reason is not that static geometry is important for its own sake. The fundamental interest is in how and why economic patterns occur. Identifying the pattern is but one of the important pieces of the puzzle.

Remember the perspectives introduced in Chapter 2. Pattern affects process; for example, separation usually means higher movement costs than proximity, and those costs affect prices, which in turn affect demand. In addition, a pattern is an indicator of how a process is working, and it is an indicator of what the process can do in a period of time (see Section 2.2.1). Furthermore, there is a pattern to a process itself; for instance,

markets will have identifiable distributions just as do wheat cultivation and steel manufacturing.

When we consider spatial order as an aspect of the national interest, the distinction between pattern and process is being blurred deliberately, because over a long period of time the difference disappears. Looking into the future, it is difficult (and uninteresting) to separate processes, such as locational decision making, from the spatial structures that will result. An ordered structure is associated with efficient processes. For every process target, there are appropriate structures—and inappropriate structures. Some structures impede reaching a target, while others facilitate it. In such ways, the geometry of an economy becomes a direct concern of national policy makers.

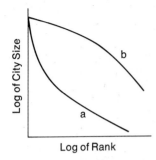

FIGURE   16.2
Two Types of Central Place Systems that May Represent Imbalances. (For explanation, see text.)

sometimes departs from what a theorist would define as the optimal decision (see Box 16.3).

When disorder or imbalance is what we see instead of order, however, it is possible that the "national interest" is not being served. For example, the rank-size rule (see Section 7.3) is believed to represent a kind of ordered urban growth process. Large, complex, long-urbanized countries show the kind of rank-size distribution illustrated in Figure 16.1. Maybe a country that has a very different distribution from this is missing cities of certain sizes from its central place hierarchy, as in Figure 16.2, line a, or has too many cities of certain sizes in its hierarchy, as in Figure 16.2, line b.

Perhaps more appropriately, it is possible to argue that there is a proper balance among the numbers of market centers at different levels in the central place hierarchy. Table 16.1 shows three expectations that result from using one technique in different ways (reflecting such real-world factors as population density and area size). Comparing the first expectation, which corresponds to the balance found in an astonishing variety of hierarchical systems in nature, with the actual system of cities and towns in Ghana, one finds an excellent fit, except for the second order of central places, which seem to be underrepresented. This might indicate that services should be added in some of the first-order places to raise them to the next higher order. Mapping the existing hierarchy would help to identify where the needs were the greatest.

This last element gets us to the heart of the geographic response to public policy. The way the spatial structure of an economy responds to national objectives is seen in the way spatial

TABLE   16.1
Number of Central Places in a Mixed Hierarchical System

NOTE: Based on the convergent mean of $k = 3$, $k = 4$, and $k = 7$ cases.

Expectation I		Expectation II		Expectation III		Actual: Ghana (reported 1964)	
Order	Number	Order	Number	Order	Number	Order	Number
8	1	9	1	6	1	6	1
7	3–4	8	3–4	5	3–4	5	4
6	10	7	8	4	14	4	11
5	37	6	21	3	56	3	35
4	118	5	56	2	218	2	92
3	256	4	151	1	729	1	258
2	518	3	256				
1	1,538	2	518				
		1	1,538				

SOURCE: Adapted from Woldenberg, J. J. "Energy Flow and Spatial Order." *Geographical Review,* vol. 58, 1968, pp. 552–574.

order is put into operation. For example, 3 large clusters of activities, evenly spaced, can represent a high degree of order, but so can 200 separate activities, evenly spaced. The key geographic issues, in some ways independent of spatial order but always important to the spatial investment decisions that cause a particular structure to develop, are these.

1. **Dispersion.** Should activities be concentrated in a few locations or dispersed in many?

2. **Connectivity.** Should present and potential foci of activity be linked fully, completely, and without restraint, or is it more desirable to limit the linkage system in some way?

BOX 16.3   SPATIAL ERROR

Actual human location and movement decisions often turn out to be different from what economic theory would say is ideal (the best for achieving the usual kinds of economic objectives). One possible reason, of course, is that the theory is off-base, although theorists don't talk about that kind of error very much.

Other possible reasons include these:

1. The decision maker was trying to take the economically optimal action but made a mistake. Most often, the reason is either that the available information was incomplete (with full information, the decision would have been different) or that the individual (or group) made an incorrect prediction about the ways conditions would change after the decision was made.

2. The decision maker was more worried about making a mistake than about finding the optimum. There are some times when people choose a safe course of action, even if they are fairly sure that it is not absolutely the best one. Consider a drive across town to attend an important meeting. By a sort of round-about route you can get there in thirty minutes, but not much faster, regardless of conditions. By a more direct route you can get there in fifteen minutes if one rail crossing is not blocked. It is blocked about 1 trip in 20, but that one time the blockage usually lasts nearly an hour. You leave for the meeting thirty minutes before it is due to start. Which route will you take?

3. The decision maker was more concerned about noneconomic objectives than economic ones. Consequently, for instance, he or she located a firm near home and family, even though location theory would have picked another location.

4. The environment did unexpected things. Even with full information and the best possible prediction, the "optimal" decision can be disrupted by things over which the regional economic system has little or no control: tornadoes, wars, and events that are a little less catastrophic.

3. **Texture.** How should the smoothness or roughness of "economic surfaces" be interpreted?

Dispersion The traditional answer to a question about the "ideal" degree of dispersion of activities comes from comparing the importance of movement costs and the distribution of the market. As we know from Chapter 7, an activity is likely to be more dispersed if (1) transport costs are high, and the source or market of the transported commodity or service is dispersed; and/or (2) economies of scale or agglomeration are relatively slight. Because types of activities vary in the answer that applies to them, a hierarchy of economic centers usually develops, with the most dispersed activities present even in the smallest centers (subject to a market threshold) but the most concentrated ones present only in the largest centers.

We know that an activity has two kinds of transport costs— (1) from sources of inputs and (2) to consumers—related to two different systems of linkages. Consequently, even if economies of scale and agglomeration are important, the impact of *both* kinds of movement costs is likely to make some degree of dispersion desirable, if both markets and factors of production are also dispersed.

But the precise degree of dispersion that is in the national interest may vary considerably according to how that interest is defined. As we have already noted, for instance, an objective of regional equity is usually associated with a more dispersed pattern of industrial production than is an objective of maximum productivity (although it may show considerable concentration for a single kind of industry).

Defining the ideal amount of economic dispersion for a country is complicated by three related problems:

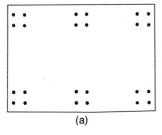

(a)

(b)

FIGURE 16.3
Two Patterns Consisting
of Regularly Spaced
Clusters.

1. **Behavioral maps.** Spatial order (that is, regular spacing) on a physical map may not be the same as spatial order on an economic map. For example, a map that is transformed to hold population density constant gives quite a different picture of what "regular spacing" means with respect to a consumer market (see Figure 7.14).

2. **Scale of attention.** In Figure 16.3, which of the two patterns is the more dispersed? The second one has three centers rather than six, but the sites within the three centers are farther apart than within the six. The geographic response to a national objective may be concentration at one scale but dispersion at another (for example, dispersion among regions but concentration within regions, or vice versa).

In considering regional development needs, a fundamental question is the size of the development unit. If aid is to be provided to Appalachia, as part of a program to encourage the decentralization of manufacturing activity, does that mean a little bit of help to many counties in eleven states or a lot of help to a few selected localities? If the latter, does the aid go to states, counties, cities, or some other kind of jurisdiction? It is hard to relate the concept of spatial order to policies "in the national interest" without settling on a *spatial focus*—the scale at which the "where" decisions will be made by government.

3. **Changing conditions of operation.** The ideal degree of dispersion at one time may not be the same as at another. For instance, a sensible pattern of grocery stores in the year 1900, based on the use of equine horsepower, would be considerably more dispersed than for 1975, with planning based on the use of automotive horsepower. Improvements in transportation and communication technology have historically played a key role in changing the spatial distribution of economic activities. The role is often a complex one, however, because a reduction in distance costs can in some cases lead to less dispersion (because the dispersed customers are more mobile), but in others it can allow more dispersion (because concentrated factors of production are more mobile or because the product can more easily be transported to centralized customers). But in any event dispersion or concentration is related to the system of linkages between localities.

As a result, it is seldom possible to identify an ideal degree of economic dispersion with much accuracy (or confidence) by using available theories and methods. Because this kind of optimization is unattainable, the job is done by "suboptimizing"—doing one's best to meet less ambitious goals. Such approaches might include analysis of the costs associated with the dispersed siting of several new facilities compared with siting them in existing concentrations, to evaluate the relative costs of dispersion; a decision to locate a minimum amount of new activity in a lagging region; or a decision to discourage the location of new activities in present concentrations (for instance, through restrictions on inputs, higher prices for services, and administrative delays—or taxes).

Connectivity Although linkages between places are usually considered desirable, we have seen that they are sometimes limited or

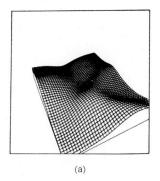

(a)

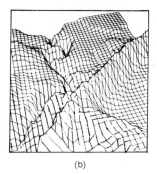

(b)

FIGURE 16.4
Two Surfaces Representing the Same General Pattern: (a) a smooth-textured surface; and (b) a rough-textured surface. (a) is in fact a mathematically smoothed version of (b).

avoided because they cost money (see Chapter 11) or because they cause problems (see Chapter 13). Generally, the extent to which the locations in an economic system are "connected up" is considered to be a matter of (1) the benefits from another link compared with its construction and operating costs and (2) the presence of boundaries that act as barriers to movement. As we know, the resulting system is hierarchical, in the sense that it is based on an ordered relationship between links of different capacities and other characteristics, and the hierarchy of links is related to the hierarchy of economic centers.

An objective of productivity usually means an emphasis on the high-capacity interregional links, whereas an objective of equity places more emphasis on the other end of the hierarchy.

Texture The most difficult issue to grasp concerns the response to evidence that economic surfaces are rough in texture rather than smooth: land rent surfaces, price surfaces. Consider Figure 16.4 as showing two different configurations of any one of these examples. Both have the same number of "peaks," "sinkholes," "ridges," and "valleys." But one is quite smooth; the price or income at one location changes gradually to that of a neighboring location. And one is rough—bumpy, even jagged. Does a smooth economic surface support higher or lower productivity? Does it mean more or less economic equity?

Table 16.2 indicates what theory would lead us to expect about the geographic texture of an economy, barring political intervention. Economic forces, together with the mobility of people and activities, are presumed to smooth most economic surfaces with time; but some texture will remain because of the intrinsic nodality of economic activity and changing circumstances.

In very broad terms, a national objective of equity means that rough economic and social surfaces are viewed as undesirable. In contrast, a national objective of productivity gives the texture of economic surfaces a lower priority than other matters; it often means that peaks and valleys are viewed as inevitable in the short run, due to time lags in adjustments to changing patterns of advantage. Consequently, an objective of raising average incomes in the country as a whole, rather than achieving an equitable distribution between places, may even lead to a strategy of raising the peaks in the income surface in hopes that (in effect) a lot of the new dollars near the mountaintops will eventually roll down into the valleys.

As with the other issues, of course, texture has meaning only with respect to behavioral maps; it may depend on the scale of attention; and it is constantly changing.

TABLE 16.2

Theoretical Expectation for the Texture of Economic Surfaces, without External Controls

Surface	Within a Region	Between Regions
Land rent surface	Moderate texture, with high points related to accessibility to agglomerations and transport networks	Depends on environmental conditions; otherwise smooth
Price surface	Smooth, relatively flat (gently sloped upward from market centers due to transportation costs)	Moderately smooth; most marked changes in slope found at service area boundaries
Income[a] surface	In the short term, depends on environmental conditions, mainly historical and political; in the long term, smooth, relatively flat	In the short term, moderate (depends on the mobility of labor in low-income areas); in the long term, smooth

[a] "Real income" (Box 16.1).

16.2.3 *Location Decisions and National Objectives*

The economic geography of a country reflects and symbolizes its national objectives (formally stated or not) because location decisions that are made in accord with the objectives affect the geographic dispersion, connectivity, and texture of the economic system. Some of these decisions are made by government. Others are made by private decision makers who are influenced by government incentives. Still others are made by private decision makers who support the objectives themselves or who wish to earn the approval of a society that does.

To repeat our familiar example, a country that places a very high priority on regional income equity would be expected to have a more dispersed pattern of economic activity than a country that gives the objective a low priority. In affluent countries today, an objective of productivity usually means that large activities are clustered in a few regions, but because of the diseconomies of extreme concentration, the activities are increasingly dispersed within those regions. An objective of equity often means that large new activities are located in regions that lack significant agglomeration economies, resulting in a more dispersed pattern between regions but a less dispersed pattern within regions.

This indicates how national interest, defined in ways that consider social and political goals as well as economic theory, can cause the dispersion, connectivity, or texture of economies to differ. In fact, when the link between objectives and economic geography is clear (for example, dispersal of industry or equity in incomes), the map of economic activities is a dramatic piece of evidence of what a country does, not just what it says it stands for.

Actually, neither an objective of equity nor an objective of productivity is very realistic in the extreme. A focus on equity with no concern for efficiency can waste so many resources that very little gets done for any place; equity is achieved at a low level of well-being. But a concern with productivity without attention to regional equity is socially insensitive and politically unsettling; in the long run it can be maintained only by repression or by the control of information. What usually happens is that the trade-offs between the two objectives get calculated in a political-economic marketplace, and some resources are allocated for each. The issues in working out the balance of priorities include (1) the mobility of the labor force, including cultural obstacles to relocation (more mobility means that regional inequities are more likely to be corrected by migration without government intervention); (2) the "opportunity costs" of dispersion and added connectivity: the value of things that have to be given up in order to reach such goals (the higher the opportunity costs of equity, the lower is usually the equity target); and (3) the costs of agglomeration at centers of concentrated investment, including congestion and pollution (the higher the costs, the less likely it is that objectives of productivity and equity will lead to significantly different locational strategies).

16.3   *ELABORATING THE BASIC CONCEPTS*

What does all this mean for lower Slobbovia, which wants central government help in persuading some new basic activities to locate there? Its concern is with particular location decisions: where is that large new fertilizer plant going to be built, and what about the new plant for manufacturing copying machines, or the new headquarters for servicing insurance claims? It wants the response to national economic objectives to be a geographic pattern that better helps it meet its particular needs.

This section will consider the relation between pattern and process a little further and will review optimization as a goal.

16.3.1   *Pattern Planning*

How does *pattern planning* come about, and what does it look like? The answers are as numerous as the number of times it is tried, but many of the elements that they have in common are already familiar to us (see Box 16.4). In reviewing these elements, consider what they mean for particular places.

In general, pattern planning starts by noting the nodality that shapes the geographic structure of an economy: centers of activity are distributed across the map, connected with each other and with their surrounding areas. One schematic idea of this structure as it evolves through time was shown in Figure 12.2. It also notes the presence of "uniform regions," as differences in comparative advantages show broad similarities within areas larger than a single center. It notes the significance of boundaries: between uniform regions, between nodal regions (the hinterlands of larger centers), and between political jurisdictions. And it observes the way patterns in areas of different sizes relate to each other—often hierarchically.

But the national interest is not limited simply to observing the way things are. It extends to evaluating the desirability of what is likely to happen next. Which of the centers will grow? Where will new ones arise? Which of the connections will be most important? Where will new ones appear? What does this mean for people in this hinterland or that? And it extends still further to asking how things *should* be.

Defining the economic pattern that "should be" is a task that turns out in practice to be crudely judgmental because our available theories are based on such a simplified view of the world (for

---

BOX 16.4 PLANNING

It is tricky to associate the term *planning* with the decisions that lie behind the spatial structure of the economy. For instance, General Motors is involved in economic planning regardless of the role of governments in the economy. Planning is the process of acquiring and assimilating information so that individual decisions are in line with the objectives of the firm. It is hard to imagine a large organization operating without it. Public-sector planning, however, has a broader meaning when it represents a coordinated strategy for the kinds of actions described in Chapters 14 and 15, because its objectives relate to interests that transcend the organization itself. It occurs when society decides that all the private planning, left alone, is adding up imperfectly. In an economy, it is part of the "balance-wheel" role of government in society, and it is general or specific according to the way this role is viewed.

Planning is an ambiguous term because it makes a great deal of difference who is planning what for whom. The subjects of attention may be regions, communities, activities, or budget categories. The needs may be corporate, political, or human. And the intent may be advisory or prescriptive.

example, often holding population density, cost of distance, and resource endowments constant). Too often we are faced with a difficult decision between (1) using a theory, some of whose assumptions we know to be wrong, and (2) using guesswork, without any help from scientific research at all. It is particularly hard to take into account all the relationships between one specific activity and the rest of the economy, and the difficulty is compounded by the fact that conditions are constantly changing. Suppose, for example, that we are trying to identify the best pattern for some new hospitals, or department stores, or beer-manufacturing plants. The number of facilities eventually to be built is uncertain. Our careful computer-based solution for three facilities shows no locations in common with our solutions for four and five activities. Where should the first facility be built? The second? Which is the best of the three "best" solutions? In a world where distances are shrinking as transportation and communication technology improves and markets and resources are shifting in their location and importance, there are very few patterns that are "best" for very long. These difficulties do not mean that pattern planning is not done or should not be done. It is of very considerable value (1) as a process that clarifies the need for information and contributes to an increased understanding of what is going on; and (2) as a guide to locational decision making, to be considered along with other sources of guidance. (An example is Figure 16.5.) But this should not be confused with optimizing public policy.

16.3.2   *Optimizing Spatial Structure*

Since the special focus of spatial planning is on making the best location decisions, optimization is often considered to be a central part of a decision maker's effort: an aim that is related in complex ways to the concept of equilibrium.

Optimization   Optimization is a procedure for finding out the best result of something: the outcome that gives the most (profit, efficiency, productivity) or the least (cost, inequality), according to the concern of the seeker. In spatial planning, the search is for the best spatial pattern to achieve an objective, and a wide variety of mathematical techniques have been developed to help a decision maker evaluate the alternatives.

It is important to remember, however, that (1) an optimization problem can only be solved by simplifying it; and (2) the solution applies only to the objective that has been defined. Consequently,

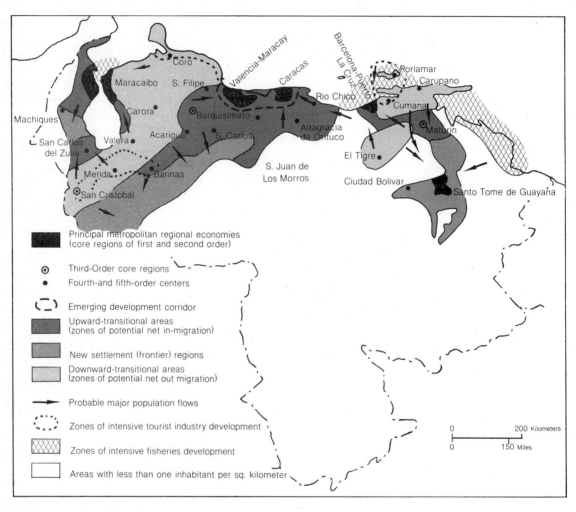

FIGURE 16.5

Pattern Planning: the recommended structure of regional development in Venezuela, 1963–1990.

optimization in spatial planning is a frequent source of controversy because various participants in locational decision making have different views of the objective and different levels of confidence in the necessary simplifying assumptions. Try, for instance, to persuade an eastern Montana farmer to support a major coal gasification industry there by telling him or her: "My model says this is the best place."

Even people who agree on objectives and general procedures can reach different conclusions, depending on the time period they are considering and the geographic area they are including. A dramatic example is the conclusion of some experts that economic productivity is best served by concentrating activities in a few places, while others conclude that productivity is best served by dispersing the activities.

There are alternatives to optimization as a goal (for example, see Box 16.5). Commonly, rather than setting as a target *maximizing* productivity or *minimizing* inequality, a national objective will be defined as achieving as efficiently as possible a target level of productivity or relative equality. Such a "cost effectiveness" approach is usually easier to reconcile with the realities of the political environment than a more idealistic "best of all possible worlds."

Equilibrium   Aside from cost minimization problems, the most tractable optimization cases are those in which opposing economic forces create predictable balance. For spatial organization, examples are (1) the value of proximity versus the higher cost of a location in a very accessible place (von Thünen); and (2) the benefits of scale versus the benefits of dispersion (central place theory). Economic decision makers make frequent reference to the kinds of spatial equilibria we considered in Chapters 4–7: the "ideal" geographic structure of land rents, prices, and other items of economic interest.

But spatial equilibria are not necessarily oriented toward the well-being of people; they may produce a structure that outlives its usefulness; and they may be hard to change. The map of prices, for example, is often insensitive to the map of needs, and the map of land rents rewards whoever is the possessor of the highest and best use. Much of the public activity in spatial planning is intended to change spatial equilibria by modifying one or more of the economic forces that define them.

BOX 16.5   SATISFICING BEHAVIOR

The usual conception of optimizing behavior for a person in the labor force is to make as much money as possible. But some people would prefer more vacation time or a shorter work week, at their same salary, to a salary increase with no reduction in the work requirement. Their main concern is not with making as much money as possible.

In a case like this, we can say that the motivation is to reach some satisfying level of income, not to achieve a maximum income. Such behavior has been called *satisficing* behavior, as contrasted with *optimizing* behavior. Below the satisficing level, a person is an optimizer but, once the level has been achieved, he or she is not very responsive to economic incentives.

Clearly, this idea is a realistic way of looking at many decisions about the use of a place or the location for an activity.

16.4   EXAMPLES

To illustrate how the national interest gets transformed into policies related to regional development and growth, we will take a quick look at four cases: the United States, Canada, Great Britain, and the USSR.

The United States   The general view in the United States has been that the national government should intervene in the economic system as little as possible. Both as a term and as a concept, *national planning* is considered a threat to the rights of private enterprise and local government; anything that sounds very much like it is acceptable only in a crisis situation.

The first real experience with regional development in the twentieth century came as a response to the economic depression of the 1930s, and the Tennessee Valley Authority remains today as an example of comprehensive federal planning to meet the problems of a particular region. But this experience was restricted to meeting what were considered to be immediate problems (for instance, people needed to be put to work, and floods needed to be controlled; TVA endeavored to solve the former by using federal money to solve the latter).

Perhaps the beginning of a broader concern with regional development was the Democratic Party primary in West Virginia for the presidential nomination in 1960. Senator John F. Kennedy campaigned hard in West Virginia, visiting many towns and talking to many people, and his victory there was a key to his eventual nomination. Reportedly, he was deeply affected by his personal observation of the economic distress of this part of Appalachia. Soon after he was sworn in as President in 1961, the Area Redevelopment Act was passed, providing economic development aid to counties that met certain criteria, which were concerned mainly with unemployment levels. The amount of support was relatively small, and for political reasons it was spread to at least one county in every state (see Figure 14.8). The most frequent uses were to attract small industrial activities and to develop recreational facilities. The impact was not dramatic.

In 1965, the Act was replaced by legislation which established the Economic Development Administration (EDA). It recognized that small areas might need help; and it provided criteria for establishing their eligibility for development grants and loans, with special attention to helping needy areas that contained potential growth centers. But it went farther to provide for larger areas overlapping

FIGURE 16.6
Interstate Economic Development Regions in the United States.

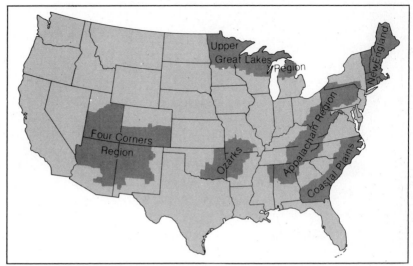

state boundaries, to be designated as economic development regions. Over the next several years six were identified (see Figure 16.6). These regions were characterized by high unemployment; low income; low-quality education, health care, and housing; a declining economy; and/or out-migration.

Each of the six regions now has a commission that prepares plans for the area, advises on economic development initiatives, and disburses some federal money. The Appalachian Regional Commission plays an especially active role. Again, the impact so far has been rather slight.

A different type of regional development support was the aid during the 1960s to American cities (for example, the Model Cities program). Much larger sums of money were allocated to meet the pressing urban needs of the time than had been provided through the EDA. These urban programs are only one example of a federal government activity that is not considered regional development as such, but that has had more substantial regional impacts than the specific programs that *are* defined as dealing with regional growth. It is fair to say that so far in the United States, the national interest—as it relates to regional development—has never been clearly enough focused to lead to a coordination of the various government programs that affect regions. Consequently, programs often work at cross-purposes, and progress is elusive.

An example of a recognition of this problem was a request in 1975 by the Technology Assessment Board of the U.S. Congress that the Office of Technology Assessment conduct a study of the relationship between energy facility siting and "national growth

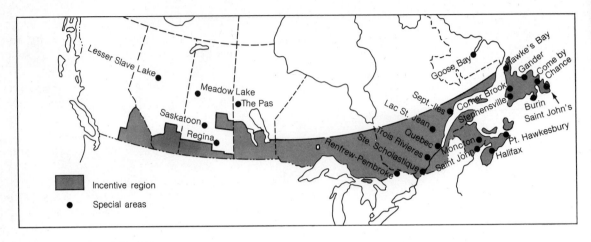

Lesser Slave Lake

Meadow Lake
The Pas

Saskatoon

Regina

Renfrew-Pembroke

Lac St. Jean

Sept. Iles

Trois Rivieres

Ste. Scholastique

Quebec

Moncton

Saint John

Corner Brook

Stephensville

Goose Bay

Hawke's Bay

Gander

Come by Chance

Burin

Saint John's

Pt. Hawkesbury

Halifax

■ Incentive region

● Special areas

FIGURE 16.7

Areas in Canada Eligible
for Industrial Incentive
Support.

policy in the United States." As stated in the request, the particular interest of the Congress is in the effect of legislation that shapes locational decisions for new energy facilities on the overall distribution of people and economic activities in the United States. By implication, if the effects are inconsistent with the national interest, the legislation may need to be changed.

Canada   The Canadian experience has in many ways been similar: some parts of the country persistently poorer than others, some central government help during the 1930s, a surge of concern with regional development problems during the 1960s. But the period since 1960 has seen a much more serious attempt than in the United States to use public policies to deal with regional economic disparities. An Agricultural Rehabilitation and Development Act (1961), designed to assist impoverished farmers, was followed by an Area Development Agency, created in 1963 to encourage economic development in areas of unemployment (mainly by offering incentives to manufacturing firms who located in disadvantaged areas: see Figure 16.7). Also in 1963, an Atlantic Development Board began operation, focusing on the provinces with the most serious economic problems. These new steps were followed in 1966 by the establishment of a Fund for Rural Economic Development, intended to provide multiyear cost-shared support to selected areas so that they could undertake ambitious programs of development. Then, in 1968, the Canadian government decided to form a federal Department of Regional Economic Expansion, with comprehensive responsibility for planning and coordinating regional development activities. By this time, so many different development policies had been tried and later changed that the basic development strategy was unclear; but the new department has showed a particular interest in the role of growth centers in large regions—and more generally in the development of healthy regional economies rather than subsidies for individual activities.

Great Britain   Great Britain, on the other hand, has shown a forty-year commitment to reducing disparities in job opportunities between regions. Legislation has evolved continuously since the mid-1930s, providing such aid to needy areas as tax incentives for industries located there, loans for new industry to go there, grants for new buildings there, and even government-built structures available for companies to use. Although the amount of emphasis on these programs has varied, depending on the political party holding the majority in Parliament, the aim has never completely disappeared from view.

Operating in a system that mixes a lot of government economic activity with private enterprise, the British approach has led to the designation of four kinds of areas needing special help: (1) areas adjacent to expanding large cities, where growth needs to be limited; (2) areas that need a wide range of help in dealing with problems of insufficient growth; (3) smaller pockets within these areas that are particularly distressed, deserving very high priority; and (4) areas that are not quite as needy as (2) but that still need a few kinds of help.

Opinions differ about the effectiveness of British regional development efforts, but the neediest areas in the 1930s (Scotland, Wales, and the north of England) remain among the neediest areas in the 1970s.

The USSR   The Soviet Union believes that in principle severe regional disparities are unacceptable, and it believes that such unacceptable situations are best dealt with by centralizing in the national government the planning and control of all economic activities. In general, the government has worked through the formal planning apparatus to reduce regional differences in two ways: by creating new centers of integrated industrial production, usually where large sources of energy are available (first coal, later hydroelectric power); and by providing educational, health, and other services to all areas of the country. It has also given a great deal of attention to the transportation system, since most of the disadvantaged areas are distant from the more affluent ones.

In many cases, the cost of helping remote areas has proven high, and it appears that regional disparities in economic benefits and opportunities in the USSR have not been reduced very much over the past forty years, in spite of a lot of economic, human, and political investment. When the national interest includes both regional equity and national productivity, such frustration may be inevitable. On the other hand, differences between regions in public services seem to have been reduced significantly.

16.5   A RECONSIDERATION

If at this point the relationship between national objectives and spatial planning seems fragmentary and impressionistic, then this chapter has done its job, because that is a reasonably accurate picture of the present state of the art. The national objectives are usually plentiful and not always consistent. And the best spatial pattern to achieve any one objective is usually a matter of informed speculation rather than confident knowledge, because the world is so much more complex than the available models can handle—and because our knowledge of pattern-process relationships is still so rudimentary.

As a result, a particular area that wants to benefit from the national objectives can choose a variety of strategies: advocating an emphasis on certain beneficial objectives at the expense of attention to certain other objectives, advocating a particular geographic interpretation of an objective, or—as a last resort—arguing that spatial planning should be based more on pragmatic political concerns than on theories that are too simple, not substantiated, or suitable only for other kinds of situations.

But what kinds of help does the area need? What should it be seeking?

MAJOR CONCEPTS AND TERMS

For definitions, see the Glossary.

Income substitutes	*Optimization*	*Regional equity*
Maximizing productivity	*Pattern planning*	*Satisficing*
	Regional equality	*Spatial error*
Minimizing inequality		

Footnote for Chapter 16

1.   Hoover, E. M. *The Location of Economic Activity*. New York: McGraw-Hill, 1948, p. 10.

CHAPTER 17

EVALUATING THE PROSPECTS OF A PLACE

*W*hat will your hometown, city, county, or state be like when you are twenty years older than you are now? If you expect still to be living there, and especially if you are trying to decide whether to stay or not, the answer to this question will shape your life.

In seeking the answer, there are two challenges: to find out what the place is like now and to find out how such a place is likely to fare in the future. We will consider these challenges by talking about a region, but the discussion can be interpreted at any scale that makes sense to a person, from a small town to a very large area.

17.1 SITUATIONS

17.1.1 The Transfer

The company you work for has offered you a promotion, but the new job is in another part of the country. If you want to get promoted, you had better move now, because if you don't take the offer it will probably be a long time before they pick you again.

The trouble is that you like the city where you live. It means friends, cultural opportunities, a good life. Your family likes it, too; in fact, your oldest child is adamant about staying there.

You decide that the choice is between (1) taking the new job and making your future with your current employer, wherever it sends you; or (2) making your future with the city, looking for advancement with other employers there. It's one way or the other.

But you decide that to make the decision you need to know a lot more about what will be happening in the city over the next twenty years or so. Where will the new jobs be? Will there be openings in other companies for somebody like you? Are you likely to end up unemployed or unfulfilled? What about your friends? Are they likely to stay or go? Are the cultural opportunities likely to continue? In short, is the city going to be a lively place or a dead end?

That weekend, some of your best friends come over for a while, and you ask them what they think about the prospects of the city. One is optimistic. One is pessimistic. A third doesn't know. A fourth doesn't care. Nobody knows how to find out for sure.

You start checking around with people who should be specialists in such things. The Chamber of Commerce says the future is bright—but what else would you expect them to say? The city planning commission gives you a foot-high stack of reports, but you can't figure out what they mean for you. The experts at the local university seem to disagree just about as much as your friends.

You decide that you will have to make your own evaluation, because you don't have very much confidence in anyone else's. But what do you do now?

17.1.2 *The Young Mayor*

At the age of 26, you have been elected major of your town in the south of Italy, because you say you will bring jobs to the town. And finding some good new jobs seems to be the only way to keep families together. Right now, nearly all the young people are leaving for the north or for countries such as Switzerland and Germany, where they can get work. As far as the people in the town are concerned, the situation has become a crisis.

Taking some money from the tiny town treasury, you embark on a trip to Milan, Turin, Bologna, and other industrial and business centers in the north. During the next month, you talk to dozens of officials of big firms, and what they tell you is very sobering. To them, your town is far from the largest markets for the products they make; the entire region is too poor to buy very much besides necessities. The labor supply from your area has a reputation of not working very hard. Your town is hard to get to—off the main roads and rail lines. The officials are simply not convinced that you have much to offer.

On the way back, you stop off in Rome to see whether the government has any plans to help your area. After several days of going from office to office, you decide that although some of the words sound nice, you had better not count on any of those people to help you out. They seem to be living in a different world from yours.

But your last stop before you head back to the railway station is at an agency involved in highway planning. There, a sympathetic secretary shows you a still uncirculated draft of a map of proposed new "autostradas"—limited access superhighways. And, lo and behold, one of them is shown as passing within 10 kilometers of your town. Since it would be linked to a national network of such highways, your village would become accessible to the rest of the country.

Sitting in your seat in the passenger car as the landscape of southern Italy slides by, sipping from a better bottle of wine than you usually buy, you resolve to return to Rome in six months or so—and if the draft map has become an actual plan, to go back to Milan and talk some more about what your town might be able to offer.

17.2   BASIC CONCEPTS

17.2.1   Regional Accounting

Suppose someone wants to evaluate your economic prospects as an individual. What would the first step be? In all likelihood, you would be given a battery of tests designed by physicians, psychologists, and educators. Your physical capabilities and limitations, your aptitudes, skills, experience, and training would be identified. You might be given a task to see how you handle it. Also of interest might be whom you know, how you are viewed by others, and where you are located. In general, a person evaluating your economic prospects would start by trying to get to know you better.

In much the same way, evaluating the prospects of a place begins with getting to know it as well as possible. Information is valuable, as we learned in Chapter 3. And where it concerns economic measurements, there are some standard ways to proceed.

One way is to construct an input-output table (see Chapter 10); another—which is more a complement than an alternative—is a localized equivalent of a "national income account." Table 17.1 shows a very simple example of such a regional account. As examples of how simplified it is, note that all government purchases of

TABLE 17.1 A Simplified Regional Income Account

Sector	Expenditures		Income	
Household	Consumption	400	Wages and salaries	445
	Personal income tax	50	Interest	15
	*Personal savings	45	Dividends	15
	Total	495	Transfer payments	20
			Total	495
Business	Wages and salaries	445	Consumption	400
	Interest and dividends	30	Government sales	100
	Corporate income tax	40	Gross investment	120
	Indirect business tax	35	Net foreign investment	10
	Depreciation	55	Total	630
	*Business savings	25		
	Total	630		
Government	Government purchases	100	Personal income tax	50
	Transfer payments	20	Corporate income tax	40
	*Government savings	5	Indirect business tax	35
	Total	125	Total	125
"Foreign" (all other economies interacting with the region)	Exports	430	Imports	420
	Total	430	*Net foreign investment	10
			Total	430
*Investment/savings	Gross domestic investment	120	Personal savings	45
	Net foreign investment	10	Business savings	25
	Total	130	Depreciation	55
			Government savings	5
			Total	130

goods and services are from the region's business sector, all transactions with the foreign sector are by the business sector (or at least any such transactions by other sectors have income that is equal to expenditures), the government is paying no wages and salaries, and all nonlocal economies are grouped as one foreign sector. Note also the way everything in the account balances with the help of an accountant's trick: the items marked by asterisks are fancy ways to say "whatever it takes to make the totals come out even."

Generally, input-output analysis focuses on interactions within the business sector, as well as between its parts and the other sectors. Regional growth theory is especially interested in the role of interactions with the "foreign sector" as a source of vigor, as well as the role of other investment/savings items. Personal well-being is centered in the household sector figures.

TABLE 17.2
A Simplified Calcu-
lation of Gross
Regional Product

Expenditures		Income	
Consumption	400	Distributed income	
Gross investment	120	Wages and salaries	445
Government purchases	100	Interest and dividends	30
Net foreign investment	10		
Total	630	Nondistributed income	
		Business savings	25
		Corporate income tax	40
		Indirect income	
		Indirect business taxes	35
		Depreciation	55
		Total	630

Table 17.2 illustrates how the regional equivalent of gross national product is calculated from such an account* and how such a regional product is related to incomes. Clearly, there are substantial problems of definition and measurement in coming up with such a figure, but economists who specialize in national income accounting have worked out many of the conceptual problems (such as the same automobile tire that is purchased twice—by the automobile manufacturer and then by the buyer of the automobile).

In spite of its neatly balanced numbers, such an account (like an input-output table) is fundamentally a conceptual framework for understanding how a regional economy works: what happens when something changes. It is primarily concerned with the identification and measurement of interrelationships.

The most general problem, of course, is the measurement requirement. It is easiest to solve when a transaction involves a money payment, which establishes a price in currency units—and as a result the numbers get less and less precise as more values have to be "imputed" (estimated). Examples of such a need include the estimated sales price of farm produce consumed on the farm, the estimated rent of owner-occupied houses, and the estimated cost of child care provided by a spouse who is not a wage earner.

Estimation is required more often for subnational units than for nations because less information is readily available and the smaller units have a more limited capability to gather additional data. Consequently, regional scientists have devoted a great deal of

* A gross national product may be seen as a total of gross regional products as well as a total of the national sector amounts.

attention to techniques for estimating values that are not directly available. As a simple example, if (1) data on characteristics A and B are available at the national level, and they have shown a consistent mathematical relationship through time; but (2) only data for A are available for each region; then (3) one option for estimating B for each region is to assume that it has the same relationship to the value of A that historically has been characteristic of the nation as a whole.

A further problem with constructing regional accounts is the importance of the "foreign sector"—the proportion of the region's transactions that crosses its boundaries. For instance, what proportion of the expenditures of the national government should be included in the region's accounts?

At any rate, the conceptual frameworks of regional accounting and input-output analysis are extremely helpful in identifying important relationships among the categories of information that would obviously be of interest: population size and composition, income employment by employment category, retail and wholesale activity, service activity by category and size, manufacturing activity by category and size, agricultural activity by crop, wage rates by skill level, land prices, transportation and communication facilities, taxes, public services, and others.

17.2.2 *Regional Assets and Limitations*

Once the people evaluating your economic prospects as an individual have learned what you are like, their next step would be to investigate how well a person with your capabilities and experience usually does. Is a person like you more likely to become a plumber, a forester, or a professor of classics? Are you likely to become a manager? Are you likely to work at night and on weekends to improve yourself? How much physical or mental stress can you handle? Their final step would be to ask whether the recent scientific evidence about human development is a good guide to the situation that lies ahead in the next twenty years. Will the profile of job openings be changing? How about the conditions that predict advancement: might your contacts, skills, sex, ethnic identity, aptitudes, or specialization be more (or less) valuable in advancing your economic well-being in the future than in the past?

Again, the process is much the same for evaluating the prospects of a region, and many of the answers are obvious to anyone who has read Chapters 5–15. For convenience, a region's assets will be categorized as economic, locational, and temporal.

Economic Assets

In any forecast of the prospects of a region, the concepts of economic base, agglomeration economies, and comparative advantage are central. A further consideration is whether or not the region has been designated for special governmental assistance (and, if so, for how long).

For example, there is good evidence that regional growth within the United States has historically been related to regional exports (economic base) and regional wage levels (comparative advantage). A region may show a high rate of growth either because it has a strong basic economy or because it is shifting labor from low-income activities to higher-income jobs in activities that are more capital-intensive (see Chapter 10).[1]

It is also quite clear that cumulative causation is a factor in regional prospects. Because it is so difficult to create agglomeration economies where none are present, a great deal of inertia is imposed by the existing economic map. Suppose, for instance, that the regional economy of Oz has a size of 1,000, while the regional economy of Id has a size of 100. Oz is growing at a rate of 2 percent a year—quite slowly. Next year, its economy will have grown to 1,020. But if Id wishes to remain no more than 900 behind, its economy must also grow by 20, which for it is a rate of 20 percent—quite a challenge.

Even more important, with economic growth may come such valuable regional characteristics as diversification, investment capacity, and big local markets. It is important to evaluate how *resilient* a place is—how prepared it is to handle the shifting effects of technological change and external competition, which will sooner or later pose problems for any important local activity. And economic diversification is an especially good sign (as is a rich cultural environment, offering adaptability and breadth of outlook). Specialization is often an indication of lack of resilience. Another sign can be a regional economy dominated by a few large firms (or other kinds of institutions), because a loss of one of those activities can be hard to balance; in this sense, economies of scale for a firm may be accompanied by potential diseconomies for the place.

Some examples of evaluations that might result from a study of economic assets are these:

1. If the employed population is relatively old or the level of labor skills is relatively low, the prospects are not very bright.

2. If part of the area has scenic value that is recognized widely, that part is likely to be preserved without much change.

3. If the region has been designated for special government aid, it is likely to attract new activities of the specific kinds that are most often attracted by the type of assistance provided.

Locational Assets

The special contribution of the perspective of economic geography is to evaluate how the region's location affects its prospects. The keys to this evaluation are two: (1) where the region is located with respect to areas of economic growth and stagnation; and (2) the relative importance of centripetal (dispersing) versus centrifugal (concentrating) forces in the spatial economy (including the role of public policy in determining the balance between them).

Because so much of the literature about economic development concerns nations rather than regions or localities, it is hard to be certain how well the standard theories are suited for evaluating the expectations of places smaller than nations, especially when they are smaller than an American state or a Canadian province. But a few ideas seem robust enough to serve at least as a starting point.

To begin with, visualize the map as a mosaic overlain by a web. The pieces of the mosaic are regions; the web is the system of connections between central places within and among the regions. The prospects of a particular region depend partly on where it fits in the mosaic and partly on how it is associated with the web.

The Mosaic For simplicity, let us divide all the pieces in the mosaic into growth regions and stagnation regions. Observation of the world tells us that more often than not, like regions will be close to each other. If we color one type blue and the other green, our mosaic will show a lot of blue pieces next to other blue pieces. This is so common, in fact, that economic development experts around the world speak routinely of a *North-South problem*. Figure 17.1 is an example; although the less advantaged section is not always on the south side (in Sweden it is in the north; in Turkey it is in the east), it is seldom scattered as small pockets throughout the entire map.

What does it mean if our own region is blue rather than green? The most widely accepted theories give us four possible answers:

1. **The difference between the types of regions will increase:** blue will become more blue. Cumulative causation makes the rich richer and the poor poorer. Polarization lies ahead: backwash effects predominate as capital and labor flow to the growth regions. Accept your fate or move.

FIGURE 17.1
Regional Economic Contrasts in Italy.

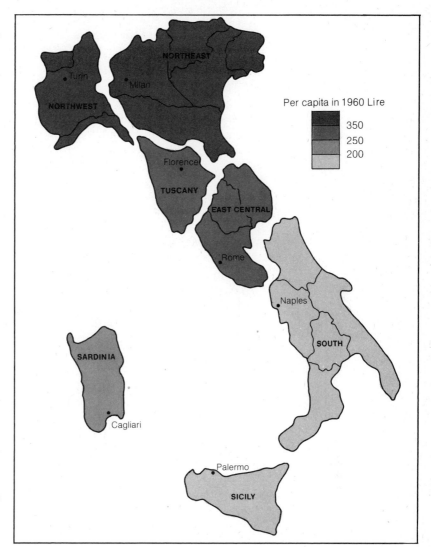

Per capita in 1960 Lire

350
250
200

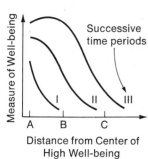

FIGURE 17.2
One Theory about Changes Through Time in the Geography of Well-being.

2.   **The difference between the types of regions will first increase but then decrease.**   At some magical point, the backwash effects will be overcome by the spread of benefits from growth regions. Jobs and income and opportunities will filter down. Be patient or move.

     An example of this idea is the model shown as Figure 17.2. In a geographic sense, an analogy would be an ice cap. As more snow falls in the middle, the weight of the accumulation pushes the edges farther and farther out. The prospects of a place depend on whether it is near the center of the ice cap, as in Figure 17.2(A), near the edge (B), or far away (C).

3. **The difference will decrease.** As labor and capital flow from poor to rich regions, the increased competition in the rich areas (and the more wide-open opportunities in the poor ones) will reduce the differences per person. It should not be necessary to be too patient.

4. **There is no way to be sure.** Growth depends on the region's export base, which may in a specific period favor either a blue region or a green one. Look to the possibilities.

Which should we believe? Theory does not give us the answer; it merely poses the question. Observation of the experience of actual regions and nations so far seems to indicate that answer 2 is a common occurrence within countries, at least up to a point, with answer 4 also a factor. Opinions differ as to whether the trend in contrasts in economic well-being between countries is best described by answers 1 or 2, although 4 is agreed to be a part of the picture (for example, the discovery of oil in a less-developed region). Answer 3 is hard to support, except as an explanation of the latter stage of 2.

The Web   It is not surprising, then, that a lot of attention has been given to how economic trends spread from one place to another, and a key to this is the web of connections between places. These connections are not just transporters of commodities, working in lock-step with the distance-decay implications of least effort. They are also the "nervous system" of hierarchic diffusion; they facilitate and shape the way a region affects and is affected by other regions, neighboring and otherwise, because they are so often the channels of communication between people—at least in industrialized societies.

The term *hierarchic diffusion* refers to the way economic relationships are usually channeled through hierarchies such as the central place system. Whether it is economic cycles, language, or style, the initial spread is often from a large center to other large centers, not to its own surroundings. Then it moves from each of the large centers to the next level of central places. And eventually it trickles down to the villages and farms.

For example, consider a decision by the central government to establish a public works program in order to reduce unemployment. Regardless of where the individual dams, buildings, stadiums, or sidewalks are built, there are likely to be administrative offices in the major economic centers—employing people, occupying office space, seeking bids for building materials, keeping records. In one sense, the money and benefits filter down through the administrative hierarchy, whose location usually corresponds with the central place hierarchy; in another sense, the economic impacts filter upward through the hierarchy from the specific sites.

As another example, consider a new coal mining activity in a remote rural area. Not only will it require a labor force and some equipment, but it will need equipment repair services, more labor union officials, sizeable loans of money, government-employed monitors of environmental quality, and many more people who are not there now. But not all these activities will be at that one mine site. Some will locate in the nearest small town; others will arise in the nearest small city, or in the larger city that meets the region's very specialized needs. Effects travel upward through a hierarchy as well as downward.

The question for evaluating a particular region is how it is situated geographically with respect to the web: centrally or peripherally? Is it covered densely or sparsely? Is it likely to be strengthened or weakened as the web evolves? These factors affect the region's access to information and the opportunities it brings. They affect its likelihood of sharing the benefits of something good happening nearby. And they affect the region's comparative advantages; the kinds of activities that usually seek peripheral areas (scenic preservation and military reservations are examples) are quite different from those that seek central locations.

Putting the Mosaic and the Web Together   In many ways, though, the answer lies not so much in the mosaic or the web as separate entities, but in how they relate. It seems clear that "spread effects" travel along the web of connections within and between regions (as do "backwash" effects). The spreading pattern illustrated by Figure 17.2 reaches out along elements of the web more rapidly than where there is no web.

It is largely because the web is there that an economic geography is not a sterile, fossilized geometry. A map is a consequence of consumer demands, producer decisions, everyday economic actions. And it is a cause of further decisions. As new ideas, people, and money flow into the economic system, they surge (or trickle) through its spatial structure as well. As a result, some appendages grow while others atrophy. For instance, Figure 17.3 extends 17.2 to show some implications of the Taaffe-Morrill-Gould model of how a spatial economy develops. Imagine yourself living through the entire sequence at places A, B, or C; as a land owner and private economic decision maker, your life would be quite different depending on where you were located.

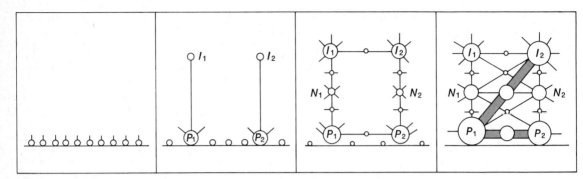

(a)

FIGURE 17.3

Some Indicators of the Development of a Spatial Economy: (a) the model (see Figure 12.2); and (b) implications of the model.

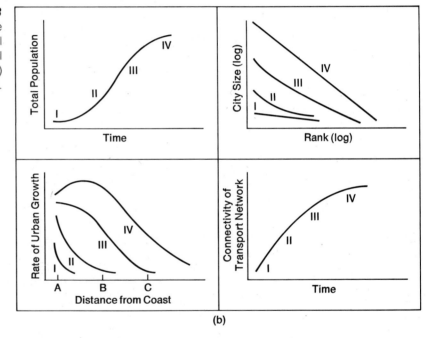

(b)

Being in a disadvantaged region that is well linked to advantaged regions is thus different from being disadvantaged and isolated. It is more risky but also more dynamic—possibly a better prospect for entrepreneurship, certainly a surer prospect for change. And a common strategy for improving the prospects of a less-developed area is to improve its internal and external linkages (see Box 17.1).

The prospects of a place may also be affected by where it lies with respect to a regional boundary. Chapters 13 and 15 have already noted the primary boundary effects when the boundary is the border of a political jurisdiction. When the mosaic is defined differently—by ecological or cultural variation—changes are usually more likely to occur in boundary zones than in interior parts of regions (which may be seen by an entrepreneur as an opportunity, but by others as a concern).

Temporal Factors

Part of the risk—and part of the opportunity—is that regional economic growth usually follows a characteristic pattern. Based on comparative advantages at a particular point in time, a region develops economies of scale and agglomeration in doing what it does best, and it grows in a way related to its size. Usually this means a sequence of acceleration followed by deceleration, as the advantages become more fully exploited. In theory, the latter, "mature" stage leads to an equilibrium situation, a little like a "climax" in ecology, which is stable. It resists change.

Suppose that two regions are stable in this way—but at an economic level that is less than they both desire. One gets a whole series of new transportation and communication linkages; the other does not. This means that the present economy in the benefited region, based on the previous set of conditions, may not be what is best suited for the new conditions. Seeking to be a leader toward the future, you start a new service firm in that region. If you succeed, the success will be great; but you may fail, either because you misread the new advantages or because the present system is too stable (too resistant to change) to respond fast enough for you to be able to pay your bills. If you had been in the other region, the prospects of success would have been much smaller, but in a familiar set of conditions the risks would have been small.

A region's prospects are therefore affected by its place on a current *growth curve* and its susceptibility to changes in the conditions that have caused the curve to take shape. It may be moving along an established curve or facing a possible change from one curve to another. Regional growth is in fact a lumpy series of growth curves (see Figure 17.4), and the movement from one path to another—responding to new conditions—is often traumatic, provoking difficult adjustments in the social and political environments of the economy. In some cases, the environmental adjustments may be considered too undesirable to allow the economic change to take place.

Some examples of evaluations based on temporal assets are these (note how they relate to the other kinds of assets):

1. If the region's economy is based partly on a disappearing resource or an obsolescent technology, it faces significant adjustments.

2. If the region itself is a growing consumer market, its prospects are relatively good for attracting consumer-oriented activities.

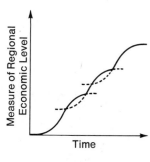

FIGURE   17.4

3.   If the region's advantages are oriented toward the use of leisure time, its prospects may be relatively bright because leisure will probably be a bigger part of our lives in the future than it was in the past.

4.   Unless it is small already, the proportion of the population employed in primary activities is likely to decrease; unless it is large already, the proportion of the population employed in tertiary activities is likely to increase.

BOX 17.1   ACCESS AND APPALACHIA

Many of the people who first settled in the valleys of the Appalachian Mountains were seeking isolation—a place where they could live independently, self-sufficiently, free from the social pressures of a more crowded world. Although the mountains were not far (in physical distance) from highly developed centers on all sides, they remained remote, both because travel by modern means was slow and because the mountain people were distinctly different from the city and lowlands people. Well into the twentieth century, many valleys could only be reached on foot or horseback, and a stranger entered them at some risk.

By the 1960s, however, this kind of life was no longer sufficient for most of the people. First, the railroad companies had cut the forests to get ties for the new lines reaching westward and to support the tunnels and roofs of mines to extract coal for the locomotives. Then the mining companies put proud mountain people in bondage to the company store. World War II, by drawing many people out for military service and to work in factories in cities in the Midwest, gave Appalachia an idea of how the rest of the world lived. And, all along, the population density in the valleys was growing.

Consequently, helping Appalachia was the first concern of the ARA and EDA in the United States, and the basic strategy was to open it up. As the reasoning went, if Appalachia is in fact a collection of the outer reaches of some vigorous cities lying all around it, its development simply requires linking it more effectively to those cities. Then the cities will spread some of their benefits into Appalachia; for example, industrialists in the cities might use the lower cost labor supply in the mountain periphery to manufacture some components for their products. It was decided to criss-cross it with interstate highways as the the first step. Schematically, the strategy took form like Figure 1. But the main effect of the strategy was to make it possible for people to get through Appalachia quicker, going from one side to another. If anything, it hurt business at the motels and restaurants along the older highways through the area.

As an alternative, the next strategy was also focused on linkages—but this time on internal ones. Not only was Appalachia not linked very well to Pittsburgh and Cincinnati, it was not linked very well with itself. Perhaps it could only hope to relate positively to the external centers if it made some

17.3   *ELABORATING THE BASIC CONCEPTS*

In digging more deeply into these concepts in order to apply them to an evaluation of a particular region, a person runs into a lot of important questions. This section will consider some of the most common ones: why some regions seem to be exceptions to all the

---

BOX 17.1 (cont'd.)

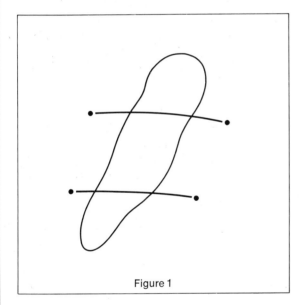

Figure 1

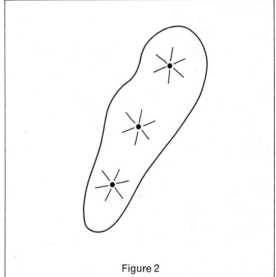

Figure 2

internal progress first. The need was to create some growth centers within Appalachia that would serve as a focus for internal development, spreading benefits and opportunities back into the "hollers." Schematically, this strategy looks like Figure 2. But it has proved difficult to persuade any member of the U.S. Congress that his or her district should not include at least one growth center, and the

concept has not been transformed into a clearly defined, well-focused policy about the allocation of federal aid.

In the meantime, the linkage system within Appalachia has developed in a fragmentary manner, with stretches of good roads interspersed with stretches that remain a real challenge.

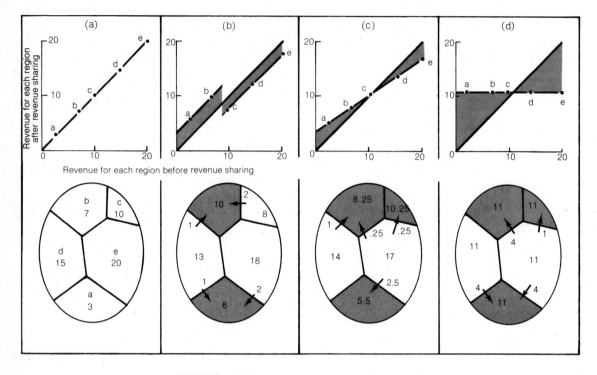

FIGURE 17.5

The Implications of Four Alternative Policies Regarding the Use of Revenue-sharing to Reduce Regional Inequities: (a) nonintervention strategy; (b) special-area strategy; (c) sliding-scale strategy; and (c) complete equalization strategy.

rules (chance or politics), how the spread of assets or limitations works, and whether national policy can actually have very much effect on the distribution of assets between regions.

17.3.1 The Role of Chance

Peter Haggett has suggested that every area is a participant in a giant resource lottery:

> *Each national territory, however defined, represents some share of the earth's stock of natural resources. In the case of agricultural resources, the pattern of environmental variation is observable and the equity or inequity of shares is well known. In the case of mineral resources, though, both the degree of geologic exploration and the changing demand for minerals make the shares more like lottery tickets.*[2]

This is a striking example of how some aspects of a region's future are hard to predict. Another example is the appearance of unusually able (or incompetent) local business or government leadership. And we can imagine many others: natural disasters, technological breakthroughs, shifts in political influence.

The most familiar contemporary case is oil. A country or region does not earn oil deposits. It can look for them, but it either has them or it does not. Libya does. Egypt does not. With the discoveries in the North Sea, Great Britain now does. France still does not. And, of course, the economic and political consequences can be enormous.

Similarly, in the 1950s and 1960s the coal reserves of Appalachia were not believed to promise much wealth for the region. Coal was a dirty energy resource that brought low prices, occupational health hazards, and environmental degradation. In the 1970s, however, once remote towns like Pikeville, Kentucky, now have a number of millionaires because of the increased scarcity and higher prices of fuels other than coal. An application of regional growth theory in 1960 would not have predicted it, but it happened.

Some things about a region's future are therefore hard to plan and hard to control, whatever the size of the area. Another example is the role of personal preference in locational decisions; regardless of the relative pros and cons of a place, as they would be assessed by an "expert," decision makers may choose it or avoid it for reasons of their own.

17.3.2 *The Role of Government Policy*

Growth theory is equally unable to predict how a country will define its national objectives and convert them into public policies, but this can also have a significant impact on a particular region (see Chapter 16). For example, Figure 17.5 illustrates the effect on the five regions in a small country of four different policies toward regional inequity: (1) leave the regions alone; (2) help the two poorest regions; (3) decrease the differences proportionally; (4) equalize the regions.

The prospects of regions A and E are sharply different with policy 1 than with policy 4. And B and C even differ noticeably between policies (2) and (3).

Consequently, it is useful to assess what a variety of possible government policies might mean to a particular region. Although the specific policy ten years from now may be impossible to forecast, such an assessment can indicate whether or not most of the possible futures give the region additional assets.

17.3.3 *The Diffusion of Change*

As we have seen, the prospects of a place are affected by the likelihood that it will be exposed to changes. And we have noted that there is a pattern to such things, associated with proximity in a mosaic or connectedness in a web. This kind of pattern is an example of the "diffusion of innovations," which is a subject that has been studied for several decades by geographers, sociologists, and others. Innovations (new ideas or objects) move across space very much like people migrate, and in a broad sense their spread is just as predictable. Generally, when a useful new idea arises in one place, it spreads to others in one of two ways:

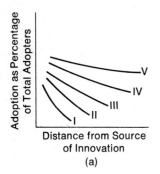

(a)

1. **Expansively.** It may spread by contacts that are more frequent over short distances (such as person-to-person communications), illustrating the concept of distance-decay (see Chapter 11). Figure 17.6(a) is a classic example of this kind of diffusion. Because on a map it resembles the spread of an epidemic, such a process is sometimes called "contagious" diffusion; common examples are the adoption of new hybrid grains and the spread of declines in fertility.

   From the point of view of a particular region that is not the source of the innovation for this kind of diffusion, its location makes a difference. New adoptions of the innovation spread like waves from the source, as in Figure 17.6(b), moving fastest along the lines of easier movement, as in Figure 17.6(c), shaped by political, physical, linguistic, and other types of barriers.

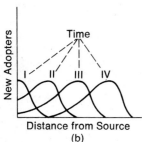

(b)

2. **Hierarchically.** It may spread through a hierarchy of centers, as indicated by Figure 17.7. It eventually becomes expansive from local centers, but first it moves through the web of connections between larger centers. Examples are economic cycles, the use of bank credit cards, and many kinds of relocation decisions.

   In this case, the prospects of a place are influenced by its position in the hierarchies to which it belongs: urban, economic, and political. Especially important in many cases are the webs of contact, information flow, and decision making within large business organizations.

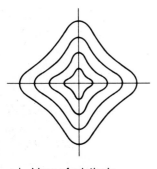

╪ Lines of relatively easy movement

╭ Adoption as percentage of total adopters, declining from the center

(c)

FIGURE 17.6
Expansive Diffusion.

Although the patterns produced by these two kinds of diffusion processes look different, the processes are similar in that both are shaped by (1) the likelihood of finding out about a new possibility, which is a consequence of the flow of information; and (2) the likelihood that a new possibility will be considered desirable by

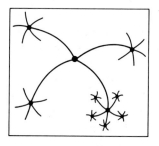

FIGURE   17.7
Hierarchical Diffusion.

decision makers who learn about it (which is a consequence of local conditions and attitudes). In expansive processes, the information networks are mosaic-oriented; in hierarchical processes, they are web-oriented. For either process, the decision-making environments—economic, cultural, political, physical—may reflect mosaics (physical conditions for cultivating a new seed, political conditions for adopting a new land use) or webs (communication or transportation requirements, more cosmopolitan cultures in more accessible locations). In every case, it makes a difference where the sources of innovations are.

Figures 17.8 and 17.9 are examples of expansive diffusions that have affected the economic prospects of places. Figure 17.8 shows how the use of marketing cooperatives for cotton production in northern Tanzania moved outward from a few innovative centers. And Figure 17.9 is a generalized map of the spread of "modernization" (economic, social, and political changes moving together) in Sierra Leone; the dominant thrust from west to east reflects the orientation of the main railway line from the coast to the interior.

An example of hierarchical diffusion within an expansive situation is the spread of banking in early America. Beginning with

FIGURE   17.8
The Diffusion of Cotton Cooperatives in Lake Province, Tanzania.

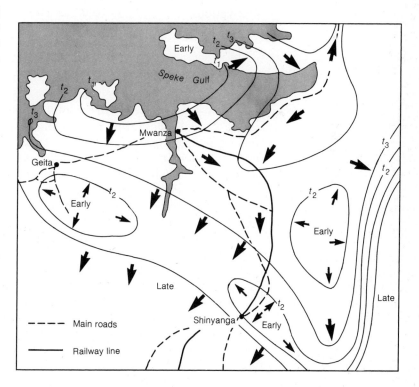

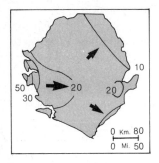

FIGURE 17.9

The Diffusion of Development in Sierra Leone. The complex actual "surface" has been smoothed in order to identify dominant elements of the pattern (see Figure 16.4).

a concentration on the northeast seaboard, banks followed the streams of westward migration down the Ohio River and around the southern flank of the Appalachians, arising in embryonic market centers as sources of credit for frontier development. From this start, adoptions of banking spread further westward; at the same time, established centers expanded their services, and gaps in the East began to fill.

One characteristic of the process was failure as well as successful adoption. Some selection took place as nearby communities competed for preeminence; but a more important factor was the reverberation of European depressions through the banking hierarchy, which proved to be the undoing of many an ambitious, overextended small bank, unable to satisfy a sudden call by a big eastern bank for the repayment of notes (so that the big bank could satisfy its obligations to the Bank of England or someone else in Europe).

These examples suggest a very important larger picture of the ebb and flow of economic changes. In any historical period, in fact, many different kinds of innovations are exhibiting the same kind of pattern (see Box 17.2), and the general outlines of the pattern can be readily identified: the centers of innovation (the collectors and marketers of new ideas) and the geography of the spread of the innovations.

17.3.4 *The Attainability of National Objectives*

In Section 17.2 it was suggested that no one is quite sure whether rich and poor regions will eventually become more alike in their levels of well-being, but in Section 17.3.2 we noted that government policies might have an effect on this. To what extent can governments overcome the inertia of an existing pattern of economic advantages to achieve their national objectives?

The evidence is uncertain. Studies of the Soviet Union indicate that in spite of major government efforts to the contrary, the concentration of industry in a few regions has gradually increased. One study of Yugoslavia concluded that without any deliberate central government effort, industrial decentralization was taking place. Does this mean that government action to modify the geography of economic activity is futile—a kind of self-serving, wasteful expression of frustration with things as they are? In fact, either naiveté or hypocrisy? One interpretation of Figure 17.10(a), which is widely accepted as the way things are now, would be that government intervention to assure equity between regions is unneces-

FIGURE 17.10

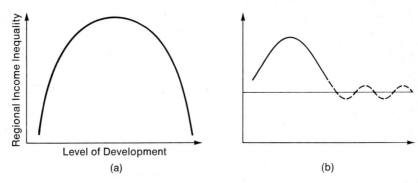

(a)   (b)

sary; with a little time and continued economic growth, the well-being of different regions will converge by itself.

But the experience of most countries, affluent or not, is that any convergence of income averages (or another measure of equity) fades away while regional differences are still substantial. For one thing, regional comparative advantages change constantly as resources are discovered, inventions are made, prices shift, and transportation technology evolves. Even a system inclined toward convergence is constantly faced with identifying new regional advantages or disadvantages and redistributing or otherwise adjusting for the resulting uneven benefits.

Another way to view Figure 17.10(a) is as a part of Figure 17.10(b). Regional income averages converge to an "equilibrium" level of moderate inequality where, unless the government intervenes, the convergence-oriented processes (such as the mobility of labor and capital) are balanced by divergence-oriented processes (cumulative causation, inertia, changes in regional environments). If this is the case, achieving equality may be as elusive as reaching the speed of light, because of opportunity costs involved in maintaining a spatial structure that is a long way from the equilibrium. And achieving greater equality than the equilibrium level would require government initiatives, with the required effort being increasingly great as the target gets farther away from the equilibrium.

17.4 A RECONSIDERATION

The most fundamental problem in evaluating the prospects of a region is not identifying its assets and limitations today. That identification requires a great deal of information, and it needs a solid understanding of economic geography; but a fairly good job can certainly be done.

The problem is that regional economic prospects depend in large part on new things that will happen *outside* the region in the future: international relations, technological changes, and so forth. And it is hard to evaluate the effect of something unknown.

There are four principal ways to take this uncertainty into account:

1. **Don't worry about it.**   Base the evaluation on what is known, and figure that unpredictable future events are as likely to improve prospects as to hurt them.

2. **Try to reduce the uncertainty by predicting the future.**   Hire a consultant or consult available predictions, and evaluate the impact of what they say will probably happen.

BOX 17.2   THE DIFFUSION OF THE INDUSTRIAL REVOLUTION

In the last several decades of the eighteenth century a group of inventions in Great Britain became the basis for a revolutionary idea about how manufacturing should be done: in large factories, using power-driven machines. This Industrial Revolution soon spread into Europe and across the Atlantic to North America, and over the next century the countries that adopted the innovations soonest came to dominate world trade and the production of manufactured goods.

The diffusion of these innovations (such as the steam engine) followed very similar patterns; for example, the figure shows how railroads, from a beginning in the industrial core of England, eventually came to cover most of Europe. A map of the date of initial industrial use of steam power would look very much like this, although the dates would be a little different.

In this way, a map of the spread of re-

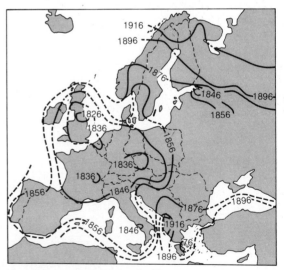

The Spread of Railways in Europe.

cent innovations can sometimes be a clue to the pattern of origin and spread of future innovations.

3.   **Develop several different evaluations based on different kinds of possible future events.**   See the prospects of the region as a family of possibilities rather than as a single best bet.

4.   **Perhaps based on 3 above, try to evaluate whether unpredictable future events, since there are certain to be some, are more likely to help the region or to hurt it.**

17.5 *TOWARD GREATER PRECISION*

Many kinds of growth take the form of an S-shaped curve on a graph: a slow start, a takeoff into a period of more rapid growth, and a subsequent slowdown again. The slowdown reflects a situation in which growth itself eventually creates conditions that limit further growth: a city gets too big to work very well, for instance.

When the S-shaped curve is symmetrical, in the sense that the second half is a mirror image of the first, it is called a logistic curve (Figure 17.11 is an example). It is often defined by this complicated-looking mathematical form:

$$Y = \frac{U}{1 + ae^{-bT}}$$

where

Y is the expected value of whatever is growing, such as the population of a city or the proportion of potential adopters who have adopted an innovation

U is the upper limit of growth

T is the time since growth started

a is the constant that can be estimated from a few observations

b is the rate of change in Y as time passes

e is a mathematical constant: 2.7183.

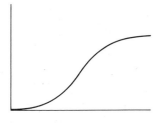

FIGURE   17.11
Logistic Curve.

Note that when T is zero, the denominator is large: $1 + a$. Y is thus small. When T is very large (a lot of time has passed), the denominator approaches the value of one, because e comes to have a larger and larger negative exponent (making the addition to one increasingly small). Y becomes very nearly the same as U.

One of the uses of a logistic curve is to predict future growth. If it can be assumed that growth is following a logistic curve (even approximately), the early years can be used to establish values for U, a, and b. And these values can be used to predict the rate of growth thereafter.

MAJOR CONCEPTS AND TERMS

For definitions, see the Glossary.

Boundary zones	Growth curve	Regional accounting
Expansive diffusion	Hierarchic diffusion	Regional product
Geographic inertia	North-South problem	Regional resilience

Footnotes for Chapter 17

1. Borts, G. H. and Stein, J. C. *Economic Growth in a Free Market.* New York: Columbia University Press, 1964.

2. Haggett, Peter. *Geography, A Modern Synthesis,* 2nd ed. New York: Harper & Row, 1975, p. 460.

CHAPTER 18

HOW A PLACE CHANGES ITS PROSPECTS

Regions, like people, want a doctor only when they are sick.

E. M. HOOVER, 1971

*W*hat if the economic prospects of a region—or a country, city, or community—are unattractive? The area seems likely to stagnate and fall behind. Or perhaps it seems likely to grow so fast that it will lose many of the qualities that make it an attractive place to live.

Can a place pick itself up by its own bootstraps? Can it affect its own destiny? If so, what are the factors it may be able to control?

18.1 SITUATIONS

18.1.1 Borrowing a Good Idea

It has been a long day at the convention, and you are hoarse from trying to talk to people all day in the noisy, smoky lobby. Back in your room, you take a shower and stretch out on the bed to read the local newspaper before you go to sleep.

As you browse through the paper, a story in the second section catches your eye. With the help of a loan from the state government, an association of local businesses has leased a very large computer that will be used on a cooperative basis. The association will provide a small staff of computer systems analysts, programmers, and key punchers; and each business will pay the association for the use it makes of the facilities and staff. Most of the participants intend to use the computer to handle their personnel records, payrolls, and inventory records; several plan to use it for billing and other mailings to customers; and a few hope to experiment with some research. In addition, the computer will have a lot of unused capacity, and the association believes that the facility will attract new business and industry to the city.

This strikes you as a good idea. You believe that such an arrangement could save your own company money; there has already been some discussion of leasing a small computer, but the company is not anxious to set up a computer staff of its own. And your city has had a hard time attracting new economic activities lately; for one thing, its air pollution level is so high that a new activity adding any pollution at all is prohibited by the current air quality standards, unless an existing activity can be persuaded to reduce its emissions.

So you take the idea home with you. Within eighteen months, aided by the enthusiastic advice of a representative of a firm that sells computers, your city becomes only the third in the country to put a large computer into operation as a cooperative venture. You are a bit of a local hero. And three small firms with large data-handling needs have already been in contact with city leaders about setting up an office there.

18.1.2 *Image Making*

Like many other people from your region, when you travel you are a little defensive about where you are from. You overhear people joking about it. On TV, it is frequently the place that a comedian mentions when he or she wants to give the audience the mental image of a backward, "hick" place. You know that many smart people would resist moving there to accept a job, because they can't imagine making their lives in such a place. It is not only a personal embarrassment; it is a constraint on the opportunities available to people who live in the region.

As a stubborn person, you decide that somebody should do something about this, because you believe that the impressions are wrong. It's an area most people would like, if they knew more about it.

After several years of talking to local officials, making speeches, and writing letters, you are able to persuade your state government to allocate a couple of million dollars a year for an effort to inform the rest of the country about the good things in the state. And you are put in charge.

Turning down a recommendation that you spend the money on magazine advertising, you decide to use it to bring influential

		Source of Resources	
TABLE 18.1 Approaches to Improving the Prospects of a Region for Economic Growth, with examples		*Internal*	*External*
Locus of Economic Decisions	*Internal*	Reducing unit labor costs by raising labor productivity	Grants or loans for locally initiated resource exploration or research aimed at inventions
	External	Local tax breaks for newly arriving business	Transportation system improvements to improve accessibility to the region

people to the state to see it first hand: providing incentives for conventions to come there, holding conferences and retreats, sponsoring a couple of high-visibility sports events, cultivating journalists from the national media.

A few years later, the state is the subject of cover stories in *Newsweek* and *Fortune*: "The Good Life in Columbia." Population statistics are starting to hint at an increase in the movement of people into the state each year. The state industrial development staff reports a definite change in the response of the firms it contacts. And, maybe most important of all to you, now you love to tell people where you are from.

18.2   *BASIC CONCEPTS*

How can a sick region get well? Like a person—either by doctoring itself, by paying a doctor to do it, or by finding someone else to pay for the doctor. Then, after the initial diagnosis and treatment, the region can either provide its own medicine or seek someone else's help in getting it. These are the basic options.

Translated into more familiar terms, this means that a region can improve its prospects for economic well-being in four kinds of ways. Table 18.1 illustrates the alternatives when well-being is associated in the region's thinking with regional growth.

Consider, for example, a little more complicated version of the multiplier concept that was introduced in Chapter 8. According to this point of view, regional income can be accounted for by this formula:

$$Y = \frac{I + E + G}{(1 - c) + m + r}$$

where

Y = regional income
I = autonomous investment
E = net exports
G = government expenditures
$1 - c$ = marginal propensity to save
m = marginal propensity to import
r = tax rate

The regional income "doctor" can operate from within, increasing E through resource discoveries or higher labor productivity, or from outside, increasing I or G by channeling external savings into the region.

Because regional development experts have been concerned mainly about decisions at a national scale, the one of the four alternatives identified in Table 18.1 that has been most studied so far is influencing external decisions with external resources (especially influencing decisions about where to locate new capital). Many of the conceptual models, in fact, imply that growth is determined mainly by what happens *outside* a region. The special concern of the development-oriented portion of this work has been with helping problem regions*: "situations where things have definitely gone awry."[1] But from the point of view of your own region, the other three alternatives are important as well because (1) the external resources may be limited; (2) there will certainly be a lot of competition for them; and (3) your own interest may be in a place that is not enough of a problem for the external folks—but not enough of a success for you.

In any case, whether the resources are internal or external, the first question is whether to adopt a strategy of changing the behavior of decision makers *within* the region or inducing decision makers *outside* the region to do things differently.

18.2.1 *Improving Prospects from Within*

Can a region change its prospects by itself, by changing the activities of decision makers inside it? The prospect of changing the behavior of one's neighbors should be a sobering one, to be approached with caution and sensitivity; but there are several ways that this can improve a region's economic prospects.

---

* The focus of much of the general theoretical work has been on equilibria *among* regions rather than how a particular region can be induced to grow.

Some of the possibilities involve (at least initially) only the activities of just a few key people. For example,

1.   **A region can become its own source of innovations, rather than waiting for waves of change from somewhere else to reach it.**   This can occur (1) by internal invention (although the pattern of spread of an invention is predictable, good ideas can be first discovered and adopted anywhere); or (2) by perceptive borrowing (spotting and using somebody else's idea that would not have arrived in the region by its own accord for a long time yet).

Borrowing is an especially promising approach because it depends on information, hard work, and ingenuity rather than on unpredictable local genius. Studies of the diffusion of innovations in business, for example, indicate that the early adopters are seldom the largest firms, with the largest research budgets; they are usually less cautious smaller firms, willing to take risks to improve their position ("when you are Number Two, you try harder").

The classic case of successful borrowing in recent world economic history has been Japanese industry. Whether the product is optical instruments, small cars, or portable television sets, Japanese manufacturers have been able to take someone else's basic product idea, improve it a little, implement it with good quality control and at a relatively low cost, and sell the product competitively in the area where the idea originated. In effect, the Japanese were connecting with the diffusion hierarchy near the top and then creating their own marketing process quickly enough to get for their products a share of the adoptions that eventually took place in lower levels of the hierarchy.

The major opportunities for borrowing arise when economic changes can be anticipated. Once a still-developing need is identified, a region can seek ways to meet it before others do: new technologies (solar heating in place of gas heating), input substitutions (printed circuits in place of wires), institutional changes (new roles for government), resource changes (new agricultural capabilities due to climatic change), consumer demand changes (pet rocks, beansprouts, instant coffee, tennis). Remember that a head start is a significant comparative advantage (see Box 18.1).

2.   **A region can find resources that no one had sought there before, changing the mosaic of comparative advantages.**   As Chapter 9 suggested, the resource endowment of an area is usually a reflection of how hard people have looked so far.

Consequently, some additional looking may result in a larger endowment.

This, too, involves risks, because it is a kind of purchase of "resource lottery tickets," with an uncertain chance of payoff; but it rewards ingenuity. For instance, a Mexican desert plant has been found that can provide an oil to take the place of whale oil, which is in short supply because the world's whale population has been seriously depleted. The plant promises to be a valuable crop, capable of being grown in areas that would have previously been considered resource-poor for agriculture. As another example, consider the effect on peanut growing of research that discovered how many uses of the peanut were possible. Or the fact that, with oil bringing a higher price, oil wells can be drilled deeper—bringing an area like southern Alabama a new oil boom as deeper wells strike reservoirs that shallower ones missed.

3. **A region can increase the market for its goods and services by finding new and different ways to provide them.** In the terminology of Chapter 7, its local economic decision makers can either expand the range or reduce the threshold of what they have to offer. Consider some possible strategies as examples. A firm producing several component parts for RCA television and stereo sets is limited in its sales to RCA's needs. If a new line of products can be marketed directly to local stores selling electronic components, the market of the firm will be increased. Or reflect on the case of a small coal mine that is usually limited to selling its product to small users of coal or to middlemen who pay less than final consumers (because a large user prefers to sign a single contract with a large pro-

---

BOX 18.1 SPOTTING USEFUL INNOVATIONS

In Section 18.1.1, a good idea was spotted by accident, but there ought to be some way to figure out where to look on purpose. The most promising method was hinted at in Chapter 17, in Box 17.2: there are some places that seem time after time to be ahead of the rest in developing and adopting successful new ideas. Clearly, they are good places to watch.

Another approach is to identify "regional analogs": areas very much like yours. Anything that works there ought to be useful where you are. It is simply a matter of comparing what they do with what your region does—and evaluating the differences to see if they suggest any possibilities.

ducer). If several small coal producers join together in a cooperative marketing arrangement, their prospects for access to big markets and higher prices may be much brighter. And finally, in a general sense, a region can focus its attention on services rather than products (see Box 18.2).

These kinds of management innovations are in fact a special case of the first option, and they can do as much to improve the prospects of a place as a new idea about a technology.

Other "bootstrap" alternatives rely less on the outcome of a resource lottery or the inspiration of a select few. They call for changes in the behavior of many people in the region. For instance, a government may increase the amount of personal income that is saved—by taxing the income and saving it in the public sector. Or it may increase regional exports, using controlled price increases to reduce local consumption. Such policies are widely used throughout the world, and they are indubitably effective at a national level. But two other strategies are worth special note because they focus on positive social actions rather than painful economic sacrifices:

1. **Reducing unit labor costs by increasing labor productivity.** A classic way to compensate for disadvantages in relative location is to offer lower unit labor costs (Chapter 6). This usually reflects either lower wage rates (not a very popu-

BOX 18.2 SERVICES AS A GROWTH SECTOR

Traditionally, when less-developed regions have searched for foci for growth, they have looked to heavy industry, specialized agricultural production, or mineral extraction. It used to be, for instance, that nearly every country wanted a steel mill. It was a sort of regional or national status symbol. But we have seen that employment has historically tended to fall in agriculture, stabilize in industry—but *rise* in services. This suggests that the long-term growth sector is not industry but services such as education, health care, government functions, research, tourism, legal transactions (for example, quickie divorces in the Dominican Republic or the registry of ocean tankers in Liberia), marketing, banking, consulting, shipping, warehousing, and data processing.

Basing regional development on service functions is still an unconventional idea, but there are some examples of it: the concentrations of high-value research activity in Southern California and northern Colorado, because they are attractive places to live; Lebanon as a banking center (until the recent civil war); Brasilia, the capital of Brazil, as a new government center in an area needing development.

lar suggestion) or a higher ratio of capital to labor in the economy (not always possible to achieve from a region's own assets). Another possibility, however, is to work harder. Recent evidence, for instance, indicates that workers who identify their own interests closely with the success of their firm are more productive; organizational loyalty is associated with a smaller turnover in the work force, fewer sick days, fewer errors on the job, and other things that affect the cost of production. Policies such as profit sharing and the involvement of a wide range of employees in the management structure of firms may therefore help to reduce unit labor costs in a region, enabling it to improve its competitive position in the national economy.

2.   **Developing comparative advantages through cooperation.** Things that individual people and firms in a region may not be able to accomplish alone they may be able to do together. For example, by cooperating in the use of transportation, communication, and computing facilities, firms may be able to eliminate redundancies, use the facilities closer to their capacities, and avail themselves of new economies of scale. And in a broader sense, if the people in a region approach their problems in a spirit of cooperation rather than antagonism, new ideas flow more freely, less time and money are spent in litigation and other kinds of disputes, and other economic advantages may result. As we noted in Chapter 4 (pages 67–68), competitive individual decision makers, acting perfectly rationally, sometimes do not profit as much as if they had gotten together and agreed to coordinate their actions.

18.2.2   *Improving Prospects from Outside*

A different approach to improving the economic prospects of a region is to change the actions of private decision makers elsewhere: to get them to make decisions that help the region. Economic patterns are an accumulation of strategy decisions by individuals and organizations trying to benefit themselves. If a place can be made to be (or appear) more attractive, some of these economic decisions will be affected. Examples include judgments about where to relocate an existing office, where to establish a new branch office, and where to buy or sell an item. The strategies are a matter of either increasing advantages or changing images.

1.   **Adding comparative advantages.** Either by internal or external action, the region's utility can be increased. As we have seen, comparative advantage is relative and often changeable.

For changing it, there are three principal (and interrelated) approaches:

a. **Provide compensating substitutes for advantages that are lacking.** When a region lacks accessibility or agglomeration economies, these disadvantages can sometimes be balanced by lower taxes, reduced risk (guarantees of loans are an example), financing at a lower interest rate, or other kinds of subsidies. This is a common policy in dealing with "problem regions" (the Area Redevelopment Act in the United States and the Distribution of Industry/Industrial Finance Act in Great Britain have been well-known cases of this). The major problem with the approach is that the continuation or termination of subsidies at some time in the future may become a controversial matter.

b. **Add advantages by public investment.** If the need is great enough, governments may decide to allocate some of their resources to increase the comparative advantages of a region. The most frequent action is to improve the area's infrastructure: building roads and other new or better transportation facilities, improving power and water supply, providing training programs to upgrade the skills of the labor force. Other possibilities are to improve public services, such as education and health care, or to add attractive cultural and recreational amenities.

c. **By careful planning, create agglomeration economies.** As the earlier discussion of the "growth center" approach to regional development indicates, there may be ways to create for a place some of the agglomeration economies that play such a powerful role in economic-geographic decisions. One option is to use subsidies, infrastructure improvements, and the location of government facilities to accelerate the growth of a particular center. An alternative approach is to plan a new economic "complex": a combination of new activities any one of which would be unwilling to come to the region by itself, but that would be happy to come if all the others do (see Box 18.3).

2. **Changing external mental maps.** But an improvement in a region's comparative advantages is wasted if no one knows about it. For this reason, and many others, a region is affected not only by the way it is, but by the way outsiders think it is. Stereotypes such as the bigoted South, the unsafe big city, and the expensive East have a strong influence on location deci-

sions. As a result, a region can look to the mental maps of economic decision makers (the principal role of "industrial development" commissions in most countries, states, and large metropolitan areas). In part, the job is making sure that information about advantages is circulated and appreciated; in part it involves interpreting disadvantages as positively as possible (for example, poverty = low wage rates, remoteness

---

BOX 18.3   AN INDUSTRIAL COMPLEX FOR PUERTO RICO*

In the early 1950s Puerto Rico was finding it very difficult to establish enough basic industry to stimulate economic development on the island. As was to happen later in Appalachia, the cheap labor there had attracted some garment factories since World War II, providing needed jobs; but these factories hardly promised to be the start of an industrialized economy.

A group of people from the University of Pennsylvania, headed by Walter Isard, was asked to come up with some suggestions. They found that, except for tourism, the prospects were not bright; it was hard to identify any comparative advantage (except the cheapness of needlework) that could support any kind of large industrial development. In fact, several of the better possibilities, such as a shoe factory and a bottling works, had already been tried without success.

"Then one day, in an unpredictable fashion, an idea came up." Maybe some combination of activities would be profitable, even if no one of the activities could make it alone. Suppose the activities were closely linked—one's outputs being another's inputs. Transportation costs could be reduced, by-products that are usually discarded could be used, and items to be used by several activities could be produced with economies of scale. Specialized labor or services could be shared. Perhaps if a bunch of activities linked in these ways were located in one place, the savings would be enough to overcome Puerto Rico's comparative disadvantages.

Working with this idea, the group came up with a promising combination: an oil refinery for Venezuelan crude oil (the most accessible natural resource), fertilizer production from refinery by-products (fertilizers were a large import item), and the production of synthetic fibers from some of the oil (the demand in the United States was growing rapidly, and Puerto Rico already had a start in the garment business).

Several versions of this combination were analyzed, although it was hard to be very certain about projections that were based partly on roughly approximated numbers. In the end, the Puerto Rican government was convinced enough of the potential of one of the alternatives that it established a sizeable subsidy to get the complex going.

And the resulting petrochemical industry has certainly had a positive effect on the Puerto Rican economy (see Section 10.4.1), although Isard has noted that some of the social impacts were less desirable.

*Based on Walter Isard, *Introduction to Regional Science*, Englewood Cliffs, N.J.: Prentice-Hall 1975, Chapter 17.

= insulation against the stresses of large metropolitan concentrations).

In addition to providing information to others, this kind of marketing effort is an important source of internal information about the way the region is viewed, and it may suggest remedial actions that can be taken. In complex and important ways, it affects the region's self-image: what are we proud of? What are we not? What do we want to preserve? What do we want to change? And the effect of thinking about these questions can go far beyond a simple measure of the growth of the region's economy.

18.3   *ELABORATING THE BASIC CONCEPTS*

The preceding section outlined some ways that a region's prospects might be improved. Before we become aggressive regional developers, however, we need to think a little further about how changes in fact come about. We have to consider how alternative strategies should be evaluated. We must be aware of the possibility that there are some limits to what can be achieved. And we should remind ourselves that the aim of some regions is to stop growth, not accelerate it.

18.3.1   *How Changes Are Made*

By now, we know a lot about why things are done where they are done. But why do these uses of places change? A region's perspective is not quite the same as that of an individual economic actor. Returning to our isolated island of Chapters 8–10, let's indicate two possible uses of a location as two curves on a graph: I and II in Figure 18.1(a). The dotted line indicates situations where benefits equal costs; anything below it is unlikely to be considered. Each curve shows, for a given land use, the level of benefit that is associated with each level of cost. x_I is the level of activity (investment, work) that maximizes net benefits for activity I, x_{II} for II. Although in some cases a person might choose to maximize absolute benefits rather than net benefits, for convenience we will assume that our decision makers are mainly interested in net benefits; they are unwilling to spend $2 to make $1.

In one sense, each local decision maker constructs such curves in his or her head (or computer) for each alternative and each location that he or she knows about. Within that range of alternatives and locations, the strategy is to maximize the total of net benefits.

Changes take place for one of four reasons:

FIGURE 18.1

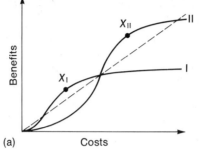

(a)   Costs

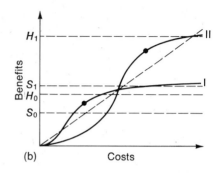

(b)   Costs

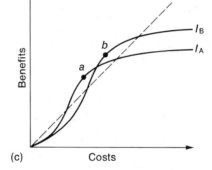

(c)   Costs

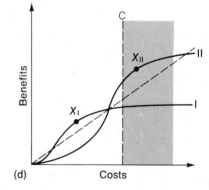

(d)   Costs

1. **A new alternative is identified that promises a *significantly higher net benefit*.**   (If the net benefit is only a little larger, it may not cause a change, because the change itself means some initial costs—such as the purchase of new equipment—and the benefits of the change are less certain than for the current activity).

2. **People's aspirations change.**   For example, in Figure 18.1(b), suppose that there is a level of benefit H that satisfies all the desires of society and a lower level S that is the least that allows it to survive. Perhaps a traditional society living by hunting and gathering (represented by I) is represented by levels S_0 and H_0. Its way of life is quite satisfactory—close to H_0. There is no reason to change to II, even if it is known to be an alternative. As its population density increases and it has greater contact with the rest of the world, however, the society's satisfaction levels rise to S_1 and H_1. Hunting and gathering are now barely sufficient for survival, much less happiness; and a change to land use II (for instance, simple cultivation) becomes increasingly attractive.

3. **The curves may be reevaluated.**   In Figure 18.1(c), a redefini-

tion of the curve from I_A to I_B would, with no change in the activity, mean that it would be pursued more intensively.

4. **The available resources may be increased, if that has been an inhibiting factor.**   Figure 18.1(d) shows that if available resources are limited to C, II is not an option even though it would have higher net benefits.

Note that information plays a more prominent part in this list than capital investment, although capital investment is more often chosen as the way to induce economic change. This suggests that a region that handles information especially well may have special advantages compared to other regions.

But a discussion of change would be incomplete without recognizing that change is often resisted. Partly, this is because economic change, however desirable for its own sake, may bring about cultural, social, political, or ecological changes that are not viewed as desirable. Economic changes affect the environments of the economy as well as being affected by them. But an even more general factor is that almost any change involves risk. Even though a new pattern of activity seems likely to provide more benefits, it is hard to be certain that it will do so. To some people, this kind of uncertainty is a compelling reason for caution, and most people would eliminate an extremely risky option unless it were the only possible way to deal with a crisis.

The point that some people are more cautious than others is an important one. In the United States and many other countries, major economic decisions increasingly involve the participation of a wide range of interests in society—not only the economic decision makers themselves but several layers of government, national and local citizens' groups, and special-interest groups of all sorts. In this sense, major economic decisions are a product of a process of political accommodation, in which resistance to change is usually a powerful point of view (and must therefore be accommodated by information, compensation, or some other strategy for resolving disagreements).

18.3.2   *Evaluating and Comparing Possibilities*

When a region contemplates the options for improving its economic prospects, it faces choices. The resources are seldom sufficient for doing everything that might be done, and some of the possibilities may even be mutually exclusive (for example, calling for different uses of the same piece of land). Consequently, an evaluation and comparison of the available ideas is needed.

One general approach to this has become standardized as part of the environmental impact statement procedure in the United

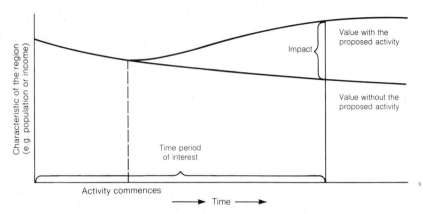

FIGURE 18.2
Evaluating the Impact of a Proposed Activity.

States. Essentially, the impact of each option on the region's income, employment, population size, and so on, is projected as diagrammed in Figure 18.2. In arriving at the projections, the plant to manufacture agricultural products, or the clothing manufacturing firm, or any other business might, for instance, be subjected to an estimate of its multiplier effects on income, jobs, and population; input-output analysis to trace connections with other kinds of economic activities in the region; and applications of location theory to estimate the effect of the proposed activity as a locational attraction for other activities from outside the region. This analysis is somewhat different from that of the developer, whose concern is with benefits for his or her firm, not the region.

A second approach is to compare every option with a generalized measure of doing nothing more venturesome than putting the available development money into a bank and earning interest on it. The logic works this way. Any decision to spend money on one thing is also a decision to forego spending it for other things. Connected with any decision, then, are what can be called *opportunity costs*, the value of which is roughly approximated by the prevailing interest or discount rate. For this reason, a method has been developed for estimating the *true value* of an option—its value above and beyond what an available interest rate would bring by itself:

$$\text{Discounted net present value} = \frac{N_0}{(1 + i)^0} + \frac{N_1}{(1 + i)^1} + \frac{N_2}{(1 + i)^2} + \ldots + \frac{N_t}{(1 + i)^t}$$

where

N = the expected income from the option during a time period, usually a year

i = the interest rate on money, for instance the bank discount rate

Applying this method is often called *cost-benefit analysis*. Although it is seldom easy to calculate N, taking into account depreciation and repair, and to choose a value for i, the formula is a powerful tool for evaluating a possible expenditure. Note, though, that its form is heavily weighted in favor of options that provide most of their benefits sooner rather than later. At a relatively modest interest rate of 8 percent, a huge benefit thirty years later is being divided by nearly 12. Note also that there is a difference between N, a total net benefit, and a proportional profit. A supermarket can operate quite happily on a 2 percent profit (grossing 2 percent above costs) if it has a large enough volume: 100 times 2 percent is greater than 10 times 8 percent. Other bases of comparison are available as well. For instance, options might be evaluated with respect to their contribution to equity. Which option does the most for the most disadvantaged part of the region or segment of the population?

These estimates share all of the problems of forecasting that were mentioned in Chapter 16, but at best they serve as an aid to policy making (and at worst they help policy makers to be more confident that no major points have been overlooked).

18.3.3   *Limits on Change*

Section 18.3.1 suggested that there are some kinds of limits on what changes can take place: lack of information, lack of need or aspiration, and lack of resources (money, land, labor). We encountered other limits as well in earlier chapters: production quotas, limits on the size of market areas, the concept of a carrying capacity, and the very real inertia that is an element of our maps of economic activities.

Opinions differ as to whether any such limits are absolute and irresolvable (see Chapter 20), but for any area at a particular time they are quite real. Many "problem regions," for example, are disadvantaged in so many ways that an investment in improving one thing may have little effect. Their prospects are limited by the sheer magnitude and diversity of the changes that would be needed to improve the situation.

As a result, some of the alternatives that are judged to be attractive for a region may not in fact be feasible: the steps necessary to bring the decision about may require resources that are not available or sacrifices that are not acceptable. But the threshold at which an option is judged not to be feasible is usually determined on social and political grounds, not economic ones.

18.3.4   *Slowing Down Growth*

But what if the objective is not to improve a region's prospects by helping it grow faster—but by keeping it from growing as fast as it seems likely to (see Section 10.3.4)? What if the concern is not with creating locational advantages but with eliminating them? This attitude is an increasingly frequent part of our lives (see Chapter 20).

As has been mentioned before, our concepts are directed mainly at understanding growth so that it can be induced. But the understandings can be used to retard growth as well. For example, (1) economic or locational assets can be counterbalanced by artificially created liabilities, such as taxes or red tape; and (2) barriers can be used to slow down the receipt of and response to growth-inducing ideas—or the innovation-diffusion process can be accelerated if it brings cultural and social changes that reduce the importance of economic growth. It can be useful to review the concepts of the book, one by one, and to consider how each one can be used in creating a strategy to slow down growth (for example, at the periphery of a city that is getting too large, its center too far from the countryside).

18.4   *EXAMPLE*

This time, it is your turn to fill in the blank. For the place that concerns you most, what can be done to increase the chance that its future will be what you would prefer?

18.5   *A RECONSIDERATION*

From the perspective of an individual or a small group of people, the most frequent challenge in trying to change the prospects of a region is that the change-inducing resources are limited but the needs are plentiful. Spreading the resources too thinly will have little effect.

Although it is not always workable, the *bottleneck* concept is worth considering in such a situation. Is there one gap that can be plugged, one obstacle removed, one factor added that will affect many parts of the regional economy? Is there a key—transportation, information, water, local leadership, the removal of a cultural or political barrier? If so, even scarce resources can be focused to have a significant impact, and even a few people can make a difference.

MAJOR CONCEPTS AND TERMS

For definitions of terms, see the Glossary.

Borrowing innovations	*Development bottlenecks*	*Regional pathology*
Cost-benefit analysis	*Industrial complex analysis*	*Retarding growth*
		Services as a growth sector

Footnote for Chapter 18

1.   E. M. Hoover. *An Introduction to Regional Economics.* New York: Knopf, 1971, p. 261.

CHAPTER 19

THE IMPLICATIONS OF PLACE PLANNING

*T*here are two dangers lurking behind the perspective of the past three chapters. First, when we say we are thinking about the economic prospects of a *place*, that is often a kind of shorthand way of referring to a concern about the well-being of the *people* who live there. Certainly, when a national objective is to help "problem regions or areas," the reason is that the people in those locations need help, not that a disembodied several thousand square miles of area is deserving of special attention. One danger of a focus on helping places is that it does not necessarily help very many people (see Section 8.3.3).

The second danger is that helping one region will hurt another. Just as only one player in the Monopoly game can own Boardwalk, in some ways different places are competing for the same things. And there are both winners and losers.

As a kind of reminder and caution before we leave this part of the book, this chapter will briefly consider these dangers.

19.1 PLACE PROSPERITY AND PEOPLE PROSPERITY

Even when the national interest is defined as people-oriented, it is usually expressed largely by decisions about places. Some of this is unavoidable, because policy tools such as the location of public facilities and the improvement of transportation networks cannot be used without getting geographic. And even when other tools are to be used, most of the people problems have a geographic dimension; such problems as poverty, hunger, unemployment, and lack of opportunity are usually centered in a few kinds of areas (see Chapter 3), and solving them requires decisions about alternative futures for those areas. In addition, administratively it is handy to carry out any national government policy by allocating money to governmental subunits, and at one level or another these units are nearly always defined geographically. It is very difficult to plan for people without planning for places (unless society believes that what is best for people is no planning at all).

But improving the prosperity of a place is not the same as helping people, for two basic reasons: (1) it does not necessarily deal with who within a place gets the help; and (2) it is possible that in the long run people actually might be helped more if the place's economy is not artificially propped up.

19.1.1   *Intraregional Distribution of Benefits*

Consider a national program to help lagging regions that is successful in getting several new industries to locate in a poor place. Who benefits? Often, in the poor place those who are helped the most are the ones who need it the least: property owners, realtors, banks, utilities. Certainly, there are more jobs in the area; but the new industries came there partly because wages were low, and they probably brought with them some of the individuals to fill higher paid positions.

Consequently, it is possible that a program to reduce differences in regional income averages—motivated by the highest social ideals—will have little effect on income differentials among people. Any of the three arrows in Figure 19.1(a) achieves the specific objective of the program, but only A offers any certainty that the social effect has gone beyond the mere manipulation of statistics.

In focusing on regions to solve people problems, the usual rationale is either that increasing the benefits of some will eventually bring benefits to all (multiplier effects, for example) or that, as long as inequalities within the individual regions are not *increased*, inequities throughout the nation will have been reduced—compare Figure 19.1(b) with 19.1(a). Although either is possible—and in fact hard to prove wrong—*evidence* that it is true is much scarcer than a *belief* that it is true. For instance, regional growth is more likely to benefit a lot of people within a region when the region's economy is already well developed—full of the characteristics we associate with agglomeration economies—but such regions are less

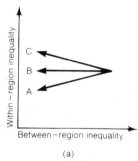

(a)

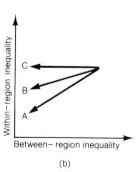

(b)

FIGURE   19.1

likely to be the targets of national efforts to encourage regional development.

A program concerned with people must pay attention to the "who" as well as the "where."

19.1.2 The "Rights" of Places

Even more complex is the question of whether helping a problem region actually hurts people by wasting resources. It is a very short step from arguing that less advantaged *people* deserve help to arguing that less advantaged *places* deserve help. It is only a little farther along to say that people have the right to live well wherever they want (see Box 19.1).

This idea is an attractive one, both for those who believe that a sense of place has cultural and psychological value and for those who have an economic or political interest in what happens to particular places. In some countries, including the United States, it may even be the dominant approach to dealing with the problems of society, because of the political influence of local interests.

But suppose that a region with no development potential has a lot of needy people. Is it better to help those people there or to help them somewhere else, where potentials are brighter? There is no simple answer to this, but parts of an answer lie in these directions:

1. The less mobile the needy people are, the more desirable it is to help them where they are now.

2. The more mobile the helpful new economic activities are, the more feasible it is to help the people where they are now.

BOX 19.1 GEOGRAPHIC DISCRIMINATION

In most countries it is against the law to discriminate against an individual because of his or her race or creed. This means, for example, that people of different races are entitled to equal education, health care, and job opportunities. In 1967, a President's National Advisory Commission of Rural Poverty in the United States went on record in favor of a national commitment "to give residents of rural America equal opportunity with all other citizens. This must include access to jobs, medical care, housing, education, welfare, and all other public services, without regard to race, religion, or place of residence." Denying a person access to a job because of his or her location would be considered a form of discrimination, just as if the denial were based on the person's race.

No such commitment has been made by the United States government, and many people would oppose it; but the idea is a logical extension of an emphasis on place prosperity, combined with a concern for economic and social equity.

3.   The less development potential the region has, the more desirable it is to help the needy people move to a more promising place.

From an economic point of view, maintaining people in locations where they are less productive can be very costly. It reduces
the productivity of the national economy, raises prices for consumers, and costs the taxpayers money. Taken by itself, such a
view is rather cold-blooded, but it is nonetheless a part of the truth.
Migration may sometimes be better for needy people (and for ambitious entrepreneurs) than regional improvement. And when, for
"noneconomic" reasons, migration is not the best solution, it
should be understood that a resulting trade-off is some economic
costs.

One approach to the problem has been to try to separate support for the well-being of people, wherever they may be, from
long-term support for places. Income maintenance and health care
programs, for example, are more clearly focused on needy, relatively immobile people than are programs to subsidize industrial
development in an area (unless the subsidies are targeted for "infant industries" that should eventually be able to sustain themselves without outside help—see Chapter 13).

19.2 *COMPETITION BETWEEN PLACES*

When places are competing for a desirable new activity, such as a
big branch office or a government research facility, only one of
them will be the winner. Even when an activity is not new but is
moving from somewhere else, the benefits (and costs) associated
with the activity are transferred from one location to another. In
this sense, a place sometimes enhances its prosperity at least partly
at the expense of other places (it is difficult to read Chapter 18
without sensing a bit of gamesmanship).

In a free, competitive economy, such enhancement is one of
the effects of the market mechanism, responding to changes in locational factors. It is roughly analogous to the concept of natural
selection in ecology, except that the environmental conditions of an
economy change more often. But society may believe that such a
market allocation of economic activities or resources is not fully
satisfactory, either because it leads to a distribution of well-being
that is inequitable or because it causes stresses in the physical or
political environments of the economy (for example, environmental

degradation or political instability). The result can be action to allocate things differently.

In reality, though, many of the tools that help a problem area do their job by steering resources away from other places. These other areas often believe that the resources—money, energy, new industry—would have been theirs if economic markets had been allowed to operate. For this reason, identifying the geographic scale of attention is a key to evaluating development alternatives. What a region would like best may not be in the national interest; what is judged to be in the national interest may not be what a region would prefer. Controversies about regional development policies often revolve around issues of this sort (see Box 19.2). Similarly, differences are common between perceptions of national and international interests—and state versus local interests.

Competition between places, however it is resolved, is not limited to what they all want. It also includes attempts to avoid things that they do not want, such as pollution and reductions in the quality of life. New Jersey and Massachusetts, for instance, are wrestling with the conflicting desires to have enough natural gas for homes and industries but to avoid environmental problems (especially from coastal area development) that might result from developing natural gas and oil resources off their shores. Meanwhile, gas-producing states in the Southwest, which might prefer to keep most of their gas to stimulate their own internal development, view the delays in offshore energy development as attempts by northeastern states to get the benefits of natural gas without having to bear the environmental costs of producing it. Of such differences in perspective and vested interest are stubborn conflicts born.

When the total amount of economic benefits or costs (for example, jobs) is the same for a country, and the only question is how the regions divide up the pie, the situation is what is often called a "zero-sum game." Any win is balanced by a loss; the overall gain adds up to zero.

But not all alternatives are of this sort. As the previous section indicated (also see Chapter 13), in some cases the winners may get less than the losers pay. In other cases, however, the winners get more, and there is a net gain for the whole country. The discovery of a new oil field is one obvious example of a net gain. Other examples are less clear-cut, because different people evaluate benefits and costs in different ways; but a characteristic of "positive-sum" policies may be that the resulting capabilities, wherever they are developed, can eventually contribute to the national economy at a variety of places. Another characteristic is that the policy, program, action, or expenditure has a lot of secondary effects. For instance, general adult education programs in disadvantaged areas may result in an improvement in the learning environment for children, improving their quality and increasing their mobility as an eventual part of the labor force. In such a case, the long-term total benefits to a country greatly exceed the short-term benefits to the target regions.

Clearly, advantage can seldom exist without corollary disadvantage. A program to help one place, or a decision to allow the market mechanism to allocate resources, usually means that one or more places bears a burden. Because these issues are a continuing part of the process of defining the government's role in shaping a

BOX 19.2 EXTENDING THE WATERWAY

The Kerr-McClellan navigable waterway extends from the Mississippi River up the Arkansas River to near Tulsa, Oklahoma (see the figure). For some years now, the U.S. Army Corps of Engineers has been studying the possibility of extending it farther north to near Wichita, Kansas.

A study of the economic and demographic impacts of such an action concluded that it would bring impressive economic growth to the counties in Oklahoma and Kansas that would be crossed or bordered by the new waterway. Ponca City, for example, would probably become the site of a large number of new grain elevators to store wheat for transport down the waterway (for eventual overseas shipment). For these counties, the benefits from the canal (in economic terms) would be many times its cost.

But much of that same wheat which would be stored at Ponca City and shipped to New Orleans is now stored in grain elevators in Enid, Oklahoma, and shipped by rail to Houston, Texas, to be loaded on seagoing ships. If the economic costs of the waterway to Enid, Houston, and the railroads are subtracted from the benefits to Ponca City and

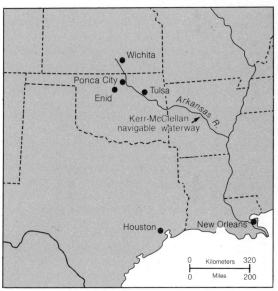

New Orleans, the net benefits are sharply reduced. From a regional or national point of view, in fact, it is questionable whether the benefits are greater than the costs.

As a result, opinions about the waterway are likely to differ between Tulsa and Houston, and the outcome may depend mainly on whose representatives have the most political clout.

country's economic geography, it is important to try to distinguish between positive-sum, zero-sum, and negative-sum options for using scarce resources.

Although these questions are not always the most important ones to individual decision makers, they are a part of the world in which they act. Individuals and profit-making groups, using the concepts outlined in Chapters 4–13, interact with institutions that are intended to represent the best interests of society at large, which use the concepts and tools discussed in Chapters 14–19.

In the end, the outcomes of this interaction depend on what people want most—how they define "development" in their minds and by their actions. In the end, our economic geographies are the product of human attitudes rather than economic laws. In the end, we find ourselves seeking new concepts to help explain why exceptions to the rules are often more common—and more important—than the rules themselves.

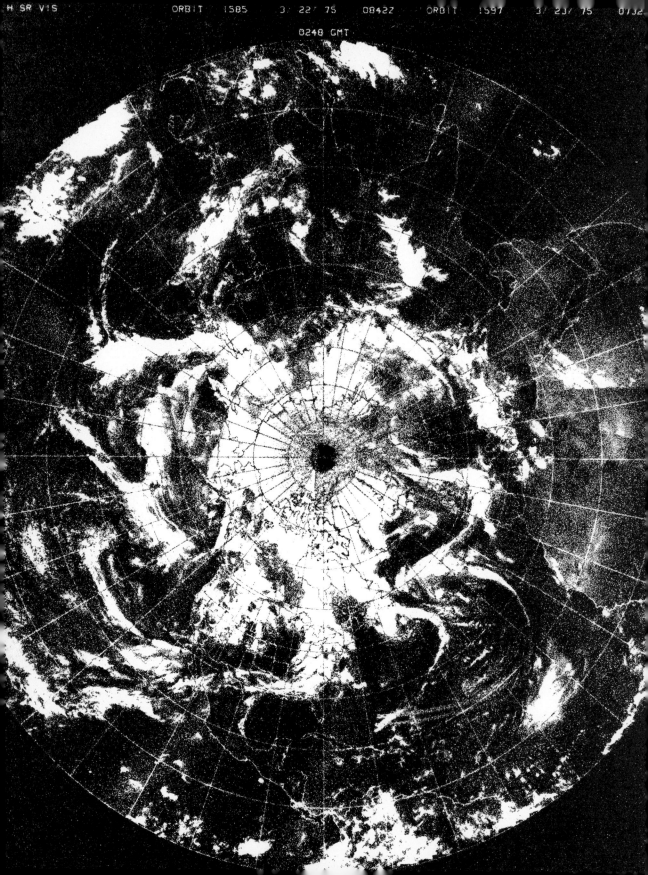

PART VIII

IN CONCLUSION

*J*ust *as economics focuses on only a part of reality, economic geography represents only one approach to understanding our world. And its concepts and perspectives, although often useful, are also a bit peculiar. They are the product of a limited range of things people have chosen to study, and a product of a limited range of ways they have chosen to do their studies.*

Consequently, we need to finish this book by reminding ourselves of the limitations of what we have learned—and of the questions that remain.

CHAPTER 20

QUESTIONS THAT REMAIN

*P*erhaps the most intriguing thing about economic geography is how little we really know after many decades of study. Our predictions are not often very accurate, the advice we get from our models is frequently overruled by "noneconomic" factors, and our preoccupation with growth has in some cases turned out to be harmful. Given this kind of record, we need to finish by trying to put the material from the earlier chapters into perspective.

First, we will consider some of the limitations of economic geography at this stage in its development. Then, we will take a brief look at the possibility that economic geography should be focused on less growth rather than more. And, finally, we will return to the question of our own future.

20.1 LIMITATIONS OF ECONOMIC GEOGRAPHY

The limitations of economic geography include these: (1) "noneconomic" things defined as outside the scope of economic geography are also important in the way people behave; (2) our knowledge of even the economic things is incomplete; and (3) our concepts are an expression not only of what we have observed so far but also of the motives of the observers, which means that they may be poorly suited for people with other motives.

20.1.1   The Relative Importance of Economic and Noneconomic Factors

Since Chapter 9, we have time and again recognized that an economy is interlocked with political systems, social systems, and the physical environment. Each of these systems has certain aims; for example:

1. **Economy:**   to maximize the provision of goods and services per person

2. **Society:**   to achieve order and satisfaction in relationships among people

3. **Physical environment:**   to achieve stability in relationships among physical objects and processes

Whether an economic aim should be preeminent is a continuing question in all of our lives. Do we work overtime to make more money or go home to work on a hobby? Do we turn down the thermostat to save on energy bills or leave it high enough so that our hands are not cold? Do we take a new, higher-paying job a thousand miles away or turn it down to stay closer to family and friends? Do we want a piece of vacant land to be used for new houses whose occupants will shop at our store, or do we want it used for a park where we can have Sunday picnics? Are we eager enough to make a lot of money playing professional football to take the chance that we will be unable because of knee injuries to walk down stairs after we are fifty years old? Our communities and countries face similar choices every day.

The focus of economic geography is on locational decisions to achieve economic aims. When our priorities rank other aims higher, the focus is less useful—serving mainly as a basis of comparison, a way to estimate the economic trade-offs of our other objectives.

20.1.2   How Much Do We Not Know?

It is as important to appreciate what is *not* known as it is to understand what *is* known. While philosophers debate whether it is actually possible to know more than we do, let us consider what we do not:

1. **We are uncertain how broadly our general concepts apply.**   Most of the concepts of economic geography are based on remarkably few careful studies of information from actual places. As a result, it is usually not clear if a concept that appears true for Iowa is also true in northern China, or if a concept that appears true for Western Europe is a dependable

guide for the Willamette Valley. When we are changing geo-graphic scale or studying a different culture, the "standard" concepts and techniques may or may not be appropriate. Much remains to be learned about whether, for example, the usual generalizations about trends in regional income in-equalities apply as well in central Africa as central North America, or whether generalizations based on information about very large regions work as well when the regions are very small.

2. **We have a limited ability to predict the occurrence of trend-changing events.** The concepts of economic geography are quite useful for analyzing a well-defined situation: given en-vironmental characteristics, technology, and other key factors. But they are not well suited for anticipating changes in these factors, which are usually defined by theory builders as "exogenous."

   Think, for instance, about the impact of the tractor on a preindustrial von Thünen land use pattern. Or the impact of the airplane on a landlocked economy. Or the impact of the wheel, the electric light, the computer, the flow diagram, the OPEC oil embargo. Most of these have transformed economic patterns where they have occurred, and our concepts help us to anticipate their effects. But they are of less help in an-ticipating the *appearance* of events that have such powerful effects. In this sense, the concepts of economic geography are essentially reactive; taken alone, they turn most decision mak-ers into counterpunchers. And in the age of "future shock," with significant events occurring at an increasing pace, this is a severe limitation.

3. **We have a limited ability to trace the relationships between economic things and noneconomic things.** No one would disagree that social geography, political geography, and phys-ical geography have important effects on economic geography (and vice versa), but we are seldom able to trace these effects between systems as well as we can deal with each system by itself. We know that taxes are tied to political factors, operat-ing costs to physical environmental factors, market organiza-tion to political ideology, and occupational choice to social mobility; but—partly because of traditional boundaries be-tween academic disciplines—most of our concepts require us to make assumptions about these things as fixed, unchanging constraints, rather than inviting us to deal with them in a realistically complicated way.

None of the limitations means that our concepts are not useful, especially if they are used to stimulate thought and the careful study of particular cases; but we need to be careful not to claim more precision for the ideas than they merit.

20.1.3   *Why Do We Seek to Know?*

Another limitation, subtle but significant, is that how a person studies economic geography can affect what he or she finds out; our concepts are the product not only of the places scholars have studied, but also of the techniques they have used and the motives that have driven them.

Think about the questions we can ask of any learned article we see in a respected academic journal. Why did the author choose that question? Where did the information come from? What judgment decisions did the author make (every investigator must make some)? Could you check whether the study is accurate? What if the author had asked the question a little differently, or gathered more information or analyzed the information in a different way? Would the results have been different? What seems to have been ignored? Is the author's view of reality similar to the views of the people in the area being studied? Since every one of our concepts is both partly true and partly not true (too simplified, often misleading), we need to identify how and why each concept is articulated the way it is. In doing so, in fact, we usually discover interesting new questions; one test of a useful concept is that it is fruitful in suggesting further ideas.

But even in pursuing a concept critically, we may be adopting the view of the world of the person who developed the concept. Some of the judgment decisions that lie behind any concept are moral ones, based on personal opinions of what ought to be. And our concepts are often difficult to extricate from these moral judgments, even if we disagree with them.

In economic geography, the strongest criticism of conventional concepts from a moral standpoint has come from scholars who use Marx's theory of political economy to develop distinctly different interpretations of urban and regional economic processes. They argue, for example, that economic "rent" cannot be considered an "objective" valuation established by the highest and best use—that it is a manifestation of a particular kind of political-economic system in which priorities are set in a uniquely selfish way. If in a different kind of system, priorities are established in some other way, concepts based on "rent" as a cause of an economic pattern are fallacious. And the associated economic geographies will be different.

20.2 *LIMITS TO GROWTH*

One of the most consistent orientations of economic geography, reflecting the society that has shaped it, has been that problems are solved by growth. Growth is desirable; therefore the aim of economic decision makers should be to have more of it. Lack of growth means stagnation, a loss of comparative advantage, limited opportunities, unemployment. Neediness is connected with terms such as *less developed*, which means *has experienced less economic growth*. Well-being is associated with vigorous growth, massive consumption of resources, forever more goods and services.

Once upon a time, this view was rarely challenged, but times are changing. States such as Oregon and Colorado find that their citizens see economic and population growth as a threat to their quality of life. Countries are discovering that at some point growth begins to mean environmental pollution, crowding, and other undesirable circumstances. And the world is beginning to realize that it is actually a "Spaceship Earth," capable of exhausting its chemical and biological building blocks and capable of poisoning itself to death.

Consequently, as the earlier chapters of this book have indicated several times, many decision makers want to learn about economic geography in order to slow growth down, not to accelerate it. Their purpose is to repel new people and activities by reducing comparative advantages (for example, compensating for beautiful scenery by placing a very high tax on new housing contruction).

In most cases so far, these efforts to limit growth have reflected the attitudes of people who associate a high quality of life with places that are not very crowded, polluted, or intense. Although individually we define such attributes very differently, we all feel territorial imperatives of some sort, and nearly all of us realize that small things are often more personal and more precious than large ones.

But some people argue that limits to growth are not simply a matter of environmental psychology; they are in fact a matter of human survival. They see a grim future for a world preoccupied with growth: depleted resources, infertile land due to overuse, rising pollution, food shortage—and eventually (perhaps at some time between the years 2050 and 2100) a dramatic collapse in the size of the world population.

Whether or not this is likely to happen depends mainly on four issues:

1. **Whether nonrenewable resources, such as fossil fuels and metallic ores, can be replaced by renewable resources.** Some experts believe (trust?) that they can: solar energy replacing coal, modern chemistry finding substitutes for naturally occurring metals. Others are less optimistic.

2. **Whether environmental pollution can be controlled without limiting economic growth.** Perhaps, by improving technologies or finding substitutes for them, we can learn to control crop pests, make industrial chemicals, and to meet other needs while at the same time reducing their adverse environmental impacts. If not, limiting growth may be the only way for us to avoid poisoning ourselves.

3. **Whether future food supplies will be adequate.** For a growing population, demanding an increasing amount of nourishment per person, food requirements will certainly grow for the foreseeable future. But there seem to be limits to the amount of land that can be cultivated, and there is substantial competition for the water, chemicals, and other inputs that agricultural expansion would need. Growing may eventually mean starving.

4. **Whether world population growth will level off as economic growth proceeds—without a food, pollution, or resource crisis.** If zero population growth, more or less, can be achieved, the amount of economic growth required to increase goods and services per person will be less, and the likelihood of a negative answer to any of the other three questions is lessened.

These are serious issues because they go beyond what is comfortable to what is possible. But either strong optimism or strong pessimism at this stage must be classified as a quasi-religious belief rather than a scientific conclusion, because all we know for certain is that the future is uncertain (see Box 20.1).

20.3   *ALTERNATIVE FUTURES*

This uncertainty reminds us that our lives and our places have many possible paths of development before them. Some of the possibilities will be foreclosed by circumstances that we cannot control. But others will be eliminated by decisions that we make in the next few years.

Section 2.2.1 introduced the idea that individual and group decisions develop as a series of "contingent events." And we know by now that many of these contingent events involve locational decisions: the best use for a place (affecting later uses there and nearby), the best place for an activity (affecting later locations for that activity and other activities to which it is linked), the next place for a person (affecting information, opportunities, experiences, personal contact networks), the route to be used, the spatial arrangement to be tried, and so on. These actions affect the future—our future.

This suggests that, if a person cares about such things, it is useful to spend a little time identifying and evaluating alternative futures for ourselves, our livelihoods, and our places. With a clear view of where we want to go (and why), it is easier to make decisions in the meantime that help us go that way.

It is remarkable how seldom this is done by places: communities, states, regions, countries. "Planning" more often means the projection of current trends, without a careful consideration of alternatives by the people who will be most affected by them.

But the concepts introduced in this book—used with the kind of caution that it has suggested—can be a starting point for a different way. All that is needed is for someone to put them to work.

BOX 20.1   POEMS

A Conservationist's Lament

The world is finite, resources are scarce,
Things are bad and will be worse.
Coal is burned and gas exploded,
Forests cut and soils eroded.
Wells are dry and air's polluted,
Dust is blowing, trees uprooted.
Oil is going, ores depleted,
Drains receive what is excreted.
Land is sinking, seas are rising,
Man is far too enterprising.
Fire will range with Man to fan it,
Soon we'll have a plundered planet.
People breed like fertile rabbits,
People have disgusting habits.

Moral:
>   The evolutionary plan
>   Went astray by evolving Man.

The Technologist's Reply

Man's potential is quite terrific,
You can't go back to the Neolithic
The cream is there for us to skim it,
Knowledge is power, and the sky's the limit.
Every mouth has hands to feed it,
Food is found when people need it.
All we need is found in granite
Once we have the men to plan it.
Yeast and algae give us meat,
Soil is almost obsolete.
Men can grow to pastures greener
Till all the earth is Pasadena.

Moral:
>   Man's a nuisance, Man's a crackpot,
>   But only Man can hit the jackpot.

Kenneth Boulding. In Thomas W. L. (ed.), *Man's Role in Changing the Face of the Earth.* Chicago: University of Chicago Press, 1956, p. 1087. Reprinted by permission of the Wenner-Gren Foundation for Anthropological Research, New York, and the University of Chicago Press.

GLOSSARY

(the number following each term indicates the chapter in which it is discussed)

A

accessibility (5, 12)   the quality of being easy to reach

agglomeration economies (7, 10)   advantages to an economic activity because of the presence of other economic activities nearby; also, advantages to a place where many economic activities are clustered

amenities (14)   conditions or facilities that make a place more pleasant

autarky (13)   national or regional economic self-sufficiency and independence

B

backwash effects (12)   due to economic activity in growing centers, the loss of capital, labor, comparative advantages, and services to other areas that are not growing as fast (see also *spread effects* and *relative deprivation*)

basic activities (8)   economic activities that serve the needs of people outside the host city or region, thereby bringing in money and other resources (see also *economic base* and *nonbasic activities*)

borrowing innovations (18)   the notion that an economy or an entrepreneur may be innovative by adapting and using original ideas or devices developed by others; imagination and skill in application may in some cases serve as substitutes for more basic inventiveness

boundary zones (17)   areas in the vicinity of boundaries which share distinctive characteristics as a result

brain drain (13)   the persistent loss of a country's or region's most capable people (especially their young people) because of the lure of opportunities and benefits elsewhere

C

carrying capacity (9)   the maximum intensity at which a parcel of land can be used, under specified conditions, without a loss of valued qualities of the land

central place theory (7)   a theory about the spatial arrangement of central places (see also *central places, equilibrium spacing,* and *hexagonal pattern;* for more detail, see Chapter 7)

central places (7)   nodes of settlement and economic activity, i.e. cities and towns (see also *nodes*)

circulation (4)   the movement of goods, services, activities, and individuals through an economic-geographic system

comparative advantage (10, 12)   a situation where, due to its economic and environmental characteristics, a place can provide a particular economic good or service under conditions that allow it to compete successfully with other places

competition (4)   a market condition in which buyers and sellers with relatively equal standing seek to improve their economic well-being by securing favorable terms for exchange (see also *competitive economy* and *exchange*)

competitive economy (4)   an economy in which a large number of independent buyers and sellers interact freely, entering or leaving markets freely, determining market behavior by their competition with other buyers and sellers (see also *competition*)

complementarity (12)   a relationship in which some of the locational advantages of one region correspond with some of the locational disadvantages of another, and vice versa, so that the two regions benefit by trading with each other

conflict resolution (15)   processes or methods for reaching decisions when parties to the decisions are in opposition to each other

consumers (4)   those who use goods and services in order to satisfy their wants

cost-benefit analysis (18)   a technique, or body of techniques, for calculating the net value of a proposed activity

cumulative causation (10)   suggested by Myrdal, the idea that market forces tend to increase inequalities between regions

D

demand (4)   a desire for a commodity; the willingness to use goods or services under specified conditions; often implies different levels of willingness (i.e., quantities purchased) at different prices

development bottleneck (18)   particular factors, situations, or conditions that obstruct development, even though other conditions would permit it

distance decay (11)   the concept that human interaction generally declines with distance

dualistic development (13)   a pattern of economic and social development in which some parts of a country or region resemble advanced economies while others resemble traditional economies

E

economic base (8)   the idea that the economic growth of a city or region is related to an expansion of basic activities (see also *basic activities* and *export theory of growth*)

economic efficiency (10)   the relationship between the value of output and the value of input (that is, a higher ratio means higher efficiency); also, an objective of maximizing or improving the relationship

economies of scale (7)   efficiencies (that is, reductions in the unit cost of production) due to increasing the size of an enterprise

ekistics (12)   a quasi-discipline concerned with the integrative study of human settlements and how they develop

eminent domain (15)   the authority of a government to appropriate any property within its jurisdiction for necessary public use, subject to reasonable compensation

employment sector minimum (8)   the idea that a city or region of a particular size and economic structure must have at least a certain minimum percentage of its employment in a specified sector (see Chapter 8)

environment (9) things and processes that are not part of an economy but affect it and/or are affected by it

environmental advantage (9) a comparative advantage given a place due to characteristics of its environment (see also *comparative advantage* and *environment*)

environmental determinism (9) the idea that differences among people and their activities are caused by differences in their physical environments (generally discredited)

equilibrium (7) a state of balance between opposing forces (see also *equilibrium spacing* and *spatial price equilibrium*)

equilibrium spacing (7) a spatial arrangement in which the various processes influencing the spacing of elements are in balance; sometimes implies a resistance to change; also implies a normative position about which a spatial arrangement tends to fluctuate

exchange (4) an act or process of reciprocal transfers of goods or services

expansive diffusion (17) the transmission of innovations to neighboring locations or decision points, reflecting a relationship between proximity and interaction (see also *distance decay*)

export/import restrictions (13) limitations on exports or imports in order to achieve a particular objective (see also *quotas*, *tariffs*, and *government regulations*)

export theory of growth (8) the idea that the economic growth of a region depends mainly, or at least partly, on a surplus of exports over imports

external diseconomy (4) a cost to an economic enterprise due to actions outside the enterprise (see also *external economy*)

external economy (4) a benefit to an economic enterprise, such as an increase in efficiency, due to actions outside the enterprise for which it does not pay; also, an opportunity to improve social welfare through actions external to individual enterprises

F

factor mobility (11) the degree to which factors of production, such as labor and capital, move easily and quickly from region to region in response to differences in factor prices and other measures of benefits and opportunities

factors of production (10) the major ingredients used in order to produce goods and services, usually aggregated into very general classes such as land, labor, capital, and technology

fiscal federalism (14) a system in which government functions and jurisdictions are arranged so that those who receive particular services from a public facility are also those who pay for them (through taxes, fees, or other ways of generating revenue)

functional region (9) a region characterized by a common structural relationship to a function (see also *region*)

G

geographic inertia (17) the marked tendency for a geographic pattern to resemble antecedent patterns

government regulation (15) the use by government of rules having the force of law in order to achieve an objective

governmental jurisdiction (14) see *jurisdiction*

gravity model (11) a theory of the relationship between human interaction and distance; also a formula for predicting interaction (see Chapter 12)

growth center (12) a location where economic growth can be stimulated relatively easily, triggering subsequent growth at other locations (see also *growth pole*)

growth curve (17) a generalized graphic or mathematical expression of a typical, projected, or planned rate of growth over time

growth pole (12) a part of an economy where economic growth can be stimulated relatively easily, triggering subsequent growth in other parts (see also *growth center*)

H

hexagonal pattern (7)   a pattern consisting of six-sided cells, usually regular polygons

hierarchic diffusion (17)   the transmission of innovations upward or downward through a system of ordered centers, locations, or decision points (such as a central place hierarchy: see also *central places* and *hierarchy*)

hierarchy (7, 11)   a series of elements arranged in graduated classes, such as classes of central places or classes of roads

highest and best use (5)   the use of a parcel of land which realizes its greatest possible contribution to economic production (see also *rent*)

I

income substitutes (16)   goods, services, or other benefits received without the expenditure of household money income

industrial complex (10)   a group of co-located economic activities directly linked by production and marketing relationships, benefiting from economies of proximity (see also *industrial complex analysis*)

industrial complex analysis (18)   an eclectic methodology for evaluating the prospects of particular industrial complexes (see *industrial complex*)

infant industry (13)   economic activities, often in less developed areas, that have little chance of success unless they are protected from competition during their early stages of development

infrastructure (14)   installations and facilities that provide a basic framework for an economy, such as the transportation, communication, and power supply systems

input-output analysis (10)   an analytical framework which expresses linkages among the sectors of an economy and is used to investigate the direct and indirect effects on the sectors of actual, anticipated, or hypothetical changes in the economy (see also Chapter 12)

intensive land use (5)   land use characterized by the expenditure of relatively large amounts of labor and capital per land unit, as opposed to "extensive"

interaction potential (11)   an estimate of the likelihood that a particular place will interact with other places, as a basis for comparing it with other places (see Chapter 12 for a way of calculating potential values)

interregional input-output analysis (12)   a form of input-output analysis that accounts for transactions between regions as well as between sectors of a regional economy (see *input-output analysis*)

isodapane (6)   lines connecting points of equal transportation cost for an industrial facility, taking into account the transportation of materials from sources to the production site and the transportation of products to markets

isotims (6)   lines connecting points of equal transportation cost for a particular material or finished product (see also *isodapane*)

J

jurisdiction (15)   the limits within which a power may be exercised, such as the territory within which a government exercises its authority

L

lobbying (15)   activities and processes intended to influence government decisions

location factor (6)   a significant consideration in determining the best location for an activity

location quotient (8)   a method of comparing the concentration of an activity in a particular region with its average concentration in a larger area

locational conflict resolution (14)   processes or methods for reaching decisions on the location of facilities when parties to the decisions disagree with each other

locational pull (6)   the force of attraction exerted by a place or an area when alternative locations for an activity are being considered

locational specialization (10, 12)   in order to realize economic benefits, the focusing of the economy of a place on activities for which it has comparative advantages

locational triangle (6)   a simple graphic technique for determining the area within which the least-transport-cost location for an industrial facility will be found

locational vulnerability (13)   the degree to which the well-being of a place depends on decisions and actions taken in other places

M

market area (7)   the area in which the consumers of an enterprise's goods or services are located

market orientation (6)   location of an economic activity at or near the location of consumers of its goods and services

material-source orientation (6)   location of an economic activity at or near the source of a material used in producing a good

maximizing productivity (16)   the objective or process of reaching the highest possible level of economic output per unit of labor (or per unit of another factor of production) per unit of time

mercantile model of settlement (7)   the idea that the evolving pattern of urban places in an area is heavily influenced by competition between merchants located outside the area, concerned with external markets; it does not just reflect competition for internal markets between the urban places themselves

minimizing inequality (16)   the objective or process of reducing inequalities or inequities to a minimum (usually very low) level (see also *regional equality* and *regional equity*)

modal choice (11)   the processes and actions of choosing the best transportation mode(s) for a purpose

monopolistic economy (4)   an economy in which one buyer or seller can determine market behavior (for example, by controlling prices)

multinational firm (12)   a firm whose subsidiaries operate in, and often are incorporated in, more than one country

multiplier (8)   a general expression of the effect on total regional income or employment of an increase in basic activities (see *basic activities*)

N

nodal region (9)   a region characterized by a common structural relationship to a node (see *nodes* and *region*)

nodes (5)   central points; usually implies that the central points have a function or functions which cause them to be foci for activities at other locations

nonbasic activities (8)   economic activities that serve the needs of people within a city or region but do not bring money or other resources into the area from outside (see also *basic activities*)

nonrenewable resources (9)   resources that, once used, are not replaced by natural processes (or are replaced too slowly for humans to be able to continue to use them indefinitely)

north-south problem (17)   an expression referring to regionalized differences in standards of living between the developed and less-developed countries, e.g., between North and South America or Europe and Africa; may also refer to regionalized differences in standards of living within a country

O

oligopolistic economy (4)   an economy in which a limited number of buyers or sellers can collectively influence the market (e.g., cause prices to be higher or lower than in a competitive economy)

optimal location (6)   the best of all possible locations for an activity

optimization (16)   the objective or process of reaching the most favorable or effective level of utility or satisfaction possible

P

pattern planning (16)   the process of determining future geographic patterns as policy objectives, including the evaluation of alternatives and the selection of implementation instruments

periodic market (7)   a market that circulates among different locations on a regular schedule; also a market that operates at a location only occasionally, at regularly spaced intervals

permissible activities (15)   economic and other activities considered acceptable by society, in some cases subject to certain constraints

planning (15)   the process of developing policies and procedures for a decision-making unit, including the establishment of goals and often including the creation of graphic representations of a preferred future

political environment (15)   political conditions and processes that affect and/or are affected by an economy

potential productivity (9)   under specified conditions, the highest level of production possible for a parcel of land, as contrasted with its present level

price (4)   the amount of money at which something is offered or obtained

primary activities (4)   extractive activities, such as agriculture and mining

producers (4)   those who convert factors of production into useful goods and services (see also *factors of production*)

production function (10)   a quantitative expression of the level of economic production as a function of various combinations of factors of production (see also *factors of production*)

productivity (4)   the relationship between the amount of production and the effort required (see also *economic efficiency*)

proximity (5)   nearness—a state or quality that in economic geography is usually assumed to have value

public facilities (14)   government-owned installations that perform particular functions, such as hospitals, schools, public housing, and roads

public interest (14)   an expression of what is best for the people of a region or country as a whole

public lands (14)   lands owned or held in trust by government bodies; may also include resources in or under bodies of water

public sector (14)   those organizations and activities accountable to the people of a region or a country as a whole rather than, for example, to a smaller group of owners

Q

quotas (15)   an agreed or specified maximum or minimum level of production or trade

R

range of a good or service (7)   the maximum effort (i.e., distance) that a consumer is willing to accept in order to purchase a good or service provided at a particular location

region (9)   an area of any size that is approximately the same in some respect; often implies an area larger than a city but smaller than a large country

regional accounting (17)   the process or activity of measuring or estimating regional income and output by sector

regional equality (16)   an objective or a condition where all regions are described by approximately equal values for a quantitative indicator of the standard of living

regional equity (16)   an objective or a condition where all regions have equivalent levels of economic and social benefit, cost, risk, and opportunity

regional pathology (18)   regional deviations from an assumed "normal" state, including their nature, causes, and effects

regional product (17)   the money value of the total output of goods and services in a region during a given period of time, usually a year

regional resilience (17)   the capability of a region to recover its economic health after a change in conditions that results in stress, loss of comparative advantages, or a significant drop in the viability of the regional economic structure

regionalizing (9)   the activity or process of subdividing a larger area into smaller areas in order to minimize variation within an area and maximize variation between areas

relative deprivation (13)   an effect of an action or process such that some areas or people, even though they receive some benefits, fall farther behind other areas or people in their overall well-being

renewable resources (9)   resources that, through natural processes, are (or may be) replaced at the same rate as they are used

rent (5)   the value of a parcel of land (or some other unit) as a factor of production, usually assumed to be equivalent to the monetary value of that parcel (or unit) to the "highest and best" user (see *highest and best use* and *factors of production*)

rent gradients (5)   the slope of a rent surface at each of a number of points on the surface (see *rent surface*)

rent surface (5)   an expression of the spatial distribution of rents as a surface, where high rents are high points on the surface and low rents are low points (see *rent*)

retarding growth (18)   a policy objective of reducing the rate of economic and/or demographic growth because the costs of growth are judged to be greater than the benefits; also, the processes by which the growth rate is decreased

S

satisficing (16)   the objective or process of reaching a level of utility or satisfaction that is acceptable, even if not necessarily optimal

scarcity (4)   a quality or state in which something is not abundant enough to be free; also, a deficiency in quantity compared with the demand at a relatively low price

secondary activities (4)   manufacturing activities

sectoral transformation (10)   the shift of factors of production (*see*) among sectors of an economy in response to changing conditions and needs (e.g., shifts of labor from agriculture to manufacturing and services as a region becomes more industrial)

services as a growth sector (18)   the notion that useful actions that do not produce tangible commodities may serve as a basis for the economic growth of a region; examples include legal and financial services, education, and health care (see also *basic activities* and *economic base*)

shadow effects (13)   due to a particular action, constraints on other possible actions nearby (or not so nearby) in space or time

social welfare (14)   overall well-being, taking into account social, cultural, environmental, and aesthetic factors as well as conventional indicators of economic welfare

spatial efficiency (6)   the relationship between spatial arrangement and economic efficiency (see *economic efficiency*); also, an objective of maximizing or improving economic efficiency, by assuring that a spatial arrangement is optimal

spatial error (16)   differences between actual spatial arrangements or decisions and optimal arrangements or decisions

spatial price equilibrium (11)   a condition where, because the movements of goods between locations are optimal, the prices of the goods at the different locations are stable, although not equal

spatial symmetry (11)   a quality of balance or regularity in a spatial arrangement, often associated with efficiency and equilibrium (see also *equilibrium spacing, economic efficiency, pattern planning,* and *spatial efficiency*)

specialization (4) limitation in scope or function to a particular good or service or to a narrow range of goods and servies

spread effects (12) economic benefits that spread from centers of activity to other, usually nearby areas (see also *expansive diffusion* and *backwash effects*)

stabilization (15) intervention in an economic market to reduce fluctuations of prices or other indicators of concern (such as employment)

supply (4) a quantity available for use; the process of making goods and services available for use; often implies different quantities at different prices

T

tariffs (15) a tax or duty imposed on goods as they enter or leave a country; also, a schedule of rules or rates for trade or transportation

technical coefficients (10) ratios that express proportional input requirements from particular economic sectors in order to increase production in particular sectors

tertiary activities (4) service activities, as contrasted with extractive and manufacturing activities

threshold for a good or service (7) the minimum size of a market at which it is economically feasible to provide a good or service

transfer costs (11) in economic geography, the costs of the transportation of goods and the transmission between locations of energy, information, and other "intangibles"

U

uniform region (9) an area that is approximately the same throughout in terms of a particular characteristic

uniform surface (5) an area that is exactly the same throughout—a common assumption in theory-building in geography, in order to examine spatial structure under idealized "laboratory" conditions

utility (4) usefulness for some purpose, especially in satisfying human wants

V

von Thünen model (5) a theory about the best location of economic activities with respect to their distance from a central market

W

weight loss (6) the loss in the weight of a material used in a finished product as a result of the production process; e.g., the difference between the weight of a length of copper wire and the ore required to produce it

Z

zones of land use (5) areas within which land uses are similar (see also *regionalizing* and *zoning*)

zoning (15) a process by which government can restrict the uses of certain areas within their jurisdictions

BIBLIOGRAPHY

GENERAL REFERENCES

Abler, R., J. S. Adams, and P. Gould, *Spatial Organization*. Englewood Cliffs, N.J.: Prentice-Hall, 1971.

Coates, B. E., R. J. Johnston, and P. V. Knox, *Geography and Inequality*. Oxford: Oxford University Press, 1977.

English, P. W. and R. C. Mayfield, eds., *Man, Space, and Environment*. New York: Oxford University Press, 1972.

Haggett, P., *Geography: A Modern Synthesis*, 3rd ed. New York: Harper & Row, 1979.

Haggett, P., A. D. Cliff, and A. E. Frey, *Locational Analysis in Human Geography*, 2d ed. London: Arnold, 1977.

Hoover, E. M., *An Introduction to Regional Economics*. New York: Knopf, 1971.

Lloyd, P. E. and P. Dicken, *Location in Space*, 2nd ed. New York: Harper & Row, 1977.

Richardson, H. W., *Regional Economics*. London: Weidenfeld and Nicolson, 1969.

Also see the leading geographic and related journals, such as the ANNALS OF THE ASSOCIATION OF AMERICAN GEOGRAPHERS, ECONOMIC GEOGRAPHY, JOURNAL OF REGIONAL SCIENCE, CANADIAN GEOGRAPHER, PAPERS OF THE REGIONAL SCIENCE ASSOCIATION, GEOGRAPHICAL REVIEW, *and others shelved nearby in a library.*

CHAPTER 1

See the general references. Regarding economic-geographic concepts and processes at the scale of an urban area:

Abler, R., ed., *A Comparative Atlas of America's Great Cities*. Minneapolis: University of Minnesota, 1976.

Berry, B. J. L., *The Human Consequences of Urbanization*. New York: St. Martin's, 1973.

Berry, B. J. L. and F. E. Horton, *Geographic Perspectives on Urban Systems*. Englewood Cliffs, N.J.: Prentice-Hall, 1970.

Berry, B. J. L. and F. E. Horton, *Urban Environmental Management*. Englewood Cliffs, N.J.: Prentice-Hall, 1974.

Bourne, L. S., ed., *The Internal Structure of the City,* 2nd ed. New York: Oxford University Press, 1978.

Bourne, L. S. and J. W. Simmons, eds., *Systems of Cities,* New York: Oxford University Press, 1978.

Gottman, J., *Megalopolis.* Cambridge, Mass.: MIT, 1964.

Yeates, M., *Main Street.* Toronto: Macmillan, 1975.

Yeates, M. and B. J. Garner, *The North American City,* 2nd. ed. New York: Harper & Row, 1976.

CHAPTER 2

Regarding economic geography's perspective on the world, see the general references and:

Bunge, W., "Theoretical Geography." Lund, Sweden: *Lund Studies in Geography,* Ser. C: no. 1, 1962.

Chorley, R. J. and P. Haggett, *Models in Geography.* London: Methuen, 1967.

Haggett, P., "Changing Concepts in Economic Geography." In Chorley, R. J. and P. Haggett, eds., *Frontiers of Geographical Teaching.* London: Methuen, 1965.

Harvey, D., *Explanation in Geography.* New York: St. Martin's, 1970.

Lanegran, D. A. and R. Palm, *An Invitation to Geography.* New York: McGraw-Hill, 1973.

McCarty, H. H. and J. B. Lindberg, *A Preface to Economic Geography.* Englewood Cliffs, N.J.: Prentice-Hall, 1966.

Smith, R. H. T., E. Taaffe, and L. J. King, eds., *Readings in Economic Geography.* Chicago: Rand McNally, 1967.

Taaffe, E., *Geography.* Englewood Cliffs, N.J.: Prentice-Hall, 1969.

Regarding space as contingency in 2.2.1:

Pred, A., "The Choreography of Existence." *Economic Geography,* vol. 53, 1977, pp. 207–221.

Regarding 2.2.2, see Abler, Adams, and Gould and Haggett, Cliff, and Frey (general references) and:

Haggett, P. and R. J. Chorley, *Network Analysis in Geography.* New York: St. Martin's, 1969.

Hudson, J. C., "Pattern Recognition in Empirical Map Analysis." *Journal of Regional Science,* vol. 9, 1969, pp. 189–200.

Hudson, J. C. and P. M. Fowler, "The Concept of Pattern in Geography." In P. W. English and R. C. Mayfield, *Man, Space, and Environment.* New York: Oxford University Press, 1972, pp. 545–550.

Nystuen, J. D., "Identification of Some Fundamental Spatial Concepts." *Papers of the Michigan Academy of Science, Arts, and Letters,* vol. 48, 1963, pp. 373–384.

Regarding "mental maps" in 2.2.3:

Downs, R. M. and D. Stea, eds., *Image and Environment: Cognitive Mapping and Spatial Behavior.* London: Arnold, 1974.

Lowenthal, D., "Geography, Experience, and Imagination." *Annals,* Association of American Geographers, vol. 51, 1961, pp. 241–260.

Lowenthal, D., ed., *Environmental Perception and Behavior.* University of Chicago Department of Geography Research Paper #109, Chicago, 1967.

Lynch, K., *The Image of the City.* Cambridge, Mass.: MIT, 1960.

Gould, P. R. and R. R. White, *Mental Maps.* Harmondsworth, UK: Penguin, 1974.

Regarding 2.2.4, see the general references and:

Berry, B. J. L., "Interdependence of Spatial Structure and Spatial Behavior." *Papers,* Regional Science Association, vol. 21, 1968, pp. 205–228.

King, L. J., "Analysis of Spatial Form and Its Relation to Geographic Theory." *Annals,* Association of American Geographers, vol. 59, 1969, pp. 573–595.

Regarding 2.3, see the general references and references for 19.1.

CHAPTER 3

Regarding 3.1:

Brunn, S. D. and J. O. Wheeler, "Spatial Dimensions of Poverty in the United States." *Geografiska Annaler,* vol. 53, 1971, pp. 6–15.

Knox, P. L., *Social Well-Being: A Spatial Perspective.* Oxford: Clarendon Press, 1975.

Morrill, R. L. and E. H. Wohlenberg, *The Geography of Poverty in the United States.* New York: McGraw-Hill, 1971.

Smith, D. M., *The Geography of Social Well-Being in the United States.* New York: McGraw-Hill, 1973.

Regarding 3.2.2, See Haggett, Cliff, and Frey, (general references) and:

Amedeo, D. and R. G. Golledge, *Introduction to Scientific Reasoning in Geography.* New York: Wiley, 1975.

Babbie, E. R., *Survey Research Methods.* Belmont, Cal.: Wadsworth, 1973.

Berry, B. J. L. and D. F. Marble, eds., *Spatial Analysis.* Englewood Cliffs, N.J.: Prentice-Hall, 1968.

Blalock, H. M., Jr., *An Introduction to Social Research.* Englewood Cliffs, N.J.: Prentice-Hall, 1970.

Duncan, O. D. et al., *Statistical Geography: Problems of Analyzing Areal Data.* New York: Free Press, 1961.

Ferber, R. and P. J. Verdoorn, *Research Methods in Economics and Business.* New York: Macmillan, 1962.

Festinger, L. and D. Katz, eds., *Research Methods in the Behavioral Sciences.* New York: Holt, Rinehart, and Winston, 1953.

Fielder, J., *Field Research.* New York: Free Press, 1975.

Greer-Wootten, B., *A Bibliography of Statistical Applications in Geography.* Washington, D.C.: Association of American Geographers, 1972.

Hays, W. L., *Statistics for the Social Sciences,* 2nd. ed. New York: Holt, Rinehart, and Winston, 1973.

Huff, D. and I. Geis, *How to Lie with Statistics.* New York: Norton, 1954.

Hyman, H. H. et al., *Interviewing in Social Research.* Chicago: University of Chicago, 1954.

Johnson, J. M., *Doing Field Research.* New York: Free Press, 1975.

King, L. J., *Statistical Analysis in Geography.* Englewood Cliffs, N.J.: Prentice-Hall, 1969.

Kish, L., *Survey Sampling.* New York: Wiley, 1952.

Monkhouse, F. J. and H. R. Wilkinson, *Maps and Diagrams.* 2nd. ed. London: Methuen, 1963.

Robinson, A. H. et al., *Elements of Cartography,* 2nd. ed. New York: Wiley, 1978.

Sawyer, W. W., *Mathematician's Delight.* Harmondsworth, U.K.: Penguin, 1950.

Selltiz, C., L. S. Wrightsman, and S. W. Cook, *Research Methods in Social Relations,* 3rd. ed. New York: Holt, Rinehart, and Winston, 1976.

Siegel, S., *Nonparametric Statistics for the Behavioral Sciences.* New York: McGraw-Hill, 1956.

Tufte, E. R., ed., *The Quantitative Analysis of Social Problems.* Reading, Mass.: Addison-Wesley, 1970.

Webb, E. J. et al., *Unobtrusive Measures.* Chicago: Rand McNally, 1966.

Yeates, M., *An Introduction to Quantitative Analysis in Human Geography.* New York: McGraw-Hill, 1974.

CHAPTER 4

See the last three books listed under general references, along with surveys of economic theory such as:

Ferguson, C. E. and C. Maurice, *Economic Analysis*, 3rd. ed. Homewood, Ill.: Irwin, 1978.

Heilbroner, R. L. and L. C. Thurow, *Understanding Macroeconomics*, 6th ed. Englewood Cliffs, N.J.: Prentice-Hall, 1978.

Heilbroner, R. L. and L. C. Thurow, *Understanding Microeconomics*, 4th ed. Englewood Cliffs, N.J.: Prentice-Hall, 1978.

Samuelson, P. A., *Economics*, 10th ed. New York: McGraw-Hill, 1976.

Wonnacott, P., *Macroeconomics*, rev. ed. Homewood, Ill.: Irwin, 1978.

Also see:

Heilbroner, R. L., *The Worldly Philosophers*, 4th ed. New York: Simon and Schuster, 1972.

CHAPTER 5

Regarding 5.2 and 5.3, see:

Alonso, W., *Location and Land Use.* Cambridge, Mass.: Harvard University, 1964.

Beckmann, M., *Location Theory.* New York: Random House, 1968.

Chisholm, M., *Rural Settlement and Land Use.* London: Hutchinson, 1962.

Dunn, E. S., *The Location of Agricultural Production.* Gainesville, Fla.: University of Florida, 1954.

Goldberg, M. A., "Transportation, Urban Land Values, and Rents: A Synthesis." *Land Economics*, vol. 46, 1970, pp. 153–162.

Hansen, W. G., "How Accessibility Shapes Land Use." *Journal of the American Institute of Planners*, vol. 15, 1959, pp. 73–76.

Huff, D. L., "A Note on the Limitations of Intra-Urban Gravity Models." *Land Economics*, vol. 38, 1962, pp. 64–66.

Kain, J. F., "An Economic Model of Urban Residential and Travel Behavior." *Review of Economics and Statistics*, vol. 46, 1964, pp. 55–64.

Mills, E., "Urban Density Functions." *Urban Studies*, vol. 7, 1970, pp. 5–20.

Sinclair, R., "Von Thünen and Urban Sprawl." *Annals*, Association of American Geographers, vol. 57, 1967, pp. 72–87.

Regarding 5.4, see:

Blaikie, P. M., "Spatial Organization of Agriculture in Some North Indian Villages." *Transactions*, Institute of British Geographers, vol. 52, 1971, pp. 1–40.

Gregor, H. F., *Geography of Agriculture.* Englewood Cliffs, N.J.: Prentice-Hall, 1970.

Harvey, D. W., "Locational Change in the Kentish Hop Industry and the Analysis of Land Use Patterns." *Transactions*, Institute of British Geographers, vol. 33, 1963, pp. 123–144.

Horvath, R., "Von Thünen's Isolated State and the Area around Addis Ababa, Ethiopia," *Annals*, Association of American Geographers, vol. 59, 1969, pp. 308–323.

Peet, J. R., "Spatial Expansion of Commercial Agriculture in the Nineteenth Century." *Economic Geography*, vol. 45, 1969, pp. 283–301.

Yeates, M. H., "Some Factors Affecting the Spatial Distribution of Chicago Land Values, 1910–1960." *Economic Geography*, vol. 41, 1965, pp. 57–70.

CHAPTER 6

Regarding 6.2 and 6.3, see:

Harris, C. D., "The Market as a Factor in the Localization of Industry in the United States." *Annals*, Association of American Geographers, vol. 44, 1954, pp. 315–348.

Hoover, E. M., *Location of Economic Activity*, 2d ed. New York: McGraw-Hill, 1972.

Isard, W., *Location and Space-Economy*, New York: Technology Press, 1956.

Isard, W. and T. Smith, "Location Games." *Papers*, Regional Science Association, vol. 19, 1967, pp. 45–82.

Karaska, G. and D. Bramhall, eds., *Locational Analysis for Manufacturing*. Cambridge, Mass.: MIT, 1969.

Scott, A. J., "Location-Allocation Systems: A Review." *Geographical Analysis*, vol. 2, 1970, pp. 95–119.

Smith, D. M., *Industrial Location*. New York, Wiley, 1971.

Webber, M. J., *The Impact of Uncertainty on Location*. Canberra: Australian National University Press, 1971.

Regarding 6.4, see the general references and:

Kennelly, R. A., "The Location of the Mexican Steel Industry." *Revista Geografica*, vol. 15, 1954, pp. 109–129; vol. 16, 1955, pp. 199–213; vol. 17, 1955, pp. 60–77.

Lindberg, O., "An Economic-Geographical Study of the Localization of the Swedish Paper Industry." *Geografiska Annaler*, vol. 35, 1953, pp. 28–40.

CHAPTER 7

Regarding 7.2 and 7.3, see:

Barton, B., "The Creation of Centrality." *Annals*, Association of American Geographers, vol. 68, 1978, pp. 34–44.

Beavon, K. S., *Central Place Theory*. London: Longmans, 1977.

Berry, B. J. L., *A Geography of Market Centers and Retail Distribution*. Englewood Cliffs, N.J.: Prentice-Hall, 1967.

Berry, B. J. L. and A. Pred, *Central Place Studies: A Bibliography of Theory and Applications*. Philadelphia: Regional Science Research Institute, 1965.

Clarke, W. A. V., "Consumer Travel Patterns and the Concept of Range." *Annals*, Association of American Geographers, vol. 58, 1968, pp. 386–396.

Christaller, W., *Central Places in Southern Germany*. Englewood Cliffs, N.J.: Prentice-Hall, 1966.

Estall, R. C. and R. O. Buchanan, *Industrial Activity and Economic Geography*, 2d ed. London: Hutchinson, 1970.

Garner, B. J., "Models of Urban Geography and Settlement Location." In Chorley, R. J. and P. Haggett, eds., *Models in Geography*. London: Methuen, 1967.

Hoover, E. M., "Transport Costs and the Spacing of Central Places." *Papers*, Regional Science Association, vol. 25, 1970, pp. 245–274.

Hotelling, H., "Stability in Competition." *Economic Journal*, vol. 39, 1929, pp. 41–57.

Lösch, A., *The Economics of Location*, trans. by W. Stolper. New Haven: Yale, 1954.

McNee, R. B., "Functional Geography of the Firm." *Economic Geography*, vol. 34, 1958, pp. 321–337.

Olsson, G., "Central Place Theory, Spatial Interaction, and Stochastic Processes." *Papers*, Regional Science Association, vol. 18, 1967.

Parr, J. B. and K. G. Denike, "Theoretical Problems in Central Place Analysis." *Economic Geography*, vol. 46, 1970, pp. 568–586.

Rose, H. M., "The Structure of Retail Trade in a Racially Changing Trade Area." *Geographical Analysis*, vol. 2, 1970, pp. 135–148.

Rushton, G., "Postulates of Central Place Theory and Properties of Central Place Systems." *Geographical Analysis*, vol. 3, 1971, pp. 140–156.

Simmons, J., *The Changing Pattern of Retail Location*. University of Chicago, Department of Geography Research Paper 92, Chicago, 1964.

Smith, R. H. T., and A. M. Hay, "Theory of the Spatial Structure of Internal Trade in Underdeveloped Countries." *Geographical Analysis,* vol. 1, 1969, pp. 121–136.

Teitz, M., "Locational Strategies for Competitive Systems." *Journal of Regional Science,* vol. 8, 1968, pp. 135–148.

Törnqvist, G., "The Geography of Economic Activities: Some Critical Viewpoints on Theory and Application." *Economic Geography,* vol. 53, 1977, pp. 153–162.

Vance, J. E., Jr., *The Merchant's World: The Geography of Wholesaling.* Englewood Cliffs, N.J.: Prentice-Hall, 1970.

Woldenberg, M. J., "Energy Flow and Spatial Order." *Geographical Review,* vol. 58, 1968, pp. 552–574.

Woldenberg, M. L. and B. J. L. Berry, "Rivers and Central Places: Analogous Systems?" *Journal of Regional Science,* vol. 7, 1967, pp. 129–39.

Regarding 7.4, see Berry, 1967 (above) and:

Berry, B. J. L., H. G. Barnum, and R. Tennant, "Retail Location and Consumer Behavior." *Papers,* Regional Science Association, vol. 9, 1962, pp. 65–106.

Borchert, J. and R. Adams, "Trade Centers and Trade Areas in the Upper Midwest." Urban Report 3, Upper Midwest Economic Study, Minneapolis, 1963.

Brush, J. E., "The Hierarchy of Central Places in Southwestern Wisconsin." *Geographical Review,* vol. 43, 1953, pp. 380–402.

Dickenson, R. E., *City and Region.* New York: Humanities Press, 1964.

Green, H. L., "Hinterland Boundaries of New York City and Boston in Southern New England." *Economic Geography,* vol. 31, 1955, pp. 283–300.

King, L., "A Multivariate Analysis of the Spacing of Urban Settlements in the United States." *Annals,* Association of American Geographers, vol. 51, 1961, pp. 222–233.

Philbrick, A. K., "Principles of Areal Functional Organization in Regional Human Geography." *Economic Geography,* vol. 33, 1957, pp. 299–336.

Skinner, G. W., "Marketing and Social Structure in Rural China." *Journal of Asian Studies,* vol. 24, 1964, pp. 3–43.

CHAPTER 8

See Hoover and Richardson, listed under general references; also:

Isard, W., *Introduction to Regional Science.* Englewood Cliffs, N.J.: Prentice-Hall, 1975, Chapter 7.

Tiebout, C. M., *The Community Economic Base Study.* New York: Committee for Economic Development, 1962.

Tiebout, C. M., "Exports and Regional Growth." *Journal of Political Economy,* vol. 64, 1956, pp. 160–164 and 169.

CHAPTER 9

Regarding 9.2 and 9.3, see English and Mayfield, section 5, and:

Barnett, H. J. and C. Morse, *Scarcity and Growth.* Baltimore: Johns Hopkins, 1963.

Burton, I. and R. W. Kates, eds., *Readings in Resource Management and Conservation.* Chicago: University of Chicago, 1965.

Burton, I., R. W. Kates, and G. F. White, *The Environment as Hazard.* New York: Oxford University, 1978.

Chorley, R. J., ed., *Water, Earth, and Man.* London: Methuen, 1969.

Clarkson, J. D., "Ecology and Spatial Analysis." *Annals,* Association of American Geographers, vol. 60, 1970, pp. 700–716.

Duncan, O. D. and R. Cuzzort, "Regional Differentiation and Socioeconomic Change." *Papers,* Regional Science Association, vol. 4, 1958, pp. 163–178.

Firey, W., *Man, Mind, and Land: A Theory of Resource Use.* New York: Free Press, 1960.

Gould, P. R., "Man Against His Environment: A Game Theoretic Framework." *Annals,* Association of American Geographers, vol. 53, 1963, pp. 290–297.

Grigg, D., "Regions, Models, and Classes." In Chorley, R. J. and P. Haggett, eds., *Models in Geography.* London: Methuen, 1967.

Grigg, D., "The Logic of Regional Systems." *Annals,* Association of American Geographers, vol. 55, 1965, pp. 465–491.

Isard, W. et al., "On the Linkage of Socioeconomic and Ecologic Systems." *Papers,* Regional Science Association, vol. 21, 1968, pp. 79–100.

Manners, I. R. and M. W. Mikesell, eds., *Perspectives on Environment.* Washington, D.C.: Association of American Geographers, 1974.

Simmons, I. G., *The Ecology of National Resources,* 2d ed. London: Arnold, 1980.

Spengler, J. J., ed., *Natural Resources and Economic Growth.* Washington: Resources for the Future, 1961.

Sprout, H. and M. Sprout, *Toward a Politics of the Planet Earth.* New York: Van Nostrand Reinhold, 1971.

Stoddart, D., "Organism and Ecosystem as Geophysical Models." In Chorley, R. J. and P. Haggett, eds., *Models in Geography.* London: Methuen, 1967.

Turner, B. L. II, R. Q. Hanham, and A. V. Portararo, "Population Pressure and Agricultural Intensity." *Annals,* Association of American Geographers, vol. 67, 1977, pp. 384–396.

White, G. F., ed., *Natural Hazards.* New York: Oxford University, 1974.

Wolpert, J., "Departures from the Usual Environment in Locational Analysis." *Annals,* Association of American Geographers, vol. 60, 1970, pp. 220–229.

Wolpert, J., "The Decision Process in Spatial Context." *Annals,* Association of American Geographers, vol. 54, 1974, pp. 537–558.

Zelinsky, W., *A Prologue to Population Geography.* Englewood Cliffs, N.J.: Prentice-Hall, 1966.

Regarding economic regions, see:

Bogue, D. L. and C. L. Beale, *Economic Areas of the United States.* New York: Free Press, 1961.

Fox, K. A. and T. K. Kumar, "The Functional Economic Area." *Papers,* Regional Science Association, vol. 15, 1965, pp. 57–86.

Oxford Regional Economic Atlas of the United States and Canada, 2d ed. New York: Oxford University Press, 1975.

Thompson, J. H., *Geography of New York State.* Syracuse: Syracuse University, with supplement, 1977.

Regarding 9.4, see:

Belli, P., "The Economic Implications of Malnutrition." *Economic Development and Cultural Change,* vol. 20, 1972, pp. 1–23.

Detwyler, T. R., ed., *Man's Impact on Environment.* New York: McGraw-Hill, 1971.

Hart, J. F., "The Demise of King Cotton." *Annals,* Association of American Geographers, vol. 67, 1977, pp. 307–322.

Krutilla, J. V., "Water Resources Development: The Regional Incidence of Costs and Gains." *Papers,* Regional Science Association, vol. 4, 1958, pp. 273–312.

Meinig, D. W., *On the Margins of the Good Earth.* Chicago: Rand McNally, 1963.

Meinig, D. W., "The Mormon Culture Region." *Annals,* Association of American Geographers, vol. 55, 1965, pp. 191–220.

Thomas, W. L., Jr., ed., *Man's Role in Changing the Face of the Earth.* Chicago: University of Chicago Press, 1956.

White, G. F., *Choice of Adjustment to Floods.* University of Chicago, Department of Geography Research Paper 93, 1964.

Zelinsky, W., *The Cultural Geography of the United States.* Englewood Cliffs, N.J.: Prentice-Hall, 1973.

CHAPTER 10

See the general references and:

Denison, E. F., *Why Growth Rates Differ*. Washington: Brookings Institution, 1967.

Hague, D. C. and J. H. Dunning, "Costs in Alternative Locations: The Radio Industry." *Review of Economic Studies,* vol. 22, 1955, pp. 203–213.

Hoag, L. P., "Locational Determinants for Cash-Grain Farming in the Corn Belt." *Professional Geographer,* vol. 14, 1962, pp. 1–7.

Keeble, D. E., "Models of Economic Development." In Chorley, R. J. and P. Haggett, eds., *Models in Geography*. London: Methuen, 1967.

Kerr, D., "Some Aspects of the Geography of Finance in Canada." *Canadian Geographer,* vol. 9, 1965, pp. 175–192.

North, D. C., "The Spatial and Interregional Framework of the United States Economy." *Papers,* Regional Science Association, vol. 2, 1956, pp. 201–209.

Perloff, H. S. and V. W. Dodds, *How a Region Grows*. New York: Committee for Economic Development, 1963.

Perloff, H. S. et al., *Regions, Resources and Economic Growth*. Baltimore: Johns Hopkins, 1960.

Pred, A., "Industrialization, Initial Advantage, and American Metropolitan Growth." *Geographical Review,* vol. 55, 1965, pp. 158–189.

Pred, A., *The Spatial Dynamics of Urban Industrial Growth, 1800–1914*. Cambridge, Mass: MIT, 1966.

Richter, C. E., "Impact of Industrial Linkages on Geographic Association." *Journal of Regional Science,* vol. 9, 1969, pp. 19–28.

Spencer, J. E. and R. J. Horvath, "How Does an Agricultural Region Originate?" *Annals,* Association of American Geographers, vol. 53, 1963, pp. 74–92.

Steed, G., "Changing Milieu of the Firm." *Annals,* Association of American Geographers, vol. 58, 1968, pp. 506–525.

Tiebout, C. M., "Location Theory, Empirical Evidence, and Economic Evolution." *Papers,* Regional Science Association, vol. 3, 1957, pp. 74–86.

Ullman, E. L., "Regional Development and the Geography of Concentration," *Papers,* Regional Science Association, vol. 4, 1958, pp. 179–200.

Warntz, W., *Macrogeography and Income Fronts*. Philadelphia: Regional Science Research Institute, 1965.

Warntz, W., *Toward a Geography of Price*. Philadelphia: University of Pennsylvania, 1959.

CHAPTER 11

Regarding 11.2 and 11.3, see the general references and:

Carrothers, G. A. P., "An Historical Review of the Gravity and Potential Concepts of Human Interaction." *Journal of the American Institute of Planners,* vol. 22, 1956, pp. 94–102.

Golant, S. M., "Adjustment Processes in a System: A Behavioral Model of Human Movement." *Geographical Analysis,* vol. 3, 1971, pp. 203–220.

Haggett, P. and R. J. Chorley, *Network Analysis in Geography*. New York: St. Martin's, 1969.

Huff, D. L. and G. F. Jenks, "Graphic Interpretation of the Function of Distance in Gravity Models." *Annals,* Association of American Geographers, vol. 58, 1968, pp. 814–824.

Kain, J. F., "The Journey to Work as a Determinant of Residential Location." *Papers,* Regional Science Association, vol. 9, 1962, pp. 137–160.

Kansky, K., *Structure of Transport Networks*. University of Chicago Department of Geography Research Paper 84, 1963.

Lowe, J. C. and S. Moryadas, *The Geography of Movement*. Boston: Houghton Mifflin, 1975.

Lukerman, F. and P. Porter, "Gravity and Potential Models in Economic Geography." *Annals, Association of American Geographers*, vol. 50, 1960, pp. 493–504.

Olsson, G., "Distance and Human Interaction." *Geografiska Annaler*, vol. 43B, 1965, pp. 3–43.

Olsson, G., "Explanation, Prediction, and Meaning Variance: An Assessment of Distance Interaction Models." *Economic Geography*, vol. 46, 1970, pp. 223–233.

O'Sullivan, P., "On Gravity and Eruptions." *Professional Geographer*, vol. 29, 1977, pp. 182–185.

Warntz, W., "Transportation, Social Physics, and the Law of Refraction." *Professional Geographer*, vol. 10, 1958, pp. 6–10.

Wilson, A. G., "A Family of Spatial Interaction Models and Associated Developments." *Environment and Planning*, vol. 3, 1971, pp. 1–32.

Wilson, A. G., "Inter-Regional Commodity Flows: Entropy Maximizing Approaches." *Geographical Analysis*, vol. 2, 1970, pp. 255–282.

Wilson, A. G., *Urban and Regional Models in Geography and Planning*. New York: Wiley, 1974.

Regarding 11.4, see the general references and:

Bederman, S. J. and J. S. Adams, "Jobs, Accessibility, and Underemployment." *Annals, Association of American Geographers*, vol. 64, 1974, pp. 378–386.

Girt, J. L., "Distance to General Medical Practice and Its Effect on Revealed Ill-Health in a Rural Environment." *Canadian Geographer*, vol. 17, 1973, pp. 154–166.

Olsson, G., *Distance and Human Interaction*. Philadelphia: Regional Science Research Institute, 1965.

Zipf, G. K., *Human Behavior and the Principle of Least Effort*. Cambridge, Mass.: Harvard University, 1949.

CHAPTER 12

Regarding 12.2 and 12.3, see the general references and:

Bressler, R. G. and R. A. King, *Markets, Prices and Interregional Trade*. New York: Wiley, 1970.

Fulton, M. and J. C. Hoch, "Transportation Factors Affecting Locational Decisions." *Economic Geography*, vol. 35: 1959, pp. 51–59.

Gauthier, H. L., "Geography, Transportation, and Regional Development." *Economic Geography*, vol. 46: 1970, pp. 612–619.

Grotewold, A., "The Growth of Industrial Core Areas and Patterns of World Trade." *Annals, Association of American Geographers*, vol. 61, 1971, pp. 361–370.

Isard, W. and M. J. Peck, "Location Theory and International and Interregional Trade Theory." *Quarterly Journal of Economics*, vol. 68, 1954, pp. 97–114.

Lachene, R., "Networks and the Location of Economic Activities." *Papers, Regional Science Association*, vol. 14, 1965, pp. 197–202.

Mabogunje, A. L., "Systems Approach to a Theory of Rural-Urban Migration." *Geographical Analysis*, vol. 2, 1970, pp. 1–18.

Maizels, A., *Exports and Economic Growth of Developing Countries*. Cambridge: Cambridge University, 1968.

Ohlin, B., *Interregional and International Trade*, rev. ed. Cambridge, Mass.: Harvard University, 1967.

Smith, R. H. T., "Concepts and Methods in Commodity Flow Analysis." *Economic Geography*, vol. 46, 1970, pp. 404–416.

Taaffe, E. J. and H. Gauthier, *Geography of Transportation*. Englewood Cliffs, N.J.: Prentice-Hall, 1973.

Taaffe, E. J., R. L. Morrill, and P. R. Gould, "Transport Expansion in Underdeveloped Countries: A Comparative Analysis." *Geographical Review*, vol. 53, 1963, pp. 502–529.

Tiebout, C. M., "Exports and Regional Economic Growth." *Journal of Political Economy,* vol. 64, 1956, pp. 160–164.

Regarding 12.4, see the general references and:

Barloon, M. J., "The Interrelationship of the Changing Structure of American Transportation and Changes in Industrial Location." *Land Economics,* vol. 41, 1966, pp. 169–182.

Garrison, W. L. and others, *Studies of Highway Development and Geographic Change.* Seattle: University of Washington, 1959.

Gauthier, H., "Transportation and the Growth of the São Paulo Economy." *Journal of Regional Science,* vol. 8, 1968, pp. 77–94.

Smith, P. E., "A Note on Comparative Advantage, Trade, and the Turnpike." *Journal of Regional Science,* vol. 5, 1964, pp. 57–62.

Thoman, R. S. and E. C. Conkling, *Geography of International Trade.* Englewood Cliffs, N.J.: Prentice-Hall, 1967.

Ullman, E. L., *American Commodity Flows.* Seattle: University of Washington, 1957.

CHAPTER 13

See records and proceedings of the sessions of the United Nations Conference on Trade and Development and:

Balassa, B., *Studies in Trade Diversification.* Baltimore: Johns Hopkins, 1967.

Deutsch, K. W., *The Analysis of International Relations,* 2nd ed. Englewood Cliffs, N.J.: Prentice-Hall, 1978.

Dunning, J. H., ed., *International Investment: Selected Readings.* Harmondsworth, U.K.: Penguin Books, 1972.

Frankel, J., *National Interest,* New York: Praeger, 1970.

Hay, A. M., "Imports versus Local Production: A Case Study from the Nigerian Cement Industry." *Economic Geography,* vol. 47, 1971, pp. 384–388.

Kindleberger, C. P. and P. H. Lindert, *International Economics,* 6th ed., Homewood, Ill.: Richard D. Irwin, 1978.

Manners, G., "Regional Protection: A Factor in Economic Geography." *Economic Geography,* vol. 38, 1962, pp. 122–129.

Nurkse, R., *Problems of Capital Formation in Underdeveloped Countries.* Oxford: Blackwell, 1953.

Olsson, R., "Commodity Flows and Regional Interdependence." *Papers,* Regional Science Association, vol. 12, 1963, pp. 225–230.

Rothstein, R. L., *The Weak in the World of the Strong.* New York: Columbia University, 1977.

Russett, B. M., ed., *Economic Theories of International Politics.* Chicago: Markham, 1968.

CHAPTER 14

Brunn, S. and W. Hoffman, "Geography of Federal Grants-in-Aid to States." *Economic Geography,* vol. 45, 1969, pp. 226–238.

Brunn, S., *Geography and Politics in America.* New York: Harper & Row, 1974.

Cox, K., D. Reynolds and S. Rokkan, eds., *Locational Alternatives to Power and Conflicts,* New York: Halsted, 1974.

Dikshit, R. D., "Geography and Federalism." *Annals,* Association of American Geographers, vol. 61, 1971, pp. 97–115.

Godlund, S., *Population, Regional Hospitals, Transport Facilities, and Regions: Planning the Location of Regional Hospitals in Sweden.* Lund, Sweden: Lund Studies in Geography, ser. B: no. 21, 1961.

Kavesh, R. A. and J. B. Jones, "Differential Regional Impacts of Federal Expenditures." *Papers,* Regional Science Association, vol. 2, 1956, pp. 152–173.

Massam, B. H., *Location and Space in Social Administration.* London: Arnold, 1975.

Murphy, T. P., *Science, Geopolitics, and Federal Spending.* Lexington, Mass.: Heath Lexington, 1971.

Revelle, C. S. and R. W. Swain, "Central Facilities Location." *Geographical Analysis,* vol. 2, 1970, pp. 30–42.

Rushton, G., *Optimal Location of Facilities.* Hanover, N. H.: Dartmouth College, 1975.

Schultz, G., "Facility Planning for a Public Service System: Solid Waste Collection." *Journal of Regional Science,* vol. 9, 1969, pp. 291–308.

Teitz, M. N., "Toward a Theory of Urban Public Facilities Location." *Papers,* Regional Science Association, vol. 21, 1968, pp. 35–52.

Ullman, E. L., "Amenities as a Factor in Regional Growth." *Geographical Review,* vol. 44, 1954, pp. 119–132.

Wilbanks, T. J. and H. Huang, "The Regional Impact of a Guaranteed Annual Income." *Proceedings,* Association of American Geographers, vol. 7, 1975, pp. 282–288.

Wohlenberg, E. H., "Interstate Variations in AFDC Programs." *Economic Geography,* vol. 52, 1976, pp. 254–266.

Wolpert, J., A. Mumphrey, and J. Seley, *Metropolitan Neighborhoods: Participation and Conflict Over Changes.* Washington, D.C.: Association of American Geographers, 1972.

CHAPTER 15

Regarding 15.2 and 15.3, see:

Boal, F. W., "Urban Growth and Land Value Patterns: Government Influences." *Professional Geographer,* vol. 22, 1970, pp. 79–83.

Jackson, W. A. D. and M. S. Samuels, eds., *Politics and Geographic Relationships,* 2d ed. Englewood Cliffs, N.J.: Prentice-Hall, 1971.

Jones, S. B., "Boundary Concepts in the Setting of Place and Time." *Annals,* Association of American Geographers, vol. 49, 1959, pp. 241–255.

Kaiser, E. J. and S. F. Weiss, "Public Policy and the Residential Development Process." *Journal of the American Institute of Planners,* vol. 36, 1970, pp. 30–37.

Kasperson, R. E. and J. V. Minghi, eds., *The Structure of Political Geography.* Chicago: Aldine, 1969.

McNee, R. D., "Regional Planning, Bureaucracy, and Geography." *Economic Geography,* vol. 46, 1970, pp. 190–198.

Mund, V. A. and R. H. Wolf, *Industrial Organization and Public Policy.* Englewood Cliffs, N.J.: Prentice-Hall, 1971.

Musgrave, R. A., ed., *Essays in Fiscal Federalism.* Washington: Brookings Institution, 1965.

Smith, D. M., *Human Geography: A Welfare Approach.* London: Arnold, 1977.

Soffer, E. and E. Korenich, " 'Right to Work' Laws as a Location Factor." *Journal of Regional Science,* vol. 3, 1961, pp. 41–56.

Warren, K., "Steel Pricing, Regional Economic Growth and Public Policy." *Urban Studies,* vol. 3, 1966, pp. 185–199.

Williams, W., "Impact of State and Local Taxes on Industry Location." *Journal of Regional Science,* vol. 7, 1967, pp. 49–59.

Regarding 15.4, for other examples see:

Fielding, G. J., "The Role of Government in New Zealand Wheat Growing." *Annals,* Association of American Geographers, vol. 55, 1965, pp. 87–97.

Hamilton, F. E. I., "Aspects of Spatial Behavior in Planned Economies." *Papers,* Regional Science Association, vol. 25, 1970, pp. 83–108.

Jensen, R., "Regionalism and Price Zonation in Soviet Agricultural Planning." *Annals,* Association of American Geographers, vol. 59, 1969, pp. 324–347.

Leontief, W. et al., "The Economic Impact—Industrial and Regional—of an Arms Cut," *The Review of Economics and Statistics,* vol. 47, 1965, pp. 217–228.

CHAPTER 16

See the general references, especially Hoover and Richardson. Also see:

Boudeville, J., *Problems of Regional Economic Planning.* Edinburgh: Edinburgh University, 1966.

Friedmann, J. and W. Alonso, eds., *Regional Development and Planning,* 2d ed. Cambridge, Mass.: MIT, 1974.

Myrdal, G. M., *Rich Lands and Poor.* New York: Harper & Row, 1957.

Nourse, H., *Regional Economics.* New York: McGraw-Hill, 1968.

Richardson, H. W., *Regional Growth Theory.* New York: Halsted, 1973.

Regarding 16.2.1, also see:

Bowen, I., *Acceptable Inequalities.* Montreal: McGill-Queen's University, 1970.

Chinitz, B., "Appropriate Goals for Regional Economic Policy." *Urban Studies,* vol. 3, 1966, pp. 1–7.

Mera, K., "Tradeoff between Aggregate Efficiency and Inter-regional Equity." *Quarterly Journal of Economics,* vol. 81, 1967, pp. 638–674.

Teriba, O. and O. A. Philips, "Income Distribution and National Integration." *Nigerian Journal of Economic and Social Studies,* vol. 13, 1971, pp. 77–122.

Regarding 16.2.2, also see:

Harvey, D., *Social Justice and the City.* London: Arnold, 1973.

Harvey, D., "Social Processes and Spatial Form." *Papers,* Regional Science Assocation, vol. 25, 1970, pp. 47–70.

Janelle, D. G., "Spatial Reorganization: A Model and Concept." *Annals,* Association of American Geographers, vol. 59, 1969, pp. 348–364.

Johnson, E. A. J., *The Organization of Space in Developing Countries.* Cambridge, Mass.: Harvard, 1970.

von Boventer, E., "Spatial Organization Theory as a Basis for Regional Planning." *Journal of the American Institute of Planners,* vol. 30, 1964, pp. 90–100.

Regarding 16.2.3, also see:

Darwent, D. F., "Growth Poles and Growth Centres in Regional Planning." *Environment and Planning,* vol. 1, 1969, pp. 5–32.

Friedmann, J., "Poor Regions and Poor Nations." *Southern Economic Journal,* vol. 32, 1966, pp. 465–473.

Friedmann, J., "Regional Economic Policy for Developing Areas." *Papers,* Regional Science Association, vol. 11, 1963, pp. 41–62.

Hansen, N. M., "Regional Planning in a Mixed Economy." *Southern Economic Journal,* vol. 32, 1965, pp. 176–190.

Hansen, N. M., ed., *Growth Centres in Regional Economic Development.* New York: Free Press, 1972.

Kuklinski, A., *Growth Poles and Growth Centers in Regional Planning.* Paris: Mouton, 1972.

Kuklinski, A., "Regional Development, Regional Policies, and Regional Planning: Problems and Issues." *Regional Studies,* vol. 5, 1971, pp. 269–278.

Leven, C. L. et al., *An Analytical Framework for Regional Development Policy.* Cambridge, Mass.: MIT, 1970.

Lianos, T. P., "Interregional Allocation of Labor: A Measure of Economic Efficiency." *Annals of Regional Science,* vol. 4: no. 1, 1970, pp. 93–104.

Nelson, P., "Migration, Real Income, and Information." *Journal of Regional Science,* vol. 1, 1959, pp. 43–74.

Perloff, H., "Key Features of Regional Planning." *Journal of the American Institute of Planners,* vol. 34, 1968, pp. 153–159.

Schramm, G., "Regional versus Interregional Efficiency in Resource Allocations." *Annals of Regional Science*, vol. 4: no. 2, 1970, pp. 1–14.

Teitz, M. B., "Regional Theory and Regional Models." *Papers*, Regional Science Association, vol. 9, 1962, pp. 35–52.

Regarding 16.3.1, especially see Haggett and Abler, Adams, and Gould; also see:

Logan, M. I., "The Spatial System and Planning Strategies in Developing Countries." *Geographical Review*, vol. 62, 1972, pp. 229–244.

Wolpert, J., "The Decision Process in Spatial Context." *Annals*, Association of American Geographers, vol. 54, 1964, pp. 537–558.

Regarding 16.3.2, also see:

Amedeo, D., "An Optimization Approach to the Identification of a System of Regions." *Papers*, Regional Science Association, vol. 23, 1968, pp. 25–44.

Mera, K., "On Urban Agglomeration and Economic Efficiency." *Economic Development and Cultural Change*, vol. 21, 1973, pp. 309–324.

Mills, E. S., "The Efficiency of Spatial Competition." *Papers*, Regional Science Association, vol. 25, 1970, pp. 71–82.

Morrill, R. L. and P. Kelley, "Optimal Allocation of Services." *Annals of Regional Science*, vol. 3, 1969, pp. 55–66.

Sakashita, N., "Regional Allocation of Public Investment." *Papers*, Regional Science Association, vol. 19, 1967, pp. 161–184.

Regarding 16.4, also see:

Alonso, W., "What Are New Towns For?" *Urban Studies*, vol. 7, 1970, pp. 37–56.

Cameron, G. C., *Regional Economic Development: The Federal Role.* Baltimore: Johns Hopkins, 1970.

Chisholm, M. and G. Manners, eds., *Spatial Policy Problems of the British Economy.* Cambridge: Cambridge University, 1971.

Friedmann, J., *Urbanization, Planning, and National Development.* Beverly Hills, Cal.: Sage, 1972.

Hansen, N. M., *Rural Poverty and the Urban Crisis.* Bloomington, Ind.: Indiana University, 1970.

Klaassen, L. H., W. C. Kroft, and R. Viskvil, "Regional Income Differentials in Holland." *Papers*, Regional Science Association, vol. 10, 1973, pp. 77–81.

Knox, P. L., "Spatial Variations in Level of Living in England and Wales." *Transactions*, Institute of British Geographers, vol. 62, 1972, pp. 1–24.

MacKinnon, R. D. and M. J. Hodgson, "Optimal Transportation Networks: A Case Study of Highway Systems." *Environment and Planning*, vol. 2, 1970, pp. 267–289.

CHAPTER 17

Regarding 17.2.1, see:

Borchert, J. et al., *Upper Midwest Economic Study.* Minneapolis, 1963.

Bramhall, D. F., "Projecting Regional Accounts and Industrial Locations." *Papers*, Regional Science Association, vol. 7, 1961, pp. 89–118.

Hirsch, W. Z., ed., *Elements of Regional Accounts.* Baltimore: Johns Hopkins, 1964.

Hirsch, W. Z., ed., *Regional Accounts for Policy Decisions.* Washington: Resources for the Future, 1966.

Isard, W. et al., *Methods of Regional Analysis.* New York: Technology Press, 1960.

Leven, C. L., "Regional and Interregional Accounts in Perspective." *Papers*, Regional Science Association, vol. 13, 1964, pp. 127–146.

Ray, D. M., "The Spatial Structure of Economic and Cultural Differences: A Factorial Ecology of Canada." *Papers,* Regional Science Association, vol. 23, 1969, pp. 7–24.

Thompson, J. H. et al., "Toward a Geography of Economic Health: The Case of New York State." *Annals,* Association of American Geographers, vol. 52, 1962, pp. 1–20.

Regarding 17.2.2, see the general references and:

Alonso, W., "Urban and Regional Imbalances in Economic Development." *Economic Development and Cultural Change,* vol. 17, 1968, pp. 1–14.

Benedict, B., ed., *Problems of Smaller Territories.* London: Athlone Press, 1967.

Berry, B. J. L., "The Geography of the United States in the Year 2000." *Transactions of the Institute of British Geographers,* vol. 51, 1970, pp. 21–54.

Bogue, D. J., *Principles of Demography.* New York: Wiley, 1969.

Bourne, L. S. et al., *Urban Futures for Central Canada.* Toronto: University of Toronto, 1974.

Brown, H., "Shift and Share Projections of Regional Economic Growth." *Journal of Regional Science,* vol. 9, 1969, pp. 1–18.

Cant, R. G., "Territorial Socio-economic Indicators in Development Plans in the Asian Region." *International Social Science Journal,* vol. 27, 1975, pp. 53–77.

Chapin, F. S. and S. F. Weiss, eds., *Urban Growth Dynamics in a Regional Cluster of Cities.* New York: Wiley, 1962.

Chisholm, M. D. I., A. E. Frey, and P. Haggett, eds., *Regional Forecasting.* London: Butterworth, 1971.

Church, R. J., "Some Problems of Regional Economic Development in West Africa." *Economic Geography,* vol. 45, 1969, pp. 53–62.

de Jouvenal, B., *The Art of Conjecture.* New York: Basic Books, 1967.

Hansen, J. C., "Regional Disparities in Norway with Reference to Marginality," *Transactions,* Institute of British Geographers, vol. 57, 1962, pp. 15–30.

Hodge, G., "The Prediction of Trade Center Viability on the Great Plains." *Papers,* Regional Science Association, vol. 15, 1965, pp. 87–118.

Hodge, G., "Urban Structure and Regional Development." *Papers,* Regional Science Association, vol. 21, 1968, pp. 101–124.

Klimm, L., "The Empty Areas of the Northeastern U.S." *Geographical Review,* vol. 44, 1954, pp. 325–345.

Kuznets, S., *Modern Economic Growth.* New Haven, Conn.: Yale, 1966.

Lankford, P. W., *Regional Incomes in the United States, 1929–1967.* Chicago: University of Chicago Department of Geography Research Paper 145, 1972.

Lee, E. S. et al., *Population Redistribution and Economic Growth, 1870–1950.* Philadelphia: American Philosophical Society, 1957.

Lonsdale, R. E. and C. Browning, "Rural–Urban Locational Preferences of Southern Manufacturers." *Annals,* Association of American Geographers, vol. 61, 1971, pp. 255–268.

Morrill, R. L., *Migration and the Spread and Growth of Urban Settlement.* Lund, Sweden: Lund Studies in Geography, ser. B: no. 26, 1965.

Northam, R., "Population Size, Relative Location and Declining Urban Centres in the U.S." *Land Economics,* vol. 45, 1969, pp. 313–322.

Parr, J. B., "Out-Migration and the Depressed Area Problem." *Land Economics,* vol. 42, 1960, pp. 149–160.

Robinson, E. A. G., ed., *The Economic Consequences of the Size of Nations.* London: Macmillan, 1960.

Rodgers, A., "Migration and Industrial Development: The Southern Italian Experience." *Economic Geography,* vol. 46, 1970, pp. 111–135.

Schwind, P., "Spatial Preferences of Migrants for Regions: The Example of Maine." *Proceedings*, Association of American Geographers, vol. 3, 1971, pp. 150–156.

Stilwell, F. J. B., "Regional Distribution of Concealed Unemployment." *Urban Studies*, vol. 7, 1970, pp. 209–236.

Tachi, M., "Regional Income Disparity and Internal Migration of Population in Japan." *Economic Development and Cultural Change*, vol. 12, 1964, pp. 186–204.

Williamson, J. G., "Regional Inequality and the Process of National Development." *Economic Development and Cultural Change*, vol. 13, 1965, pp. 3–45.

Wood, W. S. and R. S. Thoman, eds., *Areas of Economic Stress in Canada*. Kingston, Ont.: Queen's University, 1965.

Regarding 17.3.3, see:

Berry, B. J. L., "Hierarchical Diffusion: The Basis of Developmental Filtering and Spread in a System of Growth Centers." In Hansen, N. M., ed., *Growth Centers and Regional Economic Development*. New York: Free Press, 1971.

Brown, L., *Diffusion Dynamics*. Lund, Sweden: Lund Studies in Geography, ser. B: no. 29, 1968.

Brown, L., *Diffusion Processes and Location*. Philadelphia: Regional Science Research Institute, 1968.

Gould, P., *Spatial Diffusion*. Washington: Association of American Geographers, 1969.

Hägerstrand, T., *Innovation Diffusion as a Spatial Process*, trans. by A. Pred. Chicago: University of Chicago, 1968.

Hale, C., "Mechanics of the Spread Effect in Regional Development." *Land Economics*, vol. 43, 1967, pp. 434–445.

Hudson, J. C., "Diffusion in a Central Place System." *Geographical Analysis*, vol. 1, 1969, pp. 45–58.

Morrill, R. L., "The Shape of Diffusion in Space and Time." *Economic Geography*, vol. 46, 1970, pp. 259–268.

Stabler, J. C., "Exports and Evolution: Process of Regional Change." *Land Economics*, vol. 44, 1968, pp. 11–23.

Tornqvist, G., *Contact Systems and Regional Development*. Lund, Sweden: Lund Studies in Geography, ser. B: no. 35, 1970.

Wilbanks, T. J., "Accessibility and Technological Change in Northern India." *Annals*, Association of American Geographers, vol. 62, 1972, pp. 427–436.

CHAPTER 18

See the general references, especially Hoover, Richardson, and Lloyd and Dicken's Chapter 7, and:

Balassa, B., *The Theory of Economic Integration*. Homewood, Ill.: Irwin, 1961.

Bourne, L., "Spatial Allocation: Land-Use Conversion Model of Urban Growth." *Journal of Regional Science*, vol. 9, 1969, pp. 261–272.

Brookfield, H., *Interdependent Development*. London: Methuen, 1975.

Dicken, P., "Some Aspects of the Decision Making Behavior of Business Organizations." *Economic Geography*, vol. 47, 1971, pp. 426–437.

Firn, J. R., "External Control and Regional Development: The Case of Scotland." *Environment and Planning*, vol. 7, 1975, pp. 393–414.

Goddard, J. B., *Office Location in Urban and Regional Development*. London: Oxford University Press, 1975.

Graham, R. E., "Factors Underlying Changes in the Geographic Distribution of Income." *Survey of Current Business*, vol. 44, April 1964, pp. 15–32.

Harper, R. A., T. H. Schmudde, and F. H. Thomas, "Recreation-Based Economic Development and the Growth Point Concept." *Land Economics,* vol. 43, 1966, pp. 95–102.

Harvey, D. W., *Social Justice and the City.* London: Arnold, 1973.

Isard, W. and E. W. Schooler, "Industrial Complex Analysis, Agglomeration Economies, and Regional Development." *Journal of Regional Science,* vol. 1, 1959, pp. 19–33.

Keeble, D. E., "Models of Economic Development." In Chorley, R. J. and P. Haggett, eds., *Models in Geography.* London: Methuen, 1967.

McMillan, T. E., "Why Manufacturers Choose Plant Locations vs. Determinants of Plant Location." *Land Economics,* vol. 41, 1965, pp. 239–246.

Mishan, E. J., *Costs of Economic Growth.* Harmondsworth, UK: Penguin Books, 1967.

Muth, R. F., "Economic Change and Rural-Urban Land Use Conversion." *Econometrica,* vol. 29, 1961, pp. 1–23.

Pfister, R. L., "The Terms of Trade as a Tool for Regional Analysis." *Journal of Regional Science,* vol. 3, 1961, pp. 57–66.

Robinson, E. A. G., ed., *Backward Areas in Advanced Countries.* London: Macmillan, 1969.

Robinson, R., "Changing Shipping Technology and the Spatial Adjustment of Port Functions." *Tijdschrift voor Economische en Sociale Geografie,* vol. 62, 1971, pp. 157–170.

White, G. F., "Contribution of Geographic Analysis to River Basin Development." *Geographical Journal,* vol. 129, 1963, pp. 412–436.

CHAPTER 19

See the general references Hoover, Haggett, and Coates, Johnston, and Knox, along with:

Bourne, L., *Urban Systems: Strategies for Regulation.* New York: Oxford, 1977.

Gans, H. J., *People and Plans.* New York: Basic Books, 1972.

Yapa, L. S., "The Green Revolution: A Diffusion Model." *Annals,* Association of American Geographers, vol. 67, 1977, pp. 350–359.

CHAPTER 20

Burton, I. and R. Kates, eds., *Readings on Resource Management and Conservation.* Chicago: University of Chicago, 1965.

Harvey, D. W., "What Kind of Geography for What Kind of Public Policy?" *Transactions,* Institute of British Geographers, vol. 63, 1974, pp. 18–24.

Hoffman, S., ed., *Conditions of World Order.* Boston: Houghton Mifflin, 1968.

Kahn, H. and A. J. Wiener, *The Year 2000.* New York: Macmillan, 1967.

King, L., "Alternatives to a Positive Economic Geography." *Annals,* Association of American Geographers, vol. 66, 1976, pp. 293–308.

"The Limits to Growth Controversy." *Futures,* vol. 5: no. 1, February 1973, special issue.

Meadows, D., D. C. Meadows, J. Randers, and W. W. Behrens, III, *The Limits to Growth.* New York: Universe Books, 1972.

CREDITS

CHAPTER 1

pp. 4–5 From *Iberia* by James Michener. Copyright © 1968 by James A. Michener. By permission of Random House, Inc.

pp. 5–6 From *Travels With Charley* by John Steinbeck. Copyright © 1962 by John Steinbeck. All rights reserved. Reprinted by permission of Viking Penguin Inc.

pp. 6–7 From *The Road to Huddersfield* by James Morris. All rights reserved. Reprinted by permission of Pantheon Books, a Division of Random House, Inc.

pp. 7–8 From *Slowly Down the Ganges* by Eric Newby. All rights reserved. Reprinted by permission of A. P. Watt Ltd., London.

p. 9 From *The Right People* by Stephen Birmingham. Boston: Little Brown. Used with permission.

CHAPTER 2

Fig. 2.2 U.S. Geological Survey.

Fig. 2.4 From D. L. Greene et al., *Regional Transportation Energy Conservation Data Book.* Oak Ridge, TN: Oak Ridge National Laboratory, 1978, Fig. 1-34.

Fig. 2.5 From J. H. Thompson et al., *Annals*, AAG, vol. 52, 1962, Fig. 16.

Fig. 2.6a From E. C. Pielou, *An Introduction to Mathematical Ecology.* New York: Wiley-Interscience, 1969, Fig. 23a. By permission of John Wiley & Sons, Inc.

Fig. 2.6b From P. DeVise, "Misused and Misplaced Hospitals and Doctors," AAG resource paper no. 22, 1973, Fig. 2.

Fig. 2.7a From *The National Atlas of the United States*, p. 227. Published by the U.S. Dept. of the Interior.

Fig. 2.7b From V. Finch et al., *Elements of Geography*, 4th ed. Copyright © 1957 by McGraw-Hill Book Company, and used with their permission.

Fig. 2.7c From G. F. Pyle, "The Diffusion of Cholera in the United States in the Nineteenth Century," *Geographical Analysis*, vol. 1 (1969), Fig. 2.

Fig. 2.8a After B. H. Massam, "The Spatial Structure of Administrative Systems," AAG resource paper no. 12, 1972, Fig. 20.

Fig. 2.8b After D. W. Meinig, "American Wests: Preface to a Geographical Interpretation," *Annals*, AAG, vol. 62, 1972, Fig. 2.

Fig. 2.9a In T. K. Peucker, "Computer Cartography," AAG resource paper no. 17, 1972, Fig. 1.8. Program: SYMVU data: D. Mark; production: W. D. Rase.

Fig. 2.9b After M. Yeates, *An Introduction to Quantitative Analysis in Human Geography.* Copyright © 1974 by McGraw-Hill Book Company and used with their permission.

Fig. 2.10 After P. Haggett, *Locational Analysis in Human Geography.* New York: St. Martin's Press, Inc. (Macmillan & Co, Ltd.), 1965, Fig. 1.5. Used with permission.

Fig. 2.11a After T. Hagerstrand, *Lund Series in Geography*, series B, vol. 13, p. 54. Used with permission.

Fig. 2.11b After Abler, Adams, and Gould, *Spatial Organization*. Englewood Cliffs, N.J.: Prentice-Hall, 1971, Fig. 13-33. Used with permission of Prentice-Hall, Inc.

CHAPTER 3

Fig. 3.3b After O. H. K. Spate and A. T. A. Learmonth, *India and Pakistan*, 3rd ed. London: Methuen, 1967, Fig. 18.7.

Fig. 3.5 Data from *U.N. Demographic Yearbook, 1970.*

Fig. 3.6 Reprinted by permission of the New Community Press, from *Hunger, U.S.A.*, Beacon Press, 1968.

Fig. 3.7 From D. M. Smith, *The Geography of Social Well-Being* in the United States. Copyright © 1973 by McGraw-Hill. Used with permission of the McGraw-Hill Book Company.

Fig. 3.8 *Manpower Report of the President*, 1968, Chart 23. Washington, D.C.: Government Printing Office.

Fig. 3.9 From C. Harris, *Annals*, AAG, vol. 44, 1954, pp. 312, 321. © Chauncy D. Harris, 1953. Used with permission.

CHAPTER 5

Fig. 5.1 After Peter Haggett, *Locational Analysis in Human Geography*. New York: St. Martin's Press Inc. (Macmillan & Co., Ltd.), 1965, p. 159. Used with permission.

Fig. 5.9 After Walter Isard, *Location and Space Economy*. Cambridge, Mass.: The MIT Press, 1956, p. 272. Used with permission.

Figs. 5.10 and 5.11 After D. W. Harvey, "Locational Change in the Kentish Hop Industry and The Analysis of Land Use Patterns," *Transactions of the Institute of British Geographers*, vol. 33, 1963, Figs. 5 and 6.

Fig. 5.12 From Peter Haggett, *Geography: A Modern Synthesis*, 3rd ed. New York: Harper & Row, 1979. Copyright 1979 by Peter Haggett and used with permission of Harper & Row Publishers, Inc.

Fig. 5.13 From D. S. Knos, "Distribution and Land Values in Topeka, Kansas." Lawrence, Kansas: University of Kansas Bureau of Business and Economic Research, 1962, Fig. 2.

Table 5.2 From K. Cox, *Man, Location, and Behavior*. New York: Wiley, 1972, p. 276. © 1972 by John Wiley & Sons, Inc., and reprinted with their permission.

CHAPTER 6

Fig. 6.3 From J. Friedmann and W. Alonso, eds., *Regional Development and Planning*. Cambridge, Mass.: The MIT Press, 1964, Fig. 9. Used by permission.

Fig. 6.5 From E. M. Hoover, *Location of Economic Activity*. Copyright © 1948 by McGraw-Hill. Used with permission of McGraw-Hill Book Company.

Fig. 6.6 Suggested by Abler, Adams, and Gould, *Spatial Organization*. Englewood Cliffs, N.J.: Prentice-Hall, 1971, p. 305. Used with permission.

Figs. 6.7 and 6.8 After R. A. Kennelly, "The Location of the Mexican Steel Industry," *Revista Geográfica*, Tomo 15 (1954) pp. 109–129; Tomo 16 (1955), pp. 199–213; and Tomo 17 (1955), pp. 60–77.

Fig. 6.9 After O. Lindberg, "An Economic-Geographical Study of the Localisation of the Swedish Paper Industry," *Geografiska Annaler*, vol. 35, 1953, p. 124, Figure 20.

Fig. 6.10a After F. R. Drysdale and C. E. Calef, *The Energetics of the United States of America: An Atlas*. Brookhaven National Laboratory, revised October 1977.

CHAPTER 7

Fig. 7.9a After W. Isard, *Location and Space Economy*. Cambridge, Mass.: The MIT Press, 1956, p. 374. Used with permission.

Fig. 7.9b After A. Losch, *The Economics of Location*. Stuttgart: Gustav Fischer Verlag, 1954. Used with permission.

Fig. 7.12 From B. J. L. Berry, H. G. Barnum, and R. J. Tennant, "Retail Location and Consumer Behavior," *Papers and Proceedings—Regional Science Association*, vol. 9, 1962, pp. 65–102.

Fig. 7.13a After A. K. Philbrick, "Principles of Areal Organization in Regional Human Geography," *Economic Geography*, vol. 33, 1957, p. 629.

Fig. 7.13b After Borchert and Adams, "Trade Centers and Trade Areas in the Upper Midwest," *Urban Report 3: Upper Midwest Economic Study*, Minneapolis, 1963.

Figs. 7.14a and b After Abler, Adams, and Gould, *Spatial Organization*. Englewood Cliffs, N.J.: Prentice-Hall, 1971, pp. 375 [part (a), which is after Borchert], and 377 [part (b)].

Fig. 7.15b After G. W. Skinner, in B. J. L. Berry, *Geography of Market Centers*. Englewood Cliffs, N.J.: Prentice-Hall, 1967, Figs. 3.13–3.15.

Fig. 7.16 After R. A. Murdie, "Cultural Differences in Consumer Travel," *Economic Geography*, vol, 41, 1965, p. 99.

CHAPTER 8

Fig. 8.1 After J. W. Alexander, "The Basic Nonbasic Concept of Urban Economic Functions," *Economic Geography*, vol. 30, 1954, p. 250. Used with permission.

Fig. 8.2 After E. Ullman and M. Dacey, "The Minimum Requirements Approach to the Urban Economic Base," *Lund Studies in Geography*, series B, 24, 1962, p. 129.

CHAPTER 9

Fig. 9.2 From H. McCarty and J. Lindberg, *A Preface to Economic Geography*. Englewood Cliffs, N.J.: Prentice-Hall, © 1966, Fig. 3.01. Used with permission.

Fig. 9.3 Adapted from Hauser and Duncan, *The Study of Population*. Chicago: The University of Chicago Press, p. 644, Fig. 5. In W. A. Zelinsky, *A Prologue to Population Geography*. Englewood Cliffs, N.J.: Prentice-Hall, 1966, Fig. 10–5. Reprinted by permission of the University of Chicago Press.

Fig. 9.4b After *Oxford Regional Economic Atlas*, 1967, pp. 116–117.

Fig. 9.5 After J. Thompson, *Geography of New York State*. Syracuse N.Y.: Syracuse University Press, 1967, Figures 115, 119, and 117.

Fig. 9.7a After J. F. Hart, "The Demise of King Cotton," AAG *Annals*, vol. 67, 1977, p. 312, Fig. 7. Used with permission.

Fig. 9.8a After *Oxford Regional Economic Atlas: The United States and Canada*. Oxford: Clarendon Press, 1967.

Fig. 9.8b After F. R. Drysdale and C. E. Calef, *The Energetics of the United States of America: An Atlas*. Brookhaven National Laboratory, revised Oct. 1977.

Fig. 9.10 After D. W. Meinig, "The Mormon Culture Region," AAG *Annals*, v. 55, 1965, Fig. 1. Used with permission.

Fig. 9.11 After *Mosaic*, vol. 8, no. 1 (Jan./Feb. 1977), p. 22.

CHAPTER 10

Fig. 10.1 After D. E. Keeble, "Models of Economic Development." In R. J. Chorley and P. Haggett, *Models in Geography*. London: Methuen, 1967, p. 258, Fig. 8.4. (After Myrdal.)

Fig. 10.3 After W. Isard et al., *Industrial Complex Analysis and Regional Development*. Cambridge, Mass.: The MIT Press, p. 87, and used by permission.

Fig. 10.4 After J. F. Hart, "The Demise of King Cotton," AAG *Annals*, vol. 67, 1977, p. 312, Fig. 7. Used with permission.

CHAPTER 11

Fig. 11.1 After R. L. Morrill, *The Spatial Organization of Society*, 2nd ed. North Scituate, Mass.: Duxbury Press, 1974, Figure 7.11. Used with permission.

Fig. 11.3 After P. Haggett, *Locational Analysis in Human Geography*. New York: St. Martin's Press, Inc. (Macmillan & Co. Ltd.), 1965, Fig. 3-14. Used with permission.

Fig. 11.4 After W. Bunge, "Theoretical Geography," *Lund Studies in Geography*, series C, 1, 1962, pp. 183–189. Used with permission.

Fig. 11.5 After Abler, Adams, and Gould, *Spatial Organization*. Englewood Cliffs, N.J.: Prentice-Hall, 1971, Figs. 13-13 and 13-14.

Fig. 11.6 After Abler, Adams, and Gould, *Spatial Organization*. Englewood Cliffs, N.J.: Prentice-Hall, 1971, p. 279.

Fig. 11.8a and b From G. K. Zipf, *Human Behavior and the Principle of Least Effort*. Reading, Mass.: Addison-Wesley, 1949. In W. Isard, *Location and Space Economy*. Cambridge, Mass.: The MIT Press, 1956, pp. 62 and 64. Used with permission.

Fig. 11.9 After Bunge, *Theoretical Geography*. Lund, Sweden: C. W. K. Gleerup, 1966, chapter 2.

Box 11.6 In Abler, Adams, and Gould, *Spatial Organization*. Englewood Cliffs, N.J.: Prentice-Hall, 1971, p. 278. With permission of London Transport, Griffith House, London, England.

CHAPTER 12

Fig. 12.2 After E. J. Taaffe, R. L. Morrill, and P. R. Gould, "Transport Expansion in Underdeveloped Counties," *Geographical Review*, vol. 53, 1963, p. 504. By permission of the American Geographical Society.

Fig. 12.3 Chicago Area Transportation Study, Figures 18 and 22.

Fig. 12.4 After R. E. Preston, "The Structure of Central Place Systems," *Economic Geography*, vol. 47, 1971, p. 147.

Fig. 12.5 Adapted using materials in Peter T. White, "This Land of Ours—How Are We Using It," *National Geographic*, July 1976, pp. 27–35 and 40–41.

Fig. 12.6 From A. D. Philbrick, *This Human World*. New York: Wiley, 1963. By permission of John Wiley & Sons, Inc.

Fig. 12.7 After C. A. Doxiadis, *Science*, vol. 170, 1970, p. 396.

CHAPTER 14

Fig. 14.1 After Abler, Adams, and Gould, *Spatial Organization*. Englewood Cliffs, N.J.: Prentice-Hall, 1971, p. 532. Used with permission.

Fig. 14.3 From *An Introduction to Quantitative Analysis in Human Geography* by M. Yeates. Copyright © 1974 by McGraw-Hill, and used with permission of the McGraw-Hill Book Company.

Fig. 14.4 After S. Brunn, *Geography and Politics in America*. New York: Harper & Row, 1974, p. 149. Copyright 1974 by S. Brunn and used with permission of Harper & Row Publishers, Inc.

Fig. 14.5 After S. Brunn, *Geography and Politics in America*. New York: Harper & Row, 1974, p. 327. Copyright 1974 by S. Brunn and used with permission of Harper & Row Publishers, Inc.

Fig. 14.8 U.S. Economic Development Administration and Office of Regional Development, *First Annual Report*, 1966, p.8.

Fig. 14.9 After E. H. Wohlenberg, "Interstate Variations in AFDC Programs," *Economic Geography*, vol. 52 (1976), p. 256.

Figs. 14.10, 14.11 and 14.12 Data from Advisory Commission on Intergovernmental Relations, *Federal-State-Local Finances: Significant Features of Fiscal Federalism*. Washington, D.C.: Government Printing Office, February 1974.

Fig. 14.13 Data from Advisory Commission on Intergovernmental Relations, "Investment of IAIG Cash Balances by State and Local Governments, *Summary of Report A-3* (supplemental, 1965), Washington, D.C.: Government Printing Office, August 1965.

Box 14.3 After D. J. Elazar, *American Federalism: A View From the States*, 2nd edition. New York: Crowell (Harper & Row), 1972, Figs. 11, 12, and 13. Copyright 1972 by Thomas Y. Crowell Publishers.

Box 14.8 After T. J. Wilbanks and H. H. Huang. In *Proceedings of the Association of American Geographers*, 1975.

CHAPTER 15

Fig. 15.1 After Abler, Adams, and Gould, *Spatial Organization*. Englewood Cliffs, N.J.: Prentice-Hall, 1971, p. 302. Used with permission.

Fig. 15.3 From R. J. Sampson and H. T. Farris, *Domestic Transportation*. Boston: Houghton Mifflin, 1966. Reprinted by permission.

Fig. 15.4 After R. S. Morrill, *The Spatial Organization of Society*. North Scituate, Mass.: Duxbury Press, p. 137. Used with permission.

Fig. 15.7 From *Location of Reserve Districts in the United States*. Washington, D.C.: 63rd Congress, second session, Senate Document 485, 1914, p. 149.

Fig. 15.8 After J. R. Mackay, *Canadian Geographer*, vol. 11, 1958, p. 5. In Haggett, *Geography: A Modern Synthesis*. New York: Harper & Row, 1974, p. 462.

Box 15.3 After Syracuse University Environmental Policy Project, 1973.

CHAPTER 16

Fig. 16.4 From T. K. Peucker, "Computer Cartography," AAG resource paper no. 17, 1972, Fig. 4.1. Used with the permission of the Association of American Geographers.

Fig. 16.5 After J. Friedmann, *Regional Development Policy*. Cambridge, Mass.: MIT Press, 1966, pp. 226–227. Used with the permission of the MIT Press.

Fig. 16.7 Department of Regional Economic Expansion. Ottawa, Information Canada.

CHAPTER 17

Fig. 17.1 Data from L. Saville, *Regional Economic Development in Italy*. Durham, N.C.: Duke U. Press, 1967, p. 42.

Fig. 17.3 After Haggett, *Geography: A Modern Synthesis*, 3rd ed. New York: Harper & Row, 1979, p. 510. Copyright 1979 by Peter Haggett and used with permission of Harper & Row Publishers, Inc.

Fig. 17.5 From Haggett, *Geography: A Modern Synthesis*, 3rd ed. New York: Harper & Row, 1979, p. 527. Copyright 1979 by Peter Haggett and used with permission of Harper & Row Publishers, Inc.

Fig. 17.8 After Abler, Adams, and Gould, *Spatial Organization*. Englewood Cliffs, N.J.: Prentice-Hall, 1971, p. 430. Used with permission.

Fig. 17.9 After J. B. Riddell, *The Spatial Dynamics of Modernization in Sierra Leone*. Evanston: Northwestern University Press, 1970, p. 92. Used with permission.

Box 17.2 After S. Godlund, "Ein innovations Verlauf in Europa." Reprinted by permission of the Department of Geography, University of Lund, Sweden (*Lund Studies in Geography*, series B, 6, 1952).

CHAPTER 18

Fig. 18.2 Adapted from R. E. Munn, ed., *Environmental Impact Assessment: Principles and Procedures*. Toronto, Canada: International Council of Scientific Unions: Scientific Committee on Problems of the Environment, 1975, p. 22.

INDEX

A

Accessibility, 81, 236, 238–239, 243–246, 253–255, 261, 315, 317, 384–385. *See also* Distance decay; Least effort

Advantages. *See* Comparative advantage; Environmental advantages; Locational advantages

Agglomeration economies, 99, 118–119, 132–133, 148, 151, 190, 193, 199, 324, 330, 357, 360–361, 403, 413. *See also* Economies of scale

Aging activities, 263. *See also* Infant industry

Amenities, 296, 321

Assets, economic, 377–378. *See also* Comparative advantage
  locational, 378–383
  temporal, 379, 383–384

Autarky, 259, 269

B

Backwardness, 264

Backwash effects, 246, 256, 378–380, 381

Basic activities, 141–145, 148–150, 281, 282, 296–298. *See also* Economic base

Behavior, 31–34, 63–65, 84–85, 214–216, 251–253, 354–355, 365, 405–407, 418. *See also* Government as economic actor; Maps, mental

Borrowing innovations, 399–400

Boundary, 78–79, 82, 89, 221, 248–249, 295–296, 317, 325–328, 330–334, 340, 382

Boundary effects, 330–334, 340

Boundary zones, 83, 382–383

Brain drain, 269–270

Break-even distance, 78, 83

Break-even point, 221

C

Capacity of the market, 82–83

Capitalism, 68

Carrying capacity, 161–165

Cell patterns, 22, 27, 29, 31, 35, 326, 333, 378–380

Central place theory, 115, 127–133, 293, 354–355. *See also* Central places

Central places, 112–133, 378, 381
  orders of, 121–122

Centrality of location, 239

Christaller, Walter, 115–117

Circulation, 62–63, 214–216, 234–239. *See also* Migration

Classification, 83, 121

Clustering, 119–120, 132–133, 330, 360

Communication, 207, 222, 241

Comparative advantage, 101–103, 111–112, 151, 175–176, 193–220, 235, 262–263, 315, 317, 377, 402

Competition, 66–68, 122–123, 415–418

Competitive economy, 66–68

Complementarity, 235–238, 261

Concentrated pattern. *See* Clustering

Connectivity, 356, 358–359. *See also* Network patterns

Consumer, 17, 61
  government as, 288, 291, 305–307

Contagious diffusion. *See* Diffusion, expansive

Contingent events. *See* Space as contingency

Cost-benefit analysis, 351, 407–409

Cultural change, 198
Cumulative causation, 147, 198–199, 377–380
Curves, indifference, 64
    growth, 383
    logistic, 393

D

Demand, 65, 74
Density of population, 111, 215–216
Dependence. *See* Locational vulnerability
Development, bottleneck, 410
    dualistic, 264
    regions, 54–55, 58. *See also* Regions
Diffusion, expansive, 388–390
    of innovations, 338–390, 392, 399, 410
    hierarchic, 380, 388–389
Diminishing returns, 195
Dispersion, 119–120, 292, 330, 356, 357–358, 360
Distance, from market, 77–81, 85–90
Distance decay, 69, 86–87, 90, 215–216, 217–221, 227–228, 249
Distribution of benefits, 262
Diversification, 260. *See also* Specialization
Duelistic development, 264

E

Economic assets, 377–378. *See also* Comparative advantage
Economic base, 140–143, 148–150, 235, 296, 377
Economic efficiency, 203
Economic growth, 144, 146–147, 192–207, 243–246. *See also* Comparative advantage; Growth curve; Location factors; Regional development
Economic linkages, 190–196, 198–199, 201–202, 241
Economic regions, 166–168. *See also* Regions
Economic sectors. *See* Economy, sectors of an
Economies, of environment. *See* Environmental advantage

of geographic scale, 265–266
of scale, 99, 109–119, 124–133, 330, 357. *See also* Agglomeration economies
of shape, 265–266
Economy, competitive, 66–68
    external, 67–68, 146, 298–299, 315–316
    monopolistic, 66–67
    oligopolistic, 66
    sectors of an, 61–62, 199–200
    See also Capitalism; Socialism
Ekistics, 251–253
Eminent domain, 292, 329, 340
Employment sector minimum, 148–150
Energy, 24, 111–113, 176, 266–268, 301–302, 335–341
Environment, 82, 153, 155–157, 160–166, 170–177, 354
Environmental advantage, 156–158, 161–165, 171–177
Environmental determinism, 160–161, 171
Environmental influences, 160–165, 170–172. *See also* Environment
Equilibrium, 65, 119–120, 122–124, 225, 361, 365, 391
Equilibrium spacing, 119–121, 127–130, 353–359
Equity, 351
Exchange, 62
Expansion path, 195
Expansive diffusion, 388–390
Export theories of growth, 144, 146–147, 377, 380
Exports, 261–264. *See also* Spatial interaction; Boundary; Tariffs
External control, 261. *See also* Locational vulnerability
External diseconomy. *See* Economy, external

F

Factor mobility, 224–225, 378–380
Factors of production, 194, 203
Fiscal federalism, 298
Fiscal mercantilism, 322
Freight rates, 103, 106–112
Functional region, 158, 169

G

Geographic discrimination, 414
Geographic inertia, 390–391
Government, as consumer, 288, 291, 305–307
    as economic actor, 276–310
    as producer, 279–288, 290–298, 301–304
Government assistance, 300–306, 323–324, 335, 366–370, 386–387, 402–403, 417
Government jurisdictions, 295–298, 321–322, 325–328, 338–340
Graphs, 49–51
Gravity model, 218–221, 229. *See also* Distance decay
Green belt, 326
Growth center, 244, 403
Growth curve, 383
Growth pole, 244

H

Heckscher-Ohlin theorem, 197
Hexagonal pattern, 113–114, 129–130
Hierarchic diffusion, 380, 388–389
Hierarchy, 112–116, 121–122, 127–129, 132, 355, 362, 380–381, 388–389
Highest and best use, 78, 84–85, 294
Hunger, 56, 172, 177, 270–271

I

Imports. *See* Exports
Income inequalities, 351–353. *See also* Equity
Income substitutes, 352
Indifference curves, 64
Industrial complex, 202, 324, 403–404
Industry, infant, 262–263, 415
Information, 46–49, 58, 318
Infrastructure, 296, 305, 321, 324, 330, 336, 338, 403
Input-output analysis, 190–192, 201, 208–209, 237–238, 244, 374
Intensive land use, 77–80, 83–84
Interaction. *See* Spatial interaction
Interaction potential, 219, 221

Intermittent functions, 124–125
Intervening opportunities, 219, 236
Isard, Walter, 99, 208, 404
Isodapane, 99, 101–103, 105, 110–111, 317, 321
Isotims, 101–102

L

Labor shed, 250
Labor skills, 234. *See also* Comparative advantage; Locational specialization
Land rent, 78. *See also* rent
Land use, intensive, 77–80, 83–84
Land use pattern, 85, 293
Land value. *See* Rent; Rent gradient
Least effort, 32–33, 215, 217, 245. *See also* Distance Decay
Linkages. *See* Economic linkages; Accessibility; Network patterns.
Lobbying, 334–335
Location, 16, 31
  as an area, 104–105
  as teamwork, 104
  centrality of, 239
  optimal, 106, 114–115, 280–282, *See also* Optimization
Location allocation analysis. *See* Spatial allocation analysis
Location factors, 98–106, 113–114, 279–281, 315–316, 322–328, 335–341
  noneconomic, 294, 352, 422–424. *See also* Public interest; Social welfare
Location quotient, 145
Location theory, 99, 110–117. *See also* Location factor
Locational advantages, 190–200, 202–206, 378–383. *See also* Comparative advantage; Economies of scale; Agglomeration economies; Environmental advantages
Locational assets, 378–383
Locational attributes, 17
Locational conflict resolution, 292, 293, 318, 323, 340, 407, 415–418
Locational environment, 212

Locational pull, 98–106, 111–112, 148. *See also* Location factor
Locational specialization. *See* Specialization
Locational triangle, 99–100
Locational vulnerability, 259–272
Logistic curve, 393
Lösch, August, 90, 115, 120

M

Maps, 21–26, 51, 53
  mental, 33–34, 59, 216, 228, 357, 403–405
Market, capacity of the, 82–83
  periodic, 124–125
Market area, 109–116, 120–121, 123–133, 221, 226, 290, 293, 294, 330
Market orientation, 99–100, 106–112
Markets, 66, 77–80, 82–83, 85–91, 207
Material-source orientation, 99–100, 106–112
Maximizing productivity, 349–351, 359, 360–361, 365
Mental maps, 33–34, 59, 216, 228, 357, 403–405
Mercantile model of settlement, 125–126
Migration, 333–334, 415. *See also* Circulation; Factor mobility, Movement behavior
Minimizing inequality, 349–350, 351–353, 359, 360–361, 365, 386, 413
Mobility, 361. *See also* Behavior; Distance decay; Factor mobility; Movement behavior
Modal choice, 219–222
Model, 18
Monopolistic economy, 66–67
Movement behavior, 131, 214–217, 229, 236, 241–245, 250–251. *See also* Behavior; Distance decay; Movement costs
Movement costs, 103–104, 317, 320–321, 324, 335–336, 357. *See also* Transport costs; Transportation
Multinational firms, 62, 248
Multiplier, 141–143, 149–150, 309, 397–398, 408

N

National interest, *See* Public interest
Natural resources, 164–166, 234. *See also* Environment
Network patterns, 23, 27, 28, 31, 34, 103, 215, 222–225, 227, 239–243, 251, 332, 356, 358–359, 380–381. *See also* Connectivity
No-growth objective, 200, 409–410, 425–427
Nodal region, 158, 168
Nodality, 362. *See also* Nodes
Nodes, 26–27, 34, 77–80, 89, 121. *See also* Central places; Point patterns
Nonbasic activities, 141–143, 145, 148–150
Noneconomic location factors, 294, 352, 422–424. *See also* Public interest; Social welfare
Nonrenewable resources, 165, 426
North-South problem, 378–379

O

Oligopolistic economy, 66
Opportunity costs, 408
Optimal locations. *See* Location, optimal
Optimization, 17, 106, 114, 119–120, 156, 223, 225, 309, 320–330, 353–359, 363–365
Orders of central places, 121–122
Overcrowding, 164
Overpopulation, 162

P

Pattern planning, 353–359, 361–363, 364, 412–418. *See also* Spatial efficiency; Spatial structure
Pattern recognition, 13, 22–31, 85, 353–359. *See also* Clustering; Dispersion; Connectivity; Texture; Regular spacing; Cell patterns; Land use pattern; Network patterns; Point patterns; Surfaces
Pattern relationships, 30–31. *See also* Movement behavior, Pattern recognition

People–place well-being, 146, 412–415
Periodic market, 124–125
Permissible activities, 311, 316–317, 325–328, 338–340
Physical environments, 155. *See also* Environment
Place planning. *See* Pattern planning
Planning, 37, 316–318, 320–330, 350–353, 361–363, 366–370, 428. *See also* Planning regions; Regional planning; Pattern planning
Planning regions, 168–170
Point patterns, 26–27, 31, 34, 111. *See also* Clustering: Dispersion
Political environments, 156, 284–285, 315–318, 415–416. *See also* Boundary; Environment; Planning
Population growth, 143, 162–165. *See also* Economic growth; Regional development
Population potential, 221. *See also* Interaction potential
Positive-sum game, 416
Potential productivity, 162
Prediction, 17
Preference, 63–65
Price, 65, 68–69, 83, 90. *See also* Stabilization
Price controls. *See* Stabilization
Price surface, 69
Primary activities, 61–62
Producer, 17, 61
Production controls. *See* Stabilization
Production function, 195
Productivity, maximizing of, 349–350, 359, 360–361, 365 potential, 162
Proportionality, 191–192
Proximity, 74, 118
Public facilities, 281, 321–322
Public interest, 279–282, 285–288, 293, 302, 311, 315, 316, 318, 341–342, 347, 354–355, 360–362, 366–370, 412–418
Public lands, 280, 287, 293, 294, 302, 340
Public sector, 285–288. *See also* Government as economic actor

Q

Quality of life, 53, 57. *See also* Minimizing inequality; Standard of living
Quotas, 331–332

R

Range of a good, 111, 123, 293
Rank-size rule, 121–122, 354–355
Regional accounting, 373–376
Regional development, 324, 349–370, 377–387, 398–410, 412–418. *See also* Diffusion of innovations
Regional economic cooperation, 267
Regional governments, 283
Regional growth, 383. *See also* Regional development
Regional impact, 309
Regional pathology, 373–393, 397–405
Regional planning, 166–170, 366–370
Regional resilience, 377
Regionalizing, 157–159
Regions, 54–55, 58, 157–159, 367
Regular spacing, 111, 114, 116, 120–121, 357. *See also* Pattern recognition
Regulation, 319–320, 335, 341–342
Relative deprivation, 260–261, 264
Relative location, 235–236, 239, 251–255. *See also* Pattern recognition
Renewability, 198. *See also* Renewable resources
Rent, 78, 292, 425
Rent gradient, 80, 83, 89, 92
Rent surface, 89
Resource endowment, 399–400. *See also* Environmental advantage; Resources
Resource lottery, 386–387, 400
Resources, 263
  natural 164–166. *See also* Environment.
  non-renewable, 165, 426
  renewable, 165, 426
  See also resource lottery.
Restricting interaction, 261–264
Retarding growth, *See* No-growth objective

S

Satisficing, 365
Scale, 14, 358
Scarcity, 16, 32
Scatter diagram, 50–51, 87, 228, 333
Secondary activities, 61, 62
Sectoral transformation, 199–200
Self-sufficiency. *See* Autarky
Services as a growth sector, 401
Shadow effects, 265
Social and cultural environments, 156, 164, 198. *See also* Environment
Social distance, 321. *See also* Maps, mental
Social welfare, 281, 295, 309–310, 315, 318. *See also* Public interest
Socialism, 68, 425
Space, as context, 18–20, 36
  as contingency, 18, 21–22, 427–428. *See also* Time geography
  as dimension, 18–20, 36
Space packing, 113
Spacing, *See* Regular spacing; Equilibrium spacing; Point patterns; Network patterns, Cell patterns; Clustering; Dispersion
Spatial allocation analysis, 114–115
Spatial efficiency, 114, 353–359
Spatial equilibrium. *See* Equilibrium
Spatial error, 356
Spatial focus, 14, 358
Spatial interaction, 214–222, 226–229, 234–239, 241–251, 258–261
Spatial order, 353
Spatial price equilibrium, 225
Spatial pricing, 225–226
Spatial process, 25
Spatial structure, 22–31, 32, 34, 85, 341, 353–359, 363–365, 378–383 *See also* Pattern planning
Spatial symmetry, 215, 217, 353–354
Specialization, 62, 80, 121, 196–199, 234–235, 259
Spread effects, 246, 378–380, 381
Stabilization, 317–318, 328–329
Standard of living, 9–11. *See also* Quality of life
Substitutability, 197
Supply, 65

Surfaces, 27–30, 31, 35, 69, 89, 228, 249, 357, 359–360, 390. *See also* Uniform surface; Rent surface; Texture

T

Tariffs, 331–332
Taxation, 306–308, 317, 321–322, 324, 337
Technical coefficients, 192
Technological change, 198
Technology environments, 156, 163, 198. *See also* Environment
Temporal assets, 379, 383–384
Tertiary activities, 61, 62
Texture, 357, 359–360. *See also* Surfaces
Threshold of a good, 111, 123, 293
Time-geography, 21–22, 105
Trade, 235
Trade area. *See* Market area

Transfer costs, 215–216. *See also* Transport costs
Transfer tax, 316–317
Transferability, 236
Transient movements, 244–245. *See also* Movement behavior
Transport costs, 69, 98–104, 106–112, 320. *See also* Movement costs; Transfer costs
Transportation, 207. *See also* Accessibility; Distance decay; Modal choice; Transport costs
Transportation terminals, 103
Transshipment, 103, 111

U

Uncertainty, 84–85, 104–105, 120–121, 123, 244–245, 392–393, 422–425
Underpopulation, 162
Uniform region, 158, 168, 169, 362

Uniform surface, 80–82, 127–130
Urban geography, 14–15
Utility, 63–65, 74

V

Value, 17, 63–65, 73. *See also* Social welfare
Von Thünen, 80–81, 84–85, 90, 138, 365

W

Weber, Alfred, 99
Weight loss, 99

Z

Zero-sum game, 416
Zones of land use, 79–80
Zoning, 316–317, 325–328

80 81 82 6 5 4 3 2 1